Women Organizing

AN ANTHOLOGY

DISCARDED

by

Bernice Cummings

and

Victoria Schuck

The Scarecrow Press, Inc.
Metuchen, N.J., & London
1979

Library of Congress Cataloging in Publication Data
Main entry under title:

Women organizing.

    Includes index.
    1.   Feminism--United States--Addresses, essays, lec-
tures.   2.   Women's rights--United States--Addresses, essays, lectures.   3.   Women--United States--Political activity.
4.   Political clubs.   I.   Cummings, Bernice, 1924-
II.   Schuck, Victoria
HQ1426. W644   301. 41'2'0973   79-18956
ISBN 0-8108-1245-2

To All Women, Allied in

Conviction, Spirit and Deed

ACKNOWLEDGMENTS

Women Organizing had its genesis in the Women in Politics Symposium, sponsored by Adelphi University, Garden City, Long Island, in September 1975. The editors wish to express their deep appreciation to Dr. Timothy Costello, President of Adelphi University, for his endorsement of the conference and his support in the preparation of the manuscript for this anthology.

CONTENTS

PREFACE

Her wings are clipped and it is found de-
plorable that she does not fly.
                    --Simone de Beauvoir

The essays in this anthology are written for those students, professionals, and general readers, interested in equality for women. Although all the articles are of contemporary
interest, there are some that are of such significance as to
be considered classic research material for future study.

Any movement, if it is to survive, must explore meth-
odologies for developing effective lines of power. To do this,
the movement must find a definite focus to unify its constituency.

As total equality is the quintessential focus of the
women's movement, gaining individual and group power are
the means of achieving this goal.

For women, the problems involved in gaining power
and thus equality pivot around the need for a shared effort
to generate that power for change.

Because political involvement and effectiveness, as
well as the political process per se, are of primary significance in gaining power and equality, there is considerable
emphasis in this book on the subject of politics.

There is also emphasis on the need for solidarity,
created and sustained, in order to achieve the goal of equal-
ity--with women seeing themselves as part of a larger whole
--as women organizing.

There is a distinct advantage to collective behavior
that arises out of a collective consciousness. When what

most women want is social change which will give them parity, they may get it by organizing effectively.

One requirement for social change is the development of new male and female norms. This means mounting an attack on traditionalism that requires an enormous multi-level effort. Without this total commitment by organized women, there can only be the slow incursions into the male dominated social and economic structure that we have been seeing.

In this anthology, we read about women who are sensitive to the injustice of sex discrimination, who are political and who see the exercising of unified strength as an important vehicle for social change.

Some of the most interesting and vital problems concerning women, their political life in contemporary society and their need for organized effort, are analyzed in this collection. The 21 authors explore some of society's major trends, dominant patterns and cultural norms; they offer, wherever possible, an alternative point of departure.

INTRODUCTION

Historical Overview

The process of women organizing is deeply rooted in humanity's ability to effect social cooperation and to adapt to change. Believing that the feminist cause can be aided by scholarly investigation and the sharing of first hand experience, we have selected a group of original essays that relate to women gaining equality through their organizational efforts. Inherent in the focus of this anthology is the implication that women are blocked from entering the dominant social system which is customarily guarded against intrusion and attempts to change the social order.

Seen in perspective, women's organized attempts to correct this problem in the United States date as far back as the American Revolution and the Antebellum period. Visionary and courageous women, believing in a feminist ethos, blazed a path for those who followed. For the most part, women in pastoral America of the eighteenth century were as involved as men in a world of meaningful work and community. Then, as now, however, women were not accepted as equals, even though they enjoyed a sense of work and purpose.

As entire families moved off the farms and into the cities during the Industrial Revolution, the critical effect of city life cut across all class and sex lines. Leaving behind their familiar agrarian security, both women and men made extraordinary personal adjustments to urbanization. All too quickly it produced a complex of problems: separation of the sexes, overpopulation, inadequate housing, economic and educational deprivation, criminality, prostitution, and rampant illness being most apparent.

Men, learning to cope with the exigencies of city living in a work-a-day world, left their women at home to struggle with the far greater discontinuities in their own lives. As a result of newly defined attitudes, middle- and upper-class women were importuned to know their "place," surrounded by a mythology that both idealized and rendered them powerless.

The First Round

Antebellum feminists prevailed upon middle- and upper-class women to extricate themselves from such tyranny. Responding to these urgings, affluent women found satisfaction in voluntarism, viewing it as an antidote to their own boredom and frustration while helping ameliorate some urban problems. Involvement in voluntary associations afforded middle- and upper-class women the opportunity to see themselves as individuals, no longer entirely submerged in culturally determined sex roles. Women involved in forming social welfare and benevolent societies, as well as those in abolitionist and religious groups, developed a new self-consciousness characterized by active participation in challenging the traditional mores of society.

The Seneca Falls Convention of 1848 served as the culminating point of all prior attempts to end discrimination against women. With what is now a landmark document, the Declaration of Sentiments, seeking the most significant changes, proclaims all women and men equal. The cultural lag that existed between the 1848 feminists and the rest of society, however, was the root cause that prevented the Seneca Falls Convention from achieving the coveted equality for women. Though without prolonged success in its time, the legacy of Seneca Falls relates directly to the central theme of the essays presented in this anthology.

The Middle Round

Spanning a thirty year period, from 1890 to 1920, middle- and upper-class women organized around the single issue of suffrage. This phase was the second or middle round of the women's movement, the first or antebellum period having ended with the outbreak of the Civil War. The middle round, notable for the Suffrage Movement, was a pragmatic period without ideology. Leaders and constituents saw the vote as the panacea it never became. The dominance of the Suffrage Movement came to an end in 1920 with the ratification of the Nineteenth Amendment. Women had won the right to vote but ideologically, society remained traditional in its attitude toward the sexes.

The Contemporary Movement

Many women's organizations flourished as spinoffs of
the Suffrage Movement, but it was not until the 1960's that
feminism became a dynamic issue again. Beginning in 1966,
partly because of social upheaval, specific injustices, sexual
freedom, a declining birthrate and increasing numbers of
women in the labor force, the women's movement was re-
kindled, giving impetus to a variety of nationwide organizations. The new movement, adhering to contemporary social
attitudes, maintains a balance between goals and social
trends, and ideas of sexual equality, autonomy and androgyny
are all symbiotically fused in philosophy and activism.

Another important phenomenon of the 1960's and 1970's
has been the consciousness-raising groups that patterned
themselves on past civil rights sessions. These structureless, leaderless groups attracted women who recognized their
need for sharing experiences, problems and emotional support with others of their own sex. Unlike the national organizations, consciousness-raising groups were not action
oriented but rather played an important role in developing
and supporting the feminist ideology of the women's movement. The growing collective feminist consciousness has
become part of other changes in society not necessarily associated with the women's movement. Feminism has had
an impact upon business and employment practices, education
policies, day-care for children, wages and working conditions,
medical practices as well as government policy toward affirmative action. Undoubtedly other significant societal alterations will emerge.

Contemporary feminists mark the third round of the
women's movement with the broad and varied scope of their
activities, thus bridging the distance between themselves and
their disaffected, antebellum sisters of the first round. Noting these years, we make the observation that our pluralistic
society, despite its discrimination, allows for the diversity
which has made possible the women's movement.

* * *

Part One of <u>Women Organizing</u>: An Anthology, explores theoretical alternatives to traditional patterns and attitudes about the uses of power as well as the real and un-
realized power of four Black Congresswomen. Although

only one Black Congresswoman remains in office at the time of publication, the implications of this essay remain intact.

The second section focuses upon women's alienation from society, their frustration and struggle, stemming from discrimination. The centrality of these essays is sustained in both a personal account of a political career and an article describing the use of lobbying as a construct for change.

The third part explores in detail selected women's organizations that have been influenced by the women's movement. How and why these organizations developed and where their futures lie are some of the issues examined.

Part Four relates to the economic problems facing women who are not financially independent, whose incomes are low and who are divorced, widowed or otherwise single.

The fifth section includes a substantial spectrum of the political scene, focusing on various aspects of political life such as, female political volunteers, women in the Republican Party, women who have political ambitions as well as female political candidates and the Women's movement.

The last part continues the theme of the book, women organizing, by exploring discrimination, new occupational roles, inequality in the jury system and an analysis of the Equal Rights Amendment.

Although the anthology expresses the overall theme of women organizing, it also seeks to support a range of thoughtful and provocative ideas based upon diverse theories.

PART I

POWER! THE ETERNAL ENIGMA

INTRODUCTION

In the opening essay of the anthology, Nancy C. M. Hartsock connects the suffragists of the nineteenth century with the present and explores the state of the contemporary feminist movement. In contrast to those who have argued that the women's movement is dead or dying, she argues that it is instead at a critical turning point. Feminists' avoidance of exercising power over other feminists had a creative impact in the early years of the movement. Currently, this avoidance of exercising power blocks the construction of feminist organizations and strategies for the future. Hartsock urges a reconsideration of the issue of power in order to challenge some common feminist assumptions.

In the essay that follows, Inez Smith Reid analyzes the women's movement using it as a backdrop for her detailed discussion of the four Black Congresswomen who held office before the 1978 elections.

In this work of fundamental importance, Reid explores their political positions, styles and convictions; their similarities and differences; the demands made upon them as well as the problems they have faced--and their power.

Chapter 1

FEMINISM, POWER, AND CHANGE:
A THEORETICAL ANALYSIS

by Nancy C. M. Hartsock

In recent years, the media have been full of reports
about the women's movement--its essence, its reasons for
being, and most recently, its demise. The current state of
feminism is indeed an important issue. At the same time,
it is very difficult to construct a clear account from media
reports. For example, one reads newspaper reports such
as a note that a female editor of Esquire has pronounced the
women's movement dead because it did not meet the needs of
middle class women. 1 Or one finds a statement by an aerobic dance instructor that she is involved in the women's
movement because she is providing "a mental release for
women...." Aerobic dance "gives [women] a feeling of independence and self-reliance. This is what the women's movement is all about. "2 Then there is the statement by a radical woman convicted of weapons possession who says, "I
don't have any political theories. I wonder sometimes how
some people claim themselves Maoists, Leninists, and all
that. I ask myself, what am I? And the only thing I could
come up with was feminist. "3

Many reports, especially those in the feminist press,
indicate that the women's movement is, if not dying, at least
in trouble. Those who argue that the women's movement is
dead or dying put forward a variety of explanations for why
this is the case. Different people contend that the movement
has been co-opted by liberals; taken over by socialists, man-
haters (here, read lesbians), and other crazies; has been dis-
rupted by government agents; is falling apart because it col-
lided with the fears of "ordinary" women; or because it has
not met the needs of poor and working class women. Still
others claim that the women's movement has become too
caught up in cultural or spiritual feminism to pay attention to
politics, and too intent on process to get results. 4 In addition, the generation gap is coming to feminism. There is a
new generation of women who have grown up without facing

2

some of the most blatant kinds of sexism, and who tend to
think the problems have been solved.

Although it is extremely difficult to discover any coherence in all these arguments, the simple fact of their appearance over the last several years suggests that some important changes are occurring in the women's movement.
The articles demonstrate the very wide scope of the movement since women of very diverse background and in very
different situations are moved to comment on their relationship or lack of relationship to the movement as a whole.
Given this evidence of widespread interest and impact, it is
perhaps strange that we should find, especially within the
feminist press, arguments that the movement is dying.
Clearly an assessment of the progress or lack of progress
of the women's movement is in order.

Perhaps Elizabeth Cady Stanton's remarks of one hundred years ago are applicable today as a starting point for
such an assessment. She wrote to Lucretia Mott in 1876:
"Could we have foreseen, when we called that [Seneca Falls]
convention, the ridicule, persecution, and misrepresentation
that the demand for woman's political, religious, and social
equality would involve; the long weary years of waiting and
hoping without success, I fear we should not have had the
courage and conscience to begin such a protracted struggle,
nor the faith and hope to continue the work. Fortunately for
all reforms, the leaders, not seeing the obstacles which
block the way, start with the hope of a speedy success. Our
demands at the first seemed so rational that I thought the
mere statement of woman's wrongs would bring immediate
redress. I thought an appeal to the reason and conscience
of men against the unjust and unequal laws for women that
disgraced our statute books, must settle the question. But
I soon found, while no attempt was made to answer our arguments, that an opposition, bitter, malignant and persevering,
rooted in custom and prejudice, grew stronger with every new
demand made, with every new privilege granted. "[5]

This discovery of the difficulty of making change is
not unique to feminists. In the context of another movement
for change Leszek Kolakowski has commented that "achieving
even the simplest improvement in social conditions demands
the mobilization of such a huge amount of collective energy
that if the full extent of the disproportion between results and
effort expended became public knowledge the result would be
so disheartening, and would so paralyze men's courage and

strivings, that any social progress would be impossible. The
effort must be so great as to be wasteful if the results are to
be at all visible. ... [Thus] in order to muster the energy
needed to arrive at any change in human relations, this mon-
strous disproportion must be largely mitigated in men's minds
by an artificial and mythological inflation of expected results
as compared to the sum of expended effort, a sum which cannot be concealed since it is felt directly. "[6]

Here I will argue that the women's movement is neither dead nor dying; rather it has approached a critical turning point, a point at which the difficulty of the tasks for feminists are clear, although the organizational and ideological
tools for undertaking that work are as yet undeveloped. Feminists are, then, at a point where the critiques of feminism,
in spite of their varied and contradictory appearances, should
be carefully examined. The problems they point to may be
the real ones, or failing that, may lead us to the real and
important problems. What has been called the third wave of
feminism is coming of age as a movement.[7] At this stage,
its future progress depends on a clear understanding of what
has been done and what must yet be done. Such large questions cannot be answered here, but only posed. An assessment of the state of the women's movement can only be a
collective enterprise, not something done by a single individual or group.

As I have looked at articles on the state of the wom-
en's movement and listened to debates within the movement I
have been struck with the central importance feminists have
given to issues of power, and with the fact that feminist opposition to the exercise of power within the women's movement was the basis for what I see as the movement's single,
most important contribution to political change. (I do not
mean to imply by this that feminists have made only one important contribution but rather to argue for what I see as
most fundamental.) Feminist avoidance of exercising power
allowed feminists to work out a mode of analysis, a way of
asking questions and looking for answers. During the 60's
and 70's, the women's movement developed a mode of analysis whose power is rooted in everyday life and which leads
to the transformation of everyday life. And the significance
of contemporary feminism lies in this rediscovery, in a
practical way, of a mode of analysis which itself has the
capacity to comprehend and thereby transform everyday life.
That is, I will argue that the American feminist movement
has collectively recreated Marx's method. By contrast,

those who claim possession of Marx's theory, the male-
dominated Left in America, have fundamentally lost touch
with everyday life. For much of this American Left, "the
real struggle was not lived--only the struggle as a doctrinal
'principle.'" The contrast I want to draw here is between
what Antonio Gramsci recognized as "real action," action
"which modifies in an essential way both [human beings] and
external reality," and "gladiatorial futility, which is self-
declared action but modifies only the word, not things, the
external gesture and not the person inside."[8] Because the
women's movement developed in such close contact with
everyday life, feminists can make important and even essential contributions to other movements for change.

My task here, then, is to outline the main features
of the method feminists have developed in order to demonstrate both that it is a singular contribution to movements
for social change, and also that the avoidance of exercising
power was fundamental to the development of that method.
Feminists were correct in the early years of the women's
movement to give central importance to issues of power within the women's movement. But, ironically, as the women's
movement has developed and grown, feminist avoidance of
exercising power has become a liability rather than an asset.
Many feminists still tend to think that getting and using power are somehow parts of a "male trip," something unworthy
of or unnatural for women. Of course, avoiding the exercise of power is hardly the only thing that keeps the women's
movement from succeeding. Feminists are part of a society
which is itself increasingly in crisis and increasingly un-
willing to meet feminist demands. They are part of a Left
which is experiencing even more of the splits, tensions, and
lack of direction we find in the women's movement. However,
feminists cannot solve the problems which confront them without first understanding how they have reacted to the use (and
the abuse) of power. Feminist avoidance of exercising power
within the women's movement, useful as it was, grew out of
a confusion about the nature of power--a confusion which
should not be surprising because of its important social roots
and its powerful place in social life. This confusion, however, must be overcome if the women's movement is to develop a strong feminist community and work out a revolutionary strategy.

Up to this point, I have spoken in unitary terms about
a divided and diverse movement. Women who call themselves
feminists disagree on many things. To talk in such unitary

terms about a social movement so diverse in its aims and
goals seems at first to be a mistake. There is a women's
movement which appears on television, has national organizations, is interested in women's full participation in capitalist
society, and is easy for the media to reach and put forward
as representative of feminist thought. But there is a second
movement--one which is hard to find--a movement made up
of small groups and local organizations, a movement which
has worked on specific local projects, a movement which
came together around the immediate and real needs of wom-
en in a variety of cities, a movement whose energies have
gone directly into work for change. These latter groups
form the basis for my discussion of feminist theory. Those
groups were concerned with practical action--rape crisis
centers, women's centers, building women's communities,
etc.... But in coming together as feminists to confront the
problems which dominate their lives every day they have
built a movement profoundly based on practice. Indeed, one
of the major tasks for the women's movement is precisely
the creation of revolutionary theory out of an examination of
practice. [9]

Developing a Feminist Mode of Analysis

When we look at the practice of the women's movement in all its diversity we find a common mode of analysis,
a world view which differs from the practice of most so-
cialist movements in advanced capitalist countries, and which
is at the same time surprisingly close to Marx's world view.
It is this mode of analysis as well as the concrete theories
which have been developed out of it that form the sources of
feminism's power. This is the reason I can argue that
through this practice, feminists have not only re-created
Marx's method but have become the most orthodox of Marx-
ists. As Georg Lukács argued, orthodoxy in Marxist theory
refers exclusively to method. [10] In this sense, to refer to a
feminist mode of analysis is, more precisely, to refer to the
fact that feminists as a group re-created Marx's method in a
form which could be easily taken over by other movements
for social change in the late twentieth century. At base,
feminism is a mode of analysis, a method of approaching
life and politics, rather than a set of political conclusions
about the oppression of women. Feminists have applied that
method to their own experience as women in order to transform the social relations which define their existence. By
using this method, the women's movement has been able to

deal directly with American daily life--something which accounts for its rapid spread.

      The practice of small group consciousness raising--
with its stress on examining and understanding experience,
and on connecting personal experience to the structures which
define women's lives--is the clearest example of the method
basic to feminism. Through this practice feminists learned
that it was important to build an analysis from the ground
up--beginning with personal experience, and then drawing connections between personal experience and political generalities about the oppression of women; indeed using personal
experience to develop those generalities. Through this process, feminists came to understand their experience in a way
that transformed both that experience and their sense of
self. [11] Through this experience of change, feminists were
able to see new possibilities for growth.

      The power of the method feminists developed grows
out of the fact that it allows everyday life to be connected
with an analysis of the social institutions which shape that
life. Using a feminist method means that the institutions of
capitalism (including its imperialist aspect), patriarchy, and
white supremacy cease to be abstractions to read about.
Feminists concentrate instead on the impact these forces
have on everyday life, on the ways they structure daily experience and activity. In this way feminists come to understand both the institutions and the concrete inter-relations
among them.

      A secondary result of the concentration on everyday
life has been a redefinition of the role of theory within the
feminist movement. The task of theorists has become what
Antonio Gramsci argued it should be: to work out and make
"coherent the principles and the problems raised by the
masses in their practical activity."[12] Feminism as a mode
of analysis, especially when consciousness raising is understood as basic to that method, requires a redefinition of the
concept of intellectual or theorizer, a recasting of this social
role in terms of everyday life. That is, the contemporary
women's movement has developed a different kind of intellectual, one Gramsci would describe with approval as a person who participates in "practical life, as constructor, or-
ganiser, 'permanent persuader' and not just a simple orator...."[13] Feminists' initial overemphasis on leaderlessness
was an important aspect of this redefinition. By stressing
the absolute equality of all participants, by developing strate-

gies for meetings without chairpersons and organizations without hierarchies, the women's movement affirmed that every
woman is capable of analysis and reflection, and that theory
grows out of an understanding of one's own experience.

Because every woman is a theorist, education comes
to have a very different role in the women's movement than
in the rest of the Left today.   The kind of political education
feminists are doing for themselves differs fundamentally from
what I would call instruction, i. e. from being taught certain
truths.   It differs fundamentally from "learning the correct
political line. "   Education, as opposed to instruction, is or-
ganically connected to everyday life. [14]   It both grows out of
and contributes to an understanding of daily life.

Personal and Political Change

Feminist emphasis on everyday life leads to a second
area of focus, described best by Marge Piercy when she
wrote "If what we change does not change us, we are play-
ing with blocks. "[15]   Feminism as a mode of analysis relies
on the idea that people come to know the world (to change it
and be changed by it) through everyday activity.   Even the
deepest philosophical questions grow out of a concern to understand one's own life--in particular, in all its concreteness.
Focusing on daily life and experience makes it clear not only
that human beings are active in creating and changing their
lives, but that as Marx put it, reality consists of "sensuous
human activity, practice. "[16]   By working out the links between the personal and the political, and by working out the
links between daily life and social institutions, feminists have
begun to understand existence as a social process, the product of human activity.

Feminism as a method makes it clear that human
activity is also self-changing.   As both Gramsci and Lukacs
have argued,

> to transform the external world, the general system
> of relations, is to potentiate oneself and to develop
> oneself.   ... [Individuality] cannot be realized and
> developed without an activity directed outward,
> modifying external relations both with nature, and
> in varying degrees, with other men, in the various
> social circles in which one lives, up to the greatest
> relationship of all, which embraces the whole hu-

> man species. For this reason one can say that
> man is essentially "political" since it is through the
> activity of transforming and consciously directing
> other men that man realizes his "humanity," his
> "human nature."17

Thus, a fundamental redefinition of the self is an integral
part of action for political change. Developing an independent
sense of self necessarily calls other areas of one's life into
question. Feminists are led to ask how relationships with
other persons can foster self-definition rather than dependence.
That is, if one's individuality is the ensemble of one's social
relations, "to create one's personality means to acquire consciousness of them and to modify one's own personality means
to modify the ensemble of these relations."18

Clearly, since people do not act to produce and reproduce their lives in a vacuum, changed consciousness and
changed definitions of the self can only occur in conjunction
with a restructuring of the social (both societal and personal)
relations in which each person is involved. Thus, by calling
attention to the specific experience of individuals in its lived
complexity, feminism calls attention to the totality of social
relations, to the social formation as a whole.19 Although
feminists recognize that human activity is the structure of the
social world, this structure is imposed not by individuals
but by generations, each building on the work of those who
came before. The shape of social life at any point in time
depends on a complex of factors, on needs already developed
as well as embryonic needs--needs whose production, shaping,
and satisfaction embody a historical process. The process
of self-changing and growing in a changed world leads feminists to a sense that their lives are linked to and structured by larger processes: to change their lives or the
shape of society itself, feminists must change both.20 As
Marx himself pointed out: "the coincidence of the changing
of circumstances and of human activity or self-changing can
be conceived and rationally understood only as revolutionary
practice."21

Process and Totality

A third aspect of the mode of analysis feminists developed is an understanding of the importance of process
and totality. By beginning with everyday life and experience,
feminism has been able to develop a political outlook which

incorporates stress on process and on the importance of ap-
propriating the past as an essential element of political action. 22 Women who are feminists constantly confront new
situations in which they act out of their changed awareness
of the world and themselves and in consequence experience
the changed reactions of others. What some socialists have
seen as static, feminists grasp as structures of relations in
process--a reality constantly in the process of becoming
something else. Feminist reasoning "regards every historically developed social form as in fluid movement and therefore takes into account its transient nature not less than its
momentary existence. "23 Applying the method feminists
have developed, then, leads to an understanding that each of
the interlocking institutions of capitalism, patriarchy, and
white supremacy conditions the others, but that each can also
be understood as a different expression of the same relations. 24 As Marx put it, they are "members of one totality,
different aspects of a unity.... A mutual inter-action takes
place between these various elements. This is the case with
every organic body. "25 A feminist mode of analysis begins
with an understanding that possibilities for change in any
area are tied to change occurring in other areas. The precise forms of human activity as it appears in the family, the
work place, or anywhere else, can be understood only in the
context of the whole society--including both its past and its
future.

        Capitalism is more than an economic system; it does
not simply reproduce the physical existence of individuals.
As Marx pointed out, "rather it is a definite form of activity
of these individuals, a definite form of expressing their life,
a definite mode of life on their part. ... [and this coincides
with] both what they produce and how they produce. "26 A
mode of life is not divisible. It does not consist of a public
part and a private part, a part at the workplace and a part
in the community--each of what makes up a certain fraction,
and all of which add up to 100 percent. A mode of life, with
all its aspects, takes meaning from the totality of which it
forms a part.

        Feminist attention to the concrete situation, and to the
whole in giving significance to the parts, is especially important today. The importance of an understanding of the
totality of social relations has taken on a new significance in
advanced capitalist societies where the relations between different aspects of our lives have become increasingly complex.
As Gramsci pointed out, using a military analogy, the super-

structures of modern society are like the trench systems of
modern warfare, and when one attacks the state, the whole
structure of civil society comes to its support. [27]   That is,
in the monopoly phase of capitalism, we find a new relation
between politics, ideology, and the economy--one which both
shifts the boundaries of the economic and the political and
redefines the content of these terms. [28] In part because of
these changes, and because of the increasing inter-connections
between the state apparatus and the economy (through means
as varied as public education and government regulation of
industry), it becomes even more necessary to emphasize that
one can only understand and transform reality as a totality.

Feminism and Power

Feminists have developed (or re-created) a very important method for understanding reality.   It was the opposition to the exercise of power (or even in some cases, to
leadership) within the women's movement that was fundamental
to developing this mode of analysis.   The refusal to exercise
power gave every woman a role in working out a way of asking questions, and provided the time and space to try out
new ideas and analyses.   Consciousness-raising, and the understanding of social existence as a process of self-creation
--all this was facilitated by avoiding the exercising of power
within feminist organizations.   At present, however, feminists' avoidance of power stands in the way of the future
progress of the women's movement.

To make clear how this happened, and how avoidance
of exercising power was important at an earlier stage, but
now is one of the most important problems feminists have to
face, I will make direct use of the method feminists developed.
For feminists, theory is the articulation of what practical
activity has already appropriated in reality.   As Marx expressed it, as the struggle develops, theorists "no longer
need to seek science in their minds; they have only to take
note of what is happening before their eyes and to become its
mouthpiece." [29] Forming theory out of practice, articulating
what is taking place, does not come quickly or easily, and
it is rarely clear what direction the theory will finally take.
It requires close attention to practice, and to what diverse
groups of people are doing.

Contemporary feminism in the United States finds itself in a situation in which the very substantial struggles of

women have not yet been "theorized." To put this practical
activity into theoretical form, feminists must take up and
examine what they find within themselves, attempt to clarify
what they already, at some level, know. Theory itself,
then, can be seen as a way of taking up and building on experience. This is not to say that feminists reject all knowledge that is not first hand, or that they learn nothing from
books or from history. Rather it is to stress that not only
is the philosophy of each person "contained in its entirety in
[her] political action," but in addition, that in creating theory,
it is necessary to start from what one already knows. [30] The
mode of analysis developed by Marx and re-invented by the
contemporary women's movement suggests that the unity of
theory and practice refers to the use of theory to make coherent the problems and principles expressed in practical
activity. The role of theory is to articulate what is already
known at the level of practical activity, to bring out and make
conscious the philosophy embedded in that activity.

If we are to address the question of how feminists
have avoided exercising power, and how that avoidance was
at one time helpful but now is harmful, and if we are to
show how feminists have misunderstood the nature of power,
we must examine the practice of feminist organizations over
the last ten years. We must look for the theory contained
within that practice. What do feminists know about power?
What is the understanding of power contained in the political
action feminists have undertaken? What do feminist organizational forms and practices tell us about the way power is
understood? I do not intend here to write a history of this
most recent wave of feminism. Rather, I will simply call
attention to several characteristics of the contemporary wom-
en's movement which illustrate the ways the movement has
avoided exercising power, and use them to demonstrate how
avoiding power has hindered the movement as a whole in developing successful strategy. In this task, the various critiques and analyses of the women's movement can be very
helpful.

The Concept of Power in Feminist Practice

Several features of the women's movement are particularly significant in making clear the analysis of power which
has been accepted. First, consciousness raising groups have
historically been the basis for feminist organizations. Many
small groups of grass-roots activists have in fact been ex-

tensions of consciousness raising groups. Women's centers
too have often functioned on the "CR" group model. They
have frequently been based on personal, structureless politics,
and have been concerned with making a place where each
person could feel comfortable and accepted. Women's centers have traditionally opposed structures in which individuals
have power. Decisions about the work to be done in the following year have often been made in meetings where anyone
who came had as much right to participate as those who had
kept the center going during the previous year.

A second important characteristic of the women's
movement (for our purposes here) is the widespread opposition to leadership--an opposition which was overwhelming in
the early years of this wave of feminism, and is still very
strong. This opposition grew in part from the strong influence of anarchist thought in the United States. But it came
more immediately from feminist desires to eliminate bureau-
cratic structures and elitist leadership. [31] Some have argued
that the opposition to leadership meant that any woman who
was competent or could accomplish things was likely to be
"trashed" for being a leader. [32] Feminists were reacting to
the experience of leadership in the male-dominated Left--the
experience of leaders who were also those who dominated the
group, the experience of leaders who were an elite unre-
sponsive to the (female) members of the organization. Because women had been oppressed by leaders in these groups,
they reacted by refusing to designate any leaders at all.
This strategy, however, simply allowed the media to designate leaders. The point which emerges from these two features of the women's movement is that feminists attempted to
avoid appointing, electing, or selecting anyone who would
then be in a position to exercise power over them. They
recognized very clearly the important effects structures could
have on the exercise of power, and attempted to avoid those
effects by refusing to build more than minimal structures.

Feminist insistence on working collectively constitutes
a third important feature of the contemporary women's movement. Some collectives have insisted that the work done by
each member of a group should be identical with that of
every other--a way of avoiding the division of labor which has
in the past been associated with elitism. Although not all
groups which call themselves collectives function in this way,
many do. These latter are the objects of my concern here. [33]
Just as the women's movement erred in its almost universal
condemnation of leaders and its mistaken identification of

women who achieved things with those who wanted to dominate others, feminists, in working through collectives, have
often simply reacted against the isolation and competitiveness
of the capitalist workplace. Yet the lack of formal structures
often led to informal rather than formal domination of some
members of the collective by others. The attempt to avoid
hierarchy by avoiding formal structures altogether frequently
led to the creation of informal (and therefore more difficult
to dislodge) structures of domination. The theoretical control of the entire group over the work became the actual
domination of some members of the group by others. Some
members of the group may lose control over their work to
those who are more aggressive, although perhaps not more
skilled.

By insisting that every member of a collective do
every activity that the group as a whole is engaged in, the
collective, in practice, treats its members as interchange-
able parts. It reproduces the assembly line of the modern
factory, but instead of running the work past the people,
people are run past the work. Yet there is an important
statement about the nature of power contained in this practice. By implication, collectives of this sort are a statement that any differences are likely to lead to inequality and
relations of domination. This form of collective, one which
insists on the identity and interchangeability of its members,
is another way feminists have tried to avoid exercising power
by avoiding the creation or reinforcement of differences
among women which might allow some to gain a position from
which to dominate others.

A fourth major characteristic of the feminism of the
sixties and seventies has been an emphasis on process. I
argued in the first part of this essay that the emphasis on
process was fundamental to the development of a feminist
approach to politics. Feminists, however, have sometimes
become so concerned about the way things are done that
nothing is accomplished. Emphasizing the importance of
"the growing self," or the "evolving consciousness," can be
a way of avoiding the real political struggle. [34] In addition,
many feminists are familiar with the problems caused by
bringing matters up for discussion again and again until
everyone present has agreed to the policy; or the frequent
practice of re-making and re-thinking decisions when a new
woman shows up at a meeting for the first time and questions the decisions a group has already taken. The great
weight feminists have given to making sure everyone is satis-

fied with decisions makes clear their reluctance to use the power of the majority to dominate anyone (whether members of the organization or not) who might be present.

Fifth, I want to call attention to the way separatism has developed in the women's movement. First, feminists responded to male domination by insisting that they could only work separately. The split between Blacks and other minorities, and whites was a similar response to a similar situation. When it became clear that heterosexual women were oppressing lesbians and trying to make them invisible within the women's movement, and that middle and upper class women were oppressing working class women in the movement, the natural response was to split into smaller units. These units meant that no woman had to work with others who might be in a position--whether through class, race, or heterosexual privilege--to exercise power over her.

Finally, and related to separatism of various sorts, we have seen the creation of women's spaces, women's communities, and a women's culture. This is in part an attempt to overcome some of the differences among women, but is also in part a repetition and strengthening of the patterns of avoiding those who might have power over women. That is, feminists attempted to create spaces in a capitalist and patriarchal society where they could be free of their oppression as women--a world of women's music, women's businesses, coffeeshops, bars, living communities, etc. Each of these actions (I hesitate to call them conscious tactics) can and to some extent has become a way of avoiding either exercising or confronting power. They are ways of making comfortable spaces for feminists to exist. They can be places where women attempt to work out personal solutions. But personal solutions are part of the capitalist and patriarchal ethic of "getting yours." Moreover, such personal solutions will inevitably fail, since feminists cannot cut themselves off from the society which surrounds them.

It is fundamental to point out that each of the features of the women's movement to which I have called attention represents actions which were unquestionably correct at the time they developed. Although each of these actions can become a way for feminists to escape conflict, it is important to stress that it was fundamental to the survival and sanity of feminists, both as individuals and as a movement, to create "safe" spaces however defined, spaces where feminists could grow and learn and experiment. These safe spaces, however, must be a base for political action rather than an alternative to it. 35 Feminists still need places where they define the terms (as women, as lesbians, as Third World people, as working class people) and places to celebrate the success of the women's movement. But to make these things substitutes for struggling for political power will lead feminists away from the possibility of making fundamental change.

Domination, Capacity, and Community

There is an understanding of power implicit in all these actions of the women's movement. Up to this point, I have treated the nature and exercise of power as unproblematic, as something everyone understood. To a certain extent, feminists have in fact seen power as unproblematic, and the confusion to which I wish to call attention grows from this source. There are a number of vantage points from which the constellation of practices which surrounds political power can be understood. One of them is characteristically male-oriented, or patriarchal. The other two are more characteristically female-oriented. This is not to say that one cannot find women supporting patriarchal understandings of power, or men who describe more feminist understandings. Rather I am suggesting that there are some systematic differences in female and male experiences in patriarchal societies, and that these different experiences manifest themselves in the accounts often given of power. Moreover, it must be noted that these understandings of power are not altogether separable, and that each aspect of power has links to the others. It is very much a question of which features of power dominate the analysis, or which vantage point on the issue is chosen.

The characteristically male-oriented concept of power centers around power as "the ability to compel obedience or as control and domination."36 Power must be power over someone--something possessed, a property of an actor such that he can alter the will or actions of others in a way which produces results in conformity with his own will. 37 Such theorists have argued that power, like money, is something possessed by an actor which has value in itself as well as being useful for obtaining other valued things. Power as domination of others (or the use of power to "purchase" certain behavior) is what most people (especially women) confront. On this understanding, power is exercised in situations in which one person gets another to do something the

latter is disinclined to do, by threatening some consequences
that the second person will dislike more than taking the required action. [38] Some authors have gone so far as to attempt to make explicit the connection of this understanding of
power to virility and masculinity. [39]

        Feminists have experienced the exercise of power most
clearly in situations where there are conflicting objectives--
situations which involve one party (unwillingly) doing something the other wants.   Although feminists recognize that
power relations are part of this society as a whole, women's
experience of power has rarely been that of holding power
and most frequently has been that of having power exercised
over them.   The experience of oppression has led feminists
to accept the patriarchal understanding of power, and to believe that the exercise of power is equivalent to the exercise
of domination.   Moreover, the women's movement has often
traced the ability to dominate the personal characteristics
such as sex, race, sexual preference etc.   Consequently,
feminists have tried to develop forms of organization (very
amorphous forms) in which the question of power based on
differences in personal attributes or on differences in position within the group do not lead to differences in power--
i. e. , structureless groups where there are no differences of
sex, sexual preference, class, and so on. [40]

        There are, however, alternative understandings of
power which do not require domination of others, and it is
these understandings which have been stressed disproportionately by women who have written about power.   Berenice
Carroll, for example, points out that in Webster's International Dictionary (1933) "power" is first defined not as domination but as "ability, whether physical, mental, or moral,
to act; the faculty of doing or performing something" and is
synonymous with "strength, vigor, energy, force, and ability. "[41] This understanding of power does not require domination of others; energy and accomplishment are understood
to be satisfying in themselves.   This kind of power is much
closer to what the women's movement has sought, yet this
aspect of power is denied to all but a few women.

        Interestingly, a similar notion of power appears in
Hanna Pitkin's Wittgenstein and Justice, where she stresses
the distinction between "power to" and "power over. " Pitkin argues that there is power over someone which is distinct
from the power to influence someone.   But these two sorts
of power do not differ from each other in such a way that

they are obviously and easily distinguishable. [42] Adrienne
Rich, too, describes a more female-centered understanding
of power. She argues that women's power has been felt as
an energy looking for objects into which to pour itself, has
even been felt sometimes as a demonic possession. [43] Important in all these descriptions of power is a sense of power as energy, as the ability to transform oneself and the
world, of power as part of a process of change which can
be moved forward and directed.

There is a third aspect of power which has received
all too little attention from scholars. Power is always exercised within a community, as part of a relationship. The
notion of community and its relation to the exercise of power
is less clearly divisible into a patriarchal as opposed to feminist understanding. Hannah Arendt is perhaps the clearest
commentator on the issue of community and its relation to
power. She defines power as "the human ability not just to
act but to act in concert. Power is never the property of
the individual; it belongs to a group and remains in existence
only so long as the group keeps together."[44] The power of
men over women, then, can be understood to derive from the
power of men as a group. It can only be met with a like
kind of power. Even though Arendt sees the activities of a
revolutionary group as violent in her terms, she contradicts
her own argument that violence is the antithesis of power
when she notes that violence or willingness to do violence in
revolution can be a means of forging very strong bonds of
group solidarity. Pitkin, too, notes the importance of the
community in power relations. She points out that language
itself involves a set of social relations and that in acting
through language we act within a social context. [45] Since
most acts which involve the exercise of power are speech
acts, they therefore involve participants in a community.

Feminists have rightly rejected the use of power as
domination, and as a property analogous to money, but in
practice, their confusions about the differences among the
possible understandings of power--or perhaps lack of recognition that there were different understandings of power--led
to difficulties about leadership, strength, achievement, structured organizations, and so on. In general feminists have
not recognized that power understood as energy strength,
and effectiveness both within a community and as a community need not be the same as power which requires domination of others.

Feminists, however, recognize and confront the world of traditional politics, in which money and power work in similar ways. Creating political change requires that feminists develop organizational forms based on power defined as energy, strength, and the possibility of community action, groups which are structured and not tied to the personality of a single individual, groups whose structures do not permit the use of power to dominate others in the group. At the same time, these organizations must be effective in a society in which power is most fundamentally a tool for making others do what they do not wish to do.

Conclusion

Perhaps the first step in responding to the current state of the women's movement is to begin to work out systematically what power exercised as a community and power exercised within the feminist community can mean. It is clear that power as domination means power exercised among unequals and power exercised over those defined as "the other." Power exercised among equals who are part of a community with shared goals and shared practices can only be something very different. As a movement, feminists have already recognized the connections between domination, inequality, and lack of community. They have not as yet, however, developed alternatives. The method of analysis feminists have developed can be a very important tool for examining the feminist movement itself. If the women's movement is able to recognize in practice that power is not necessarily equivalent to the domination of others, and that inequalities which lead to domination cannot be avoided simply by insisting that each member of a group have the same personal attributes and/or do the same work, some of the differences which have fragmented the movement may be overcome. In addition, new organizational forms--in which leaders are chosen, given power, and still kept accountable to the group--may be developed. The working out in practice of alternative understandings of power is essential to building a powerful and effective feminist community, one which can both formulate alternatives and work for real change.

NOTES

Many people have helped me formulate the ideas

in this essay. The section on the feminist mode
of analysis has profited from comments from C.
Ellison, Z. Eisenstein, J. Landes, S. Rose, and
M. Schoolman. I have had numerous discussions
about the ideas in the second section of the paper
with R. Flathman, and J. G. A. Pocock. The
Quest staff has been instrumental in helping me
formulate and develop ideas, and readers of Quest
will no doubt find many familiar ideas in these
pages.

1. The Baltimore Sun, December 9, 1976.
2. Ibid., January 15, 1977.
3. Statement by Wendy Yoshimura, The Baltimore Sun (API
    release) February 21, 1977.
4. In addition to small articles in various feminist news-
    papers (especially Sister, and Big Mama Rag) the fol-
    lowing have been especially important in making these
    and other arguments about the stage of the women's
    movement: Victoria Geng, "Requiem for the Women's
    Movement," Harper's, Vol. 253 (November, 1976),
    49-68; Naomi Weistein and Heather Booth, "Will the
    Women's Movement Survive?" Lesbian Tide (Fall,
    1976), 28-33; Carmen Kerr, "The Corruption of Fem-
    inism," Issues in Radical Therapy III, 4 (Fall, 1976),
    3-8; Charlotte Bunch, "Beyond Either/Or: Feminist
    Options," Quest: A Feminist Quarterly III, 1 (Sum-
    mer, 1976), 2-17; Red Apple, (a work group of the
    Connecticut Valley Women's Union) "Women's Unions
    and Socialist Feminism" Quest: A Feminist Quarterly
    IV, 1 (Summer, 1977), 88-96.
5. Reprinted in Sister VII, 1 (July-August), 1976, 10.
    The contemporary relevance of such a statement is
    especially clear in light of the increasingly strong re-
    sistance to the ratification of the ERA.
6. Leszek Kolakowski, Toward a Marxist Humanism (New
    York: Grove Press, 1968), pp. 145-6.
7. Victoria Schuck, "Sexism and Scholarship: A Brief
    Overview of Women, Academia, and the Disciplines,"
    Social Science Quarterly, LV, 3 (December, 1974),
    563-585.
8. Antonio Gramsci, Selections from the Prison Notebooks,
    tr. Quinton Hoare and Geoffrey Nowell Smith (New
    York: International Publishers, 1971), pp. 225, 307.
    Gramsci was one of the founders and probably most
    important theorist of the Italian Communist Party.
9. I should perhaps note here that in all this I am speaking

as a participant as well as a critical observer. The
experiences I take as a reference point are my own
as well as those of other women.

10. Georg Lukács, History and Class Consciousness (Cam-
    bridge, Mass.: MIT Press, 1971), p. 1.
11. This is not to say there have not been problems, or
    that always beginning with personal experience in every
    case led women to think in larger terms. Some groups
    have remained apolitical, or have never moved beyond
    the level of personal issues; others have become so
    opposed to any other than personal organizations that
    they are immobilized. There are, as well, problems
    about the "correct line" which are part of the current
    debate in the women's movement. On the current
    problems, see Charlotte Bunch, "Beyond Either/Or:
    Feminist Options," Quest: A Feminist Quarterly III,
    1 (Summer, 1976) 2-17.
12. Gramsci, Prison Notebooks, p. 330.
13. Ibid., p. 10.
14. Ibid., p. 43.
15. Marge Piercy, "A Shadow Play for Guilt," To Be of
    Use (Garden City, New York: Doubleday, 1973),
    p. 17.
16. Karl Marx, "Theses on Feuerbach," in Karl Marx and
    Frederick Engels, The German Ideology, ed. C. J.
    Arthur (New York: International Publishers, 1970),
    p. 121. This method also overcomes the passivity
    characteristic of much of American life. See, for
    example, the comments of Richard Sennett and Jona-
    than Cobb, The Hidden Injuries of Class (New York:
    Vintage, 1973), p. 165; and Stanley Aronowitz, False
    Promises (New York: McGraw-Hill, 1973), p. 112.
    See also Gramsci, Prison Notebooks, p. 351.
17. Gramsci, Prison Notebooks, p. 360. See also Lukács,
    History and Class Consciousness, p. 19.
18. Gramsci, Prison Notebooks, p. 352.
19. On this concept, see Nicos Poulantzas, Classes in Con-
    temporary Capitalism (London: New Left Books,
    1975), p. 21.
20. See the statement by Marx, 1844 Manuscripts, p. 141.
    See also Karl Marx, Grundrisse, tr. Martin Nicolaus
    (Middlesex, England: Penguin Books, 1973), p. 162.
21. Marx, "Theses on Feuerbach," in The German Ideology,
    p. 121. See also Gramsci, pp. 352, 360.
22. See Lukács, History and Class Consciousness, p. 175.
23. Karl Marx, Capital, Vol. I (Moscow: Foreign Language
    Publishing House, 1954), p. 20.

24. Marx, 1844 Manuscripts, p. 119.
25. Ibid., p. 13.
26. Marx and Engels, The German Ideology, p. 114.
27. Gramsci, Prison Notebooks, p. 243. Poulantzas and
     others have commented on similar phenomena by
     calling attention to the "decisive" role of ideological
     and political structures, particularly the state appa-
     ratus. (Poulantzas, Classes... p. 27; See also Ernest
     Mandel, Late Capitalism (London: New Left Books,
     1975), pp. 500-513.
28. Poulantzas, Classes... p. 168.
29. Karl Marx, The Poverty of Philosophy (New York: In-
     ternational Publishers, 1973), p. 125.
30. Here too, see Gramsci, Prison Notebooks, p. 424. A
     part of the process Gramsci describes here--convinc-
     ing people that they are philosophers without knowing
     it--had already been included in feminist practice.
     This attention to action, to what people already know,
     is strikingly similar to the work of Ludwig Wittgen-
     stein in the Philosophical Investigations, tr. G. E. M.
     Anscombe, (New York: Macmillan, 1953) and Re-
     marks on the Foundations of Mathematics, eds. G. H.
     von Wright, R. Rhees, and G. E. M. Anscombe
     (Cambridge, Mass.: MIT Press, 1967).
31. See, for example, Charlotte Bunch and Beverly Fisher,
     "What Future for Leadership," Quest: A Feminist
     Quarterly III, 4 (Spring, 1976), 2-14.
32. See the letter of resignation from the women's move-
     ment by Anselma dell'Olio and Joreen, printed in
     Chicago Women's Liberation Newsletter, (mimeo-
     graphed) July, 1970, p. 4.
33. See Ginny Berson, "Olivia: We Don't Just Process
     Records," Sister, VII, 2 (December-January, 1976)
     pp. 8-9, for an analysis of a "collective" which does
     not work this way.
34. See the articles referred to above, n. 4, for some de-
     scriptions of this process.
35. Weistein and Booth ("Will the Women's Movement Sur-
     vive?") make a similar point (see note 4).
36. See for example Bertrand Russell, Power: A New So-
     cial Analysis (n. p.: 1936), p. 35, cited by Anthony
     de Crespigny and Alan Wertheimer, Contemporary
     Political Theory (New York: Atherton Press, 1970),
     p. 22.
37. See Talcott Parsons, "On the Concept of Political Pow-
     er," in Political Power, eds. Roderick Bell, David V.
     Edwards, and R. Harrison Wagner (New York: Free

Press, 1969), p. 256.

38. See also, in addition to the works already cited, Harold
     Lasswell and Abraham Kaplan, Power and Society
     (New Haven: Yale University Press, 1950), p. 76;
     and David Bell, Power, Influence, and Authority (New
     York: Oxford University Press, 1975).

39. David Bell, Power, Influence and Authority, p. 8. See
     also Bertrand de Jouvenel, in Hannah Arendt, "Re-
     flections on Violence," Journal of International Af-
     fairs, XXIII, 1 (1969), 12, cited by Berenice Carroll,
     "Peace Research: The Cult of Power," paper pre-
     sented to the American Sociological Association in
     Denver, Colorado, Sept., 1971, p. 6. Interestingly
     enough, the aspect of power as domination is what
     Arendt has referred to as violence. She argues that
     violence is instrumental (as is power understood as
     domination) and that it is designed to multiply strength
     [On Violence (New York: Harcourt, Brace, and World,
     1969), p. 46]. Arendt adds that "Only after one elim-
     inates this disastrous reduction of public affairs to the
     business of dominion will the original data concerning
     human affairs appear or rather reappear in their au-
     thentic diversity." See "Reflections on Violence,"
     New York Review of Books, XII (February 27, 1969),
     24, cited by Hanna Pitkin, Wittgenstein and Justice
     (Berkeley: University of California Press, 1973),
     p. 277. It might be observed here that the under-
     standing of power as domination is only one aspect of
     the dualism which Adrienne Rich argues characterizes
     patriarchal thought. She notes that a world in which
     having power means that there must be someone with-
     out power and over whom power is exercised simply
     reflects a split in the conceptual world between the
     inner and outer, the self and the other [Of Woman
     Born (New York: Norton, 1976), p. 67]. She points
     out that the characteristically female experience does
     not follow this pattern. She cites several examples of
     female experience, among them, the experience of
     pregnancy, which overcome the dichotomy of "me"
     and "not me." (Ibid., pp. 64, 36, and 167.)

40. This strategy indicates the extent to which feminists
     have failed to challenge their own liberal and capi-
     talist assumptions. Rather than look directly to the
     pattern of social relations, the shape of society as a
     whole, feminists have often tried to find the sources
     of their difficulties in the personal attributes pos-
     sessed by individuals. C. B. MacPherson, in The

Political Theory of Possessive Individualism (London: Oxford University Press, 1962) has made clear the connections between this approach to politics and the development of capitalist society.

41.   Carroll, "Peace Research," p. 7; See also Christian Bay, The Structure of Freedom (New York: Atheneum, 1968).

42.   Pitkin, Wittgenstein and Justice, p. 279.

43.   Rich, Of Woman Born, pp. 69, 101.

44.   Arendt, On Violence, p. 44.

45.   Ibid., p. 67.

Chapter 2

HOW POWERFUL IS POWERFUL?
The Women's Movement and the
Four Black Congresswomen

by Inez Smith Reid

To examine the power of four Black female members
of Congress is to conduct an analysis in a vacuum.   To pre-
cede that analysis with a glimpse into the power of the total
women's movement places the inquiry into some meaningful
context.

Can one speak of the power of the four Black Congresswomen, or the power of the total women's movement?
Must one discuss the women's movement as a middle class
fad?   Or must it be reckoned with as a revolutionary force?
Must one quietly accept the four Black female Congresswomen as the gentleladies of the legislature?   Or must they
be regarded as the amazons of the political arena, or at
least the Black political arena?   If the women's movement
is powerful, or if the four Black Congresswomen are powerful, how powerful is powerful?   A search for answers to
these questions may provide some tentative conclusions about
the power of the women's movement and that of four Black
women who have been positioned in the halls of the United
States Congress.

Is the Women's Movement a Middle Class
Fad or a Revolutionary Force?

Is the women's movement a middle class fad or a
revolutionary force?   This is one of those common questions
which clouds the complexities of a striking movement but
which nonetheless is capable of yielding conclusions about the
power of the women's movement.   Of course it is middle
class.   Few realists would negate that proposition.   In fact,
however, most protest groups and individuals in the forefront of potential change have their origins in middle class
homes.   Angela Davis, Kathy Boudin, Martin Luther King,

25

Jr., the NAACP (W. E. B. DuBois and Charles Houston),
and George Wiley of the National Welfare Rights Organization
are illustrative. As Juliet Mitchell has written in Women's
Estate: "... poverty alone cannot protest itself. It is never
extreme deprivation that produces the revolutionary."[1]

Of course it's not a fad. It's been with us, historically, at least since 1848. Or, if one prefers not to identify the current women's push with the early feminist strug-
glers, it's been with us at least since mid to late 1960's.
And while some women devote great energies to the movement, it is difficult to describe them as being entangled in
a "craze" or as manifesting some type of "exaggerated zeal."

Of course it's not a revolutionary force. Juliet
Mitchell misleads us all when she writes: "... in concept
and organization, [the women's liberation movement] ... is
the most public revolutionary movement ever to have existed."[2] To which one must raise an incredulous eyebrow
and ask: More publicly revolutionary than the Algerian FLN,
than the PAIGC in Guinea-Bissau, than the Panthers, than
the SDS? Hardly.

So, now, if the women's movement is middle class
but neither a fad nor a revolutionary force, what is it? Or,
more pertinent, perhaps, what does it do? What has it accomplished?

First, the women's movement is a dynamic force composed of women anxious to extricate themselves from fundamental psychological oppression. Movement women--White
women in particular--have been struggling to get a hold on
themselves, to discover what makes them tick in fright and
terror on the streets, in the home, in the university, on
their jobs. Particularly nerve-racking to them is the apparent malady which afflicts bright, educated, middle class
young women. Jesse Bernard, the sociologist has written
about that malady. Matina Horner, the psychologist, has
spent hours and hours pouring over psychological data to
shed some light on that puzzling malady. It is a malady
which cannot be dismissed with a shrug of the shoulders or
with a grain of salt because it has enormous implications
for a movement which wants to address itself to more than
the esoteric problems of an idiosyncratic segment of our
society.

What is that malady? Depending on whether one wants

to view it negatively or positively it is "fear of success" or
"avoidance of success." Women underachieve, goes the
theory, because they literally fear success, or they avoid
success because they clearly believe that success and femininity are incompatible. As Matina Horner has stated: "Unusual excellence in women [is] clearly associated for them
with the loss of femininity, social rejection, personal or
societal destruction or some combination of the above."[3]

The writings of Bernard, Horner and others under-
score the apprehension of White women in particular, and
their anxiety to bounce away from psychological oppression.
But how can this "bouncing away" process be accomplished?
What is the formula? "Through consciousness-raising" comes
the chorus from the women's movement. Consciousness-raising
usually occurs in small groups, six to twenty-five individuals,
where the topics generally covered are: family, childhood
and adolescence, men, marital status, motherhood, sex,
women, behavior, age, ambitions and movement activity.[4]

While consciousness-raising is important, and while
one cannot deny that the women's movement has done a superb job in this area, inevitably the question must be posed
starkly: So what if women's consciousness is raised? One
consciousness-raising session, broadcast over radio station
WBAI-FM in New York City, was devoted to men and violence. It explored men's "control" of the streets, men's
tendency to resort to violence against women.[5] The last
words uttered during the program ended on an extremely
pessimistic note, seeming to internalize fear and a conviction
of powerlessness:

> It seems to me that the reason we have such dif-
> ficulty responding adequately either to being at-
> tacked or being put down or being used in some
> way, being disregarded, whistled at or whatever,
> is that on the one hand there is objectively a great
> deal of real danger, and to a certain extent if
> we're sensible we're going to back away. I mean
> that's a sensible reaction to real danger. But on
> the other hand we have internalized our fear of in-
> voking male anger, and that we carry around with-
> in us--this powerlessness. We've allowed it to
> shape us on the inside so that internally we're de-
> bilitated and there are also external conditions that
> are really threatening. The combination of the two
> really, I think, is too much.[6]

With such pessimism permitted to "hang in the air"
it is little wonder that some are beginning to raise questions
about consciousness-raising. As Juliet Mitchell put it:
"Some of the women's liberation 'consciousness-raising'
groups have suffered the fate of the whirlpool. Individual-
small group-individual. Lonely women have left home and
gone back home. "[7] One participant in a consciousness-raising session described her experience and mounting frustration
in these terms:

> I kept asking myself, What is the point of just con-
> tinuing to talk about ourselves? Why bother?
> Where is it leading? Some evenings we didn't get
> down to serious discussion until 10:30 or 11:00
> when everyone was ready to go home. Some meet-
> ings degenerated to the level of comparing bra
> sizes and talking about vitamins we bought at the
> health food store. At these meetings we were all
> unconsciously expressing our frustration with our
> purposelessness. I left because the group did not
> change and I needed to relate to the women's move-
> ment in a different way. I felt nothing could be
> accomplished by becoming more and more intimate
> with a small group of women and that if women's
> groups are not political then they are nothing more
> than amateur therapy or social clubs. [M]y stay-
> ing in a small group which just talks and which
> does not relate to the rest of the movement is
> stagnation. [8]

Maybe this woman was in a bad, in the sense of ineffective,
consciousness-raising group. Yet, she forces two essential
inquiries: What kind of consciousness is being developed?
What follows consciousness-raising?

Unless some kind of political-social-economic consciousness is being raised for the purpose of addressing
labyrinthic political-social-economic problems, then one
might validly ask: What's the point? As Juliet Mitchell reminds us: "If we simply develop feminist consciousness (as
radical feminists suggest) we will get, not political consciousness but ... simply a self-directed gaze, that sees only the
internal workings of one segment; only this segment's self-
interest. Political consciousness responds to all forms of
oppression. "[9]

The women's movement is a dynamic force bent on

terminating psychological oppression. Yet, it may have fallen
short of the mark because women are not being molded to address complex socio-economic and political issues.

Second, the women's movement is a force which has
not yet adequately addressed itself to hard social and economic problems; rather, it has wallowed almost exclusively
in interpersonal, personal, and artistic concerns.

Rebirth of Feminism[10] supposedly, according to Catherine Stimpson's review, is a valuable "political and intellectual history. "[11] As such, it should tell us what the movement accomplished--at least during the period 1961-1971.
What it tells us is that the movement achieved some success
in the areas of the media, abortion, child care, education,
professions, and the church. It attacked "Blondes have more
fun, " or "Camay keeps the girls different from the boys. "
It called in question discrimination against women employees
by Ladies Home Journal, Newsweek, Time, Washington Post,
San Francisco Chronicle, and the New York Times. It created its own communications network. But it didn't address
itself much to ownership and control of the media, and the
implications of ownership and control for the total oppressed
community. It didn't address itself enough to problems of
Cable TV acquisition and the availability, for purchase, of
radio stations and newspapers by the oppressed.

It did launch a highly successful attack on outmoded
abortion laws and enjoyed an enormous victory in Roe v.
Wade and Doe v. Bolton. Yet, did it heed the sighs of one
pregnant welfare recipient who muttered: "Now I have the
right to have an abortion, but I don't have the right to be
pregnant. "[12] Did it tackle, as enthusiastically, the plight
of poor women who are victims of involuntary sterilizations,
sterilizations without informed consent?

It made an assault on this country's attitudes toward
child care--especially for working mothers--mothers who are
college professors, administrators with philanthropic organizations, undergraduate and graduate students. But, did it
do more than give a nod to the plight of poor mothers anxious to work but apprehensive lest their children be left in
custodial or psychologically questionable atmospheres? Yes,
there were some attempts to establish day care "liberation
centers" in poor areas. Nevertheless, as one mother wrote:

Most of the group were White middle-class hippy

or radical type women, a third of whom had Black
children. There were no Black mothers, and most
efforts to recruit Black or Puerto Rican mothers
failed. The objection seemed to be that our nurs-
ery was non-institutional: dirty and sloppy, and
emphasis was placed on free play rather than structured learning. One Black mother did join the
group but left because she didn't feel at ease with
the other mothers who seemed like hippies to
her. [13]

An isolated experience? Maybe.

The movement, particularly through the Women's
Equity Action League (WEAL), made a magnificent assault
on sex discrimination at the elementary, junior high, high
school, and college-university level: both in terms of cur-
ricula materials and personnel. It devoted enormous attention to women in the professions. But did it really give
more than a passing consideration to the economic and employment problems of poor women--especially Black women--
who occupy the lowest economic rung in this country?

It "toyed" with the church--even questioned the alleged
sex of God. But did it address itself to the fundamental
racism of the church--nationally and internationally?

Radical feminists supposedly are more involved with
hard social problems than so-called reformist and moderate
groups. If that is true, Radical Feminism[14] ought to tell
us what they have accomplished. Disappointment oozes
through the veins as one learns that, in terms of the "wom-
en's experience" Radical feminists reflected concern for
middle-aged women whose families blamed them for their
every shortcoming, concern for gay relationships, for consciousness-raising, for the necessity for man-hating, for the
poor portrayal of females in children's books, for sexual
freedom. In terms of theory and analysis there was a concern for the need to break away from social control, for
abortion, for enforcement of Title VII of the 1964 Civil
Rights Act even though, it was admitted, "positive implementation" of that Act "would not likely result in any immediate,
drastic change in the pattern of women's employment,"[15]
for the uselessness of psychology in trying to understand
women, for sex, for the need to collectivize and industrialize
housework, for the need to regard marriage as slavery, for
the need to view rape as an act of terror against women and

as part of the ideology of sexism. In terms of building a
movement, there was concern for consciousness and the
group process. Then, a few theoretical articles, outdated
platforms of action, manifestos, and a glimpse at women in
the arts rounded out Radical Feminism. What about fundamental social problems like adult criminal justice and juvenile justice, problems on which virtually all women's
groups have been alarmingly silent? Only the Black feminists seem to have taken more than a fanciful interest in
these areas.

It may not be too farfetched to suggest that NBFO,
the National Black Feminist Organization was conceived on
the bed of deep frustration with the women's movement's
inability to address fundamental social and economic problems
which affect all oppressed groups, not just one segment.
Even Catherine Stimpson in her review of Radical Feminism
noted the lack of "a more scrupulous account of the nexus
between sex roles and class, between sex roles and money,
and between radical feminism and radical economics." She
noted, too, that the "analysis of the links between the wom-
en's movement and post industrial technology ... is often
thin to the point of transparency."[16]

The period 1971-1977 reveals some additional gains
but even those gains are not the hard social and political
variety. Moreover, the 1971-1977 period unveils the same
kind of backlash against women as against minorities who
sought to open up channels of real opportunity in American
Society. While Roe v. Wade still stands, Federal funds to
pay for abortions not necessary due to conditions threatening
the life of the mother apparently are no longer available.
While a woman's bank opened up in New York City, women
by no means have the economic weapons which would permit
them to exercise effective power at all levels of American
Society. While society knows, at least theoretically, that
sex discrimination is not to be tolerated at the elementary
and secondary school level, vocational education schools still
do not offer meaningful educational opportunities for females.
And although Juanita Kreps and Patricia Harris ascended to
national cabinet posts, women neither hold the reins of national political power, nor solely control even one string in
the total rope of national power.

Third, the women's movement is composed of a large
body of women, not all but a large body, who persist in ignoring an analysis of power and thus fail to analyze their

strategies in light of a broader conceptualization of power.
One of the most illuminating articles written on the women's
movement is one fashioned by Elizabeth Janeway. In her
article "The Weak Are the Second Sex,"[17] Ms. Janeway
pens the following words of wisdom which deserve repeated
readings:

> When women ask for equality, this should be seen
> as an example of what happens when the weak chal-
> lenge the powerful. I do not believe that one can
> ... make a case for Women and only for women,
> and I believe that until women see this they will
> waste time and energy fighting all men as if every
> issue that arises between them were political. In
> my view, the case for women is a paradigm, a
> brief in a class action for subordinated groups as
> a whole against clumsy, inefficient and stupidly
> solipsistic power center.[18]

Examining the power dynamic as it relates to men
and women is crucial. As Ms. Janeway notes: "Equality
for women brings more competition (to men), but for those
who think of themselves as fair competitors, that isn't shat-
tering. Equality with women, however, is something else.
If you have been brought up to know that women are inferior
--deservedly inferior--how can you accept that? It's shock-
ing, it's insulting, it's UNFAIR."[19] Not only is the "equality with" instead of the "equality for" difficult to accept, but
also the ultimate reality of accepting the "equality with"
proposition. For "closing the male/female split means a
drastic rearrangement of the barriers between the weak and
the powerful. Then not women, but the weak become the
second sex, subordinate, submissive, subject to rape."[20]
That is, the simply weak (women), powerful (male) dichotomy
will disintegrate with a new sexless dichotomy: weak and
powerful with some of both sexes in each category. Thus,
"the demand that women be given a share in power" not only
"upsets men" but also "forces upon men a review of their
own position."[21] What they may see in such a review is a
picture of women "ready to storm the bastions of the Establishment" while they who have failed to storm "live out their
lives in submission and resignation." As they reside in their
"cells of submission and resignation ... suddenly ... bursting
out of the slave quarters come women--the inferiors--invad-
ing the corridors of power as if, by merely being human,
they had a right to be there."[22]

Not only would a power analysis bare the danger of men reacting devastatingly to relegation to "the second sex" but it would also disabuse women of the belief that they "are going to climb easily into positions of power because fairness demands that they be represented according to their numbers."[23] Stinging and bitter lessons have been learned through the cases of Cissy Farenthold whose name was tacked onto the IRS (Internal Revenue Service) review list by the Nixon Administration, and Congresswoman Shirley Chisholm, threatened with prosecution over relatively paltry sums of money.

Naiveté and politics never mix well. And what an analysis of power can teach is that power may know no justice; power may have no sensitivity to tearful pleas; power is as cold as a nose gripped and bitten by 25 below zero degree weather. Much more could be said on the subject of power. Suffice it to say, however, in the words of Ms. Janeway: "I believe ... that women would profit by a study of power and its workings."[24]

The women's movement is not a fad; it is middle class; it is not a revolutionary force but it has raised political consciousness to such an extent that thousands of women (including 8,000 to 10,000 in the State of New York) turned up for state women's meetings in connection with the National International Women's Year Conference held in Houston, Texas in November 1977. It is beginning to get women of all social classes to at least think about social issues other than rape and abortion. It is beginning to reveal the seeds of power--enough to get female cabinet appointments-- but it has not yet been able to alter the fundamental bases of power in this country.

How powerful is powerful with respect to the women's movement? Clearly there is power of the voice, power of powerless numbers, power of moral outrage, and to a certain extent power of the mind but there is not yet power of the purse, or power of the communications media, or power of the strategic move.

Are the Black Female Congresswomen Gentleladies or Amazons?

Are the Black female Congresswomen gentleladies or amazons? This is one of those questions which might be dismissed quickly as an unfair and biased inquiry. Yet, the conclusions which it produces might help answer questions about the power of the four Black female members of Congress.

Gentle connotes soft, compliant, wellborn, refined, and docile. Amazon suggests warrior, aggressive, strong, masculine, tough, and powerful. Is it possible that Black Congresswomen may be (or at least are perceived to be) both gentle and amazon-like? Is there power in gentleness? Does power inevitably flow to the Amazon?

Our inquiry must be examined within an analytical framework which focuses on: the context in which the Black female legislators perform their congressional role, the demands made upon them as national legislators, the style with which they have chosen to operate, the goals which they seem to have adopted, and the yield of their efforts (in power terms).

One cannot begin to address questions of the power of Black female members of Congress without first confronting some disgraceful statistics. By the early nineteen seventies there were some 520,000 elected officials in the United States. Of these some 337 were Black women. The 337 figure included many who held school board positions. For example, of the 37 Black female elected officials in New York State in the early nineteen seventies, thirty-five served on school boards. The number "four" stands out as ridiculous in the context of half a million, or even in the context of almost half a thousand.

Most American citizens learn at a very young age that a man or a woman shall not be exposed to double jeopardy. Indeed, the American Constitution specifically states that one may not be put in jeopardy twice for the same set of circumstances. Yet, it is clear that Black women have been entangled in the evil net of double jeopardy for centuries--the jeopardy which comes from being Black (racism) and the jeopardy which stems from being a woman (sexism). Not to be missed is that the double jeopardy has led also to economic deprivation or powerlessness in the purse.

In 1963 Lorraine Hansberry, author of Raisin in the Sun and To Be Young, Gifted and Black described in the latter book (New York: New American Library, 1969, pp. 225-6), "America as seen through the eyes of the TV tube." Her description ran as follows:

1. Most people who work for a living (and there
   are a few) are executives and/or work in the
   same kind of office.
2. Sex is the basis of all psychological, economic,
   political, historical, social--in fact, known--
   problems of man.
3. Sex is very bad.
4. Sex is very good and the solution to all psychological, economic, political, historical, social--
   in fact, known--problems of man.
5. The present social order is here forever and this
   is the best of all possible worlds.
6. The present social order is here forever and this
   is the worst of all possible worlds.
7. The present social order is all in the mind.
8. Women are idiots.
9. Negroes do not exist.

Leave no doubt about it.   The four Black Congresswomen
have been subjected to racism, sexism and economic deprivation.   They now hold a public office which should shield them
from the harsher effects and manifestations of racism, sexism, and economic deprivation but which will not permit them
to escape the impact altogether.   All this prompts the question: can one subjected to racism, sexism, and economic
deprivation be powerful?

Relevant to an understanding of the power or powerlessness of the four Black Congresswomen are the demands
made upon them.   Heaped upon these women are both indi-
vidual-organizational-group demands and issue demands.   Undoubtedly these demands are made because these women are
Black, female, local politicians, natural politicians, and public figures.   There are the demands of governors, mayors,
heads of state and local agencies, members of the industrial
and financial world, public interest firms, advocacy groups
(those in behalf of women, other ethnic minorities, the poor,
the aged, the handicapped, the addicted, the alcoholic, etc.),
civic, social and other clubs.   The issue demands are stag-
gering: health (medicare and medicaid, health planning, dis-
eases [cancer, hypertension, heart disease], sterilization,
abortion, immunization, etc.); labor (manpower training,
CETA programs, youth employment, supported work for ex-
fellows, etc.); education (public elementary and secondary
school assistance, private school assistance, desegregation,
racial isolation, vocational education, student financial assistance for college, graduate and professional schools, Black
colleges, discrimination against teachers, professors, access

to high level administrative position, boards of education,
boards of higher education, etc.); public assistance (welfare
reform; benefit for survivors, the aged, the blind; Aid to
Families with Dependent Children, etc.); commerce (aid to
minority business, assistance to firms willing to locate in
inner cities and other economically depressed areas); housing
(construction and maintenance of public housing, construction
and maintenance of middle income housing, mortgage discrimination and other household financing issues, etc.); energy (cost of gasoline, cost of heating, staffing in the new
Energy Department, etc.); justice (the state of the penal system, treatment of juvenile offenders, increasing the number
of Black judges, Black United States attorneys, impediments
to civil suits by the economically poor, decisions emanating
from the United States Supreme Court which are adverse to
women and minorities, etc.). The list of demands is mind-
boggling and prompts the question: can one on whom so
many demands are heaped be powerful or be perceived as
powerful if each and every demand is not met?

What kind of women are being asked to meet so many
varied demands and address a mind-boggling variety of issues?
They range in age from 41 to 52. Their signs vary from
Pisces to Virgo to Sagittarius to Libra. Their fathers struggled as janitor, factory worker, laborer, and Baptist pastor/
warehouse assistant. Their mothers worked as real estate
agent, seamstress, nurse, and homemaker. Two studied
law (at the University of Southern California and at Boston
University). One concentrated on education (at Columbia).
One began college (Northwestern) but left to do stenographic
work. Two initially commenced legal careers. One launched
a career as an educator. The third concentrated on sten-
ography, then became an accountant, then an auditor. Three
interrupted their chosen careers to serve in the state legislature: The California Assembly, the New York Assembly, and
the Texas State Senate. A fourth helped her husband in his
political career (including service in the United States Congress) until his untimely death in an airplane crash.

One arrived in Congress in 1968, two in 1972, and
one in 1973. One is comely and calm. Another is thin and
fiery. Yet another is relatively average size and circum-
spect. The last is heavy set and imposing. None rose from
the Black intelligentsia, or the Black bourgeoisie, or the
Black lumpen-proletariat. Each is bright, shrewd, and im-
bued with common sense and political instinct.

None may easily be labeled within the four political styles identified by Jeane J. Kirkpatrick in <u>Political Woman</u>.[26] At least one or all may be a "leader." ("The leader has a special concern with authority and influence.") At least one or all may be a "moralizer." ("The moralizer is distinguished by the priority of her involvement with questions of right and wrong, good and bad and her tendency to emphasize the moral dimension....") None or all may be a "personalizer." ("The personalizer is preoccupied with interpersonal relations, more specifically with the search for approval and affection ....") At least one or all may be a "problem solver." ("The problem solver is a truly multivalue personality whose commitments to family and policy-oriented public service coexist peacefully.")[27]

The four do not form a cohesive unit. They do not represent a monolithic voice. They do not exert influence as a foursome, but they do share interests. Each has addressed women's issues: sterilization and abortions. Each has paid some attention to social welfare issues. Each has an abiding concern about racial discrimination--both institutional and personal.

Yvonne B. Burke

She is quiet, attractive, not visibly threatening. She was a model; then served as a deputy corporation counsel. She was a hearing officer for the Los Angeles Police Commission that investigated the 1965 Watts riots. People like her. People seek her out. Yale wanted her as a Chubb Fellow. Harvard lured her as a Fellow at the Institute of Politics (attached to the John F. Kennedy School of Government). The Democratic National Committee asked her to co-chair sessions at the 1972 Democratic Convention. The Congressional Black Caucus called upon her leadership skills for a term. She is warm, collegial. She is respected, admired. She is charming, persuasive, but she is not like a centerpiece--to be savored for beauty alone.

Yvonne Burke reflects a quiet power--the power of the word, the power of a constituent organization. When Vernon Jordan, head of the Urban League, came into disfavor in the summer of 1977 for his negative comments on the accomplishments of the Carter Administration in behalf of the poor and the disadvantaged, Yvonne Burke did not hesi-

tate to rush to his defense.   "We must stand behind what
Jordan said, " was her message. [28]   When she disapproved of
the treatment granted to Vietnamese refugees by the Ford
Administration in comparison to the handling of problems confronting the American poor and the disadvantaged, she did
not hedge nor temper her opposition to the President.   When
she disagreed with Congress's 1977 failure to approve payment of abortions for poor women with Federal funds, she
spoke out and introduced comments into the Congressional
Record, comments from those who realized the need for Federal payment for abortions on poor women.   Without such
payment (particularly if states did not agree to pay for abortions) poor women might well return to the days of the back-
room, dirty table, hideous, unsanitary, and inhumane methods of aborting fetuses.

        She returns frequently to California to oversee a con-
stituent organization and to listen to statements of need in
order to determine how those needs might be addressed.   Her
roots are in California.   That is where she grew up.   That
is where her husband has business interests, where she apparently wants her young daughter to grow up.   Her contact
with her constituency appears to be close and she molds
that constituency carefully--oozing from it the power of constituent organization.   Her individual interests and involve-
ments are compatible with those of her constituents: urban
mass transit, energy and equal employment/affirmative action.

Shirley Chisholm

        "When you are not doing anything, nobody talks about
you. "   Congresswoman Shirley Chisholm spoke those words
on September 25, 1976, before the National Hook-up of Black
Women, Inc.

        People have been talking about Shirley Chisholm for
years. [29]   When the fiery West Indian engineered an amazing
election victory and proudly took her seat in Congress in
1968, voices shouted her praises.   When the Congress wanted
to stifle her interests at the outset by placing her on what
she perceived to be a meaningless committee, the Congresswoman complained loudly--and people talked about her.   When
Shirley Chisholm announced her candidacy for the Presidency
of the United States, tongues wagged long, loudly, persistently.   No one seems to tire of talking about Shirley Chisholm--

not her friends, certainly not those who dislike her, and
most surely not those who hate her. She must be doing
something.

Shirley Chisholm understands power. She understands
best the power of the masses, the power of organization.
When people said she couldn't beat a James Farmer at the
polls, she organized. She whipped the masses into enthusiasm for her candidacy. When people said she was slipping
and could not beat back a challenge from New York City
Councilman Samuel Wright in the 1976 Congressional election,
she organized. She pulled and pushed her forces into fren-
zied and positive action. She gave Samuel Wright a Muham-
med Ali "whupping"--taking about 53 percent of the vote.

Shirley Chisholm also comprehends the power of moral persuasion. She commenced her career as an educator.
She directed a child care center; she served as an educational consultant for the New York City Division of Day Care.
She has never lost her penchant for teaching. She is constantly the teacher, insisting that her pupils learn by example, by illustration. As she teaches, her moral position
is hard to confront successfully. So, in spite of the dis-
content, even outrage expressed by male members of the
Black Congressional Caucus, Congresswoman Chisholm ran
for the presidency of the United States. By her daring entry
into the presidential race she taught that Black women need
not, should not step back and allow Black men to lead simply
because they were born into the male sex. Most important,
perhaps, she taught that she firmly believes in the power of
Black women.

Shirley Chisholm knows that political power is elusive
and may result only from the power of work, especially if
one does not possess wealth. In the face of the horrendous
unemployment rate among American teenagers, especially
Black and Puerto Rican teenagers, Shirley Chisholm did not
stand back and simply wait to vote for the 1977 youth unemployment bill. She worked closely with the Employment Opportunities Subcommittee to make certain that there would be
a billion-dollar youth employment bill and to guarantee that
poor youth would receive the benefits of the bill. On welfare reform issues Shirley Chisholm is visible. On food
stamp legislation she lets her views be known. The House
Education and Labor Committee demands much of her time,
and gets it. As a member of that Committee she struggled
for a meaningful vocational education bill that could begin to
eradicate sex and race bias in vocational education schools.

Shirley Chisholm understands that energy into an ex-
citing political arena must not be allowed to mask reality.
She comprehends the importance of the question: How powerful is powerful? In fact she might ask, more bluntly, how
powerful can power be if one is Black and female? Certainly she will not soon forget the psychological and "raw" power
of the American Government savagely directed against her as
the GAO accused her of campaign finance irregularities with
respect to her $99,000 campaign for the presidency of the
United States. Not until 1974 did the Justice Department
clear her of the GAO allegations.

Cardiss Collins

The least complicated and least enigmatic of all the
Black Congresswomen is Cardiss Collins. Someone who dares
step directly into the Congressional arena without a history of
deep entrenchment in state politics, or without immersion in
the field of law or government, or without an education in one
of the finest private or state colleges or universities in the
country is courageous and merits the plaudits of the less
daring. Somehow, though, applause for Cardiss Collins
seems inappropriate because she is best viewed as a natural
politician. This is true not only because she apparently has
a set of specific, people-oriented goals but also because she
keeps an ear close to the ground of her constituency.

On women's issues Cardiss Collins has been most vo-
cal. She is an advocate of the right to an abortion and of
the right to an abortion paid with public funds if a woman is
economically poor. She decries uninformed sterilizations;
never again does she want to see a teenager rudely and
abruptly deprived of her right to bear children without prior,
full awareness of that deprivation. She fought a determined
struggle to have medicaid funds used for breast protheses.

Without fanfare Congresswoman Collins stepped up to
chair the Manpower and Housing Subcommittee of the Government Operations Committee. She keeps a close watch on the
Community Services Administration, the successor to the Office of Economic Opportunity; she held oversight hearings to
determine how to improve service delivery in CSA.

Addressing hard social policy issues is a must for
her if she is to service her district successfully. With a
large mass of urban poor in Chicago she must be sensitive

to AFDC (Aid to Families with Dependent Children) issues,
welfare reform, day care services, supplemental security income, and a host of other social concerns.

While Cardiss Collins may not evidence power of the
word, power of the voice, she clearly understands the power
of the purse and seems destined to devote strong energies to
loosening and tightening (for effective administration) the purse
strings of the federal social welfare program coffers.   It
seems clear that she wants the power to make the lives of
Chicago's urban poor less miserable and more tolerable.

Barbara Jordan

Of all the Black Congresswomen Barbara Jordan
emerges as the most enigmatic.   Talented, moody, unpredictable, brilliant, testy, abrasive, cold, sociable, warm.
All these terms might easily fit her.   Is the enigmatic label
traceable to her tendency not to grant interviews to journal-
ists, notwithstanding the 1977 Barbara Walters ABC-TV interview?   Is it attributable to her rapid rise to prominence
in the days of Richard Nixon's battle against impeachment,
her manifestation of the heights of persuasive oratorial power
at the 1971 Democratic Convention, and her absence from the
cabinet of the Carter Administration?

An attempt to comprehend Congresswoman Jordan may
have to begin with Lyndon Johnson.   Lyndon Johnson was an
astute politician.   He succeeded in part because he mastered
the rules of parliamentary procedure, the rules of Federal
agencies, and innerworkings of Federal bureaucracies.   But
Lyndon Johnson rose rapidly in political circles also because
he charmed, persuaded, even bullied individuals into march-
ing with him on certain issues.   Barbara Jordan emerged in
the political arena when Lyndon Johnson enjoyed and exercised power, virtually without fear.   She stepped into a
Texas political arena that had sent Sam Rayburn and Lyndon
Johnson to Washington.   She walked into a Washington political arena marked by the legacy of Rayburn and Johnson.

Unlike Lyndon Johnson, Barbara Jordan does not engage in extroverted behavior, at least not openly.   She tends
to shy away from most people, even hide from them.   She
does not exude the charm of a Johnsonian warm embrace.
She is not enthusiastic, at least not outwardly, about her relationship with other members of Congress, even the Black

Caucus. In that respect she is not Johnsonian. Yet, she is
Johnsonian in her determination to master the rules of the
game, in her effort to understand what rules must be followed
if power is to be aggregated.

In Barbara Jordan's search for power she is Johnsonian. She is uncomfortable without power, or without an
effort to obtain it. Unlike Johnson, she is quiet in her
search for power. Few realize that in her short Congressional career she has managed to obtain seats on three presti-
gious and influential House Committees: Judiciary, Government Operations, and the Steering and Policy Committees of
the House Democratic Caucus. She also serves on several
subcommittees, including Government Information and Government Relations, Energy and Natural Resources, and Monopo-
lies and Commercial Law. Tenure on these committees and
subcommittees represents tracks to the world of the power-
fully powerful.

Barbara Jordan is clothed with power of the word,
power of the voice, power of the mind. She can hold an audience spellbound--get individuals to hang onto her every
word--demanding more. She can make an elementary civics
lesson sound profound. She can make one believe in the value
of a Constitution which has not protected racial minorities,
aliens, women or the poor. She can weave a rationale for
rejoicing in the bicentennial of a country which for centuries
has denied equal justice. Her speeches are not threatening.
They are not strident. They are not abrasive. They do not
make unreasonable demands. As an orator, she is not antagonistic. She is determined. She is not monotonous.
She speaks words with the same kind of love with which
Leontyne Price sings opera. She is not vacuous. She
preaches from the text of history with the same power and
force with which Martin Luther King, Jr. preached from the
text of religious doctrine.

The power of the word, the power of the voice, the
power of the mind did not bring a cabinet post under the
Carter Administration. Some said she was foolish to demand
just one position--that of Attorney General of the United
States. Why would the President give her that position rather than a Judge Leon Higginbotham? Rather than a southern
lawyer or jurist? True, the power of the word, the power
of the voice, the power of the mind did not bring a cabinet
post under the Carter Administration, but that power conveyed
a message: A position within the Administration without the

influence and power to change (even radically change) attitudes and policies is worthless. A position of power within
Congress--a commanding seat on the Judiciary and Government Operations Committees--with hope for an eventual chair
--could have more nationwide impact than an Assistant Secretary, or the head of the Community Services Administration.
A distinguished congressional career could even lead to a
judicial appointment--to the Court of Appeals, even to the
United States Supreme Court. And when one is 41 there is
time, time to wait, time to build.

     Lyndon Johnson believed in power, sought power,
scrambled for power. Yet, power was not an end for Lyndon Johnson. As Doris Kearns put it in Lyndon Johnson and
the American Dream: "The desire to benefit others was ever
the prime motive for his quest for power."30 In another
passage Professor Kearns wrote: "His mother had taught
him ... that power had value only when used to benefit people."31 Barbara Jordan quietly believes in power, seeks
power, struggles to obtain power. Is Barbara Jordan convinced that power has value "only when used to benefit people?" The answer is not clear. Congresswoman Jordan remains an enigma. Only time will tell whether her concept
of power truly is of the Johnsonian vintage. Only time will
tell how powerful is powerful.

Conclusion

     The four Black Congresswomen are not the gentle-
ladies of the Congress in the sense of being soft and compliant. Nor are they amazons in the sense of being tough
warriors who march with a masculine strength. One may
embody power of the word, power of the mind, power of the
voice. Another may display the power of moral outrage.
Still another may aspire to power of the purse. Yet another
may aggregate extremely well the power of constituent organization.

     The women's movement is not a revolutionary force.
Its numbers have been subjected to sex discrimination for
years, but the activities, goals, and achievements of its numbers must be acknowledged even though they may not have
addressed hard and pressing social issues. The four Black
Congresswomen are not amazons. They and their ancestors
have been attacked by race and sex bias for centuries, but
the individual accomplishments of these women cannot be cast

aside as insignificant. Under any conception of power both
the women's movement and the four Black Congresswomen
are powerful, or, at least have planted the seeds of power.
The only significant question remaining for deeper analysis
is: how powerful is powerful?

NOTES

1.   Juliet Mitchell, Women's Estate, New York: Vintage,
      1971, p. 21.
2.   Ibid., p. 13.
3.   Ms. Reader, New York: Warner Books, Inc., 1973,
      p. 28.
4.   Koedt, Levine, and Rapone, Editors, Radical Feminism,
      New York: Quadrangle Books, 1973, p. 280.
5.   Ibid., pp. 63-71.
6.   Ibid., p. 71.
7.   Ibid., p. 63.
8.   Ibid., pp. 282-284.
9.   Mitchell, op. cit., pp. 93-94.
10. Hole and Levine, Rebirth of Feminism, New York:
      Quadrangle Books, 1971.
11. Ms. December 1973, Vol. 2, No. 6, p. 35.
12. Eve Cary, "Pregnancy Without Penalty," Civil Liberties
      Review, Fall 1973, Vol. 1, No. 1, pp. 31-48; p. 32.
13. Hole and Levine, op. cit., pp. 311-312.
14. Koedt, Levine, and Rapone, op. cit.
15. Ibid., p. 177.
16. "The Women's Movement and How It Grew--Book Re-
      view," Ms, December 1973, p. 36.
17. Elizabeth Janeway, "The Weak Are the Second Sex,"
      Atlantic, December 1973, Vol. 232, No. 6, pp. 91-
      104.
18. Ibid., p. 92.
19. Ibid., p. 95.
20. Ibid.
21. Ibid., p. 96.
22. Ibid.
23. Ibid., p. 103.
24. Ibid., p. 104.
25. Lorraine Hansberry, To Be Young, Gifted, and Black,
      New York: New American Library, 1969, pp. 225-
      226.
26. Jeane J. Kirkpatrick, Political Woman, New York:
      Basic Books, 1974.
27. Ibid., pp. 174-176.

28. Chicago Tribune, July 30, 1977.
29. See Inez Smith Reid, "Together" Black Women, New
     York: Third Press, Second Edition, 1974.
30. Doris Kearns, Lyndon Johnson and the American Dream,
     New York: New American Library, 1976, p. xii.
31. Ibid. , p. 56.

PART II

ALIENATION AND FRUSTRATION:
MOTIVATION FOR CHANGE

INTRODUCTION

Alienation, frustration and struggle have been hand-maidens of history. Women's estrangement from society, stemming from discriminatory practices, is convincingly depicted in this chapter.

The central theme of this book, the need for women to organize in order to bring about ameliorating changes, is never more apparent than in the first selection. Here we are keenly aware of women's isolating experiences.

In the second piece, we detect a source of frustration, unexpected by the authors of the essay and in the last selection, we see a transcendence to what is primarily an effective construction.

Karen Burstein's essay is a remarkably singular reminder of the omnipresent problem facing the individual woman, be she office worker or government official. This is a fascinating anecdotal study of a state senator's early experiences. Again we see, all too well, women's need for the strength and power of numbers.

The next article in this section explores in interesting detail, the implications of women's emergence into politics, using local school boards as a possible springboard for such entry. Marilyn Johnson and Kathy Stanwick analyze this concept in terms of its effectiveness. Many questions arise as to the relationship of the characteristics of local school boards and organized participations of women in any public sphere.

Lobbying is one of the most effective methods available for making changes in our society. Chapter 5, a selection by Anne Costain, strongly attests to the power of the unified effort. In a highly informative essay, Costain explains the organizational skills required for lobbying to be executed with efficacy. This very detailed work can readily serve as a model for future lobbying.

Chapter 3

NOTES FROM A POLITICAL CAREER

by Karen Burstein

I saw it first in law school. I was sitting around a
luncheon table with some other students, all of them male.
Generally, we met to complain about the rigidity of our conservative institution and to plot anti-war political action.
This day, we started discussing William Styron's Confessions
of Nat Turner. We'd been together for such a long time and
we were so attuned to each other's rhythms that all of them
had forgotten I was "a girl." Talk turned to the portion of
the book where Turner, driving his owner's daughter in a car-
riage, is aroused by her innocently seductive banter. His
servitude makes acknowledging the sexual attraction between
them impossible. Frustration at his position produces rage.
In interior monologue, he speaks of wanting to rape her.
One of our discussion participants said: "You know how it
is. You get one of those smart Smith students, who talks
and talks in some abstract way. You say to yourself: 'I'll
shut her up; I'll just jam it up her and shut her up.'"

That moment was a revelation. It demonstrated how
much anxiety and anger even progressive men could feel towards women, particularly women who appear confident and
assertive. I glimpsed a hard truth. Law and social institutions are not the only bars to woman's progress towards
equality. Psychological barriers are thrown up as well, barriers created by the worry, mostly unacknowledged, that men
have about their own worth, about their right to control the
world's activities. (I will talk about women's introjection of
these concerns later.)

That worry is kept at bay by women's absence from
places where decisions are made, by their silence in de-
liberations. It surfaces, as our visibility heightens, as we
begin demanding recognition. Before Maryann Krupsak, Carol
Bellamy and I were elected in 1972, few women had been
state senators. Before, only one had sat at a time. (How
lonely and isolated each must have been.) Our entry in tan-

49

dem was much publicized. Our reception, however, was not
auspicious. The Majority Leader, criticized for a resolution
untimely put before us, responded: "Gentlemen, without rules,
we'd just be sixty happy fellas--I mean, uh, 57 and 3." The
tension implicit in "and 3" shortly manifested itself in a more
direct and disturbing way.

One Sunday night, very late, at an hour no secretary
or aide could be expected to subject herself to exploitation,
I entered the legislative office building. A few days earlier,
a regulation had been passed exempting elected officials from
the necessity of presenting identification. The burly six-foot
guard at the door barred my way to the elevator, saying that
I must show him a pass. I insisted that as Senator Burstein
I was under no such obligation (against my own socialized instincts to yield). Our colloquy continued for a short time:
his reiterating the demand, my denying it. Finally, bravely,
I informed him I was going to my room, as I had work to
do. Not five minutes later, a knock came at my door. I
slowly opened it. He pushed forward and--between clenched
teeth--commanded: "YOU SHOW ME YOUR PASS." Reluc-
tantly, I gave it to him. He held it in his hand, turned it
over several times and finally said, with loathing: "My God,
it kills me to call girls Senator."

It would be comforting to dismiss this incident as a
product of the difference in our positions. A female legislator threatened the guard, one might argue, because her
achievement, in his mind, devalued his own status. Unfortunately, he was merely more explicit about his feelings than
others at other levels of state government. Title, I discovered, did not guarantee absence of anxiety; it only masked
its expression.

I remember, for example, attending a conference on
education with the then chair of the Senate committee. I
made an impassioned presentation to the gathered parents,
which was greeted by enthusiastic applause. He looked dis-
gruntled throughout my performance. At the moment I sat
down, he whispered to me: "You know, Karen, somehow I
just can't think of you as a Senator. I think of you as a
girl. Is that awful?" I answered by suggesting that I thought
of myself as a woman without that interfering with my conception of my professional role. If, in the privacy of his
room, he chose to reflect on my questionable charms, he
had every right to do so. In a forum like this, I gently suggested, it would be more appropriate if he conceived of me

as his colleague only and directed his attention to the sub-
stance of my talk.

That year, Constance Cook, a woman of authority and
intelligence, headed the Assembly Committee on Education.
She had too mature and imposing a presence to be dismissed
as "just a girl." So, I would hear suggestions that she really didn't run the committee, that she sat there like a "mother hen, clucking" while male cohorts did the actual work.

The need to resolve the tension and threat of women's
presence as legislators sometimes resulted in an unconscious
denial of our existence--a denial illustrated by an experience
of Linda Winikow's. (After Maryann Krupsak became Lieutenant Governor, Linda Winikow joined Carol Bellamy and
me as the third woman State Senator.) Being driven to Albany one day by her young male aide, Linda decided to make
a special effort to keep within the 55 mile per hour speed
limit (a rare accomplishment for any legislator). When they
entered the Thruway, they saw a police car traveling in their
direction. The police car was preceded by a bus. She reasoned that the police car was likely to keep her faithful to
her intention to drive slowly and so she instructed her aide
to follow it. As it pulled out, her car pulled out. As it
pulled back, she pulled back. Suddenly, screaming sirens
sounded and she was flagged to the side of the road. A
state trooper looked into the window and, glancing unbeliev-
ingly from the young men to her, asked: "Who's the Senator?" It seems that the bus was transporting prisoners.
They'd radioed that a car with Senate license plates, driven
by a "teenager" with a female passenger, was closely tagging
the escorting police vehicle. Obviously, a prison break was
intended. It simply did not occur to the dispatch officer that
the Senate license plates might signal the presence of a legislator. He had "forgotten" (he later apologized) that three out
of the sixty of us were women (and had been for the past
three years).

It is important to realize that such incidents, however
funny or irritating or frightening, do not render women legislators incapable of performing their duties. They manage to
draft significant programs and shepherd bills through floor
passage to gubernatorial signature. The attitudes these incidents illustrate, however, make legislative work more difficult and frustrating for women. But there are benefits for
the general polity in the fact that women are not warmly accepted into the club, that they are not easily assimilated as

"one of the boys." To understand this benefit one must understand the club. Its cardinal rule is that members protect each other from outside criticism and that new, young participants defer to their elders, however unwise. The goal is to persevere long enough to move into a position where one becomes a leader. At that point, one may finally express the views which have till then been restrained out of deference to the system. The problem is that it generally takes so long to reach leadership positions that one forgets, on attaining power, the original reasons that sent one into politics.

Women, excluded from the climb from the beginning, outsiders by biological accident, have no stake in preserving the game intact. More, they are likely to regard it with a sufficiently jaundiced eye to make loud noises about its obvious failings. I have called this "the naked emperor phenomenon."

Toward the end of my first year, a massive piece of legislation appeared on our desks, still wet from the printer. It created the Adirondack Park Agency (around which, I might note, controversy still rages). It was clear from our initial questions that no one, including the Majority Leader, had read all 107 pages of the measure. However, we were assured, the Daily News had printed excerpts. Presumably, then, the Daily News was familiar with its contents. Carol Bellamy protested that her constituents had not elected the Daily News to represent them. She asked that the bill be laid aside until the next day so all Senators might have a chance to understand it. That, it developed, was impossible. No one wanted to stay an extra day. Governor Rockefeller had scheduled a press conference the following morning to announce, with a flourish, his signing it. It was too late to make new arrangements.

Carol and I then announced that unless it were laid aside, we would use the two-hour debate rule to read the legislation on the floor, out loud. This produced even more grumbling. We were, it was suggested, going to pass it anyway, as the majority of members supported the concept. It was now 7:00 p.m. and a cocktail party meeting, thrown by a powerful Assembly leader, was called for eight; Republican Senators wanted to attend. Why couldn't we just make a brief statement on the bill, let the representatives from the affected area speak out so the newspapers might quote them, vote and adjourn?

We couldn't, because it was wrong. I admit to wanting to agree. For years, important legislation had been passed this way and the state continued to exist. It had been, till then, a difficult session for us and we were just becoming bearable to our colleagues. To persist would be to alienate again those we worked with. But the fact is the ordinary way cheated the people, who had elected us to make reasoned decisions about their lives.

So for nearly two hours, Carol Bellamy and I stood on our ultimately weary feet, spelling each other, reading dry, technical material. At the end, having yielded to the two Adirondack area legislators, we sat down and voted yes. Almost all of the rest of the body was in a rage at us. Three of Carol's bills were, perhaps coincidentally, laid aside for the rest of the session. The upstate papers, torn between admiration and shock, handled their discomfiture by devaluing our effort in headlines reading: "fillybuster." But, interestingly, the practice of mindlessly passing unread measures tapered off. It has finally ended.

The willingness to question established conventions, to tell uncomfortable truths, doesn't always produce change in procedures. But it almost always makes it harder to do foolish or harmful things. I recall Constance Cook, exasperated by the debate on the accessibility of contraceptives to minors, suggesting wryly that the best way to limit adolescent sexual activity was to forbid the sale of beds in the State of New York. She didn't win, but some Assembly members voted for the bill out of embarrassment. And the press covered her statement widely, insuring that the issue wasn't buried by its Albany defeat.

Indeed, raising issues, widening the grounds of discussion, protesting the closed, insular nature of legislative activity have been major contributions of women elected to the New York State Senate and Assembly. As our numbers have grown, a consciousness change has occurred among those employed as support people and among our male colleagues. I discover that most of the awful experiences, the funny/painful stories about females in politics date to my early terms. I know certainly that the insistence of women who have sat with me that women's specific concerns be addressed has affected the tone and tenor of legislation. New York is now in a better position to assure its female citizens access and opportunity nearer that offered men. Still, things are not fine. The fact that one can even write about

this subject signals distress.   No one in the world would pub-
lish a journal on political men.   Until we can say the same
thing of women, of the 51. 3 percent of our population, we
are compelled to ask what more we must do.

I believe with Emma Goldman that "the right to vote,
or equal civil rights, may be good demands, but true emancipation begins neither at the polls nor in courts.   It begins in
woman's soul...." The anger and fear of men, their dis-
comfort at having to share power with women, would be easier to overcome, to transform, if women didn't introject that
hostility, didn't assimilate and act on attitudes about female
inferiority.

During the fight to gain approval of the New York
State equal rights amendment, we discovered that the major
organized opposition came from ad hoc women's groups,
named WUNDER and HOTDOG (Housewives Opposed to the
Degradation of Our Girls).   It was disheartening to have male
allies tax us with the defection from our ranks of our sisters
and to know, in fact, that socialization of women as second-
class citizens had occurred with such effectiveness that they
would frustrate an effort that benefited their own sex.   We
simply didn't have enough time to educate women to their
true situations.   Instead, we were overborne by shibboleths
and myths that centuries of discrimination have written in
our souls.   After all, it is always difficult to give up the
known for the uncertain, even when the known is not terribly
attractive.   Women have so long been taught not to risk
themselves that they can, some of them, stand against important and productive change.   In doing so, they of course
deprive others of necessary rights and obligations.   They
also add to the isolation of women inside the political system.   Absence of support, obstacles to the formation of a
united womanfront outside the system confirm men in their
conviction that the present dispensation is fine.   We elected
women are more readily dismissed as odd and unrepresenta-
tive and not to be listened to.

We have our own psychological difficulties in counter-
vailing that presumption.   A major obstacle to joint fervent
action are lapses in our perception of an experiential com-
monality among all women.   In New York, people of Black
and Puerto Rican descent make up a small percentage of
legislative membership.   All of them have banded together
regardless of the economic and social backgrounds from which
they come.   Clearly, there are differences in style and sub-

stance among them, but each is convinced, however favored
he or she might have been, that racism in our society creates obstacles to the progress of every individual of color.
Therefore, only if all individuals of color join together, in
separate caucus, can any know ultimate success.

Unlike the Blacks and Puerto Ricans, the women in
the legislature have no caucus.   This is partly a function of
our being of different parties, besides being from varied
backgrounds.   It is also partly a function of our numbers
which are probably too small for such a forum.   Fundamentally, though, we suffer from the fact that the prejudice that
binds us together is more subtle and complex than that which
binds individuals of color.   Sexism has a gentle face.   The
oppressors, men, are also lovers and husbands, fathers and
sons.   It is true racism scars whites; Lincoln once noted
that the slave pulls the slaveholder down into the very ditch
in which the slave is mired.   Still, it is relatively difficult
for a black person to feel pity for a bigoted white.   On the
other hand, it is relatively simple for a woman to be sympathetic to the anguish of men, walled off from their instincts
for tenderness and nurturing.   Consequently, it is possible
for women to be torn between the demands of their sex for
acknowledgment and of the opposite sex for compassion.   It
becomes hard to sustain ongoing unity among women.   More
than likely we coalesce around specific issues and then break
back down into our component party parts.

Notwithstanding that, there are some threads of similar experience which bind us, to which we can refer, occasionally which we can evoke when the going is very rocky.
Our capacity to make common cause among ourselves and
between us and women outside politics will depend increasingly on our identifying those threads more precisely.   As
we learn to articulate better the nature of our experience,
it will be seen, and properly, as only a special type of the
general condition of womankind.   As a result, female citizens will understand their stake in our success and will rise
up, not in opposition to what we do, but in affirmation of it.

Even then, our ability to foster productive solidarity
will continue to be affected by our credibility as public officials.   The peculiar historical position of women creates a
problem for those of us who are vanguard participants in the
political process.   We must constantly try and strike a balance between speaking for women and speaking for general
constituencies.   The balance is difficult to maintain because

of our own consciences and the expectations of the media and
male colleagues. Carol Bellamy noted that until recently she
could issue ten reports on mortgage and banking matters and
not receive a line in the press. Let her show up at an anti-
rape conference and she is the featured individual on the evening report.

Our first term yields a vivid example of the dilemma
we face. In the beginning, we rose almost daily to protest
the exclusion of female names on the Governor's appointment
lists and to object to language which presupposed that only
males did certain things, e.g., "young men in New York cannot get into medical school. " After a while, our colleagues'
growing irritation with our role as defenders of our sex began to make us uncomfortable. We decided to mute our protest. We specifically chose not to discuss a measure amending a statute to read "police officer" instead of "policeman. "
The federal government had ruled that absent the amendment,
which would allow men and women to compete for law enforcement jobs on an equal basis, no money would flow to
the state. Although it was evident that New York had no
choice, debate raged for more than an hour and eventually
descended into idiocy. One Senator first claimed that women
should not be permitted to be patrol officers since they would
be frightened to enter a bar at three o'clock in the morning
if a brawl were in progress. Having been persuaded that
women who sought patrol officer designation would, in fact,
get out of their cars under such circumstances, he went on
to assert that they would become so unnerved by the violence
that they would pull out their guns and shoot everybody in the
place. By now, we had become extraordinarily restless.
Nonetheless, since we were certain of the bill's success, we
restrained our tongues. Then a male colleague leaned over
and tapped Senator Bellamy. "Get up, " he whispered, "this
is one of your issues. " In a sudden rage, she turned and
said: "I don't always have to talk about women. "

The fact, however, is that to some degree or another,
women legislators do have to talk about women whenever the
subject of women arises, or whenever it doesn't and should.
For the progress that has been made in New York State since
the appearance of women in some numbers in the halls of
government has been geometric compared to what occurred
prior to our accession. It is evident that if women are not
present, no one will speak for us. Yet, if we talk only about
women, who, after all, count for less than men in our present social value system, we are devalued in our colleagues'

eyes. More, there are legitimate competing demands for
our attention and energy; problems of the joint community of
men and women need to be addressed and resolved. Our
constituents can become convinced that we are single issue
representatives and turn away from us, depriving us of the
power to attack the roots of women's disabilities. So, we
have to walk a narrow line--maintain a delicate balance.
And it is not always clear when the line is crossed. It will
only cease being our charge when women enter all fields of
endeavor in proportion to their numbers. The question of
striking the appropriate balance will answer itself when it is
commonplace for women to stop making coffee and start
making policy, or to do both simultaneously, as men must.

Contemplating the vast sea-changes in our social order
that will be necessary if women are to be full co-participants
in the world's affairs, we elected women, indeed all of us,
can become overwhelmed. Depression produces inertia. One
feels silly, for example, about insisting that language be re-
formed, that sexist phrases be eschewed. Yet, one must insist, for the way we say things shapes our perception of
reality. As our great native philosopher, John Dewey, taught
us, "to name a thing is to know it." I sometimes let floor
debate proceed during which a legislator will exclusively use
a male pronoun. Mostly, however, I object. Increasingly,
colleagues are saying "he and she," "men and women," as
they describe the activities and concerns of citizens of New
York.

That consciousness that men and women are both to
be attended to has made it possible to change the laws of
this state and to offer broader opportunities to both sexes
here. Institutional change has been accompanied by attitu-
dinal changes, however slowly and painfully arrived at. The
guard who gritted his teeth at my being a Senator apologized
at the conclusion of my remarks on the New York State equal
rights amendment. The same Majority Leader who had
greeted us with "uh, and 3" closed debate on the ERA with
an impassioned, enlightened speech in its favor.

The changes that have occurred are especially to be
celebrated because of the psycho-historical difficulties mili-
tating against them. Fear and self-doubt in men and women
are deep rooted. We are badly socialized as people. Little
boys learn to kill the tenderness inside of themselves as little girls learn to deny their capacity to be assertive and independent. Denial of this kind, suppression of part of us,

must generate anger. That anger is easily directed at the
other, at the ones who have what it is we are forbidden to
enjoy.

It is evident that the efforts and energy of a few
elected women (even aided by a number of sensitive male
allies) cannot alone transform the laws and customs that give
objective form to such feelings of rage and jealousy. While
remedial legislation must be developed and passed, the work
of transformation has to begin earlier and its focus has to
reach beyond government (to education, the economy and social relations). While I believe that simultaneous pressure
at all points on the spectrum of human activity is urgently
required, special attention should be directed to the lives and
experience of children. If we can create conditions which insure against rigid sex role stereotyping and encourage full
development of human personality in all boys and girls, we
will produce healthy, generous and free men and women.

The challenge which invites us was eloquently formulated by Eleanor Holmes Norton in a commencement address
at Wellesley College. She said, in part: "The question has
been asked, 'What is a woman?' A woman is a person who
makes choices. A woman is a dreamer. A woman is a
planner. A woman is a maker and a molder. A woman is
a person who makes choices. A woman builds bridges. A
woman makes children and makes cars. A woman writes
poetry and songs. A woman is a person who makes choices.
You can't even simply become a mother any more. You
must choose motherhood. Will you choose change? Can you
become its vanguard?"

If our responsibility is, as I believe, to reshape the
prevailing system so that it is open for choice, women must
necessarily be in the vanguard. They have the most visible,
immediate stake in a reordered society. But men will clearly benefit as well. Indeed, they themselves can begin to
make genuine choices, only when women fully realize their
capacity to choose. With our growing commitment to that
end, some breaching of barriers has taken place. More and
more, I notice a willingness to understand the motivations
and unconscious drives which shape public action. More and
more, I have witnessed a willingness to confront the shibboleths and myths that lack of acknowledgment of anxiety
sustains.

I read textbooks now that are unmarred by sexism.

I know such change has been effected not only by the Congress in passing Title IX, but as well and predominantly by
the insistence of women in education, parents and teachers.
I watch TV occasionally and see female doctors, lawyers,
detectives, along with homemakers.   I know these images
reflect the pressure of women in media.   I receive reports
from women office workers and applaud the bravery of secretaries and assistants who have banded together to demand a
proper respect for the services they render this economy.

These vanguard victories help us delimit the ground
upon which future struggle needs to be waged. But each victory has to be defended vigorously, for the closer we come
to the core of the problem of sexism, the deeper the resistance to its elimination will be. Sexism reminds me of
those intricate Russian dolls, smaller ones totally encapsu-
lated in larger ones. When one imagines one has reached
the last, another doll remains.

Several years ago, after considerable struggle, we
succeeded in redrafting the rape law. No longer did all elements of the act have to be corroborated by evidence, independent of the testimony of the victim. No longer might the
defendant introduce material relating to the prior general
sexual conduct of the plaintiff. It seemed that the legislature
had finally acknowledged that women could be competent witnesses to their own violation.

This session, as a natural extension of the concept,
we submitted a measure that protects a woman, separated
for six months by judicial decree, order or agreement, from
her spouse's violent sexual assault. The measure calls that
assault what it is--rape. The bill recently failed in the
Senate committee. Colleagues, previously sympathetic on
the broad issue, balked. After all, one suggested, an es-
tranged wife and husband might make up sexually. Then,
angry with him again, she would scream "violation." When
I pointed out that the same elements of proof available in all
criminal matters would operate to protect against unwarranted
charges, he suddenly blurted out: "Well, your legislation
will interfere with the sanctity of marriage."

The medieval resonance of that phrase rocked me.
Unconsciously, my colleague was reformulating Blackstone's
dictum: in marriage, the husband and wife are one, and the
one is the husband. His opposition was bottomed on the unacknowledged idea that a woman's body is the property of the

man to whom she is wed. Evidently, her claim to physical
and mental integrity appeared, to his mind, less compelling
than the need of her spouse to experience his own power.
So long as any individual imagines that that power confers
status, that one sex is valuable in relation to the lesser value
of the other, we cannot create a sane and loving community.

In admitting this disheartening fact, in acknowledging
how slowly our long march proceeds, I still see enough evidence to warrant a continued, strong effort. Even during
the darkest moments, impulses toward decency emerge. At
the conclusion of the debate on the police officer bill, which
I detailed above, a black Senator, representing Bedford Stuy-
vesant, rose. He reported that women were riding patrol
cars with males in one of the toughest districts in the city.
Their presence was an experiment and they were proving
their worth. "In fact," he said, "they have been superb."
He was moved to add: "You know, one good woman is worth
a thousand lousy men." My logical head discounts the exaggerated numbers. Nonetheless, the formula does my
troubled heart good.

Chapter 4

LOCAL OFFICEHOLDING AND THE COMMUNITY:
The Case of Women on New Jersey's School Boards*

by Marilyn Johnson and Kathy Stanwick

Although school boards are often omitted from the
study of politics, they are neither unimportant as governing
bodies nor irrelevant to the political interests of women.
They constitute 20 percent of all the local governing bodies
in the United States.[1] Of more significance than sheer numbers, school boards are closely involved in the governance
of local communities. They are involved not only in ways
that affect the educational system and the rearing of future
generations of adults but also in ways that ramify to affect
a variety of salient public issues such as taxation, integration or civil liberties.

Profoundly relevant to the status of women is the major responsibility that school boards currently have for directing the implementation of federal and state mandates to
remove sex discrimination from the schools. Commentators
have concentrated on the actions of teachers and administrators and on the manner in which local groups of women can
influence the process of implementation. But one of the
more direct means by which equity can be achieved may be
through increased participation of women on school boards.
For example, past research has shown that women on school
boards have more positive attitudes toward the employment
of women administrators than do their male colleagues.[2]

*The author is indebted to the Russell Sage Foundation for
support enabling the research reported here. I also wish to
thank Dr. Eugene Keyek, formerly Executive Director, and
Dr. Linda Morton of the New Jersey School Boards Association for generously giving of their time in making available
data on male/female membership, and Linda L. Laskay of
the National School Boards Association for her prompt and
capable attention to my several inquiries.

In addition to their potential effects on the status of
women in education, women bring to school boards skills
and emphases that may broadly affect educational governance.
Women on school boards place more emphasis than men on
representation of the public, on school-community relations,
and on educational philosophy, instruction and curriculum. [3]

If women were to be adequately represented in any
public sphere, one would predict substantial participation on
bodies making educational policy.   Teaching is an accepted
feminine occupation; the active membership of the PTA is
largely female; traditionally, mothers are more immediately
concerned than fathers with the education of children.   Unlike other public offices, in which female occupants typically
have no minor children, [4] school board members of both
sexes are overwhelmingly parents of school-aged children. [5]
Moreover, the local, part-time, largely unsalaried nature of
school board membership suggests a high degree of corres-
pondence with the traditional voluntary and community service
activities of women.

Despite the "logic" of a high degree of female participation, the proportion of women among school board members nationwide has remained under 20 percent for several
decades[6] and only now appears to be increasing beyond the
peak of 18 percent in 1958 to a current estimated 18 to 22
percent. [7] A national survey of school board members in
1974 by the National School Boards Association (NBSA) found
widespread absence or tokenism regarding women. [8] Of the
male respondents, 39 percent reported no women on their
boards; an additional 35 percent were on boards with only
one female member.   Similarly, 46 percent of the women
said they were the lone female on their boards.

The sources of this poor representation--whether located in a reluctance of women to serve or in resistance of
the political environment--remain largely unexplored.   Forty
percent of the women board members in the NSBA study felt
that being a woman impaired chances of obtaining office, especially if the board already contained a woman.   Yet, to
our knowledge, there are no studies of the public's attitudes
toward women as board members that would either confirm
or refute these perceptions.   If community sentiment is reflected in the attitudes of male board members and superintendents, there is a depressingly familiar pattern of stereotyping and exclusion.   Although the objective qualifications of
women in the NSBA study were at least equal to those of the

men, male board members often perceived women in stereo-
typical terms. In addition, twice the proportion of women as
men reported discouragement from other school board members and from administrators as obstacles to office that they
had to overcome. The author of a report of superintendents'
attitudes toward school board members summarizes their attitudes toward women in an imaginary want ad: "... Will
also consider docile, unemotional, well-educated female candidates with work background other than homemaking (suscepti-
bility to recurrent attacks of acute laryngitis desirable but
not essential). "[9]

To be sure, the under-representation of women is not
uniform across all communities. Some school boards have
no women; a few have a majority or near majority. Very little is known about the conditions associated with such variation; limited past research has indicated only that women are
relatively more likely to be found on school boards in the
Northeastern and Pacific states, in the larger cities and on
decentralized boards, and on boards whose members are
elected rather than appointed. [10]

The apparent variation in the "receptiveness" of communities to the membership of women on boards leads one to
ask whether a closer study of such variation might not permit description of the socio-political environment most favorable to local office-holding by women. Current arguments
abound over the sources of women's low participation in the
policy. Some have argued that the barriers lie in the socio-
political environment, i.e., in political and cultural resistance
to public participation by women. Others have argued that
the answers are more complex but inhere most fundamentally
in the general position of women in the society--in the motivations that arise from the socialization of women, in the
peculiar constellation of domestic roles that pre-empt time
for political activity, in the confinement of women in the occupational sphere to traditionally "female" occupations.

The analysis of women on New Jersey school boards
to be presented here addresses the first set of interpretations
and is concerned with the kinds of socio-political local environments that encourage or discourage officeholding by wom-
en. The analysis deals with women's school board membership in 1975 and with changes in the five-year period 1971-
1975. This research was initiated in the expectation that
identification of the kinds of communities in which relatively
more women serve in public office could improve understand-

ing of the barriers to office and how they might be removed.[11]
As the reader will discover, our results are highly ambiguous and do more to illustrate the complexity of the subject
of women and the polity and the need for additional research
from many perspectives than they serve directly to explain
or assist women's participation.   Nevertheless, we present
our analysis as of some value in raising issues of interpretation, in clarifying some dimensions of the problem, and in
indicating directions for future research.

Women on School Boards vs. Women on Municipal Councils

    To the degree that conditions associated with women
holding office are general regardless of the type of office,
the proliferating body of research on women in politics is
also cumulative.   Under such circumstances, a study of
women in state legislatures, for example, would inform us
equally about women on school boards.   Or a study of women
on school boards would tell us much about women on municipal councils.   However, to the degree that differing offices
recruit differing kinds of women through diverse processes,
then the task of understanding the low participation of women
in the polity becomes the more complex task of specifying
the relevance of women's status to each type of office.

    Our data discourage assumptions that results of research on women in one kind of office are applicable to women in other offices, even at the local level.   In examining
the correlation between numbers of women on school boards
and the presence or absence of municipal councilwomen within
the districts, we find little or no association.[12]   The correlations are only -.09 for districts with five-person boards,
.25 among districts having seven-member boards, and .10
among nine-member board districts.   These low correlations
are consistent with the findings of a recent analysis conducted
by the Center for the American Woman and Politics, in which
the proportion of women among members of state boards and
commissions was found to be unrelated to the presence or
absence of women in state cabinet posts and only moderately
associated with the proportion of women among state legislators.[13]

    Evidence is limited, but what little there is supports
the conclusion that school board members and municipal
councilors are recruited from differing segments of the female population.   A comparison of the characteristics of

women school board members as reported by the National
School Boards Association[14] with the characteristics of wom-
en on municipal councils as reported in the Center for the
American Woman and Politics[15] reveals noteworthy differences in education, employment and domestic status.[16] Sixty-
two percent of the female school board members report 16
or more years of formal schooling but only 38 percent of
women on municipal councils are college graduates. Among
school board members, 62 percent were not employed when
they entered office, in contrast to the 56 percent of municipal councilors who report holding full or part-time jobs in
addition to officeholding. Nearly all (97 percent) of the school
board members, but only 75 percent of municipal councilors,
are married. Only 23 percent of the women on school boards
have no children in public schools, a figure that does not
take into account children of pre-school age or those in private schools. By contrast, 52 percent of women on councils
report no children under 18 years of age. Perhaps reflecting
differential stages of the life cycle, school board members
appear on the average to be two or three years younger than
councilors and to have lived in the same community a few
years less, although both groups are typically in their forties
and both have typically lived fifteen or more years in the
same community.

Such differences invite speculation about the differential social situations conducive to school board and council
participation. The school board attracts women with children
in the schools, but this higher involvement with children results in recruitment of an elite who can afford to be out of
the labor force. The educational and employment status of
school board members is, in combination, an indirect indi-
cator of relatively high family economic status. In addition,
the connection of school boards with education may make
formal educational credentials relatively important. Women
on councils, although an educational and economic elite relative to the general population of women, hold offices with less
direct connections to education and to children. The office
is more likely to recruit women who are occupationally active
but not necessarily of elite status.

Given the differences in personal characteristics of
women in two different types of local office and given the fact
of little association between the participation of women on
school boards and on municipal councils among local communities in New Jersey, serious questions arise of whether research findings from one office may be generalized to another.

An implication of the differing patterns is that explanations for women's uniformly low participation in public policy-making must be based on a careful sifting of those causes peculiar to each position.

Women's School Board Membership in New Jersey

Sources of data for the analysis of school boards include the U.S. Census of Population for 1970 adjusted to school district boundaries by the Department of Health, Education and Welfare, statistical data published by the New Jersey Education Association, and data on numbers of women supplied by the New Jersey School Boards Association. Complete or partial information is available for 70 five-member, 42 seven-member and 377 nine-member boards.[17] Eighty-six percent of these 489 boards serve a single municipality; the remainder represent consolidated or regional districts. Sixteen percent of five-member, 36 percent of seven, and two percent of nine-member boards are appointive rather than elective.

As shown in Table 1, women comprise 24 percent of the 350 members of five-person boards, 28 percent of the 294 members of seven-person boards, and 21 percent of the 3393 members of nine-person boards. Both appointive and elective boards with seven members have slightly higher percentages of female membership than boards of other size. Contrary to the evidence of past research, appointive boards of every size do have slightly higher percentages of women.[18] Although some have argued that appointment requires the kind of sponsorship not likely to occur on the part of a male-dominated elite, who are likely to appoint people like themselves, an argument to the contrary can be made. Community elites have been found to be more "liberal" or "tolerant" than the electorate in general.[19] Those with the power to appoint may be more receptive than the electorate to the participation of women. Moreover, the appointive process may encourage a more explicit "balancing" of community interests in board representation, a process that may lead more readily than election to the membership of women.

A common explanation of the variable presence of women in occupations and public office is that they are concentrated in the less "important" positions.[20] Accordingly, one might expect to find a smaller proportion of women on boards operating full K-12 districts or regional high schools

TABLE 1

Percentages of Female Board Members in New Jersey, 1975

Percentage Board Members Who Are Women Among	Five-Member	Seven-Member	Nine-Member
All Districts	24%	28%	21%
Total number	(350)	(294)	(3393)
Appointive Districts	27%	31%	26%
Total number	(55)	(105)	(54)
Elective Districts	23%	26%	21%
Total number	(295)	(189)	(3339)
Elementary Districts	24%	28%	22%
Total number	(245)	(140)	(1530)
K-12 Districts	25%	34%	24%
Total number	(95)	(154)	(1458)
Secondary Districts	10%	---	15%
Total number	(10)	(none)	(405)

than on those operating elementary districts only. The data in Table 1 confirm this hypothesis only for secondary districts. These regional districts have somewhat lower proportions of women on their boards. There is little difference between elementary and K-12 districts in the percentage of female board membership. Indeed, seven-member boards have slightly higher percentages of women in K-12 than in elementary districts. That the type of district operated is not clearly related to the percentage of female board membership is paralleled in the finding that the size of the school population has only a very low correlation with the number of women on a school board. [21] The Pearsonian correlations between the size of district enrollment and number of women on school boards are only .19, .11 and .04 for five-, seven- and nine-member boards respectively. [22]

The Distribution of Female Membership Among Boards

Women are not evenly distributed among the boards in our study, as can be seen in Table 2. Five-member boards are more likely to have no women at all (30 percent) than are boards with seven (5 percent) or nine (11 percent) members. Although five-member boards more often have no women, they are also more apt than the larger boards to

TABLE 2

Percentages of N. J. Boards with
Given Numbers of Women in 1975

No. of Women	Five-Member	Seven-Member	Nine-Member
0	30%	5%	11%
1	37%	21%	28%
2	20%	50%	30%
3	13%	20%	22%
4	0%	2%	8%
5	0%	0%	1%
Total boards (= 100%)	(70)	(42)	(377)

have a majority of women: thirteen percent of five-person boards have a majority but only two percent of seven-member and one percent of nine-member boards are dominated by women.

The majority of boards, regardless of size, count only one or two women among their membership. Does this modality point to a distinct pattern of tokenism as a conscious or even unwitting decision of community electorates and appointers? That is, given the fact that overall school board membership is less than one-quarter female, can the uneven distribution of this one-quarter among boards be interpreted to mean widespread policies of tokenism?

This question is more difficult to answer than might first appear. In order to address it, it is useful first to imagine a situation in which gender is irrelevant to school board membership, in which case one would expect approximately half the total school board members in the state to be women. It does not follow from this expectation that every board would be composed of half females. Instead, sheer random fluctuation would create a situation in which many boards would have 50 percent women but some would have a majority of men, some a majority of women, and an occasional board would even be composed entirely of males or females. That is, the distribution of boards according to their sex composition would tend to describe a normal curve. The right-hand column of Table 3 illustrates, for boards of each size, the percentages of boards that would have particular numbers of women if sex were irrelevant to school board membership and if women overall were 50 percent of all

TABLE 3

Actual Percentages of N. J. Boards with Given Numbers of Women in 1975, Compared with Percentages Expected by Chance Distributions

Five-Member Boards No. of Women	Actual	Expected by Chance Given Current 24%	Expected by Chance Under Equality, 50%
0	30%	25%	3%
1	37%	40%	16%
2	20%	25%	31%
3	13%	8%	31%
4	0%	1%	16%
5	0%	1%	3%

Total boards = 100% (70)

Seven-Member Boards No. of Women	Actual	Expected by Chance Given Current 28%	Expected by Chance Under Equality, 50%
0	5%	10%	1%
1	21%	27%	6%
2	50%	32%	16%
3	22%	21%	27%
4	2%	8%	27%
5	0%	2%	16%
6	0%	0%	6%
7	0%	0%	1%

Total boards = 100% (42)

Nine-Member Boards No. of Women	Actual	Expected by Chance Given Current 21%	Expected by Chance Under Equality, 50%
0	11%	12%	0% (.19%)
1	28%	29%	2%
2	30%	30%	7%
3	22%	20%	16%
4	8%	7%	25%
5	1%	2%	25%
6	0%	0%	16%
7	0%	0%	7%
8	0%	0%	2%
9	0%	0%	0% (.19%)

Total boards = 100% (377)

school board members.   Comparison with the actual percentage distributions in the left-hand column is a further drama-
tization of the under-representation of women.

A condition of equality would mean that women would
comprise roughly half the school board membership.   The
actual representation in New Jersey is far less than half.
The middle column of Table 3 presents the percentages of
boards that could be expected to have particular numbers of
women under an assumption of random distribution of current
female board membership. 23   Comparison of the left-hand
and middle columns in Table 3 reveals that the actual distribution of female board membership closely approximates a
random model.   Among nine-person boards, the correspond-
ence is nearly exact.   The only notable departure from
chance expectation occurs among seven-member boards, in
which there are more boards with two women than a random
model would predict.   In short, it is possible that the presence of only one or two women on the majority of boards is
merely a function of the generally low numbers of women entering school politics rather than evidence of tokenism as a
barrier to participation.   If tokenism were operating as a
distinct pattern, it is plausible to assume that the percentages of boards with one or at most two women would far exceed chance expectations.   The fact that they do not does not
prove an absence of tokenism but does indicate that patterns
of participation could have arisen from other processes operating to discourage women's officeholding.

Community Characteristics and Variations in
Board Composition

In an effort to explore the manner in which differing
types of communities may produce varying numbers of women
in local office, a large and relatively diverse set of ecological variables describing the school district and its population
was selected for examination.   Table 4 lists these characteristics, along with the simple correlations between each variable and the numbers of women on school boards of varying
size. 24

On the whole, these correlations are low in magnitude even though each, singly or in combination, as characteristic of political women or of the socio-political environment, has been proposed to explain the participation or lack
of participation of women in politics.   Among five- and nine-

TABLE 4

Simple Correlations Between the Number of Women
on N. J. School Boards in 1975 and
Characteristics of School Districts

	Five-member N= 61	Seven-member N= 35	Nine-member N= 350
POLITICAL			
% Democratic vote in 1975 elections to lower house of state legislature	. 09	. 33	. 02
Degree of partisanship (4-point scale) in vote for legislature	-. 11	. 22	-. 12
Presence of one or more women on municipal council(s) in district	-. 09	. 25	. 10
SCHOOL DISTRICT			
Size of district enrollment (correlates . 95 with district population)	. 19	. 11	. 04
Operation of secondary school only (nine-member boards)	---	---	-. 18
Appointed board (seven-member boards)	---	. 18	---
ETHNIC			
% Persons of foreign stock	. 05	-. 04	. 07
% Black	-. 06	. 30	-. 03
% Hispanic	-. 28	. 31	-. 11
SOCIOECONOMIC			
Median years schooling of population aged 25+ years	. 15	. 15	. 27
Median family income	. 24	. 07	. 29
FAMILY			
% Families with female head	. 05	. 26	-. 10
Mean number children born to ever-married women aged 25-34 yrs. in 1970	-. 03	-. 14	-. 15
RESIDENTIAL STABILITY			
% Persons residing in same house 1965-70	-. 12	-. 06	-. 11
EMPLOYMENT OF WOMEN			
% Females aged 25-64 yrs. in labor force	-. 11	. 14	-. 14
% Employed females in professional managerial positions	. 39	. 24	. 28

person boards, the SES of the community--education, income
and the professional-managerial status of employed women--
seems to have a weak but positive effect. Among seven-
member boards, there is a suggestion of the interaction of
urban political and social characteristics with SES. Among
these boards, larger numbers of women are in minor degree
associated with a high Democratic vote, a high level of parti-
sanship, the presence of women on councils, a relatively
large Black or Hispanic population, and a high percentage of
families headed by females.

Despite steps taken to reduce redundancy in the selection of independent variables, the simple correlations tend to
be so low that some of the interactions among the community
characteristics are higher than are their correlations with the
numbers of women on school boards. This becomes apparent
when we ask the extent to which the variables in Table 4 in
combination account for variation in the representation of
women on school boards. Utilizing multiple regression procedures and adjusting the percentage of explained variation
for the number of cases and the number of variables, we find
a maximum of 30 percent of the variation is explained among
five-person boards, 42 percent among seven-person boards
and only 14 percent among nine-member boards. [25]

Given the number of variables examined, in no case
is an impressive amount of the variation explained. Moreover, the weak patterns that do emerge do not easily fit
within a consistent conceptual framework. Instead, it would
seem more reasonable to conclude that knowledge of the type
of community, as described by the variables utilized, is of
little assistance in predicting whether and how many women
will be found in local office. This finding is contrary to expectations and to casual experience. Yet other researchers
have come to much the same conclusion, as a result of an
analysis of the role of ecological characteristics in the candidacy and election of women to city councils. [26]

Such a "negative" finding raises many issues of interpretation that must await further research. Several avenues
for the further pursuit of these issues are open. One is
that district characteristics are relevant but that we have
failed to identify and measure relevant aspects of the socio-
political environment. Yet we have employed the "standard"
ecological variables often found in past research to differen-
tiate communities in important ways. If the findings are not
an artifact of the research procedures but reflect a reality of

women's public participation, then the barriers to women's
political participation may occur uniformly in all kinds of
communities--if not in the form of active resistance to wom-
en in public life, then through the indirect effects of a cultural milieu that everywhere operates to discourage female
participation.   But if barriers are uniform, what accounts
for the variation from community to community in the participation of women?   One possible answer is that such variation reflects little more than random fluctuation, and we have
seen in Table 3 that, given the relatively low overall percentages of women on school boards, their distribution among
districts approaches a random model.   The important issue
then becomes one of accounting for the low overall percentage either by identifying and explicating the common factors
among communities in resistance to women's political participation or by focusing on the social-psychological aspects
of women's lives--their sex-role socialization and the peculiar constellation of roles they occupy--that reduce their political activity. 27

Changes in Rates of Women's School Board Membership

During the five-year period 1971-1975, New Jersey experienced a notable increase in the presence of women on
school boards.   In 1971, five-member boards consisted of
only 13 percent women but had increased to 24 percent by
1975.   Parallel increases for seven-member boards were
from 17 percent to 28 percent, and for nine-person boards
from 13 percent to 21 percent.   Table 5 compares 1971
and 1975 with respect to the numbers of women on boards
of given size.   During the five-year period, the number of
boards with no women decreased dramatically; those with
two or three women show correspondingly dramatic increases.

Not all boards followed this general trend, however;
a sizable minority of boards actually decreased the number
of women over the period.   Sixteen percent of five-member,
seven percent of seven-member and ten percent of nine-member boards lost one or more female members over the five
years.   Contrary to the general trend of increase, boards
which had a female membership approaching a majority in
1971 were more likely to lose than to gain female members.
Of the 11 five-member boards with two or more women in
1971, seven lost at least one woman; only one gained.   Of
the two seven-member boards having three women in 1971,
one lost two women, one remained the same.   Among nine-
member boards, 37 had three or more women in 1971.   Of

TABLE 5

Percentages of N. J. Boards with Given Numbers of Women,
1971 and 1975, by Size of Board

No. of Women	Five-Member		Seven-Member		Nine-Member	
	1971	1975	1971	1975	1971	1975
0	44%	30%	10%	5%	29%	11%
1	41%	37%	63%	21%	37%	28%
2	13%	20%	22%	50%	24%	30%
3	2%	13%	5%	22%	9%	22%
4		0%		2%	1%	8%
5		0%		0%	1%	1%
	(68)	(70)	(42)	(42)	(370)	(377)

these, 17 had fewer women in 1975, 17 remained the same,
and only three added female members.

The pattern of loss among boards which in 1971 had
a majority or near-majority of women, during a period in
which most other boards were increasing their female
membership, points to an important barrier to sexual equality
in representation. The current barrier is not to the inclusion
of a token woman but to the inclusion of women in numbers
that would give them a majority or near-majority. Not entirely facetiously, we note that sexual equality of membership cannot be achieved for any particular school board.
Since the boards have odd numbers of members, either men
or women must numerically dominate. If the hard line of
resistance to women is to their becoming a majority on any
particular governing body, then aggregate equality of representation must paradoxically await the crumbling of resistance
to majority rule by women on particular boards.

Community Characteristics and Changes in Women's Partici-
pation

As we have seen, the ecological characteristics of the
district do not assist in identifying boards likely to have
larger or smaller numbers of women. A possibility not yet
examined is that such characteristics may be of help in
identifying the types of districts most likely to change in line
with the general trend. Table 6 describes the correlations
between district characteristics and the numbers of women
lost or added to the district's board. As was true of the

TABLE 6

Simple Correlations Between 1971-1975 Change in the Number of Women on N. J. School Boards and Characteristics of the School District

	Five-member N= 61	Seven-member N= 35	Nine-member N= 350
POLITICAL			
% Democratic vote in 1975 elections to lower house of state legislature	.04	.22	.06
Degree of partisanship (4-point scale) in vote for legislature	-.00	.04	-.13
Presence of one or more women on municipal council(s) in district	-.06	.09	.06
SCHOOL DISTRICT			
Size of district enrollment (correlates .95 with district population)	.29	-.01	.01
Operation of secondary school only (nine-member boards)	---	---	-.05
Appointed board (seven-member boards)	---	.04	---
ETHNIC			
% Persons of foreign stock	.27	.06	.12
% Black	-.00	-.04	-.10
% Hispanic	-.42	-.16	-.09
SOCIOECONOMIC			
Median years schooling of population aged 25+ years	.04	.09	.18
Median family income	.13	.10	.19
FAMILY			
% Families with female head	.06	.01	-.14
Mean number children born to ever-married women aged 25-34 yrs. in 1970	.04	-.09	-.07
RESIDENTIAL STABILITY			
% Persons residing in same house 1965-70	.03	.13	-.13
EMPLOYMENT OF WOMEN			
% Females aged 25-64 yrs. in labor force	-.06	-.04	.18
% Employed females in professional managerial positions	.19	.19	.19

cross-section correlations for 1975, the correlations are low.
Utilizing multiple regression procedures similar to those for
1975, we find that our variables are even less capable of explaining change in the sexual composition of boards than they
were of explaining the composition at a single point in time.
Only 23 percent, six percent and seven percent of the variation in change[28] among five, seven and nine-member boards
respectively is explained by district characteristics.

Conclusion

The principal stimulus for our exploration of links between the nature of local communities and the presence of
women on school boards has been the assumption that specific
socio-political environments encourage or discourage political
activity on the part of its female residents.   If these environments could be identified, this understanding could be applied
to strategies for increasing women's participation.   The results have failed to support our basic assumption.   We find,
instead, a series of mostly negative observations: school
and municipal council membership by women are unrelated;
district characteristics are unrelated either to the number of
women on school boards or to change in numbers; the distribution of women on school boards approximates a random
model, except for the disproportionate presence of two wom-
en on seven-person boards.   The only "positive" clue to the
underrepresentation of women on boards is that boards approaching a majority of women members are likely to lose
women in subsequent elections.

In raising the issue of women's participation on school
boards at the beginning of this paper, we noted the apparently greater involvement of women with education as a type of
experience that should lead to the participation of women on
school boards.   Yet a recent survey of public attitudes toward school boards casts doubt on this assumption:

> Contrary to a widespread impression in education
> circles that women are more knowledgeable about
> school matters than men, there is very little dif-
> ference between men and women in this survey.
> In fact, to the extent that there are any differences,
> it tends [sic] to be in the direction that men are
> more knowledgeable. [29]

Thus 41 percent of men but only 34 percent of women could

name a recent action of their school board. Men and women
did not differ in reported contact with the schools, or in believing that the board represents their views. Unless these
findings reflect some hidden sample or response bias, [30] a
closer look at the way in which men and women in the local
community relate to their school systems is indicated. Perhaps the two sexes participate in differentiated networks that
carry differing opportunity to learn about and influence school
policy. If, for example, the local PTA is largely devoted to
bake sales and lectures from teachers of the how-to-get-along-
with-your-adolescent-child variety, then the participation of
women in parent organizations may not be a channel for the
communication of the political structures and policies of the
educational system. Perhaps men are likely to learn about
school politics through local associations of professional businessmen and politicians from which women are largely ab-
sent--organizations in which male board members and politicians are also likely to participate. If so, then the lack of
participation of women on school boards is simply one more
manifestation of the general sexual allocation of roles--an
allocation that pervades both private and public life, formal
and informal organization. The interconnectedness of sexual
distinctions in diverse social spheres implies a slow and difficult process of change in any single institution, for particular changes become dependent upon general alterations in the
status of women.

The issue of whether such changes can best be brought
about through attacking environmental obstacles to opportunity
or the socialized motivations and expectations of individual
women is a prominent but probably spurious controversy. An
ascribed characteristic such as sex that forms a basis for
social differentiation cross-cutting institutional spheres is inevitably structured both organizationally and in the personalities of individuals. Our failure to discover meaningful
differences in the barriers or facilitators presented by local
environments invites neither exclusively individual nor exclusively structural interpretation. The present results merely
indicate, should they be confirmed by future research, that
obstacles to women's local political participation operate uniformly among local environments. Such obstacles undoubtedly include the intersection of culture and individual that defines the internalized expectations, motivations and role priorities of individual women.

NOTES

1. The 1972 Census of Governments reports 15,781 school districts among the 78,218 operating local governing bodies in the U.S. United States Bureau of the Census, Governmental Organization, the U.S. Census of Governments, vol. 1 (Washington, D.C.: Government Printing Office, 1972), p. 1.

2. Suzanne S. Taylor, "The Attitudes of Superintendents and Board of Education Members Toward the Employment and Effectiveness of Women as Public School Administrators," in Sex Bias in the Schools: The Research Evidence, eds. Janice Pottker and Andrew Fishel (Rutherford, N.J.: Fairleigh Dickinson University Press, 1977), pp. 300-310; Marilyn Boyd Neidig, "Women Applicants for Administrative Positions: Attitudes Held by Administrators and School Boards" (Ph.D. dissertation, University of Iowa, 1973).

3. Trudy Haffron Bers, "Local Political Elites: Men and Women on Boards of Education" (Paper delivered at the Annual Meeting of the Southern Political Science Association, Atlanta, Georgia, November 4-6, 1976), pp. 16-26; National School Boards Association, Women on School Boards (Washington, D.C.: National School Boards Association, 1974), pp. 46-50. Perhaps related to the differing attitudes and emphases of women and men on school boards is a recent discovery that boards with large numbers of women more often display persistent patterns of split votes in decision-making. See Paul D. Blanchard, "If You're Jittery or Embarrassed Because Your School Board Is 'Divided,' Maybe You Shouldn't Be," American School Board Journal 164 (July 1977), p. 36.

4. Marilyn Johnson and Kathy Stanwick, "Profile of Women Holding Office," in Women in Public Office: A Biographical Directory and Statistical Analysis, Center for the American Woman and Politics (New York: R. R. Bowker Company, 1976), p. xxxiii.

5. National School Boards Association, Women, pp. 17-18.

6. National School Boards Association, Fifty State School Boards Associations (Washington, D.C.: National School Boards Association, 1975), p. 2; Andrew Fishel and Janice Pottker, "School Boards and Sex Bias in American Education," Contemporary Education, 65 (Winter 1974): 85-89; Robert H. Brown, "The Composition of School Boards," American School Board Journal, 141 (August 1954): 23-24; George S. Counts, The

Social Composition of Boards of Education: A Study
in the Social Control of Public Education, Supplemen-
tary Education Monographs, no. 33 (Chicago: University of Chicago Press, 1927).

7. Bernadette Doran, "The Feminist Surge Has Hit School
Boards, and They May Never Be the Same Again,"
American School Board Journal, 164 (April 1977): 25.

8. National School Boards Association, Women, pp. 5-6.

9. Carolyn Mullins, "If Superintendents Could Pick Their
Own School Board Members, Here's the Kind They
Say They'd Choose," American School Board Journal,
161 (September 1974): 25.

10. Fishel and Pottker, "School Boards and Sex Bias," p.
87; National School Boards Association, Women, p. 30.

11. The present analysis is preliminary to planned research
on the structure, manner of operation and policy outcomes of boards having varying numbers of women.

12. Data on councilwomen in New Jersey, adjusted for
school district boundaries, are drawn from those compiled by the Center for the American Woman and Politics, Eagleton Institute of Politics, Rutgers University.

13. Kathy Stanwick and Marilyn Johnson, Women Appointed
to State Boards and Commissions, Report of the Center for the American Woman and Politics to the Wom-
en and Power Committee of the National Commission
for the Observance of International Women's Year
(Washington, D.C.: U.S. Department of State), pp,
10-11.

14. National School Boards Association, Women, passim.

15. Johnson and Stanwick, "Profile," passim.

16. Only the general pattern of differences can be persuasive, for the two studies may lack strict comparability. The NSBA study was conducted a year earlier.
There may be differing biases of nonresponse to the
two mailed questionnaires. The data are not always
presented in parallel form. (Where the NSBA reports
means, the medians have been estimated from the
published tabulations for comparability with the Center's tabulations.)

17. These numbers represent 80 percent of the 609 boards
in New Jersey in 1975. Omitted from the analysis
are vocational, special and nonoperating districts,
districts with enrollment below 300 and Newark (because of its unusual size in relation to other districts).

18. Our data refer only to boards to which all members
are appointed. We have no data on the appointment
of women to fill unexpired terms on elective boards.

19. See, for example, the prototypical study by Samuel A.
     Stouffer, Communism, Conformity, and Civil Liberties
     (New York: Doubleday and Company, 1955).

20. Research conducted by the Center for the American Wom-
     an and Politics (Johnson and Stanwick, "Profile,") il-
     lustrates the need for careful specification of the mean-
     ing of "importance," for there are larger proportions
     of women in state legislatures and state cabinet-level
     positions than on county and municipal councils. In
     her analysis of the association between the "competi-
     tiveness" of legislative positions and the percentage of
     offices filled by women, Irene Diamond indicates one
     of the ways in which "importance" may be operational-
     ized. Irene Diamond, Sex Roles in the State House
     (New Haven: Yale University Press, 1977).

21. Correlated .95 with population size.

22. Note, however, that the smallest districts--those with
     enrollment below 300--are not included in the analysis.

23. For example, if board size = 5 and p (woman) = .24,
     p (man) = .76, then the expected or chance proportion
     of boards having:
     0 women = .76 x .76 x .76 x .76 x .76 x 1 = 25%
     1 woman = .24 x .76 x .76 x .76 x .76 x 5 = 40%
     2 women = .24 x .24 x .76 x .76 x .76 x 10 = 25%
     3 women = .24 x .24 x .24 x .76 x .76 x 10 = 8%
     4 women = .24 x .24 x .24 x .24 x .76 x 5 = 1%
     5 women = .24 x .24 x .24 x .24 x .24 x 1 = 1%

24. A number of additional variables were scrutinized and
     dropped from the analysis because their correlations
     with one or more of the variables in Table 4 were so
     high as to constitute redundancy: percentage of per-
     sons aged 30-39 years, percentage of families with
     children under 18 years, percentage of mothers of
     children under 18 years in the labor force, percent-
     age of families below poverty level, equalized valua-
     tion/pupil, size of district population.

25. A forward stepwise regression procedure was employed,
     with the addition of variables ended at the point at
     which the adjusted R^2 began to decline.

26. Albert K. Karnig and B. Oliver Walter, "Elections of
     Women to City Councils," Social Science Quarterly,
     56 (1976): 605-613. Although our data are organized
     to reflect school district boundaries and the size of
     school boards rather than municipal jurisdictions,
     limited analysis of the relation of the variables in
     Table 4 to the presence of women on municipal coun-
     cils is consistent with the negative findings of the

school board analysis and the study by Karnig and
Walter.

27. Karnig and Walter, "Elections of Women," make es-
     sentially the same points in their argument that the
     basic problem of political participation is whatever
     set of conditions discourages women from becoming
     candidates.

28. Maximum adjusted R^2's in stepwise regressions.

29. National School Boards Association, The People Look
     at Their School Boards (Washington, D.C.: National
     School Boards Association, 1975), p. 34.

30. Research findings that contradict familiar assumptions
     inevitably invite skepticism.

Chapter 5

LOBBYING FOR EQUAL CREDIT[1]

by Anne N. Costain

The Women's Rights Lobby[2]

By early 1973, when the Equal Credit Opportunity Act was being considered by the U.S. Congress, there was already an identifiable and active women's rights lobby working on Capitol Hill. This cooperative lobby consisted of both traditional women's voluntary organizations like the National Federation of Business and Professional Women's Clubs (BPW) and feminist groups like the National Organization for Women (NOW). It had arisen out of successful but largely non-institutionalized efforts to obtain congressional passage of the Equal Rights Amendment (ERA) in 1972. Although lobbying for the ERA was orchestrated primarily by members of Congress, particularly Representative Martha Griffiths, [3] a number of individuals and organizations were brought together in support of this legislation. An ad hoc committee formed to coordinate these activities began patterns of cooperation and resource sharing which would prove invaluable in the development of a more permanent cooperative lobby in support of women's rights legislation.

The stimulus for continued legislative activity in support of women's interests provided by the ERA[4] was quickly reinforced by organizational activity. The opening of Washington legislative offices by the Women's Equity Action League (WEAL) in 1972, the National Organization for Women (NOW) in 1973 and the National Women's Political Caucus in 1973 together with the formation of Women's Lobby (1972) a new group specifically designed to "effect the passage of bills in Congress for the benefit of women"[5] provided the nucleus for such a lobby. Although there had long been women's groups with lobbying operations in Washington, most notably the League of Women Voters, it was not until self-consciously feminist groups established legislative offices that the necessary catalyst for sustained lobbying in support of women's rights was present. Traditional women's organizations had been reluctant to become identified with "women's issues." This was both a product of the negative associations attached to feminism after its peak in the 1920's and also a reflection of the breadth of interest of most of these groups. Organizations like the League of Women Voters and the American Association of University Women (AAUW) carried on legislative programs encompassing issues ranging from support of the United Nations and free trade to penal and tax reform. Even when support of women's issues became popular within these organizations, it was difficult for their lobbyists to devote sufficient time to organize and direct a cooperative women's rights lobby.

The influence of this new women's lobby seemed to come largely from the ability of groups like the Women's Political Caucus and BPW to complement each other's lobbying strength. Although none of the organizations composing the lobby possessed the political or economic clout to bring great pressure in support of legislation advancing the interests of women, by coordinating their legislative efforts, they were able to create a viable lobby. In the relatively short time since the women's rights lobby began to develop, it was a significant factor in helping to pass at least two pieces of legislation, extension of the minimum wage to domestic workers (1973) and the Women's Educational Equity Act (1974).

Defining the Credit Issue

In addition to lobbying in support of pending legislation, groups involved with the women's rights lobby were also active in this early period in developing and publicizing areas of future legislative concern. One of the first issues involving women to be made public after congressional passage of the ERA was the issue of discrimination by the credit industry in granting credit to women. This issue surfaced nationally during the May, 1972, hearings of the National Commission on Consumer Finance. The staff of the commission began to notice a pattern of complaints in letters sent to them by women who had been denied credit in their own name or who were without a credit record after being married, widowed or divorced. Representative Leonor Sullivan (Democrat, Missouri), a member of this congressionally mandated special commission, decided that this problem was widespread and serious enough to warrant separate hearings by the commission on this issue. Two days of hearings were arranged by the commission staff. Members of both WEAL

and NOW's task force on credit were active in helping the
commission schedule witnesses who could present the most
effective case possible against discrimination in the credit
industry.   The hearings themselves were very successful in
arousing public concern about industry discrimination.

One congressional committee staff member who attended the hearings commented in a later interview:

> Well, those hearings in May 1972 [on sex and mar-
> ital status discrimination] were the most effective
> hearings around here, other than impeachment, in
> a long time because media coverage was terrific.
> One of the leadoff witnesses was an NBC television
> woman in Chicago who had tried to get credit cards
> shifted to her married name.   All her credit cards
> and charge accounts were cancelled because the
> creditors wanted them in her husband's name and
> her husband was unemployed because he had just
> been defeated in the campaign against Richard Daley
> for mayor of Chicago.... Those hearings were
> captivating in the information they brought out. 6

Not only did the hearings provide a graphic picture of individual cases of discrimination but they also revealed a wider
pattern of systematic discrimination based on sex and marital
status.   Studies were reported in which men and women with
similar incomes, jobs and credit records were sent to a
number of creditors to secure a loan.   The women were consistently turned down, while the men's loan applications were
approved by the same creditors.

Following these hearings women's organizations were
active in keeping this issue in the public view.   The success
of their effort is apparent in examining the New York Times
Index.   In 1971 there was not a single article dealing with
sex and marital status discrimination in granting credit.   In
1972, when the May hearings of the National Commission on
Consumer Finance were held, there were three articles in-
dexed.   In 1973 there were fifteen articles including a Times
survey of the efforts of women's groups to end sex discrimination in the extension of credit. 7   In 1974 there were an
additional fourteen articles published before a bill outlawing
such discrimination was signed into law by President Ford.
Women's groups had helped to develop this issue both inside
and outside of Congress.

Credit discrimination was defined very early by women's rights groups as a sex discrimination problem rather than as a consumer or industry problem. Issue definition is a particularly critical stage in determining the ultimate success or failure of any issue. The way in which the issue is initially framed will often determine which interests become involved and what solutions are considered by decision-makers. [8] In this instance the focus was narrowed to link credit discrimination to the issue of legal discrimination against women in American society, symbolized by the Equal Rights Amendment. By taking such action in 1972 the supportive constituency activated by the Equal Rights Amendment could be used to apply pressure for equal credit legislation as well. As one staff member on the Banking and Currency Committee of the House noted:

> They [women's groups] made a case before they even came here [to congress] that there was discrimination in the granting of credit based on sex and marital status. Whether it was widespread or not widespread, everybody was convinced that there was some discrimination and that we could pass a bill to eliminate it because it was not desirable. It was a real motherhood issue, so it was not a matter of having to lobby something through that was not popular. [9]

By 1973 then, when pressure in support of the Equal Credit Opportunity Act began to build in congress, the women's rights lobby, although relatively new as a lobby, was not without experience with this particular issue. In a very real sense these organizations had shaped it from its inception. They had encouraged the National Commission on Consumer Finance to consider it, helped the commission staff arrange hearings and finally used their memberships and resources to help publicize the issue. Largely through their efforts, credit discrimination was a "hot" issue on the agenda of the 93rd Congress.

Congressional Initiative

The women's groups lobbying for an anti-discrimination bill did not need to stimulate legislative involvement in Congress. They could instead respond to congressional initiatives. It was apparent quite early in the legislative history of the credit discrimination bill that direction of its

legislative progress would come almost exclusively from within congress. [10] Since the 1972 hearings of the National Commission on Consumer Finance publicized the problems many
women had experienced in obtaining credit, numerous bills
had been introduced to end this type of discrimination by the
credit industry. [11] Even more significantly, several members of Congress, notably Senator William Brock (Republican,
Tennessee) and Representatives Bella Abzug (Democrat, New
York), Leonor Sullivan (Democrat, Missouri), Margaret Heckler (Republican, Massachusetts), and Edward Koch (Democrat,
New York) had adopted the sexual discrimination issue as a
priority legislative concern. Sullivan's interest was of particular importance because of her position as chairperson of
the subcommittee which would be handling this legislation.
Each of their offices in varying degrees publicized the issue,
drafted bills and mobilized supportive groups to lobby for
congressional passage of a bill to end this discrimination.
Women's groups active in the women's rights lobby were approached by these supportive legislative offices both for advice on the contents of proposed legislation and for action to
sustain interest inside and outside of congress.

It is not unusual for members of congress to recruit
lobbies. As Bauer, Pool and Dexter noted in their well-
known study of tariff legislation:

> The congressman who told us that he had to tele-
> phone "his" lobby to get them going was not telling
> us a man-bites-dog story. He was describing a
> usual state of affairs. [12]

One of the reasons for the relatively rapid acceptance of the
women's rights lobby by Congress was that many members
were already introducing and voting for legislation to alter
some of the most visible inequities in the legal treatment of
American women. The pressure of changing social and political attitudes towards women in the late 1960's and early
1970's[13] seemed to stimulate this wave of legislation while
leaving a temporary void in organized support for those in
congress responding to this pressure. The organization of
a supportive lobbying operation helped to lessen the costs
for individual offices in initiating legislation to help women.
In addition, it provided a unified voice to translate women's
demands for social change into an intelligible agenda for
legislative action.

Lobbying Response

The ability of the women's rights lobby to respond to these congressional requests for help in drafting and passing credit legislation can be evaluated along three dimensions: information, access and perceived electoral impact. The information function in lobbying is obviously critical in dealing with legislation as technical as regulation of the credit industry. It was important for the women's rights lobby to make rapid and accurate assessments of both the significance of and probable judicial interpretations of proposed statutory wording in order to get the strongest legislation possible through congress.

Without good information the lobby had difficulty in achieving consensus among the groups composing the lobby, in knowing its own interests and in persuading members of congress to support those interests. Early in its legislative involvement, a variety of preferences for statutory wording arose among lobby members. Two of the organizations, Women's Lobby and the National Women's Political Caucus took much tougher positions on consumer rights than did the other women's groups which were active. This difference was made more difficult to resolve because of the apparently genuine disagreements, without much factual evidence, over the issue of whether individual damage law suits against creditors or class action suits, where an entire class of individuals similarly affected may sue as a group, were more effective in enforcing consumers' rights. This diversity of opinion led to confusion in the lobbying effort as several contradictory women's positions were circulated on the Hill.

There were several obvious causes of this weakness in information. First, women's rights lobbyists represent organizations with a wide range of legislative concerns, making it difficult for them to develop technical expertise in any single subject area. Second, credit reform was the first attempt of this cooperative lobby to influence banking legislation, so it had little general knowledge of the issues in financial regulation. Finally, and most critically, the lobby did not have the monetary resources to hire a legal consultant experienced in these matters to present an independent judgment of statutory language. What the women's rights lobby did have were two lawyers experienced in credit legislation who were willing to provide free advice.

The first and more controversial of these women lawyers was Sharyn Campbell, head of NOW's legislative task
force on credit. Campbell lobbied full-time for a number of
months, assisting subcommittee staff, drafting legislation and
consulting with women's lobby groups in developing a consensus on what legislation to support. Campbell, although
conceded to be a skilled attorney, was also an employee of
BankAmericard and therefore open to charges of conflict of
interest. Although Campbell was officially on leave from
BankAmericard during the majority of the time she worked
on the Hill, reservations were expressed by several of those
who worked with her on this legislation about her ability to
subordinate her employer's interests. Particularly controversial were her dislike of class action remedies and her
willingness to limit rather severely punitive as contrasted
with actual damages in the case of class action and individual
suits. Both were positions shared by the industry which
some felt unnecessarily weakened consumer protection.

The other attorney, Margaret Gates, did not engage
in the same sort of direct lobbying as did Campbell. Gates
as co-director of the Center for Women Policy Studies, a
non-profit tax-exempt corporation, was supervising a large-
scale study of sexual discrimination in the credit industry
financed by several private foundations. Gates, after testifying on the subject of credit discrimination at the November
1973 oversight hearings of the subcommittee on Consumer
Affairs, was asked to testify again at the follow up June 1974
hearings on credit discrimination legislation. Gates was also
asked by the committee staff to provide expert opinion on
legislative language. Because of the tax-exempt status of
her Center for Women Policy Studies, Gates was, from all
accounts, quite reluctant to work closely with women's groups
on this legislation. Although Gates took a much stronger consumer position than Campbell in regard to both class action
suits and punitive damages, she did not rally support for
these positions. Overall, then, the information available to
the women's rights lobby on credit legislation was less clear
and well-developed than would be desirable for maximum lobbying impact.

In addition to the information function of lobbying,
groups must develop access to legislative decision-makers if
they hope to communicate their own interests effectively.
Part of this access involves sufficient knowledge of the legislative process to realize when to intervene and with whom.
In the case of credit legislation, access was facilitated by

the activity of several congressional offices notably those of
Senator William Brock (Republican, Tennessee) and Representatives Leonor Sullivan (Democrat, Missouri), Margaret
Heckler (Republican, Massachusetts), and Edward Koch (Democrat, New York) in virtually recruiting women's groups to
work for this legislation. By responding to the legislative
direction of members of congress, the lobby was assured of
timely and informed participation in the legislative process.

Beyond the guidance the women's rights lobby received
from specific members of congress, they also had reasonably
good access to a variety of legislative offices. Because of
the diversity of the groups composing the women's lobby,
ranging from NOW and the Women's Political Caucus to more
conservative organizations like the AAUW and BPW, it could
select which organizations might best approach specific congressional offices. Also, the women's rights lobby had a
built-in constituency within the House. Many of the women
members of congress take an almost proprietary concern
about the activities of the women's rights lobby. The wom-
en's lobbyists interviewed reported in turn far more communication with the offices of the women in congress than
was the case for members in general. [14] Overall, the wom-
en's rights lobby had reasonably good access to members
working on credit legislation.

The final aspect of effective lobbying to be noted is
the perceived electoral impact of a lobby. A member of
congress should be convinced at some level that to ignore
this group's interests might produce negative electoral reper-
cussions. Since none of the groups lobbying for women's
rights contributed to political campaigns and only one, the
National Women's Political Caucus endorsed candidates, the
most direct actions to produce electoral impact were largely
absent at the time the credit legislation was under consideration. There was, however, some persuasive evidence to suggest that these groups did possess electoral strength. In the
case of credit legislation, between the May 1972 hearings of
the National Commission on Consumer Finance and the end of
1973, twenty-two states and the District of Columbia passed
bills guaranteeing women equal access to credit. By the
time Congress's Equal Credit Opportunity Act was signed into
law in October 1974 thirty-three states had similar laws. As
Congresswoman Sullivan observed in the hearings on credit
discrimination before her subcommittee:

In the 22 years I have served in Congress, I have

seldom seen an issue take fire as quickly as this
issue of discrimination in extensions of credit by
reason of sex or marital status and lead to so
many new state laws in a period of only 2 years
since the national Commission held its hearings in
May, 1972. [15]

The series of legislative victories won by proponents of wom-
en's rights in state houses across the country could hardly
have failed to create some impression of electoral clout.

In summary, the women's rights lobby was weakest
in its technical grasp of the issues before congress concerning credit regulation. Its access to the members involved
with this legislation was good. Similarly, its perceived
electoral impact, although not overwhelming, was sufficient
to suggest widespread support in the states for women's
rights issues.

Competing Legislative Agendas

Action on equal credit legislation was almost immediate in the Senate. In July 1973 a title (III) to Senate bill
S 2101, introduced by Senator William Brock passed the Senate
by a vote of 90 to 0. With this legislative history, Senate
support of a bill ending discrimination on the basis of sex
and marital status seemed assured and women's groups
focused their attention on the House of Representatives which
had not yet passed such a bill.

Despite or perhaps because of the high degree of congressional involvement with this issue, two competing approaches to the problem of sexual discrimination in the credit
industry quickly surfaced in the House. One approach advanced by Congresswoman Leonor Sullivan as Chairperson of
the Subcommittee on Consumer Affairs stressed the need for
a comprehensive bill dealing with a wide range of credit industry abuses, of which sex and marital status discrimination
would form only one part. Sullivan was very concerned
about the omnibus Senate-passed bill previously mentioned
(S 2101) which contained Brock's title on equal credit opportunity. Sullivan felt that the first two titles of S 2101 contained provisions which, although described as technical
amendments, weakened the Truth in Lending Act. For this
reason she preferred to have the House pass its own comprehensive bill covering all the areas dealt with in the Senate

bill, but with stronger consumer provisions, closer to those
of the final report of the National Commission on Consumer
Finance. Sullivan wanted a comprehensive House bill rather
than the more limited Equal Credit Opportunity Act to go to
conference with the omnibus Senate bill. She feared that
House conferees, without the guidelines of a broad House bill,
would end up agreeing by default to many of the provisions
of the omnibus Senate bill.

Sullivan also felt that discrimination based on sex and
marital status was part of a broader pattern of discriminatory practice within the credit industry encompassing discrimination based on race, color, religion, national origin and
age as well as sex and marital status. She consequently
favored a broader equal credit opportunity guarantee than
Brock's.

Tactically, Sullivan recognized the popularity of legislation dealing with sex and marital status and seemed to
prefer to hold it as a bargaining chip in her efforts to pass
a strong bill protecting consumers from a variety of credit
industry abuses uncovered in the National Commission on
Consumer Finance's investigation. Barring this possibility,
she hoped at least to use this provision to get a broad piece
of anti-discrimination legislation through congress. Sullivan
preferred that the issue of sexual discrimination be treated
either as a consumer or a civil rights problem rather than
as a woman's issue.

It became apparent that two members of the subcommittee had developed different legislative priorities from
Sullivan's. Edward Koch (Democrat, New York) and Margaret Heckler (Republican, Massachusetts) felt that the evidence
presented during the 1972 hearings of the National Commission on Consumer Finance concerning women having less access to education, homeownership, entrepreneurship and investment than men justified immediate action to remedy this
inequity. They both felt the fastest remedy would come
from a separate bill on sex and marital status discrimination.
They feared that the momentum accumulated for passage of
such a limited bill might be dissipated were it tied to a
wider range of legislative proposals such as those Congresswoman Sullivan suggested.

Because of their preferences, Koch and Heckler were
active in mobilizing women's rights groups and members of
the subcommittee to put pressure on Sullivan to hold separate

hearings on a sex and marital status bill. Sullivan reluc-
tantly scheduled separate hearings on the issue of sex discrimination in the granting of credit to be held June 20 and
21, 1974, but she first extracted two concessions from her
subcommittee colleagues who favored the Koch-Heckler approach. First, the bill on which the hearings were held
(HR 14856) was a broad credit discrimination bill introduced
by Sullivan, rather than the sex and marital status bill of
Edward Koch and Margaret Heckler. Second, Mrs. Sullivan
believed she had commitments from the women's rights lobby
and the co-sponsors of her bill on the subcommittee, including Koch and Heckler, to oppose any attempts to use this
bill for a joint conference and with the Senate on extraneous
provisions of S 2101. This meant, Sullivan felt, that these
members of congress would oppose using a House equal credit opportunity bill as the measure for passing the Senate
Truth in Lending amendments.

Within this framework of legislative maneuvering, the
women's rights groups interested in the passage of strong
legislation ending discrimination by the credit industry had
to choose whether to adopt Leonor Sullivan's legislative
strategy emphasizing the connection between this bill and a
whole range of consumer and discrimination problems or the
more narrow Heckler-Koch approach which also was a weaker consumer bill. Under normal circumstances in congress,
since the chairperson of the subcommittee considering the
legislation, Sullivan, was favorable to the legislative interests of the women's groups and since her bill was in fact
the basis of the legislative hearings being held, one would
expect that the main focus of lobbying by women's groups
would be directed through Sullivan's office. Such was not
the case in this instance, as most of the women's groups
instead chose to work with Koch and Heckler.

For the women's rights lobby to work for Congresswoman Sullivan's broad efforts to reform the credit industry,
they would have had to believe that they would receive their
legislative pay-off--strong legislation ending sex and marital
status discrimination. This trust did not develop. Sullivan
as the only woman in Congress to vote against the Equal
Rights Amendment was regarded with suspicion from the outset. Although she, as one of the House members on the
National Commission on Consumer Finance had originally requested that hearings be held on credit discrimination based
on sex and marital status, her privately held view was that
hearings alone without legislation would probably clear up

the problem.[17] This was not a view shared by women's rights groups.

By contrast, both Heckler and Koch had a long history of involvement with women's rights issues. Their interest in a bill limited to discrimination based on sex and marital status which could pass quickly was very much in accord with the preferences of most of the lobbyists for the women's groups. Since the women's rights lobby was a comparatively new one, the need for early achievements to keep the lobby together was felt acutely. This preference for a bill which could pass rather than a more controversial but stronger bill was reinforced by the lack of reliable information about the relative advantages and disadvantages of each bill. Without any sure way of comparing the provisions of the Sullivan bill to the Heckler-Koch alternative, it was safest to go with the more politically viable bill. Finally, the earliest involvement of these groups on this issue had taken place through Heckler and Koch's offices in the successful fight to get Mrs. Sullivan to schedule separate hearings on credit discrimination. The close working relationship which had developed between these legislative offices and the women's rights lobby was sustained throughout the course of this legislation.

In summary, the women's rights lobby chose to work closely with Representatives Heckler and Koch. They supported a simple bill, closest to the Brock amendment to S 2101, banning only sex and marital status discrimination and containing relatively weak language on provisions such as punitive damages and industry disclosure of reasons for denying credit. This was a bill which could gain the support of the credit industry as well as many Republican members of the House.

Conflict Without Opposition

Two Separate Bills

Against this background of legislative conflict, the hearings on credit discrimination finally opened before the Subcommittee on Consumer Affairs on June 20, 1974. These legislative hearings to be properly understood must be recognized as occurring on two levels. Representatives Heckler and Koch were intent on outmaneuvering Sullivan to gain control of the legislative agenda for their proposal. Formally,

Mrs. Sullivan arranged the hearings to provide discussion of
her bill HR 14856, a broad bill limiting discrimination by the
credit industry on the basis of race, color, religion, national
origin, age sex and marital status.   This was a tough consumer bill patterned on the Truth in Lending Act which had
been co-authored by Leonor Sullivan.   It contained provisions
for class action as well as individual law suits in cases of
discrimination by the industry.   It allowed individual and
class recovery of damages under both state law, where it
existed, and federal law rather than forcing a choice of
remedies.   This latter provision was important because many
of the state laws outlawing discrimination in granting credit
were weak in their consumer recovery provisions.   By not
forcing a choice between state and federal law, the individual
could start court action under state law, realize it was inadequate to recover damages and then bring action in federal
court.   The individual could err in the initial selection of
remedies and still be protected.   Finally, the Sullivan bill
put the Federal Reserve Board in charge of drawing up administrative regulations for enforcement of the legislation.
The Federal Reserve Board is generally regarded as a tough
enforcer of the Truth in Lending Act.   Since Sullivan's bill
was co-sponsored by twelve of the fifteen members of her
subcommittee, she had every reason to believe that she controlled the legislative agenda on credit discrimination.

In addition to the formal legislative agenda on credit
discrimination established by Sullivan, there was a competing
agenda developed under the auspices of Representatives Koch
and Heckler.   Both Koch and Heckler were suspicious of the
sincerity of Sullivan's commitment to passing legislation ending sex and marital status discrimination.   They noted that
it had taken Sullivan over a year from the time congress began to consider equal credit legislation until she scheduled
hearings on the subject.   Similarly, they feared that both the
inclusiveness of her bill, containing race, religion, color,
national origin and age, in addition to sex and marital status,
and the stringency of consumer remedies for industry viola-
tions would result in no bill at all.   Several individuals interviewed suggested that this in fact was Mrs. Sullivan's ultimate strategy.   This belief gained such currency within congress at the time that Sullivan felt compelled to publicly deny
this charge.   For these reasons, Koch and Heckler, working
through the minority staff of the Committee on Banking and
Currency, assembled representatives from women's organizations and from industry to draw up a separate bill from
Sullivan's.

This use of the Republican side of the staff was the
result of the perception of many Democratic members of the
subcommittee that the majority staff was "Mrs. Sullivan's
staff. " It did seem to be the case that the work of the
Democratic side of the staff was primarily responsive to
Sullivan's interests. This, however, has been true of most
subcommittee staffs, until recent procedural reforms in congress, which have attempted to make staff more available to
other majority members of subcommittees as well as the
chair. In any case, the primary coordination of this effort
to draft new legislation came from the Republican committee
staff.

In a series of meetings in minority staff offices and
in Congressman Koch's office, a new bill was put together
with the assistance of representatives of both women's rights
groups and business. The women's groups most involved in
this drafting effort were NOW, National Women's Political
Caucus, WEAL, Women's Lobby and Margaret Gates from,
but not representing, the Center for Women Policy Studies.
It was far more difficult to obtain information in which industry representatives were present for these meetings.
From the names specifically mentioned in interviews, it
seemed that most of the representatives involved were from
companies giving testimony in the hearings such as J. C.
Penney and Sears, Roebuck. A member of the staff of the
subcommittee described the first meeting between these groups
as follows:

> At the end of 1973, after the Senate bill [the Brock
> amendment to S 2101], we [the minority staff]
> asked different women's organizations if they would
> get together with people from industry who have
> representatives in town.... We asked some people
> we felt were particularly knowledgeable and well-
> informed to work on a cooperative basis, combining
> knowledge of the problems of the industry and wom-
> en's organizations, and we got a bill drafted. There
> were certain areas on which they couldn't come to
> final agreement ... and ... [staff members] said,
> "Okay, we'll resolve this. " So the staff made the
> final decisions as to how disputed language would
> be written [for this draft.]18

This initial meeting was followed by a series of meetings with women's groups, attended by both committee staff
and representatives of interested congressional offices, to try

to build consensus on a final bill.   Described by a congressional staff member, subsequent meetings proceeded in the
following way:

> We got together in Mr. Koch's office one afternoon
> and we got together every women's organization we
> could find to come in and tell us what they thought
> was wrong with this draft [completed after the first
> meeting described above].   We sat there that after-
> noon battling out changes and compromises and
> things that people could live with.   We did this
> over a period of a week or two, I guess, drafting
> language to comply with one person's idea or an-
> other's and exchanging the language over the tele-
> phone trying to get together something that every-
> body could support. [19]

Working through the minority side of the staff Democratic Congressman Koch and Republican Congresswoman
Heckler had created a triangular alliance among women's
rights groups, industry and a bi-partisan coalition on the subcommittee.   It might seem surprising that the credit industry was willing to cooperate in this way, since any bill would
entail substantial revision of credit granting procedures.
This expectation of industry opposition ignores the fact that
the credit industry had been embarrassed by the revelations
of the 1972 hearings of the National Commission on Consumer Finance, in which industry denials of discrimination
were countered with massive evidence to the contrary.   In
addition to the bad publicity, by the end of 1973 twenty-two
states and the District of Columbia had passed laws prohibiting sex discrimination in the extension of credit.   With
so many state laws already on the books the industry chose
not to fight federal legislation, but instead to concentrate on
minimizing costs to the industry, by such methods as limiting: class action law suits; punitive damages; and coverage
of the anti-discrimination provisions.   As a member of the
House subcommittee staff was quick to point out, the industry already had to revise its procedures to comply with state
laws and so a narrow federal statute would make little additional difference.

This lack of opposition from business was unexpected
enough for one staff aide working for a liberal member of
the subcommittee to turn over to us an obviously unplayed
tape from J. C. Penney as a demonstration of industry opposition.   In fact the taped message supported credit discrim-

ination reform.   The industry as a whole seemed to have
made the strategic choice to gain some good publicity by
supporting legislation to end discrimination based on sex and
marital status while working to influence the specific content
of this legislation in ways favorable to themselves.

The Triangular Alliance

It could certainly be argued that women's rights groups
and members of congress were at a disadvantage compared
with industry representatives in drafting language on credit
regulation.   The significance of alternate wording in terms of
administrative enforcement was a subject of far greater fa-
miliarity to the industry representatives than to the others
present.   Also, the Republican side of the Banking and Currency staff seemed relatively sympathetic to the industry in
interviews conducted.   One Republican staff member asserted:

> Most of the industries' position was, "We don't
> have any desire to discriminate.   We don't dis-
> criminate, but we don't want a bill that is written
> in such nebulous language that we cannot comply
> with it.   We want a bill that says clearly what is
> expected of us and spells out in adequate language
> what Congress wants in the way of compliance, so
> that we know how to comply. "   Their [industries']
> experience with Truth in Lending legislation had
> been so abominable with so many class action suits
> and what not because of the language in that bill
> not being clear.   Many of them [industries] were
> being attacked in large class action suits for tech-
> nical noncompliance. [20]

Any technical expertise which might have come from
consumer-oriented groups was absent.   This is in part a reflection of the way in which this issue had been defined as
primarily a women's rights problem.   In part it is also a
result of the failure of members of Congress or women's
groups to sell this issue to sympathetic public interest groups
and thus fashion a broader lobbying coalition.   Individuals interviewed at both Common Cause and the League of Women
Voters indicated that their organizations had been approached
to work on this legislation by women's rights groups.   After
initial interest in both organizations, plans for any sustained
involvement were discarded by both the League and Common
Cause because of perceived disorganization in early lobbying
activities in support of a credit discrimination bill.   This

disorganization stemmed from the difficulty the women's rights
lobby had initially in agreeing on legislative language in the
bill, as was described earlier. This disagreement, ironically, was largely a product of inadequate technical information
which might have been supplied by either the League or Common Cause.

In any case, by the time the legislative hearings were
to be held the Koch-Heckler bill had the support of both industry and women's rights groups. What the Koch-Heckler
bill did not have was direct access to the legislative process.
The only two bills on which House hearings were to be held
were Sullivan's bill and a very restrictive minority bill (HR
14908) introduced by Representatives Clair Burgener (Republican, California) and William Widnall (Republican, New
Jersey). The Koch-Heckler bill was therefore sent to Republican Senator William Brock's office where it was introduced in substantially the same form by the Senator on May
14, 1974. Those House members preferring this Senate
version of the bill then made an effort to contact witnesses
scheduled to testify before the Consumer Affairs subcommittee at the credit discrimination hearings to ask them to testify not only on the bills before the subcommittee, but on the
Senate version of the bill as well.

At the close of the hearings, two major amendments
to Mrs. Sullivan's bill were passed by the subcommittee,
bringing her bill into closer conformity with the Brock bill
passed by the Senate. Representative Fortney (Pete) Stark,
a Democrat from California, introduced a successful amendment to eliminate race, color, religion, national origin and
age from the bill, leaving only discrimination based on sex
and marital status. Representative Koch sponsored an amendment limiting the amount of class action recovery under the
bill.

The women's rights groups active in lobbying for this
legislation were persuaded to accept these limiting amendments on political grounds. The cooperative relationship
fostered between these groups and the credit industry convinced many of the women's rights lobbyists that this was
the best bill they could get through congress. Sharyn Campbell, NOW's representative, was also successful in persuading most of the groups to abandon a class action remedy in
favor of personal punitive damage suits, a choice later questioned by several of the participants.

A member of Sullivan's staff commenting on the hearings noted:

> We weren't sure whether the women's lobbyists
> were speaking for the women's movement as such
> or for an agreed upon position of the credit indus-
> try and the women's groups and this of course wor-
> ried me. [21]

In this truncated form, with a limited class action
remedy and non-discrimination restricted to sex and marital
status, the Sullivan bill as amended was brought to the Committee on Banking and Currency for approval.

The Race to Report Out a Bill

On October 1 at 11:00 the House Committee on Banking and Currency met to consider the Equal Credit Opportu-
ity Act as reported out by the Consumer Affairs subcommittee. The full House was scheduled to go into session early
that day, so the committee had only one hour to act on the
bill. After a delay in getting a quorum, debate began. One
observer of the proceedings described the scene:

> A member of the committee from New York state
> introduced an amendment to the subcommittee's bill
> which he could not explain and nobody could under-
> stand. As it turned out, what he intended to do
> was restore to the language of the bill race, color,
> religion, national origin and age, but with some
> limitations on the age coverage, but he couldn't ex-
> plain it. He got to Washington late. Apparently
> his assistant handed him something. He got in
> there [to the committee meeting] and offered the
> amendment, but he couldn't explain what he was
> talking about and nobody could understand whether
> he was striking age or adding age. The legislation
> was explained. The basic provisions were explained.
> The two major controversies in connection with that
> bill--the coverage of race, color, religion, nation-
> al origin and age as well as sex and marital status
> and the class action feature of that particular bill
> which was the same as the Senate class action pro-
> vision on Truth in Lending in S 2101--were ex-
> plained. But the meeting ended without a vote.
> When the meeting ended, the chairman said he

would schedule another meeting at the first opportunity, which we figured would be around the fifth
of that month. 22

The Sullivan bill did not get out of committee on October 1.

    Senator Brock's bill, which was also the Koch-Heckler
bill, had been added as a non-germane amendment to the De-
pository Institutions Amendments of 1974 (S 18745). These
Amendments as further amended by Senator Brock passed the
Senate and were scheduled to go to conference with the St.
Germaine (Democrat, Rhode Island) subcommittee of the
House Banking and Currency Committee. Mrs. Sullivan appealed to Representative Fernand St. Germaine and all the
members of that subcommittee not to take up in conference
the Senate amendments introduced by Brock, including the
first two titles of S 2101 amending the Truth in Lending Act,
as well as the Koch-Heckler version of the Equal Credit Opportunity Act. Sullivan's position was that all these amendments introduced by Brock were under the jurisdiction of her
subcommittee. She particularly put pressure on Representatives John Moakley (Democrat, Massachusetts), Angelo Ron-
callo (Republican, New York), and Matthew Rinaldo (Republican, New Jersey), who were co-sponsors of her bill as well
as conferees on the St. Germaine subcommittee, to fight acceptance of these amendments. Sullivan felt that these three
Congressmen were committed to try to block this use of
equal credit legislation as a way of amending the Truth in
Lending Act because of their previous commitment to her
when she agreed to schedule hearings on credit discrimination. They did not see their obligation in this way. 23

    Sullivan also applied pressure on the women's rights
lobby, using this same argument. There were a series of
meetings among women's lobbyists which resulted in their
setting as their first priority a completed bill outlawing credit discrimination. This meant accepting the Brock amendment. The Brock amendments were subsequently approved
by the conference committee.

"All Points of Order Against the Conference Report Are Hereby Waived."

    Sullivan was outmaneuvered again in her final attempt
to change the conference report on the House floor. The
supporters of the bill had gotten a closed rule from the House
Committee on Rules, disallowing all points of order. This

was particularly significant for this bill because House rule twenty-eight normally would have required separate House votes on non-germane amendments accepted by House conferees. Sullivan had hoped to use these votes to knock out of the bill changes in Truth in Lending legislation and perhaps the Brock equal credit opportunity provision as well. The closed rule made a separate vote impossible. The final bill passed the House with only one dissenting vote and Mrs. Sullivan not voting.

The Women's Rights Lobby: An Evaluation

In assessing the activities of the women's rights lobby in support of equal credit legislation, two basic questions need to be addressed. Would a bill have gotten through congress without its work? How good a bill did it finally get?

There is substantial evidence to suggest that the activity of the women's rights lobby may have been decisive in passing this legislation. First and not to be minimized is the role played by women's organizations in defining and publicizing the issue. From the earliest indication of interest in credit discrimination by the National Commission on Consumer Finance, women's groups were active in developing a case of sex and marital status discrimination. Through their memberships and the media they helped keep this issue alive as a women's rights issue for two years until federal legislation could be passed. By sustaining this issue as a women's issue they were able to keep the constituency mobilized by the Equal Rights Amendment, while profiting from the increasingly favorable attitude of the general population towards women's rights issues. Second, despite the popularity of equal credit legislation both within and outside of congress, any bill introduced was in danger of falling victim to the bitter congressional in-fighting which surrounded this matter. The animosity between Leonor Sullivan and some of her colleagues on the Consumer Affairs Subcommittee had reached such a level that before the start of the next Congress Sullivan would be stripped of her position as Chairperson of the Consumer Affairs Subcommittee. [24] Without the monitoring and prodding of the women's lobby it is arguable whether a bill could have survived the convoluted legislative route followed by the credit discrimination bill. The final legislation was drawn up by the minority staff, sent to the Senate, returned to another House subcommittee as a non-germane amendment, accepted in joint conference committee and

finally passed by both House and Senate and signed into law.
The ability of a piece of legislation to survive this passage
through congress testifies to the momentum behind the bill.

Finally, the Equal Credit Opportunity Act is a significant legislative achievement for the women's rights lobby because there is no direct federal precedent for this bill.   Unlike many of the women's rights bills passed, this act was
not patterned on a prior racial discrimination statute.   A
number of observers of the women's movement have credited
much of the movement's overall success in affecting national
policy to a coattails effect.   They note that gains made
through hard fights by the black civil rights movement are
later used by the women's movement either to pass comparable bills or to amend existing legislation to add "sex."   In
this instance not only was this not the case, but the women's
groups lobbying for equal credit sought purposely to prevent
other disadvantaged groups from being added to their bill.
Their argument was that a case had been developed over several years of hearings and research, documenting both industry discrimination based on sex and marital status and how it
could be remedied.   No similar work had been done on discrimination based on race, religion, color, national origin
or age.   For this reason, and because of opposition by the
credit industry to including age as an illegal form of discrimination, the women's rights lobby preferred to pass its
own bill first.   The feeling was that this bill would then
serve as a precedent for later legislation barring other forms
of discrimination in the extension of credit based on race,
color, religion, national origin and age.

Despite evidence that the women's rights lobby was an
important influence in passing credit legislation, the question
still remains, what kind of legislation did they get.   Three
major weaknesses in the bill as consumer legislation are
apparent:

1)   Punitive damages are limited to $10,000 in the
case of an individual or $100,000 or one percent of the net
worth of the creditor, whichever is less, in the case of a
successful class action law suit.   Such diverse Democrats
as Abzug (New York) and Sullivan (Missouri) considered this
an unwarranted protection of the credit industry against court
judgments.

2)   There was no provision in the final bill to make
creditors responsible for explaining why they denied an indi-

vidual credit.   Without this provision it is very difficult for
an individual or a court to know whether discrimination has
occurred.   Notification was proposed by Mrs. Sullivan as an
amendment to her own bill after the subcommittee hearings
were held.   This provision was rejected by her subcommittee.   The Federal Reserve Board in drawing up administrative regulations for this bill subsequently added this provision as necessary for enforcement of the anti-discrimination
statute.

      3) Finally, by limiting the bill to sex and marital
status, large classes of individuals who prima facie seemed
to be victims of discrimination were not covered.

      Acknowledging that the Equal Credit Opportunity Act
which passed congress was not as strong a bill as it might
have been, the question remains, could a stronger bill have
been enacted?   The only competing legislation before congress was Sullivan's bill which was a tough consumer measure.   Ignoring the issue of Sullivan's sincerity, the fact remains that Sullivan had delayed the passage of legislation
ending sex and marital status discrimination for over a year.
Republican Congresswoman Heckler (Massachusetts) had requested hearings on such a bill at the start of 1973.   No
hearings were held until June, 1974, and no bill was passed
by October, 1974.   Sullivan has made the argument that since
this legislation was without federal precedent, careful study
had to be done before a bill was enacted to make sure the
bill could adequately fulfill its stated purposes.   It is clear
that Sullivan's major priority was never passage of a sex
and marital status discrimination bill.   Whether she would
have pushed her amended credit discrimination bill to passage before the close of the 93rd Congress is therefore open
to question.   It is difficult to argue conclusively that the
women's rights lobby would have done better working for the
Sullivan bill.   They might have had a better bill or they
might have had no bill at all.

      The fundamental problem in examining the Koch-Heck-
ler bill is that the evidence is mixed concerning the political
feasibility of a stronger consumer bill following this legislative route.   The major direction of the Koch-Heckler bill
came from the Republican staff in the House and a Republican Senator, Brock, in the Senate.   The women's rights lobby itself did not have adequate technical advice on credit
legislation to appreciate fully the significance of many of the
compromises it made as part of this political alliance.   It

seems likely that the lobby might have gotten stronger legislation had it been better informed.

This case study highlights some of the strengths and
weaknesses of the women's rights lobby in 1973-1974.   For
a comparatively new lobby, women possessed an unusual
amount of influence in this early period.   This influence derived from three sources: success in passing the Equal
Rights Amendment in March, 1972; strong popular support
for women's rights in public opinion polls[25]; and the large
number of legislators available to work for women's rights
in congress.   These factors created expectations of success
among both those lobbying and those being lobbied.   It
seemed that a majority voting coalition in support of women's
issues existed in the House and Senate.[26]   The women's
rights lobby had only to activate this supportive group through
the appropriate legislative initiative to gain further victories
in congress.   The problems experienced by this lobby in
working on the Equal Credit Opportunity Act illustrate its
weaknesses within this overall position of strength.

There were two basic difficulties encountered by those
lobbying for women's rights.   First, they had inadequate information on technical aspects of the Equal Credit Opportunity Act.   Second, they lacked effective coordination among the
separate groups.   In their work on credit legislation this was
a major problem.   The failure of these groups to agree on
how much weakening of consumer protection provisions would
be tolerated in order to pass an anti-discrimination bill split
the women's groups active on this issue and confused those
in congress with whom they were working.   It forced women's
groups to achieve unity through the personalized route of rejecting Sullivan's bill and accepting the legislative compromises fashioned by Koch and Heckler.   In effect, the wom-
en's lobby through its internal disagreement was forced to
forfeit initiative on the legislation to congressional sponsors.
The lobby's ability to influence specific provisions in the
legislation became minimal.

These weaknesses in information and coordination are
not unusual for a new lobby, let alone one which is structured
on the basis of voluntary cooperation among a number of
separate groups.   Yet, the continued ability of the lobby to
retain credibility in congress seemed to depend strongly on
correcting these deficiencies.   The momentum from earlier
successes could not last indefinitely.

Of these two problems, lack of adequate coordination seems the easiest to remedy. Continued experience in working together will force women's groups to develop routinized procedures for handling disagreement or dissolve cooperative efforts entirely. Since the power of lobbying coalitions depends on agreement among separate groups, this difficulty is too basic to go uncorrected.

More serious and less likely to be self-correcting is the ability to obtain accurate and reliable data rapidly on technically complex legislation. Barring a great increase in resources, the example of work on credit legislation suggests that the most efficient way for the women's lobby to improve its information sources is by including well informed groups within its issue coalitions. Had the lobby successfully recruited Common Cause or the League of Women Voters to work on credit legislation, it is unlikely that there would have been the level of misinformation which characterized this effort.

The women's rights lobby in 1973-1974 then had influence within congress without developed knowledge of how to use this influence. The case of the Equal Credit Opportunity Act suggests that this period was a turning point for the lobby. Its "honeymoon" with congress was coming to an end. It had to improve its lobbying coordination and its sources of information or forfeit initiative on women's rights to others more skilled in legislative operations.

NOTES

1. This research is part of a larger study of lobbying for women's rights carried out under a grant awarded through the 1974-75 Florence Eagleton Grants Program. This program of grants and symposia is sponsored by the Center for the American Woman and Politics of the Eagleton Institute of Politics, Rutgers University.

I would also like to thank the Brookings Institution for providing me with facilities for my field work in Washington, and the Political Science department at the University of Colorado which granted me a leave of absence and a reduced teaching load during the period of this research. The help of W. Douglas Costain of The Johns Hopkins School of Advanced International Studies who read and commented on sev-

eral versions of this research and the interviewing
done by graduate students Carol Bray and Valerie
Gilpeer are gratefully acknowledged.

2. This case study is based on interviews conducted with
members of Congress and the congressional staff who
worked on the Equal Credit Opportunity Act of 1974.
Interviews were also held with representatives of organizations which are part of or have worked with,
the emerging women's rights lobby in Washington.
The following members of the House Consumer Affairs subcommittee were interviewed: Representatives
Sullivan (D-Mo.); Gonzalez (D-Tex.); Stark (D-Calif.);
Koch (D-N. Y.); Heckler (R-Mass.); McKinney (R-
Conn.); Rinaldo (R-N. J.) and Burgener (R-Calif.).
Additionally, twelve congressional committee staff
members who had worked on this legislation were
questioned.   (A number of the staff aides interviewed
requested not to be specifically identified.) Finally,
representatives of the following organizations were in-
terviewed: American Association of University Women,
November 19, 1974, and August 11, 1975; B'nai B'rith
Women, November 19, 1974; Center for Women Policy
Studies, October 21, 1974; Common Cause, October
30, 1974, and March 2, 1976; Federally Employed
Women, December 30, 1974, and May 7, 1975; Federation of Organizations for Professional Women,
January 3, 1975, and July 30, 1975; General Federa-
tion of Women's Clubs, October 17, 1974; League of
Women Voters, October 8, 1974, and August 14, 1975;
National Council of Jewish Women, November 1, 1974;
National Federation of Business and Professional Wom-
en's Clubs, September 20, 1974, and October 1, 1974;
National Organization for Women, October 31, 1974,
and August 5, 1975; National Woman's Party, January
23, 1975; National Women's Political Caucus, October
22, 1974; Network, March 16, 1975; United Methodist
Women, November 4, 1974; Women's Equity Action
League, November 25, 1974; Women's Lobby, December 3, 1974.

3. Gary Orfield, Congressional Power: Congress and Social Change (New York: Harcourt, Brace, Jovanovich,
1975), pp. 300-2. Jo Freeman, The Politics of Wom-
en's Liberation (New York: David McKay, 1975), pp.
213-7.

4. A more complete discussion of the ways in which the
Equal Rights Amendment acted as a stimulus for continued legislative involvement by both women's volun-

tary organizations and women's movement groups may
be found in Anne Costain's Lobbying for Social Change:
Congress and Women's Issues, manuscript in progress,
or in her "A Social Movement Lobbies: Women's
Liberation and Pressure Politics," a paper presented
at the Southern Political Science Association Convention, Nashville, Tennessee, November 5-7, 1975.

5. Flora Crater, "Women Lobbyists Incorporate for Full
Scale Action for Women," The Woman Activist, 2
(November 1972):1.

6. Interview with a member of the staff of the committee
on Banking and Currency of the House of Representatives. Conducted on July 18, 1975, in Washington,
D. C.

7. The New York Times Index 1971, 2 vols., Publication
of the New York Times Company, vol. 59 (New York:
New York Times, 1972). The New York Times Index
1972, 2 vols., Publication of the New York Times
Company, vol. 60 (New York: New York Times,
1973). The New York Times Index 1973, 2 vols.,
Publication of the New York Times Company, vol. 61
(New York: New York Times, 1974).

8. Roger Cobb and Charles Elder, Participation in American Politics: The Dynamics of Agenda-Building (Baltimore: The Johns Hopkins University Press, 1972),
pp. 30, 44-5.

9. Interview with a member of the staff of the Committee
on Banking and Currency of the House of Representatives. Conducted on July 3, 1975, in Washington,
D. C.

10. The Nixon administration, embroiled in Watergate revelations, had practically no involvement with this legislation. The White House did not take an official position on any of the bills considered, although one member of the subcommittee reported contact with Anne
Armstrong, counselor to the President. As one
senior member of the Banking and Currency Committee staff observed in an interview: "Whatever administrative push there could have been behind this legislation was absent." The White House, although requested to send a representative to testify at the subcommittee hearings, did not send anyone.

11. For a complete list of the bills introduced in the House
see: U. S., Congress, House, Committee on Banking
and Currency, Credit Discrimination: Hearings on
HR 14856 and HR 14908, 92d Cong., 2d sess., 1974,
part 1, pp. 27-9.

12. Raymond A. Bauer, Ithiel de Sola Pool and Lewis
     Anthony Dexter, American Business and Public Policy:
     The Politics of Foreign Trade, 2nd ed. (Chicago:
     Aldine, 1967).

13. The following table from The Virginia Slims American
     Women's Opinion Poll, 3 vols. (n. p. : The Roper Or-
     ganization, 1970-4), 3:3, illustrates the dramatic in-
     crease in support for bettering the status of women in
     America.

Favor/Oppose Efforts to Strengthen or Change
Women's Status in Society

	1974		1972		1970	
	Women	Men	Women	Men	Women	Men
Percentage who:						
Favor	57	63	48	49	40	44
Oppose	25	19	36	36	52	39
Are Not Sure	18	18	16	15	18	17

14. Representatives of fifteen of the women's organizations
     surveyed were given a list of the women members of
     the Ninety-third Congress and asked to indicate with
     which offices they had been in contact in the previous
     year. The results, given below, suggest high levels
     of communication between these groups and the women
     in congress. These findings are especially surprising
     since some of the organizations surveyed reported
     only minimal direct contact with Capitol Hill. Those
     organizations surveyed were: League of Women Vot-
     ers; National Woman's Party; National Women's Po-
     litical Caucus; Women's Lobby; American Association
     of University Women; General Federation of Women's
     Clubs; National Federation of Business and Profes-
     sional Women's Clubs; Federally Employed Women;
     National Council of Jewish Women; National Organiza-
     tion for Women; Women's Equity Action League; B'nai
     B'rith Women; Federation of Organizations for Pro-
     fessional Women; Network; United Methodist Women.

The Number of Organizations Surveyed Reporting
Communication with the Women Members of the
Ninety-Third Congress

	No. of Organizations
Martha Griffiths	15
Bella Abzug	14

Patsy Mink	14
Pat Schroeder	13
Shirley Chisholm	12
Corrine Boggs	11
Margaret Heckler	11
Barbara Jordan	11
Yvonne Burke	10
Elizabeth Holtzman	10
Edith Green	8
Leonor Sullivan	8
Ella Grasso	7
Cardiss Collins	6
Marjorie Holt	6
Julia Butler Hansen	5

15. U.S., Congress, House, Committee on Banking and Currency, Credit Discrimination: Hearings on HR 14856 and HR 14908, 92d Cong., 2d sess., 1974, part 1, p. 16.

16. Margaret Gates, "Credit Discrimination Against Women: Causes and Solutions," Vanderbilt Law Review 27 (April 1974):410-1.

17. Interview with Congresswoman Leonor Sullivan. Conducted on July 24, 1975, in Washington, D.C.

18. Interview with a member of the staff of the Committee on Banking and Currency of the House of Representatives. Conducted on July 3, 1975, in Washington, D.C.

19. Ibid.

20. Ibid.

21. Interview with a member of Congresswoman Leonor Sullivan's staff. Conducted on July 24, 1975, in Washington, D.C.

22. Interview. Conducted on July 18, 1975, in Washington, D.C.

23. Interview with a member of the U.S. House of Representatives. Conducted on July 28, 1975, in Washington, D.C.

24. Part of the New York Times account of this action follows: "Representative Leonor K. Sullivan of Missouri was deposed today [January 28] as chairman of the Consumer Affairs Subcommittee as leadership changes continued in the House of Representatives.

"Democrats on the parent Banking and Currency Committee elected Representative Frank Annunzio of Illinois who had not been a member of the subcommittee. The vote was 15 to 13." (New York Times,

29 January 1975, p. 13)
25. See footnote 13.
26. Favorable congressional action in 1973 on legislation backed by the lobby extending the minimum wage to domestic workers and attacking sex discrimination in the schools reinforced this belief in the existence of a supportive voting majority in congress.

PART III

WOMEN AND THEIR ORGANIZATIONS

INTRODUCTION

Women's organizations have made enormous contributions toward changing the social climate. The organizations represented in this anthology are indicative of American women united in a concerted effort.

The ability of an organization to survive rests largely
upon the perception of its effectiveness, sustained by the
members. In an interesting in-depth view of the League of
Women Voters, Ruth Clusen explains the strength and political clout of this distinctive organization.

The formation of an organization has been meticulous-
ly outlined in the next fine study of WEAL (Women's Equity
Action League). Arlene Daniels' essay suggests the power
of organizing behind an idea as every detail is chronicled in
an unusual account of struggle and development.

Chapter 8 explores the 1970's struggle of working
women to develop collective power. It is a volatile struggle
and much has happened since Barbara Wertheimer and Nancy
Seifer wrote this article in 1977. Primarily, it considers
the climate of the times that led to the creation of four new
organizations which are representative of a broader trend and
compares the circumstances of working women in the last
century to those of today.

The last article, by Rona Feit, explores the history of
the National Women's Political Caucus as an expression of wom-
en's recent interest in political power and as a result of the interaction of pragmatic politics, feminism, and the desire for
social justice.

Chapter 6

THE LEAGUE OF WOMEN VOTERS AND POLITICAL POWER

by Ruth C. Clusen

Any group seeking a foothold of power in a democratic society must eventually turn to the political arena. As only 7 percent of all current public office holders in the United States, American women have not become an irresistible force against the immovable bastions of male political power.

As successful as the woman's movement has been in recent years in exerting political pressure for equal opportunity, it has not managed to make large inroads on established power. Except for a brief time after women gained the vote in the twenties, and a more recent affirmative action effort after the 1968 conventions, the political parties have been barriers as often as routes for women seeking political office. Even while women have closed ranks as a special interest group and lobbied successfully at the state and national levels for legislation to insure and protect equal rights and equal opportunity, their isolation from the mainstream of political power continues to be a handicap. The relative handful of women who have been successful in politics have often had to find alternative routes into the political system.

Clearly, being a pressure group is not enough. While feminists are correct in insisting on equal opportunity for women to hold elective or appointed office the problem for women is to gain access to public office in the first place. With their small proportions in the business and legal worlds, women today are still forced to seek other methods to gain political office. The League of Women Voters has functioned as such a political lifeline for many women candidates. The League has re-emerged in the last decade as a strong citizen's lobbying group on national, state, and local levels of government, and as a result, is a natural training ground for women in politics.

At one time, in the years immediately following ratification of the woman suffrage amendment, the League served
as a direct route for women seeking political careers. The
organization worked closely with the national political parties
to assimilate women into full-fledged political participation.
The subsequent lapse of the women's movement and erosion
of political power left the League as virtually the only viable
national woman's organization primarily concerned with government and politics until the mid 1960s.

From its founding in 1920, the League has survived
both the disappearance and resurgence of the women's movement, but its effectiveness in producing potential women
candidates for public office has reflected the status of women
in the society at large.

Today League leaders are again likely to enter political careers as a next step after their League training. As
the number of women in public office increases, League wom-
en are more frequently appointed to public office at higher
levels of government, and female candidates for elective office are more accepted as viable candidates by the major
political parties.

A preliminary analysis of data assembled in January,
1978, by the Center for the American Woman and Politics
of the Eagleton Institute at Rutgers University shows that 21
percent of the 81 percent of women affiliated with any organization who are holding elective office or high level state
and federal appointed office are current or past members of
the League of Women Voters.

The survey, an updated version of the Center's 1976
publication Women in Public Office (New York: R. R. Bowker Company), covered municipal councils; mayors; township
councils; county councils or commissions; state legislatures;
statewide cabinet level appointments; state supreme, appel-
late and trial courts, U. S. Congress, and high level federal
appointments. Other studies also indicate a high correlation
between League background and women in office.

Whether for elective or appointive office, the League
continues to provide a unique form of access to the political
system for women. It is worth examining the reasons why
a special organization has been necessary for fledgling wom-
en politicians while men worked their way through the political party power structure--what has the League provided

to the political woman, how has the League provided it and
what will its future role be as old structures respond to
women's changing roles?

To understand why the League is an effective stepping
stone into politics, it is also necessary to look at the League
in relation to the requirements for winning elective or appointive office, and at its relation to the status of women in
today's and yesterday's America.

In assessing the status of women in politics, in its
final report in June, 1976, the Women in Power Committee
of the National Commission on the Observance of International Women's Year (IWY) noted that in lieu of the business experiences and contacts that lead men into political office,
women need an alternative form of political education:

> ... help must be given those women who are not
> yet in public life, but who are aspiring to public
> participation and who could be reached and moti-
> vated to become active. [1]

This describes the League function for potential women officials: providing an alternative link with the governmental
process which is generally unavailable to women through any
other vehicle.

While the women's movement and feminist organizations provide the impetus for women to focus on achieving
power, and women's political caucuses recruit and support
female candidates, the League's role has been to provide the
initial opportunity for a woman to assume a leadership role,
and take a close-up look at government while giving her a
taste of political power as a citizen lobbyist. In working
for change in her city government or state legislature she
can develop the political skills necessary to form coalitions
and gain public support for her goals. In effect, for many
women in public office today, the League has been the wom-
en's substitute for the experiences that usually prepare men
to become public officials.

Evidence of the League's role is ample. Two studies
by the Eagleton Institute and a study by the Democratic National Committee have indicated consistently that 40 percent
of women in politics claim the League as a political alma
mater. Some are in Congress from all parts of the country:
Yvonne Braithwaite Burke (D-CA), Millicent Fenwick (R-NJ),

Margaret Heckler (R-MA), Patricia Schroeder (D-CO), and Gladys Noon Spellman (D-MD), among others, credit the League as part of their political training. Connecticut's Ella Grasso, the first woman to be elected governor in her own right, points to the League as her initial experience in politics. [2]

Ironically, while feminists may have greater motivation to seek public office, it becomes apparent that a raised consciousness about the status of women never got a woman candidate elected or appointed. In the Democratic National Committee's study, women winners shared their insights on what it takes to run and win:

> Be issue oriented; have at least one area of expertise such as health, aging, children, or consumerism. Avoid becoming identified as the "women's issue" candidate. Campaign on issues the voters think are important. Do your homework. Candidly admit ignorance. Speak out on issues, especially when there is media coverage. Know the legislative process. Be informed about issues from the last legislative session. Do volunteer lobbying to gain expertise and information.... [3]

In examining the requirements for public office, the Women in Power Committee of the IWY Commission noted that in making appointments, officials consider competency and representation of a constituency as their main criteria for judging qualifications. Competency was characterized as

> a demonstrated ability to understand the political climate, be committed to the public good, understand basic facts and issues, be responsible in attendance and participation, express ideas without creating undue hostility, carry out the appointive tasks, and garner public support for decisions and recommendations. [4]

An individual with a constituency was described as: an effective member of an organization, who has waged or managed an effective campaign for public office or organized an effective citizens' group for change.

While men have used professional careers to develop these abilities, both the qualities cited by the candidates,

and those noted by the IWY Commission are also the kinds
of qualities developed, and demanded of League leaders. The
League, focusing as it does on "non-feminist" government issues, provides the political woman with the background to
meet these "job qualifications" for political office while teaching her how governments function at national, state, and local levels.

There is also a tremendous need for support--psycho-
logical and emotional, as well as practical and financial--
for any woman who decides to take the plunge into professional politics. First comes her need to feel self confident that
she is qualified for the job. Interviewed for a slide show
produced by the national League for its 1976 convention,
Audrey Colom, former chairperson of the National Women's
Political Caucus told the League,

> Women I've talked to who are on the state legisla-
> tive level and on the federal level have said, to
> have held some position of leadership within an or-
> ganization gives them the confidence that they feel
> is necessary in order to run. They've testified
> before Congressional hearings or state legislative
> hearings or City Council hearings. They've held
> press conferences. They've worked on, and done
> research on, specific issues. They've had some
> management, in terms of overall responsibility for
> seeing a project through, so that they have skills
> that are necessary to make them a good politician
> or a good legislator. [5]

Many League leaders would recognize themselves in
that description, and many are experiencing political ambitions while still in the League. The profile of delegates to
the League's national convention in May 1976, showed that
22 percent had been active in local politics, 5 percent in
state politics, and another 5 percent in national politics. In
addition, 7 percent had already run for office and 8 percent
were considering it as a future move. Eleven percent were
already serving in appointed offices which ranged from zoning
committees, town councils, welfare boards, commissions on
the status of women, mayor's advisory boards, human rights
commissions and boards of education to parks and recreation
boards. [6]

Most women who run for office are older--forty to
fifty years old--than the average League 1976 convention dele-

gate who was in her thirties. The League encourages all
members to run for public office. In order to maintain its
nonpartisan position however, women who are League officers
or board members must resign from leadership positions
upon declaring their candidacy. Chances are, therefore,
that those who do go on to the political arena will not be
identified as "League" during their campaign unless they publicly acknowledge the association, hoping perhaps to make it
a campaign "plus."

While the League's nonpartisan policy also precludes
the organization's endorsement of a member's candidacy, a
League candidate will generally have the benefit of her prior
relationship with both League members and other members of
the community she worked with during her League years.
Often these groups provide a cadre of volunteer workers
which compensate for the initial campaign funding so frequently lacking for female candidates.

As to why League leaders tend to become candidates
for public office, Harriet Cipriani, Director of Women's Activities for the Democratic Party muses, "I believe that
from the training that women get in the League by looking
at issues objectively and studying and lobbying, the next step
is an automatic interest in running for public office."[7]

Why? What makes League training of more value to
the potential candidate than membership in an environmental
group or a feminist organization? The answer, to paraphrase
Calvin Coolidge, is that "The business of the League is government." Except for the competition of electoral politics,
the League is most like the real world that the prospective
politician will encounter when her name goes on the ballot
and she is elected to public office.

The grass roots government of the League is one asset, paralleling the grass roots support that a political candidate must seek. League positions on political issues, and
the program of work on those issues are determined by the
membership rather than decided from on high by the leadership. Therefore, it is possible for a potential leader to develop quickly at the local level in the League by having some
voice in the determination of issues and program. The real
world of the political contest makes the same demands as
her fellow League members: to achieve her ends she must
begin at the outset to cultivate her League constituency to
seek their agreement for a study or action on a local issue

such as penal reform, property tax, sewage disposal systems, or school financing.

She must also be fairly persistent, and have her facts well marshalled to get membership support. Having overcome that hurdle, however, she must then do the same thing in regard to the city council, or if legislation is required, whatever political body has jurisdiction over the problem. In addition, the League, offering the tools for study and observing of government, gives the potential candidate a chance to develop these skills at whatever pace she may desire. The League rarely passes up new leadership, and indications that she is ready to tackle additional responsibility may mean that she is made a committee chairperson and a member of the local League board. She then becomes responsible for making decisions, delegating work, and getting it done by volunteers, a skill that every politician must have, no matter how many fat cats may be offering money to hire professional help in a political campaign.

An additional prod into public office is often the satisfaction, even exhilaration, of getting something accomplished in government. Few people realize that most local governments are hotbeds of citizen apathy, and the group that makes the effort can have a significant impact. That there is a power vacuum which citizen participation can fill is true even beyond the local level of government. A U.S. Senator remarked several years ago when told there were less than two hundred-thousand League members nationwide: "I thought there were millions of them."[8]

To refine further and expand her political education, a League leader can pursue her interest onto state or federal levels of government as well. Local Leagues often have national legislative action chairpersons who keep their local Leagues up to date on national legislative developments through the national League's Report from the Hill, and Spotmaster Service, a sort of telephone "weather report" each weekend on the status of League-targeted legislation in the U.S. Congress. Both the Report and the telephone service include specific lobbying suggestions. The quarterly National Voter carries articles with a long-range view on issues. For the astute political student, the lessons in how the power pies are divided between various levels of government are there, and can offer a realistic idea of what she might expect to accomplish in office.

Perhaps one of the most advantageous points of the political education offered in the League, is the necessity to temper advocacy with tact in order to get things done. Being an effective lobbyist demands many of the same qualities demanded of public officials. As the national League's issue oriented Campaign Handbook points out in the section on lobbying: "A first rule of lobbying is not to threaten or antagonize those whom you are trying to influence." Whether conducting a legislative campaign, or becoming a candidate for elective or appointive office, one lesson to be learned in the League is that the end goal, whether votes for legislation or votes for a candidate, will not be achieved through acrimony. A League leader who can successfully balance the sometimes apparently conflicting needs to speak out on an issue and hold down the opposition is getting an invaluable opportunity to practice the skills that she may later require in a political campaign or in holding public office. As Jeane Kirkpatrick points out in Political Woman:

> The distance from nonpartisan activity to political candidacy is less than might be supposed; both consist of group activity oriented to public goals. And though some argue that politics is distinguished from volunteer activity by the level of conflict and consensus, democratic politics is not all conflict, and non-partisan civic activities are not necessarily conflict free. The nonpartisan activist is not infrequently deeply involved in issues and causes that divide the community: school bonds, church buildings, community development, even Red Cross drives stimulate controversy and opposition. So the move into politics is not necessarily one from consensual to conflict oriented activities. [9]

The last reason why the League is an effective training ground is the most simple: because it is there. Over thirteen-hundred local Leagues are located in virtually every congressional district in the United States. In many places it is the "only game in town" for women who want to participate in, or learn more about, government. This is more important than it might sound, since most women public officials are gathering numerical strength in smaller communities rather than the big cities where the woman's movement began.

Despite the League's resumption of its role as a po-

litical training ground, women in political office lag far behind the proportion of women in the general population.   The
fortunes of women in politics have always reflected their
status in the society.   In a democratic society, the reasons
are particularly obvious.   The political candidate must count
on the voters to put her in office.

When women were seen as secondary to men, who
felt a woman's place was in the home rather than the House,
and that it was their right to discriminate against women in
civil rights, business, education, credit, jobs, and politics,
the woman political candidate was an anomaly with no constituency.   Chauvinistic political parties supported the traditional disapproval of women who insisted on careers other
than housework.   A woman candidate was seldom a viable
candidate throughout the 1950s and early 60s, and all the
League support that could be mustered could not have changed
these circumstances.   In a society where men wouldn't vote
for a woman because they disapproved of her running in the
first place, and women would not vote for her because she
presented a threat to the post World War II women's role,
a political party could claim justification, if not justice, in
refusing to support her candidacy.

Today with women increasingly choosing to eschew
traditional roles in many fields including politics, this is
changing, but is by no means guaranteed over.   Former
Republican National Committee chair, Mary Louise Smith,
told the League, "A few women are not enough.   We must
be present in far greater numbers than we are now.   And
we must be present within the political party structure because this is the system through which power flows."[11]

The League has been conscious of this since its inception.   Carrie Chapman Catt, the suffrage leader who
spearheaded the final successful effort to ratify the woman
suffrage amendment in the states, founded the League and
advised the new members: "The only way to get things done
is to get them done on the inside of the political party."
She also warned, "You won't be welcome, but there is the
place to go."[12]

As League members followed up this advice by joining the parties, male party leaders attempted to counter
their assertions of political power.   In 1921, party women
in some states were ordered to withdraw from the League
which had pledged at its national convention to fight the pre-

vailing political boss sytem. [13] In addition, the major parties
advocated a return to the convention method of choosing their
candidates so as to avoid the effect of the women's franchise
being felt in the primaries. [14]

Political parties are still cautious about supporting a
woman as a political candidate, as evidenced by the small
numbers they encourage to run. While this is improving, it
is a gradual shift, not comparable to the shift in party policy
after the 1968 conventions. Feminist pressure on the major
parties resulted in vast numbers of women becoming delegates
to the national party conventions in 1972 when 40 percent of
the Democratic delegates and 29. 8 percent of the Republican
delegates were women. If there is one thing that the League
has learned the hard way, it is that a token movement is not
enough to guarantee the base of political power. The power
base requires vigilance once acquired. Large political gains
and the constituencies necessary to maintain them, can disappear in a matter of years if they are not nurtured and
guarded. Nowhere is this better illustrated than in the history of the League's own experience from the time of its
founding.

The League was a direct descendant of the moderate
wing of the suffrage movement. Ratification of the suffrage
amendment marked the culmination of a long period of consciousness raising on the effects of sex discrimination. In
the process, differences had developed between radical feminists, who sought to wipe out discrimination in all areas of
society, and the moderates, who sought more immediate solutions through the legislative process, to the problems caused
by male chauvinist practices. No essential disagreements
existed between radicals and moderates on the fact that discrimination was the cause of practical ills which required a
remedy, but differences existed over remedial goals. Radicals were more concerned with exposing and obliterating the
underlying assumptions about women that allowed not only the
practice, but ths sanction of sex discrimination. They took
on such hallowed institutions as the Bible, the federal Constitution, marriage, divorce, prostitution, property rights,
and dress customs, in the effort to raise the society's collective consciousness.

The moderates, while also concerned about the causes,
addressed themselves to the more immediate effects of sex
discrimination. They adopted a step by step approach, dealing one at a time with laws, mostly in the states, which al-

lowed women to be legally subjected to the moral and civil
control of their husbands or fathers, paid half of men's wages
for similar work, while responsible for families over which
they were denied legal, civil, or moral authority. [15]

Different goals resulted in tactical differences between
radicals and moderates.   Radicals saw the problem as so
pervasive as to require widespread social as well as political
reform.   Moderates agreed, but saw the most pressing problems as inadequate safeguards for women in state laws, requiring a state by state legislative campaign.   Even suffrage,
which both groups agreed was vital to women's achieving political power, was such a source of division.   Radicals
wanted a federal amendment, while moderates pursued suffrage in the states. [16]

Both groups were correct in their analysis of the problems.   Radicals saw that discrimination would be eradicated
only if its underlying assumptions were challenged and erased.
Moderates viewed this task as too Herculean, if meanwhile
the immediate problems remained unsolved.   Both groups
agreed that the vote was the wedge necessary to gain a foothold in the political power structure.   The radicals provided
the reasoning.   The moderates were concerned with the practical questions of "how to" get on with the changes.   Ironically, it was the practical step by step approach of the moderates which ultimately resulted in suffrage becoming part
of the federal Constitution. [17]

The attempt to gain suffrage was stalled on the federal level until Carrie Chapman Catt took over leadership
of the National American Woman Suffrage Association (NAWSA
--an amalgamation of the radical and moderate groups which
had previously been separate organizations).   Under her
leadership, suffragists were organized in synchronization with
the political structures in each state, in a drive to gain a
share of the presidential electoral vote as well as the political leverage of voting rights.   The strategy worked.   The
presidential electors for whom women could vote jumped from
ninety-one in 1916 to three hundred and twenty-six in June
1919.   With this demonstration that women were able to exercise political power through the ballot, Congress, after
many refusals, finally passed the federal suffrage amendment
in 1919.   The campaign for ratification by three quarters of
the states again demanded that the state organizations, along
with special delegations from NAWSA, fight the opposition in
each state during the ratification process. [18]   Tennessee pro-

vided the final victory, giving women the vote in August,
1920.

The national League was organized in February of that
year, before the amendment was actually ratified, by vote on
an optimistic NAWSA, to educate women on use of the new
franchise and to lobby Congress for social reform legislation.
State Leagues, like their predecessors in the suffrage campaign, were organized around existing political structures to
lobby at state levels.

The political climate seemed friendly to women.
There was a general spirit of political reform in the country.
The Progressive Party, a formidable, reform-minded, splin-
ter group from both major parties, had provided additional
impetus for the woman suffrage campaign, as well as a
threat to the security of established politicians. [19]

Millions of women, organized into groups supporting
such diverse issues as temperance and labor laws, had fought
for suffrage as a single force. When the amendment was
ratified, Congress, wooing the women's vote, couldn't do
enough for women. The League was at the forefront of the
national lobbying for social reform legislation. Maud Wood
Park, the League's first president, did what countless League
leaders would do after her on a smaller scale: she established a coalition effort, the Women's Joint Congressional
Committee, to work for legislation on Capitol Hill.

From its inception the League, like most other national women's organizations of the time, believed that the
total battle for equal rights had already been won with the
vote. The collective voice that women had worked so long
to make audible was therefore directed at issues which reflected women's roles and responsibilities rather than wom-
en's rights. Child labor laws, maternity and infancy legislation, and public health measures became the new focus of
concern. While the League also worked on such "women's
issues" as independent citizenship rights for married women,
these rights, with suffrage won, were no longer considered
in jeopardy. The vote was viewed as the political leverage
necessary to make "women's" issues obsolete in the society.

Suffrage was viewed as such a panacea, in fact, that
the League was seen by its founding members as a temporary organization which would self-destruct in a few years for
lack of work. It was assumed that women would be assimi-

lated into the party structures whether recalcitrant men
wanted to make room for them or not.

The League was thought of as a power in politics despite its nonpartisan stance, since its leaders were also
visible members of the party structure. The Dearborn Independent, a publication sponsored by Henry Ford, complained
in 1924 that the League was infiltrating both major political
parties at the highest level with social concerns:

> It gives us food for thought when the leading wom-
> en in both the Democratic and Republican parties
> are members of the League of Women Voters which
> organization is admittedly working for pacifism and
> internationalism and is sworn to uphold the non-
> partisan movement among women. [20]

Guilty as charged.

By the end of 1924, after two successive elections in
which it became apparent that no women's voting bloc would
materialize and that many women would continue to vote with
their husbands if they voted at all, the mood of Congress
became resistant. [21]   The women's movement as a political
force had dissipated by the end of the decade and the
League's effectiveness on Capitol Hill was becoming a shadow of its former self.   In the Woman Citizen of that period,
the magazine that had been the political news organ of the
suffrage movement was offering "clubwomen" advice on dec-
orating their clubhouses.   Except for the two pages allocated
to the League of Women Voters which dealt with national
legislation and political developments, the magazine had begun to take on some of the characteristics of "the women's
pages" of the daily newspaper. [22]

The thirties, partly as a result of the Depression,
saw a greater breakdown of the women's movement.   The
League remained one of the few active women's political organizations.   The strides that were made in that period, included Eleanor Roosevelt (a League member) making the
position of First Lady one of professional status, record
numbers of women being appointed to public office and the
appointment of the first woman federal cabinet member,
Frances Perkins. [23]   At the same time the political weather-
vane pointed an ill wind for the women on another front
when the League was trounced in its efforts to defeat a provision of the federal Economic Act of 1932, which limited

government jobs to one member of a family. The League
opposed the provision on the grounds that it ignored the merit system as grounds for employment. As the League fore-
saw, when both spouses were employed, it was wives who
were dismissed from government service.[24] Despite such
League legislative victories as the extension of protective
labor legislation to men, and reform legislation such as the
Food, Drug, and Cosmetic Act, and the Social Security Act,
the League became more isolated as a woman's lobbying
group. The financial crisis of the thirties followed by the
international strife of World War II, overshadowed the minimal efforts of the women's movement to attract further attention or support for its own cause. As stated in Women
Together:

> At a time when discrimination kept women out of
> good jobs, higher education, government service
> and politics, the League offered an opportunity to
> be involved, although indirectly, with public issues
> of concern to women. The League's relative in-
> effectiveness above the state and local level mir-
> rored the general powerlessness of women in in-
> fluencing and controlling the world around them.
> It also reflected their continuing, although dimin-
> ished, interest in doing so.[25]

Lacking the consciousness raising about women's second class status that radical suffragists had provided, and
the cohesiveness of diverse women's groups nationally united
around a single goal as they had been with suffrage, the
League continued to expand its focus as a public interest
group with even less identity with "women's" issues, for
which there was almost no constituency in the larger American society.

Between then and now, things changed. Although
Rosie the Riveter, the woman worker who kept the factories
going in World War II, was hailed as a folk heroine, she
was dispatched once again to the kitchen at the end of the
war to open up higher level jobs for homecoming male veterans. Her diminished status and the closing of doors
through which she could market her talents, was reflected in
a surge of growth in the membership of the League which
nearly doubled its membership in the two decades following
the war. Despite public appearances, Rosie did not return
willingly to an isolated domestic role.

The resurgence of the women's movement in the mid 1960s was a repetition of earlier history when women were denied equal voice with men in the abolition movement. In the social ferment of the sixties when women were excluded from decision making roles, the League remained one of the few organizations which offered the opportunity to work on civil rights, for example, with no competition from men for leadership and policy making roles.

The League's relation with the larger women's movement has always been a symbiotic one, as have women's fortunes in the political arena. Never having turned its major focus from the general aspects of government, the League was an organization of women rather than for women.

The new feminist consciousness raising movement of the 1960's pointed up the need for women to organize once again on behalf of themselves as a special interest group. Thus that period witnessed the birth of such groups as the National Organization for Women, Women's Equity Action League, and the National Women's Political Caucus. The League along with other survivors of the earlier women's movement, such as the Federation of Business and Professional Women and the American Association of University Women, found its collective consciousness raised in the process, as feminists rallied around their new national goal: The Equal Rights Amendment.

The League determined to support ERA as a program priority. Since so many feminist issues of the sixties were the same as those of a half century before, it was apparent that women still had not achieved resolution of the old problems. In setting their sights on suffrage, earlier feminists had opted for the more achievable if more limited goal.

The decision by most major women's groups to abandon pursuit of an equal rights amendment after suffrage had been won was largely based on political expediency rather than opposition to equal rights for women. In the League, three factors weighed in the decision: first, members shared the general belief that the vote would be the means to eradicate the remaining problems. Secondly, they were inheritors of the moderate philosophy of suffrage--that a methodical, highly organized lobbying approach would be a surer method of attaining their goals. It had, after all, worked in winning the vote.

Third, in the course of the pursuing solutions one by
one, women had also managed to lobby effectively for protective labor legislation for women in the states which
claimed jurisdiction over working hours, wages, and other
labor issues. They saw their successful efforts to protect
women workers being endangered by the proposed federal
amendment. As in the early push for suffrage, radicals and
moderates agreed on the essential grievances still in need of
redress, but not on tactics for achieving their goals.

In the League an anti-ERA position remained in the
program until 1954. By the early 1970's it was clear that
such issues as protective labor laws, family support, social
security and welfare provisions had acquired a long history
of legal precedent in the judicial system which they had
lacked early in the century, and that such legislation would
simply be modified to include both sexes under ERA. In
1972, Leagues at all levels began to organize and coordinate
state lobbying efforts to ratify ERA. By January 1, 1977,
the national League, with the help of state and local Leagues,
had raised over $300,000 in ERA campaign funds, funneling
most of the money back to state organizations. In June 1977,
the national board of the League launched a $1 million, na-
tionwide fundraising campaign to finance a final all-out push
for ratification of the Equal Rights Amendment.

The League's national position against racial discrimination has been extended to include discrimination because
of sex since 1972 and the League has lobbied intensively for
such issues as federally funded day care, equal opportunity
in employment and education, the inclusion of affirmative
action goals and timetables in government regulations, and
the appointment of women to responsible positions in the federal government.

The League's relation to the feminist movement is
one of support rather than exclusive focus, and this is unlikely to change. And if feminist organizational goals benefit from League support, the League has also benefited from
the new feminist movement. When women began to put pressure on government officials to end discrimination in their
appointive offices and hiring practices, the League had candidates for jobs which required expertise in such non-feminist
areas as waste-water disposal and land use planning.

Despite the qualified candidates both in and outside

the League for such jobs, the pulse of political power of
women is still woefully weak. According to the census compiled by the National Women's Political Caucus for 1975-76,
there was only one woman governor, there were three lieutenant governors, eight out of six hundred and seventy-five
federal judges, eleven secretaries of state, nineteen out of
four hundred and thirty-five members of the House of Representatives, and one hundred and thirty-nine of approximately
thirteen hundred (elected and appointed) state cabinet members. [26] While the 1976 elections saw the addition of another governor and secretary of state, there were losses on
other fronts, such as one less woman in the House.

On the lower levels of the political hierarchy, the
Caucus' 1975-76 count was six hundred and ten (9 percent)
women out of seven thousand five hundred and sixty-one state
legislators, four hundred and fifty-six ($2\frac{1}{2}$ percent) of seven-
teen thousand county commissioners, and five thousand nine
hundred and forty-seven (5 percent) of approximately one
hundred and thirty-six thousand mayors, and city and township council members. The greatest proportion of women
is to be found on school boards where they hold eleven thous-
and (11 percent) of ninety six thousand five hundred and
sixty seats. [27]

A further indication of weakness is to be found in the
comparative figures for female delegates in attendance at the
national party conventions from 1920 to conventions of the
1970's, the record breaking number of women at the 1972
conventions, diminished slightly for the Democrats by 1976
(see chart). [28]

Women Delegates to National Party Conventions

	1920	1972	1976
Democrat	93 (7.3%)	1,275 (40%)	1,036 (34%)
Republican	27 (2.7%)	402 (29.8%)	703 (31.1%)

Women in Office

	1920	1972	1976
State Legislature	37	383	610 (685 elected Nov.)
U.S. House of Repre.	1 (elected)	12	19 (18 elected Nov.)
Senate	0	2	0

Sparse as they are, the figures are not entirely bleak. Each year for the past six years a third more women have run for public office. The larger number of women in offices below the state level can be seen as providing potential candidates for statewide and national offices in future years. This is important. In a Wall Street Journal article just before the '76 elections, Patricia Goldman, head of the Republican Women's Task Force, was quoted as advising women in politics to get "back to basics, push women into the system, get them in a position to raise funds and run for office at all levels. You can't just start at the top."29

The task of pushing women into the system becomes more formidable the longer it's delayed. As a 1920 edition of the Woman Citizen pointed out, if voting then was generally an exercise in machine politics where know-nothing voters cast their ballots as they were told, it was also a time of opportunity for new leadership when local governments were still evolving.30 Today the opportunity is still there but more difficult, as it is always more difficult to break into an established order.

Given the League purpose, defined by its bylaws, "to promote political responsibility through informed and active participation of citizens in government," the League will continue to be a political portal for many women at all levels of government from the first step into political waters to the assumption of higher government posts.

This function will be enhanced as increasing numbers of League women abandon traditional female roles for a professional or political career. Pressures to respond to working schedules of women members have been tugging at the League since 1974 when the image of the typical Leaguer as a middle-class housewife was shaken by a membership study. It revealed that 48 percent of the members had jobs, 25 percent full time and 23 percent part time, many of them in business or the professions. Job profiles of League women who worked showed that 22 percent were lawyers, doctors, other professionals, or working in government, while 32 percent were teachers or university professors. Twenty-eight percent worked in business or clerical positions and 16 percent held skilled labor or other types of jobs.31 This study also showed that the working women tended to be the most active League members who also belonged to organizations besides the League. While enhancing their effectiveness in the

League for some, however, the full-time job has proved too much competition for the time of other members. Thirty-six percent of the dropouts from the League were employed full time. Nonetheless, the study showed it is family responsibilities rather than professional workloads which weigh most often in a decision to drop out of the League. [32]

With employed men and women as members, some League procedures are changing. More meetings are being held at night. The tradition of thorough study of all sides of an issue before taking a position is unlikely to disappear, and the League's focus as a lobbying group will continue to expand, bolstered by the growing professional skills of its members.

Other aspects of League activities will also remain constant. Volunteers with daytime hours available will continue their services as observers of city councils and legislatures, and monitoring judicial developments in the courts, to fulfill the need for first-hand knowledge of government action on League issues. League lobbying, however, may be parcelled out among a larger number of members requiring fewer people with large blocks of time available. For the aspiring public official, the League will probably continue its on-the-job training function, but as a complement rather than a substitute for the role of political parties. Increasingly, with more women welcome in government, the League is a ready resource for advisory and management positions at federal, state, and local levels.

Oddly enough, the greatest political gains in terms of "pushing women into the system" in 1976 were made by the League of Women Voters Education Fund, without fielding a woman candidate. A Washington Post story (October 24, 1976, p. E-1), explains:

> As producer of the Presidential Debates, perhaps the pivotal event of the campaign--the League has been thrust into its greatest position of power and prominence. At no other time in its history has its decisions on policy and procedures played such a vital part in the American election process. [33]

That both presidential candidates agreed to debate under the aegis of the League of Women Voters was a testimonial from the highest level of politics to the viability and legitimacy of participation by women in public life.

NOTES

1. Report of the National Commission on the Observance of International Women's Year, ... To Form a More Perfect Union ... Washington, D. C.: U. S. Government Printing Office, 1976, p. 312.
2. Thomas Buckley, The New York Times News Service, April 27, 1974.
3. Summary of Democratic Women State Legislators' Responses to Questionnaire (Washington, D. C.: Democratic National Committee, March 1976) p. 3.
4. Report of Commission on IWY, p. 345.
5. Audrey Colom, "Are You a Potential Candidate: League Women in Politics, " (Washington, D. C., League of Women Voters, 1976) slide show audio.
6. News Release (New York City: League of Women Voters of the U. S., May, 1976).
7. Harriet Cipriani, "Are You a Potential Candidate?"
8. Judith Axler Turner, "League of Women Voters Backs Studies with Lobbying, " (Washington, D. C., National Journal, 1972) 4:21, p. 870.
9. Jeane J. Kirkpatrick, Political Woman (New York: Basic Books, Inc., 1974) p. 61.
10. Eagleton Institute for the American Woman and Politics, Women in Public Office (New York, R. R. Bowker, 1976) Table 8.
11. Mary Louise Smith, "Are You a Potential Candidate?"
12. Mary Gray Peck, Carrie Chapman Catt: A Biography (New York: H. W. Wilson Co., 1944) p. 325.
13. Carrie Chapman Catt, "Editorially Speaking, " The Woman Citizen (April 23, 1921) p. 1188.
14. Ibid. "The Direct Primary Under Fire: Women Voters Fight the Old Convention, " (May 7, 1921) p. 1210.
15. Judith Papachristou, Women Together (New York: Alfred A. Knopf, 1976), pp. 66-73.
16. Ibid. pp. 82-87.
17. Maud Wood Park, "The Winning Plan. " In Victory, How Women Won It, 1840-1940 (New York: H. W. Wilson Company, 1940) pp. 123-139.
18. Ibid.
19. Carrie Chapman Catt and Nettie Rogers Schuler, Woman, Suffrage and Politics (New York: Charles Scribner's Sons, 1923) p. 189, p. 239.
20. Dearborn Independent (March 15, 1924), as cited by Judith Papachristou, Women Together (New York: Alfred A. Knopf, 1976) p. 200.
21. William H. Chafe, The American Woman (New York:

Oxford University Press paperback, 1974) p. 33.

22. See The Woman Citizen, issues of 1930.
23. Chafe, p. 42.
24. Papachristou, p. 123.
25. Ibid.
26. Report of Commission in IWY, p. 341.
27. Ibid.
28. Convention Records: Republican National Committee, 310 First St., S. E., Washington, D. C. 20003: Democratic National Committee, 1625 Massachusetts Avenue, N. W. Washington, D. C. 20036.
29. Vol. CLXXX VIII, No. 79, October 21, 1976, p. 24.
30. Mrs. Raymond Brown, from a lecture delivered before the School of Political Education conducted by Carrie Chapman Catt following the suffrage convention in Chicago, "Politics and the Home," The Woman Citizen (June 5, 1920) p. 28.
31. Albert H. and Susan Davis Cantril, The Report of the Findings of the League Self Study (Washington, D. C.: League of Women Voters, February 1974) p. 4.
32. Ibid., p. 12.
33. "League of Women Voters Has Come a Long Way," The Washington Post, (October 24, 1976), p. E-1.

Chapter 7

W. E. A. L. : THE GROWTH OF A FEMINIST
ORGANIZATION

by Arlene Daniels

Organizational Structure

W. E. A. L. (Women's Equity Action League) is a national feminist organization formed in the late 1960's. It
developed, primarily out of the efforts of a woman lawyer,
in response to misgivings over the platform of another feminist organization, N. O. W. (National Organization for Wom-
en). Elizabeth Boyer, an Ohio lawyer who was herself one
of the founders of N. O. W., argued that too militant an approach to women's rights would offend many moderates and
prevent rather than hasten the passage of such desirable
measures as the Equal Rights Amendment. Boyer argued
that stands on such issues as abortion rights or recognition
of the rights of homosexuals and such tactics as demonstrating or picketing would alienate many women who might otherwise subscribe to the principles of equality for women in
education and employment. And so she left N. O. W. to
found another organization with a narrower focus on the redress of inequities through legislation and lobbying.

In the view of one member of the initial National Advisory Board, the split between N. O. W. and W. E. A. L. involved three main issues: 1) The abortion issue at that
time was too dangerous politically to take an affirmative
stand on it. Too many women would refuse to support a
feminist organization that would support legalized abortion
even when they agreed with all other goals of the organization. Too many legislators who might otherwise vote for
the E. R. A. in their state would withdraw support if pro-
abortion sentiments became associated with the E. R. A. movement. Particularly in states with strong Catholic constituents, such an association might be political suicide for
Catholic legislators. 2) Betty Friedan, as the founder of
N. O. W. projected too controversial an image in her own person to attract and hold women of a more conventional life

style.   3) N. O. W. became too diffuse in its purposes because of all the different cases--and causes--it supported.

In founding W. E. A. L., Boyer resolved to avoid some
of the problems she saw in N. O. W. by limiting membership
quite selectively until the shape and direction of the organization stabilized as she wished.   And so, before publicizing
the existence of this new organization, she toured the country, seeking like-minded feminists to serve on a national advisory board. 1 Ultimately, this founding board of 44 directors would encourage others to join and suggest the direction for the new organization.   Once this board of acade-
micians, legislators, lawyers, administrators and judges
(mainly women but with a sprinkling of men) was organized,
the constitution and by-laws of the organization were constructed in order to establish the special focus of the organizational goals--and to eliminate the possibility of take-
overs by feminists with a broader range of interests.   A
board of directors (officers and committee chairpersons) to
run the new organization was selected after consultation with
the national advisors.   Elizabeth Boyer was the first president.

The organization basically expressed the dream of its
founder to focus upon legal, educational and administrative
inequities facing women today.   The organization, though national, began with a base in Ohio, as a non-profit corporation.   From there, the organizational base moved to Washington, after a few years when the fourth president, Arvonne Fraser, established a Washington legislative office to
monitor and lobby issues affecting the treatment of women. 2
At the same time, various educational and research projects
were established to study the treatment of women in such
areas as credit, in divorce cases, in textbooks, in higher
education employment.

During this period, the organization also expanded to
include state divisions and some local chapters within states.
National and divisional meetings are held yearly and officers
are elected yearly from a slate produced by a nominating
committee.   A small part-time paid staff at the national headquarters manages membership and mailings.   It is joined by
the staff of the W. E. A. L. Legal and Educational Defense
Fund which prepares research and disseminates information
on sex discrimination.   But in the main, the organization is
still a volunteer effort; and it is growing slowly, relative to
the larger N. O. W. organization.

Goals of the Organization

The organization of W. E. A. L., though relatively
small, shows many signs of power, that is, the ability to
exert influence upon legislators, to lobby effectively, to contribute to the writing of federal legislation, to effect changes
in federal policy, to get wide publicity for injustices against
women, to win cases for women airing their grievances in
court and administrative actions, to produce information useful to proponents of equity for women in public hearings, to
produce expert witnesses, to conduct original independent
research and then disseminate the findings.

In addition to its own efforts, the organization leaders lend their position to joint efforts, particularly in court
actions, with other feminist organizations. Spokespersons
for all the national feminist organizations often band together to press for better federal policy concerning equal opportunity in employment and civil rights for women. The National Coalition for Women and Girls in Education, The Campaign to End Discrimination Against Pregnant Workers are
examples of coalitions in which W. E. A. L. members are active participants. In addition, they participate when coalitions are formed to establish human rights commissions at
the city or county level. W. E. A. L. members are also active in commissions on the status of women at the federal,
state and city level. For these groups are supported by national leaders from the entire structure of women's organizations. These affiliations are possible because the major
goals of all these organizations are substantially the same:
equal rights for women. Many of the differences between
them are more questions of tone and style, rather than substantive issues. There are radical women who find more
compatibility with those of similar life styles--found in
N. O. W. Some radical women feminists find even N. O. W.
too stodgy for them and band together in lesbian collectives,
anti-establishment women's health centers, consciousness-
raising groups. [3] Older women and those who adhere to a
traditional style of life find W. E. A. L. more suitable to their
goals.

The differences in style between W. E. A. L. and the
more militant radical groups affect the manner in which
goals are pursued. W. E. A. L. members are more likely to
request than to demand, to use legalistic rather than confrontation tactics, to support sex-role linked or "feminine"
behaviors. For example, W. E. A. L. members are not above

using "womanly wiles" to make their case. One spokeswom-
an told me that her state group often invited legislators to
speak on topics of interest to feminists in order to educate
the speakers more than the audience. The legislators would
learn by accepting a request to speak as "experts." They
would have to research the topic. But of more importance,
the questions posed by those in the audience, more knowledge-
able than the speakers themselves, would aid their education
in feminism.

Sympathy for the position of the antagonist (in order
to have the opportunity to change her/his way of thinking) is
frequently stressed. Elizabeth Koontz, when speaking at a
state convention in California (1972), discussed the inadequa-
cies of the school system in combatting sexism. She advised compassion rather than hostility toward counselors who
continue sexist practices. "The counselors are not doing
their job. Is that what you think too? But remember, don't
put that bag on them until they're out from under all that
testing they have to do. They are not given the time, now,
to learn how not to do sexist counseling."

Another sympathetic tactic to inveigh against sexism
among men is offered by this speaker. "No matter how
much a man is a male chauvinist pig, he may very well have
a bright daughter. You can ask him: what do you think will
happen to that bright girl? And if he thinks she's going to
do better at finding a job than others because she is so special, ask him: what about the other bright girls in his own
office; what opportunities has he offered them? People don't
understand how inconsistent they are; and you have to point
up the inconsistencies."

The differences in strategies and tactics to attain
goals which show the characteristics of W. E. A. L. as compared to more militant groups also appear in the tolerance
of "false consciousness" among women. The more radical
groups tend to be accusatory (or judgmental) to women not
committed to feminism. The leadership in W. E. A. L. coun-
sels caution and understanding. "It is important not to
hassle women who want to stay home and be mothers. We
shouldn't sneer at them when we point out that we want the
right to go and work. But not every woman has yet attained
the right to that privilege of staying home if she wishes to.
And most women at some time in their life may be forced
to work."

Through sympathy and tolerance for the housewife's perspective combined with the effort to explain the hardships faced by most women who have to work, W. E. A. L. members seek new recruits from the more moderate and conservative women of every class.

Despite differences in style or tactics, the goals of W. E. A. L. are similar to those of any feminist group: equity before the law and in every institution in society for women. Though some groups want much more as well, the major difference between W. E. A. L. and other organizations is the style for attaining goals. W. E. A. L. is reformist and believes in working in and with the current political structure.

Again, such tactics require understanding and sympathy for those in the power structure. The W. E. A. L. members sometimes criticize the tactics of the more radical group viewed as lobbying in an arrogant or high-handed way. As one W. E. A. L. official put it, "Sometimes other groups use offensive tactics or tactics that just don't work. We have to repair the damage that they do when they create bad feelings among policy makers. We dress like middle-class ladies for 'business reasons' and save our jeans for the weekend. The others find it difficult to understand that legislators sometimes won't listen to your ideas if they don't like the way you look. It may not be fair, but that's the way it is. "

This approach leads members of the group to focus upon reform as the ultimate policy change. W. E. A. L. members accept the necessity for political compromise. This approach is facilitated by the high proportion of professionals --especially lawyers--among the members. The focus of attention is upon the key or class action case which will establish precedent in some area--sick leave compensation for pregnancy, equal retirement benefits for women and men, protection of women's right in hiring, promotion, and retention on the job, abolition of sex-stereotyped employment.

The 1976 national report shows how specific directions for legislative action have developed from the national office. W. E. A. L. continued to work for ratification of the Equal Rights Amendment, to promote qualified women for appointments and salaried positions of power and influence on state and national levels. W. E. A. L. placed special emphasis on fighting discrimination in tax laws, particularly sex bias in the Social Security system. As their abilities have developed

and become known on the Washington scene, W. E. A. L. members have provided testimony on discrimination in insurance
policies, and focused on discrimination in housing and mortgage grants.

An important developing focus for W. E. A. L. has been
support of legislation to give economic recognition to homemakers. W. E. A. L. has also supported the development of
alternate work patterns to expand work opportunities for wom-
en who cannot work full time. And W. E. A. L. continues to
attack stereotypes of women in the media and discrimination
against women in employment and education in general.

New directions in W. E. A. L. encompass child care
legislation providing tax credit for working parents. And,
since eternal vigilance is required to maintain the advances
toward equity already initiated in laws and regulations,
W. E. A. L. members now have the responsibility of policing
the agencies and officials with responsibility for enforcing
Title VII of the Civil Liberties Act, Executive Order 11246,
the Equal Pay Act, and Title IX of the Education Amendments
Act of 1972. W. E. A. L. members also watchdog the Wom-
en's Education Act of 1974, (designed to encourage research
on women's issues and new programs beneficial to women)
and the Equal Credit Opportunity Act (on the maintenance of
credit records for men and women).

All these combined and sustained efforts mean that
non-professionals become acquainted with the law as they
seek changes in the society. The state and national leaders
in the organization are conversant with the anti-discrimination laws and the executive orders which spell out national
policy against discrimination based on sex. They also help
initiate legislation, such as The Women's Education Equity
Act, and they work for legislation designed to protect domestic and factory worker. They conduct new research to show
how to promote equity between the sexes as exemplified in
publications, Women Graduates and Women and Fellowships,
1976.

Recruitment and Social Control of Members

The belief in a common purpose and a shared understanding of how to attain it motivates the leadership of
W. E. A. L. Interested as they are in new members, they
share an understanding of how to recruit them. Members

who have the time, energy and commitment to work diligently
are almost assured of upward mobility in the organization.
Within the understandings of what the W. E. A. L. constitution
and bylaws permit members to do, everyone (of either sex)
is welcome. Upon payment of a nominal fee ($20. 00 a year)
one becomes a voting member. If living in an as yet unorganized state or region, one may apply for permission to
convene a division or chapter. The organization encourages
new members to construct their own projects and, if approved
by the organization, the results of the project receive the
W. E. A. L. imprimatur and are widely disseminated, as in the
case of the Texas W. E. A. L. 's investigation of the Waco
schools.

   The founder, Elizabeth Boyer, has been successful in
building an organization which reflects the persistent, focused
concern on equity for women in education and employment
which she has always stressed. This success may be a consequence of the initial recruitment method. Once the founding board of directors was chosen, Boyer's organization and
its goals were described in various national popular journals
for women and in newspapers and women's newsletters or
journals in those areas around the country where Boyer was
invited to speak. The nucleus of the membership was formed
by women who wrote to her asking for more information
about the organization and/or about a personal grievance of
their own. Elizabeth Boyer answered these letters at great
length and encouraged these women to pursue their projects,
while offering helpful suggestions about how to do it.

   The beginnings of the feminist movement in this country are characterized by the formation of networks from such
efforts. In this case, many of the women reaching Elizabeth
Boyer, through media announcements about her organization,
became leaders--members of the board of directors, convenors of state divisions, presidents and committee chairpersons. The organization also grew through their efforts
at finding and recruiting members. But this first group
which was preselected or screened by Boyer, initially attracted women by the statements about W. E. A. L. which she
presented to the media. All of these women were agreed on
the point that they would fight for equal rights, but only in
certain ways: they would not picket, demonstrate, or engage in violent and unseemly behavior. And when this group
canvassed for new recruits, they sought them among like-
minded persons.

The first wave of recruits, in addition to sharing their conventional (liberal-reform) approach to social change, were mainly professionals: lawyers, doctors, teachers, professors, administrators, architects, scientists, and engineers. All had a personal stake in the fight for equality, since their own career mobility was often seriously curtailed by sex stratification. Some were able to devote time to organizing W. E. A. L. and conducting projects in its name because they were currently unemployed or threatened with unemployment as a result of sexism in the society.

Most were busy women carrying responsibilities for job and home in addition to their responsibilities to organize W. E. A. L. In consequence, any new recruit was appreciated as an extra pair of hands. While practical, efficient members who worked well with others were preferred recruits, any person who would do something, and who was not destructive of other members, was welcomed.

In this context there was little need for formal rules. Beyond the basic limitations set by the constitution and by-laws, each member was free to set up projects and pursue them. Permission to use W. E. A. L. 's name was restricted to projects approved by the board; but this permission was relatively easy to obtain. In consequence, the specific projects undertaken in the first years of the organization reflected particular concerns of individual members; they worked dedicatedly and independently. One of the most striking of W. E. A. L. 's first successes came about through the efforts of Bernice Sandler who filed charges against universities and colleges in W. E. A. L. 's name. These charges established the existence of a widespread pattern of sex discrimination. The project took on added luster because of the backing of the organization. Even when W. E. A. L. was only a paper organization with a handful of members, its projects received national recognition. At the outset, it appeared to be more powerful and well organized than it actually was.

The disadvantage of this loose-knit scheme was its vulnerability to those who might use the organization for purposes antithetical to its goals. In the effort to guard against such dangers, the organization grew more slowly than it might otherwise have done. Persons who seemed too concerned with personal problems or too involved in other ideological perspectives than those promulgated by W. E. A. L. were permitted to become discouraged and disaffected.

Limitations were also set upon efforts to attract vast numbers of members by media appeals. Members did not wish to engage in sensational activities to catch media attention. But they could not recruit so widely nor so quickly without media coverage. The new members they wished to attract--working women and housewives who essentially adhered to traditional roles but were nevertheless concerned for women's rights under the law--were difficult to find. Not organized into readily accessible groups, they were not easily identified. When discovered, such women were exposed to feminist ideology, gradually and with great patience. The W. E. A. L. leadership was busy and hard-pressed meeting the obligations of work, home and the organization. These women had little time for recruiting and training members to replace them as leaders. Notwithstanding these difficulties, the organization grew to a membership of several thousand spread throughout the fifty states. Yet it remained a loose-knit organization, permitting members to work as diligently as they pleased. The only formal negative sanction available to the organization leaders was withholding support for a project by failing to provide interest and personal cooperation. The clearest sanction was withholding support to high office from aspirants deemed ineffective or inappropriate by the leadership. The organizational structure did not offer any other means of bringing errant members into compliance; either they agreed to work together as the consensus directed, or they could work alone, or leave the organization.

Some of the influences or tendencies within the organization which might persuade members to work together (or dissuade them from trying) can be observed at the public meetings. The assemblies at divisional (state) conventions and local chapters offer an opportunity for outside speakers on feminist issues and for the leadership from the national W. E. A. L. to address the membership--to encourage the faithful, hearten the laggards. When speakers are inadvertently chosen who do not represent the spirit of W. E. A. L., the negative response to them--and the manner in which that response is manifested--suggest something of the informal rules governing membership and the system by which deviance may be corrected. The following two excerpts (from field notes) indicate the way those who are too conservative-conventional to understand feminist stance are rebuffed in public meetings.

November, 1971: At a panel presented at a state convention, a local legislator voiced the opin-

ion that it was not important for women to have
equal access to medical school with men since
women are not the main breadwinners. Therefore,
a ratio of 10 percent admissions for women to men
should be considered reasonable. At once, many
hands shot up, waving wildly for recognition. The
legislator said angrily that he didn't come to such
a meeting to be insulted. He came as a favor and
would leave if mistreated. The moderator leaped
to her feet and entreated the audience to be polite
to this legislator who had done so much for women
in that state by voting the feminist cause on so
many issues--even risking his own political advantage to do so. The audience subsided; but when
the gentleman left, the moderator was bitterly re-
proached from the floor. The speaker from the
audience rebuked her for accepting his definition of
a show of hands as insolent and threatening. The
legislator needed education more than the audience.
Other members of the audience chimed in, pointing
out how much more polite and tolerant they had
been than more militant feminists would have been
before such provocation. The rebuke to this moderator was keenly felt and resented by her. When
we discussed it later, she rebuked me sharply for
the sympathies with the handwavers which I had
shown. Yet she also said she realized that her
views of style were too conservative for many in
this organization and she would try to accommo-
date accordingly.

November, 1972: A State Convention with about
two hundred women members and guests attending.
In the main, the audience was middle-aged and middle-class in appearance. There were three black
women in the audience, and three or four men.
The out-going state president introduced the opening speaker who began with a joke about W. E. A. L.
being at the far right of the women's movement.
She then offered congratulations to the president
whom she particularly admired as one of the best-
dressed women in the state. These remarks were
received in stony silence except for one hiss. The
speaker continued, undaunted, with homely and
folksy jokes, as: women were like kleenex, which
will stretch even though it looks fragile. (Some
rustling and a few polite sounds of laughter; but
not much enthusiasm.)

The speaker continued by saying women have to compete on the same level as men, live up to the same qualifications and goals for success. She thought it would take toughness, discipline and emotional maturity for women to learn how to work an eight-hour day and not ask for exceptions to be made for them. One male member of the audience, sitting behind me, murmured to his companion, "She sounds like a navy skipper." I was put more in mind of a top sergeant. Applause was polite but sparse at the conclusion. Later I was told by the outgoing president that she considered the speaker a disaster and had made a mistake in inviting her.

These examples suggest how the public meetings give membership and leadership opportunities to gauge the tone and style--and the direction--toward which feminist expressions are heading. While strong outbursts are rare, small contretemps of the kind noted here are noticed by everyone and continue to figure in discussions long after the event--particularly when planning the next large assemblage of members.

Public meeting, particularly national conventions, also offer opportunity to observe how the leadership protects the organization from pressures to be more radical and less conventional than the founders thought desirable. The direction of the national convention of 1972 was endangered by an effort at a takeover. Pressure was exerted to force acceptance of a resolution supporting abortion on demand. Since this was one of the issues considered politically inadvisable to link with the feminist causes advocated by W. E. A. L., and since W. E. A. L. had broken with N. O. W. over this issue, the measure was neutralized. The preceding discussion and the arguments and counter arguments for changing the original stance of W. E. A. L. are quite revealing of the organizational tactics and goals. A very few spokespersons argued against abortion on religious grounds. These arguments were countered by the position that it was legitimate self-defense for a woman to save her own life (and well being).

In the main, the arguments did not center here; rather the issue was understood in relation to passage of the E. R. A. Women from the South claimed that legislators in their home states would torpedo the Equal Rights Amendment and/or refuse to negotiate with E. R. A. spokeswomen who

also supported pro-abortion laws.   Again and again, the issue was drawn as a tactical rather than an ideological one,
how best might the ultimate goal of equal rights for women
be served?   And how might priorities be set so that one
goal might not work against the other?   The primary importance of passing the Equal Rights Amendment before taking on other issues was asserted.   By arguing in this fashion,
the most violent proponents of a strong anti-abortion stand
were placated so that a more neutral (or ambiguous) stand
on the issue might be taken.   The final resolution was worded
to say only that women should control their own bodies, without explicit reference to the use of abortion as a means to
that end.   While such a resolution would never satisfy the
most radical feminists, it served to show that the organization was willing, under pressure, to modify its strong stand
about having no part of this controversial issue.

Structure of Opportunities

As in other volunteer organizations, the most persuasive sanctions affecting W. E. A. L. members are positive
ones.   When any member of a group is free to leave at any
time s/he becomes disinterested or disaffected, only the positive mechanisms creating social solidarity really work.   In
this case, women enjoyed the companionship and sense of
unity provided by sisterhood in a common cause.   They fought
a common enemy (sexism) and they shared common histories
(similar wounds from past battles) and similar aspirations
for themselves and their daughters.   The bonds created by
membership in W. E. A. L. were strengthened at national and
state conventions, and maintained through the year by letters
and telephone calls about the current state of some project.
They rejoiced together in victories--the passage of E. R. A.
in one more state, the success of legislation to offer the
minimum wage to greater numbers of working women.   And
they worked together to stave off defeat such as the reintro-
duction of anti-abortion legislation, the weakening of the
stand by federal agencies on enforcing affirmative action programs in education and industry.

This process created strong loyalties both to other
individuals within the organization and the organization itself.
But the opportunities for such interactions were limited.
Most women had no time to elaborate the structure of
W. E. A. L. meetings because they were involved in many
other feminist activities and organizations.   It was difficult,

sometimes, to find members willing to hold office.   And in
some state organizations, even key positions--such as the
presidency--would go begging.

The very top positions (national board members and
officer of the two organization boards) had to be limited to
members with time and money to pay part of their travel
expenses (anything over the regular one hundred dollar re-
imbursement from W. E. A. L.) four times a year to the meetings. Professional working women who could rationalize this
activity as part of their jobs (educational administrators, directors of women's centers, attorneys specializing in sex
discrimination cases, professors in women's studies) were
in an excellent position to serve.   Alternatively, women with
extra time (currently unemployed, retired) could participate
if their or their husband's means permitted.   A few participated without any special facilitating circumstances because
of their enormous commitment to the women's movement.

Often the selection of these women was on a trial and
error basis.   Candidates were elected or appointed to the
board and then retained or let go after a testing time to discover their commitment, effectiveness and responsibility.
These decisions were made by the inner circle or core mem-
bers--initially recruited by Elizabeth Boyer.   Boyer removed
herself from the first board, but stayed on the second board
of the W. E. A. L. Educational and Legal Defense Fund, formed
later as the non-political arm of the group to engage in activities which could receive foundation funds.   The initial
board remained the lobbying group to which gifts are not tax
exempt.   (These distinctions were mainly for tax exempt
status and other I. R. S. purposes rather than representative
of differences.)   The first board represented the membership
for lobbying, publicity, and carried on some research and
legal action.   The second board was permitted to accept tax
exempt contributions and could operate as a foundation, spon-
soring projects, and could actively support court cases with
financial and legal assistance to litigants.

The inner circle of core members carried on the
tradition established by Elizabeth Boyer.   They kept control
of the direction of the organization (and the subsidiary organization represented by the second board) and they carefully monitored the elections of the new leaders by supervising nomination procedures as closely as possible.   Thus
far, even in those few elections which were hotly contested,
the members of the inner circle agree that the candidates
representing the initial W. E. A. L. spirit have prevailed.

The array of jobs at state and national levels cover
many parallel functions. Positions are open on membership
and nominating committees, and for treasurer, recording
secretary, and secretary, parliamentarian, resolutions committee chairperson, newsletter editor, speakers bureau and
research committee. In addition, of course, national and
state divisions have a president and vice president. The
state committee heads and officers comprise the state division's executive committee. This committee plans and ex-
pedites the annual convention, develops research projects,
decides what feminist activities the state W. E. A. L. will
officially endorse, and works to promote feminism generally
and the W. E. A. L. brand particularly. The national board
is organized somewhat differently--with members to represent various geographic areas as well as such specific concerns as membership, finance and newsletter editing. Some
of these tasks are managed by the paid staff in the national
office, with the aid of a special set of Washington-based
volunteers.   But the positions of the recording and corresponding secretaries and the president and vice president in
the national organization are parallel to state offices.

Generally, board members choose the activities which
will receive emphasis. Some of the tasks are for example,
writing grants for research projects, conducting research
and disseminating findings, forming education and consumer
credit committees, developing legal expertise and disseminating information about current cases involving sex discrimination. One board member organized a national committee on
help wanted/classified job advertising. A group undertook
microfilm research in newspapers at the New York Public
Library. A committee found that large newspapers in major
cities were in better compliance than those elsewhere; yet
much sex-segregated advertising continued to exist despite
laws forbidding employers from such practices. Accordingly,
this committee filed well over 400 complaints with the Equal
Employment Opportunities Commission (E. E. O. C.).

The W. E. A. L. Fund board has its own complement of
officers. [4] Their focus of attention is upon selecting cases
for legal action and then supporting complainants with legal
services or financial contributions or both. In its educational component, the fund has aided and reinforced antidiscrim-
ination legislation by publishing informational kits on new
federal laws and regulations. It watches the Federal Reg-
ister and prepares comments on proposed regulations affecting women, and, like the action arm of the organization, it

works with other public interest groups in Washington. The
Fund has been active in research and publicity on women in
fellowship and training programs, helping to break the male-
only tradition in the Rhodes Scholars program and to increase
the number of female White House Fellows. The W. E. A. L.
Fund also published the only condensed version of the World
Plan of Action for the Decade for Women (1976-85)--with
English, Spanish, and French versions available. Current
and future projects include an international women's resource
center and an internship program with W. E. A. L. in Washington. The organization this board represents can legally accept and receive any grants federal or private agencies may
award to it.

The business of both national boards is conducted
throughout one long weekend, four times a year. Many of
the board meetings are held at the national office in Washington. Members are invited to attend, particularly state
presidents who might wish to offer suggestions and information from their home states.

The W. E. A. L. Fund board meeting begins on Sunday
morning, usually in private homes or in member's hotel
rooms, and concludes in the early afternoon when members
leave to catch trains and planes for home. Annual convention meetings are held in hotels with convention facilities.
Board meetings are also held, during and prior to these
meetings, in the hotel.

For the majority, W. E. A. L. is only a worthwhile
"cause" they support with membership dues. Members receive newsletters and reports; they may request and receive
various kinds of technical or specialized information on legislation, politics and research about sex discrimination.
Relatively few members appear at national and state conven-
tions--the only opportunity they would have for any interaction with other members. The organization functions more
like a political interest group whose members write letters
to legislators and other governmental officials urging them
to some action. The call may go out to the members from
the leaders asking for a show of strength through letter writing on an issue. Or the leaders may write or speak publicly, urging their government representatives to some stand
while stressing the unified stance of the substantial membership which they represent on this issue. The greatest function of the rank and file is to provide this support for the
organization's action.

Some regional chapters have developed within state divisions to counteract this customary form of activity and to offer greater opportunity for sisterhood and for work on conjoint projects. But this movement is only beginning; and for the most part the membership leaves the opportunity for intense interaction to the leadership.

Within this context, the formal rewards for participation are quite limited. Election or appointment to membership on the national boards is the highest honor within the organization. Despite the hectic quality of its activities, and the personal and financial costs involved in these intensive weekends, the positions are prized and attendance is faithful. In addition, an award named for Elizabeth Boyer is now given yearly to an important contributor to feminist causes. Thus far, the award has been given twice: to Betty Ford (for her efforts on behalf of women's rights when she was first lady) and to Bernice Sandler, the board member nationally known for her crusades--and her research on behalf of women in education.

Recognition from the larger society to W. E. A. L. members is often seen as a result of service to W. E. A. L. One member of W. E. A. L. became a high-ranking official in the Ford administration--after a systematic lobbying effort in her behalf. W. E. A. L. members mounted a write-in campaign on behalf of a candidate they found extremely well-qualified for the job. Yet they feared she would be passed over without considerable pressure from women's groups. Apparently, the necessity was also seen by the candidate herself. For, after her appointment, she became a life member (a substantial donation to W. E. A. L.), Dr. Bernice Sandler, upon receiving a 1976 Rockefeller Public Service Award for her outstanding work in expanding employment opportunities, expressed her sense of gratitude to the organization giving her the initial impetus in this career, and donated a portion of the prize money to W. E. A. L.

In addition to these specific kinds of honors, some rewards may come indirectly from service to the organization. Publicity as the author of a report or as the trial lawyer in cases of sex discrimination is sometimes advantageous for the careers of professional women. In some cases, this possibility is recognized in a quid pro quo relationship. The national leaders will offer a woman the status of convener of a state division in return for some effort on her part in fulfilling some requirements of the organization. Public support is often thought helpful.

The organization is seen as an instrument for social change. The founders and leaders see themselves as breaking ground for future generations of women. All see the society as a better and more equitable environment because of their efforts. Since these women believe they are instituting social changes and participating in social reforms, they are optimistic about the future. Gains may be small, setbacks occur, but they see a trend toward equality between the sexes.

The successes are often cited. One feminist reported in expert testimony to a congressional committee on W. E. A. L. 's work concerning the subject of credit. A congresswoman asked her, "What's W. E. A. L. ?" The W. E. A. L. president, hearing about this, organized a write-in campaign to this congresswoman asking her to hold hearings on credit for women. The W. E. A. L. Washington lobby also persuaded congressional colleagues to ask this woman why she did not hold hearings on credit. The W. E. A. L. president reported with some satisfaction that "We turned her around by this information in our Washington Newsletter and by all these other requests to hold hearings. "

And members point with pride to the inroads they have made in previously resistant labor strongholds. One male pro-labor congressman complimented W. E. A. L. for fighting to maintain the clause on domestic workers in a minimum wage bill. Without such effort, the women's movement is seen as exclusively concerned with interests of white middle-class women. Working to keep domestic workers in the minimum wage bill gave W. E. A. L. points on Capitol Hill.

Legislators learn to feel the power of these women in other ways. One senator added to the foreign aid bill a feminist amendment that would focus on women as part of economic development in third world countries. Senatorial colleagues laughed at the proviso in committee meetings and dropped it. But word went out through the informal network of federal and private agency women in Washington to such groups as W. E. A. L. Once alerted, the leadership organized a letter writing campaign to the conferees of the bill. Eventually, the amendment was reintroduced. One antagonistic senator was angry; he did not know how word of the omission leaked out. W. E. A. L. prides itself on the informal network, including secretaries, that helps the leadership marshall forces at such times.

Publicity favorable to W. E. A. L. in the Washington Post and other national news media also provide evidence of success--members see these items as indicators of the growing social agreement on the worthiness of feminist causes.

Conclusion

The women who actively participate in W. E. A. L. belong to the tradition of citizen participation, actively pursuing political strategies to improve society. They come primarily from the ranks of working, professional women. As working women, they have certain strengths and weaknesses in attempting volunteer work. The women of W. E. A. L. have professional expertise to bring to this work, but they are also pressed by volunteer in addition to salaried work commitments. In consequence, they seek recruits from the ranks of more traditional volunteers--housewives without salaried employment. While active participation from such new recruits is desired, their important contribution is to swell the ranks of supporters: cash contributors, letter-writers, public relations persons who can speak knowledgeably about the justice of feminist causes to friends and neighbors in local communities. This organization, then, represents a coalition between an active, but small leadership group of volunteers having professional expertise and the general membership who lend support.

NOTES

1. The National Advisory Board included the following:
   Rep. Bella S. Abzug, Marian Ash, Elizabeth Athanasakos, Sen. Birch Bayh, Daryl J. Bem, Sandra L. Bem, Lucy Wilson Benson, Jessie Bernard, Caroline Bird, Rep. Corrine C. Boggs, Elizabeth Boyer, Rep. Yvonne Burke, Rep. Shirley Chisholm, Mary Daly, Eleanor Dolan, Nancy E. Dowding, Thomas I. Emerson, Cynthia Fuchs Epstein, Frances Tarlton Farenthold, Daisy B. Fields, Laurine Fitzgerald, Ruth Bader Ginsburg, Vera Glasser, Rep. Edith Green, Rep. Martha W. Griffiths, Ruth Church Gupta, Rep. Julia Butler Hansen, LaDonna Harris, Viola Hymes, Elizabeth Janeway, Mildred M. Jeffrey, Geri Joseph, Leo Kanowitz, Herma Hill Kay, Roberta Kilberg, Elizabeth Koontz, Olga Madar, Abigail McCarthy, Rep. Robert McClory, Rep. Patsy T. Mink, Betty

Southard Murphy, Pauli Murray, Estelle Ramey, Helen
J. Roig, Alice S. Rossi, Jill Ruckelshaus, Rep. Patricia Schroeder, Anne Firor Scott, Althea T. L. Sim-
mons, Gloria Steinem, May Lou Thompson, Bettina
Weary, Sarah Weddington, and Ruth Weyand.

2. At that time, the national board included the following
   members: President Arvonne S. Fraser, Vice Presi-
   dent Doris Seward, Corresponding Secretary Elizabeth
   K. Wright, Recording Secretary Vilma Hunt, Treasurer
   Jessie Baum, Carol Brocato, Barbara Glenn, Bert
   Hartry, Pat Massey, Carol Polowy, Norma Raffel,
   Marguerite Rawalt, Jane Robens, Bernice Sandler,
   Emily Taylor, Paula Treder, and Anne T. Truax.

3. See Jo Freeman, The Politics of Women's Liberation
   (New York: David McKay Company, Inc., 1975) and
   Maren Lockwood Carden, The Feminist Movement
   (New York: Russell Sage Foundation, 1974).

4. As of 1976 the officers were Ellen Dresselhuis, Marguerite Rawalt, Bert Hartry, Arvonne Fraser, Elizabeth Boyer, Margaret Gates, Elizabeth D. Koontz,
   Bernice Sandler, Margaret Young, Norma Raffel, Ei-
   leen Thornton, Doris Seward, Dee Hahne, Judy Wise,
   Esther Hersh, Carol Parr, Elaine Binder, and Jo
   Lee Davis.

Chapter 8

NEW APPROACHES TO COLLECTIVE POWER:
FOUR WORKING WOMEN'S ORGANIZATIONS

by Nancy Seifer and Barbara Wertheimer

Working for Wages ... and Power

The mythology that used to surround the subject of women and work seems finally to be giving way to reality. Only a few short years ago, pioneering women researchers compiled and published statistics to disprove the myth that women worked only for "pin money," or that they worked sporadically, or that they had much higher absenteeism rates than men. By the mid-1970's there was growing public recognition of the fact that most women spend part, if not all, of their adult lives in the work force; and that most of the growing numbers of women entering the work force are there to stay--not for pin money, or for a chance to "develop their potential," but for the survival of their families and themselves.

One of the most interesting phenomena testifying to this reality is the recent development of new organizations of working women. While these groups differ in many ways --from their relationships to organized labor and the feminist movement, to their structures, strategies and memberships--they share common goals: to improve the status of working women and the conditions under which they work. Working women are, in short, organizing to gain power over their lives, to change the balance of power between themselves and their employers.

This development in itself belies the lingering myths. It could not have come about unless significant numbers of women recognized the permanent nature of their participation in the labor force. To engage in a struggle for higher wages, for greater training and promotional opportunities, and for more humane working conditions and benefits, is to make a long-term commitment to change. Regardless of current

economic conditions, those involved in the struggle recognize
that it will not be easily won.

The membership of these new organizations appears
to parallel closely the composition of the female labor force
where women blue collar workers and college-educated professionals are in the minority. The vast majority are clerical and other non-professional white collar workers. One
out of every three working women holds a clerical job, making office work the largest by far of any single category of
employed women.

Today a new organizing momentum is coming from the
ranks of these women office workers--the segment of the work
force traditionally considered the most difficult to organize.
Labor organizers, who in the past have said "It couldn't be
done, " have pointed to such factors as the relative isolation
of office workers compared to plant or factory workers; the
personal loyalties of secretaries and other office workers to
their "bosses" or supervisors; the superior status that was
attached to office work, that "sheen of respectability" that
factory work lacked; and the notion that women viewed their
jobs as a temporary interlude before marriage and motherhood.

All of that is in flux. The availability of new technology has taken growing numbers of office workers out of
the isolation of one-to-one relationships with their bosses,
and thrown them into work pools not unlike the factory assembly line, where they operate dictating equipment and
word processing machines and are forced to keep to carefully supervised production schedules. Personal loyalty--per-
haps the greatest single obstacle to union organizing--is on
the decline. Instead, loyalty is more a function of tangibles
such as salaries, working conditions, and fringe benefits.

In addition, most women no longer view their jobs as
temporary; economic necessity is their prime motivation for
working. This casts a less flattering light on the trappings
of office work. The importance attached to "respectability"
becomes negligible when the average office worker's wages
are compared to those of factory workers, whose gains are
due to a high level of unionization. And while it may be
acceptable to work as a secretary, typist, file clerk or re-
ceptionist for three or four years at a time, the dead-ended-
ness of those jobs becomes unbearable for many women when
viewed as life-time occupations. The corporation or institu-

tion in this country that provides an upward mobility ladder
for clerical workers still is the rare exception.

As offices become increasingly fertile territory for organizing, labor unions are beginning to fill the void.   Those
that have won elections to represent office workers in recent
years run the gamut from the Office and Professional Employees International Union to the International Brotherhood
of Teamsters and the United Automobile Workers.   The vast
majority of office workers, however, and of working women
in general, are not yet organized.   At present, of the 40
million women who work outside their homes, only some five
and one half million--or slightly under one out of seven--be-
long to labor unions.   However, they represent close to one
quarter of all labor union members.   (Contrary to popular
belief, less than 25 percent of this country's work force is
organized into labor unions.)

As an alternative to union membership, and conceiv-
ably as a transitional step, a growing number of women are
turning for support to new organizations established to combat sex discrimination in the work place.   For some of the
members of these new groups, there may be no union to
join.   For others, there is a fear of management retaliation
against union organizing activity.   For still others, there is
lingering anti-union sentiment.

Whatever the reasons, thousands of women have chosen
to become part of the new organizations of working women
that have emerged within the past few years.   In some cases,
the women are already union members and have joined these
groups to gain added organizational support for problems related to sex discrimination and other women's concerns.   In
the area of office work, the groups are growing so rapidly
both in number and strength that there are those who have
begun to see it as a movement: the office workers' movement.

In Western societies the term "movement" has generally been associated with efforts to bring about radical social, economic and political change based on an ideological
commitment to eliminating injustice or inequality.   Viewed
in that context, it may not be appropriate to describe the
activities of office workers or other working women's groups
in terms of a "movement. "

The nucleus of the organizations in question is less

ideological than pragmatic. While they sometimes join coalitions with feminist, civil rights, environmental or other types
of organizations around broader issues, most of their energies are devoted to seeking concrete gains for women in specific work-related areas. They are less interested in bringing about radical change than they are in enforcing the legislative and policy victories already won by the civil rights and
feminist movements. While they seek to reform the established structures of our society, they are willing also to
work within them.

However, if the word "movement" is used to suggest
the potential for broad-based grass roots organization co-
ordinated through a national network, it may prove to be an
appropriate description after all. In terms of sheer numbers, the potential for working women's organizations seems
unlimited. As new and relatively small as most of them
are, they have already flexed their muscles with big business,
big unions, and big government. Their string of victories
is growing, and with it, the development of new leadership
and membership.

The organizations discussed in this article may or
may not come to resemble--as a collectivity--a movement
for social change. However, based on the experience of
only a few short years indications are that they may make
inroads in two crucial areas: 1) cementing the legislative
gains of the major movements of the past two decades--civil
rights and women's rights; and 2) democratizing and re-
vitalizing one of the most institutionalized and powerful movements of this century--the labor movement.

At present, there are signs that the collective power
of working women will be increasingly felt by their employers, by labor leaders, and by the government agencies that
are supposed to enforce the laws that protect them. The
leaders of the new organizations are educated and experienced.
Their leadership skills are the product of years of involvement in labor, civil rights, feminist and student movements
(and in some cases, several).

The goals of the organizations are clearly defined,
their tactics sophisticated. They have already made a greater impact on many of our institutions than would seem justified based on membership figures alone. Several factors,
however, raise questions about their future momentum and
direction. The discussion that follows will explore the short-

and long-range potential of these groups to develop and utilize
power on behalf of working women.

Four New Working Women's Organizations

The four organizations discussed in this article illustrate the diversity of ways in which employed women are
moving to gain power over their work lives.   These are not
the only such organizations in existence, and still others are
in formation, particularly in the area of office work.   These
four, however, represent a spectrum of organizing styles and
philosophies, and are among the oldest and "most established"
of a new breed of organization that has emerged only since
the early 1970's.

The descriptive material in this and other sections
of this article was supplied by leaders of each organization.[1]
While some of the information we sought was already re-
corded in the form of newsletters and other written documents, much of it was not.   In addition, we were less interested in making "objective" evaluations of each organization than we were in obtaining current self-evaluations from
leaders of each one.   Our goal is not to measure relative
degrees of success in gaining power, but to describe the efforts of a variety of new organizations to help women gain
dignity and control over their lives as workers.

Women Employed

WE was founded in April 1973, in response to a growing number of job discrimination problems brought to the attention of the leadership of Chicago's YWCA.   The original
members included both individual workers with specific grievances and college-educated women activists interested in the
broader issue of sex discrimination in employment.

In five years' time, WE has built an organization with
representatives in over 100 Chicago offices.   Through strategies which include public hearings, media exposés, negotia-
tions and confrontations with corporate and government officials, WE has won major back pay suits, forced large corporations to develop comprehensive affirmative action plans,
pressured the federal government to investigate discrimination in private industries, and brought about a new Illinois
state regulation banning the sale of discriminatory insurance
policies.   It has also been instrumental in organizing a na-

tionwide protest against the Department of Labor's attempts (starting in late 1976) to water down affirmative action policies.

Currently the membership of WE is reported to be one thousand. Almost all of the women work in offices in downtown Chicago--the focus of the organization. Women in management jobs are not eligible for membership. For over two-thirds of its members WE is the first organization they have joined. WE is supported by membership dues (paid on an income-related sliding scale), grass roots fund-raising activities and foundation grants.

Nine to Five

Nine to Five was launched officially in October of 1973. It grew out of a conference held at the Boston YWCA in the spring of 1972, one of whose workshops was for office workers. The ten founding members who met there felt that the time was ripe for creating a voice for women office workers, who represented one-fourth of Boston's work force and were facing increasing job and wage discrimination. In addition, they felt overlooked by the more professionally-oriented women's movement organizations. Original members included both college graduates who could not find professional jobs and ended up in office work with no channels for upward mobility, and women who had been prepared to spend their work lives in offices, but who became increasingly incensed at the working conditions.

Through an effective newsletter, public forums and hearings, demonstrations, petitions, leafletting and in-company task forces to oversee enforcement of anti-discrimination laws and suits, Nine to Five has succeeded in winning a (Massachusetts) state regulation denying licenses to insurance companies that discriminate against women; bringing about major equal pay, promotion and training reforms in several companies; and obtaining a charter from the Service Employees International Union, AFL-CIO, to establish Local 925, thus bringing Boston office workers (who choose to join) into the trade union movement. Nine to Five's early successes, along with those of WE, also served to spark the creation of similar organizations in Cleveland, Dayton, New York and New Haven.

The current dues-paying membership of Nine to Five is over 400, with active members forming the task forces in

many companies within a variety of industries and institutions
in the Boston area.   While some members had previously
been involved in the student and feminist movements, most
are new to political activity.   The organization is supported
by foundation grants, grass roots fund-raising, membership
dues ($5 per year), newsletter subscriptions, the sale of
literature, and fees for speakers and film-showings on office
workers.

Union WAGE (Women's Alliance to Gain Equality)

Union WAGE was founded on International Women's
Day, March 8, 1971, at a NOW (National Organization for
Women) conference in California.   Two of the founding members met each other there, discovered that working women
were not on the agenda, and proceeded to organize a special
panel which fifteen women attended.   They concluded that an
organization was needed to speak to the special concerns of
working women, and met the following week to establish
Union WAGE.

The founding members were trade unionists with a
feminist perspective.   However, the organization was soon
opened to all working women, regardless of the kind of job
they held or whether or not they belonged to a union.   The
original ten-point program was built around the goals of gaining equal rights, equal pay, and equal opportunities for wom-
en workers in society, in unions and in the work place.

Over the past seven years, WAGE has succeeded in
extending several protective laws in California to men (fighting the attempt of employers to abolish all protective laws
for women in the name of "equality"); in holding a number
of major conferences, including a pioneering West Coast organizing conference which brought together for the first time
representatives of independent unions organized by women;
and in publishing a highly successful monthly newspaper, as
well as a pamphlet series on historical and contemporary organizing efforts of working women.

WAGE also works to accomplish its goals by supporting union organizing drives; offering strike support for wom-
en workers; and working in coalition with other groups for
laws and policies that would improve the conditions of all
working women.   Acting independently of the labor union
movement, WAGE supports unionism at the same time that
it often takes positions critical of union bureaucracies.

WAGE has only 200 or so dues-paying members ($7.50 per year) in California (largely in the San Francisco Bay Area) and 50 more in other states. Currently there are 4 chapters (and 2 in formation), all in California. In response to requests from women in different states to form chapters, WAGE is considering the possibility of becoming a national organization. The newspaper has 700 subscribers--400 in California, the rest in other states and a number of foreign countries. The organization is supported by membership dues, newspaper subscriptions, the sale of publications, foundation grants and special fund-raising drives.

Coalition of Labor Union Women

CLUW officially came into being at a Founding Convention held in Chicago in March of 1974 to provide a national voice for union women. The 3,200 women who poured into Chicago from every part of the country represented 58 international unions. The convention was preceded by several regional meetings held in 1973, organized by prominent women trade unionists to determine the extent of interest in forming a women's organization within the labor movement. The catalyst was the growing strength of the women's movement, and particular incidents such as the visit of feminist leaders to AFL-CIO President George Meany to discuss the absence of union women in key leadership positions. The founding members felt that they should be "fighting their own battles."

CLUW's original goals included: affirmative action for women on the job and in union affairs; legislation to improve the status and condition of working women; greater involvement of women in union activities and politics at all levels; and organizing unorganized women workers. Through the considerable visibility that CLUW has gained, some of these goals are beginning to be achieved. For example, more women than ever before have been elected to the executive boards of international unions and are becoming active in their locals.

CLUW's national structure parallels that of most labor unions. It operates locally through chapters (whose membership must represent at least five different unions in order to be chartered) with committees on legislation, political action, education, organizing and strike support, many of which parallel the national CLUW standing committees. In addition to the national quarterly newsletter, most chapters also have their own newsletters.

There are currently about 6,000 dues-paying ($10 per
year) members, some of whom are members at large but
most of whom belong to some 30 active chapters across the
country, the largest of these in New York City and Los
Angeles.   Over 60 percent of the members are government,
white collar and professional workers.   In addition to membership dues, CLUW depends on financial support and in-kind
contributions (printing, mailing privileges, telephone, travel
to CLUW meetings, etc.) from sympathetic unions.   It has
no paid staff, in contrast to the other three organizations described above.

Primary vs. Secondary Organizations

All four organizations discussed here seek to have
their members understand and realize the potential of their
power as change agents.   However, the roles played by WE
and Nine to Five are distinct from those played by CLUW
and WAGE.   The first two groups can be seen as primary
organizations for their members, who (apart from those Nine
to Five members who have joined Local 925) do not belong
to labor unions.   They are the sole source of organizational
support for women struggling with immediate work-related
concerns.   By contrast, all members of CLUW and most
members of WAGE depend primarily on their labor unions
to represent their economic and other job-related concerns.
Therefore, these two groups can be viewed as secondary organizations.   Their goals relate less to the immediate needs
of individual women workers than to long-range changes for
women within the labor movement and in the workplace.

By their very nature, secondary organizations are less
essential in a survival sense to the lives of their members.
Therefore, maintaining a high level of participation and gen-
erating loyalty are among the most difficult challenges that
CLUW and WAGE currently face.   However, WE and Nine to
Five may find themselves in a similar position in the future,
depending on the course they choose to follow.   Many of the
leaders of those two groups see unionization of their members as an ultimate goal.   If they reach that goal, they, too,
will become secondary organizations.

Out of the Past, Into the Present

Only the degree to which working women are mobilizing
today is new, not the act itself.   With the introduction of the

factory system early in the 19th century, the spinning and
weaving jobs that women had always performed at home
moved to the mills and women moved with them. It was not
long before women saw the need to join together for their
mutual protection against wage cuts, machinery speed-ups,
or stretch-outs that increased the amount of work each operator had to do.

Yet as brave and determined as these women were,
most of their organizing efforts failed. Why? What is different about women in the work force today that might lead
to a more favorable prognosis for the success of their organizations?

There were ten basic factors which generally combined to foil working women's organizing efforts during the
century between 1830 and 1930. Although some of the same
kinds of obstacles exist today, circumstances have changed
dramatically. A brief comparison between the past and the
present serves to illustrate the extent of change.

Time and Experience

As recently as 1920, the average employed woman
was 28 years old. She lacked general organizing experience
and found that most trade unions barred her participation.
Moreover, she had little time for organizing. Through most
of the 19th century her work day was 13 hours or more.
Families were large, and labor-saving equipment at home a
rarity. When women did form unions, it was in response to
momentary crises, not with the intention of building on-going
organizations.

In contrast, today's working woman is considerably
older (her average age is 38) and more experienced in organizational activities, including labor unions. Her work
day is generally eight hours long, and her family is likely to
be much smaller and her household chores simplified. Still,
the latter generally remains hers alone--in part because so
many employed women are single heads of household and in
part because household responsibility has only recently begun
to be shared more equitably by the hundreds of working wom-
en. While there might seem to be more "free" time for
organizational involvement, groups like Union WAGE report
that a lack of time available to members for participation in
WAGE activities is a major problem. Critical to each organization discussed here is the maintenance of high member-

ship participation, enthusiasm and loyalty beyond the initial crisis or situation which led to the recruitment of its new members.

Money

Even if working women of the past had foreseen the need to form continuing organizations, they earned too little to support them. Their low-skilled and low-paying jobs provided them with bare subsistence, leaving them cruelly vulnerable to the recurrent economic depressions. There was simply no money to pay union dues or to maintain themselves during a strike action or any dispute with their employers.

Women still hold the lowest paid, lowest skilled jobs, whether in white collar and clerical or blue collar and factory occupations. Although real wages today are markedly higher than the starvation wages women earned in the mills and sweatshops of the past, still there is little left over from the weekly paycheck for dues or savings in the advent of a strike. All of the four groups discussed here see the lack of funds (membership dues are low and paid memberships are relatively small) as a major obstacle to developing their potential power. Currently, they all depend upon outside funding in the form of grants or other financial contributions.

Isolation

Workers of the past were isolated from each other in many significant ways. Because both public transportation and communication were poor, it was difficult to enlist the support of workers at different work sites or in other cities for local labor struggles. In addition, in the period up to World War I, so large a percentage of factory workers were immigrants that language barriers further handicapped organizing efforts and were exploited by employers to keep workers apart.

Today's world of mass communication and transportation has all but eliminated those problems. Moreover, office working arrangements increasingly resemble those in factories, reducing the internal isolation that once kept office workers so divided. Although large numbers of new immigrants continue to find work in American factories, these groups seem to be absorbed more readily, and language barriers do not serve to keep workers apart to the extent that they once did.

Legal and Economic Protection

In the past, workers had no legal protection when they protested employer abuse or exploitation. No National Labor Relations Act existed to grant them the right to bargain collectively. Neither were there built-in governmental supports such as unemployment insurance, food stamps, or welfare to keep an unemployed or striking family from starvation.

Today, Federal and State laws mandate maximum working hours, overtime payments, minimum wages, and compensation for work-related injuries. While legal protection for workers' organizing efforts does exist, its effectiveness remains limited in many cases. Food stamps and welfare are available to the unemployed, and to striking workers in some states after a penalty period.

Employers' Attitudes

As a condition of employment in the last century, workers frequently were forced to sign an "iron clad oath" pledging never to organize or join a labor union. If they broke the pledge, they were fired without recourse. In addition, an employee blacklist circulated the names of the men and women who did so, and no employer in the area would hire them.

For two of the organizations discussed in this article --WE and Nine to Five--the fear of employer hostility remains one of the greatest obstacles to organizing at present. Reprisals--in the form of firings, transfers to less attractive jobs, and the loss of promotions--are an ever-present danger to women workers who have no union protection. Even for those who are unionized, the legal protection that exists can be circumvented easily by employers, just as they can skirt enforcement of the equal employment laws.

Mores of the Times

In the nineteenth century, society frowned harshly upon the assertive woman. The courts, the press, churches and public opinion constituted strong pressure against their organizing. "Proper" women did not speak out in public, attend evening meetings alone or participate freely in gatherings with men. In spite of disapproval and ridicule, a number of women did so anyway. Women's organizations emerged and women leaders came forward, both in workers organizations and in the abolition and suffrage movements.

Clearly, times have changed. Due in large part to the women's movement and the social and cultural changes it embodied, the "assertive" woman is in evidence everywhere-- in the media, in a growing number of political and governmental roles, and in labor organizations. Though women may continue to feel unwelcome in some traditionally male-dominated organizations, increasingly they are overcoming resistance to their participation. Still, anti-union and anti-organizing sentiments--particularly on the part of women in clerical jobs--remain major barriers that the new working women's groups must overcome.

Leadership

A lack of experienced women leaders constituted a major roadblock to women's organizing efforts of the past. The tendency was to turn to men whenever they needed help. As a poignant example, lodges of women workers in the Knights of Labor (a labor federation that preceded the American Federation of Labor and began to organize women workers in 1881) frequently wrote to headquarters pleading that they be permitted to choose a man as president. In part this may have stemmed from the fact that employers negotiating with the Knights would take men more seriously; in part because few women had either the time, training or inclination to tackle the job or fight the social mores of the period.

Even today, many women still turn to men for leadership. This was mentioned by a leader of the Coalition of Labor Union Women as a concern. Women workers still must depend on support from male-dominated unions to bring their needs and concerns to the bargaining table. But with greater education and organizational experience than in the past, skilled women leaders have emerged and built support organizations of their own. Prominent among them are the four discussed here.

Working Men's Attitudes

The lack of interest on the part of men in organizing women workers has a long history. At first men sought to keep women out of the occupations where they worked. When this proved impossible, some unions began around the mid-19th century to call for equal pay for women, knowing that if employers had to pay women the same wages, they would prefer to hire men. Until well into the 20th century a num-

ber of unions barred women from membership.   While nom-
inally on record in support of organizing women workers, the
American Federation of Labor for a long time was headed by
men who favored organizing craft and skilled workers (men),
regarded women as "cheap men, " and believed that industries
where women worked would be too difficult to organize.   With
a few notable exceptions, particularly in the garment unions,
it was not until the 1930's and the advent of industrial unionism and the new Congress of Industrial Organizations (CIO),
that unions began to open doors to women and minority workers.

   Gradually men are accepting the fact that women are
in the work force to stay.   There is also a growing appreciation of the added income they contribute to the family.
Unions that once excluded women from membership no longer
do so; instead labor leaders are recognizing the potential
gains in organizing the increasing numbers of women workers.
Additionally, equal rights legislation makes unions responsible
along with management for ending discrimination in hiring,
pay and promotion.   Yet CLUW leaders report sexism in the
labor movement remains a key problem.   Even labor unions
with as high as 80 percent or more female membership are
headed by men, while few women hold key decision-making
posts in any union.   Union WAGE sees rigid union bureaucra-
cy as a great obstacle.   So is the lack of a tradition of white
collar unionization, recognized by each of the new organizations.

Education

   In the past, women's educational level was low.   Many
joined the work force at a young age, often when they were
still children.   Families put a priority on educating boys.
The low level of education also reflected the numbers of immigrant women in the work force, many of whom were illit-
erate.

   Today's working woman has more education than ever
before, sometimes more than men.   The Monthly Labor Review of February 1975 reported that among workers who have
completed high school (and have not gone on to college) over
8 percent more working women than men are graduates--
44. 2 percent compared to 36 percent.   (At the college level,
however, 16. 4 percent of working men, compared to 12. 8
percent of women are graduates.)   This rise in educational
attainment contributes to the working woman's growing aware-

ness that she is in the work force for much of her life, that
she is most often locked into a low-paying job with little
chance for upward mobility, and that she is quite often capable of performing at a higher level. This key frustration
might be the basis for a momentum never before possible.

The Presence of Women in the Work Force

Once it was true that women constituted a low percentage of the work force, were intermittent workers, and
suffered society's scorn if they worked for a living. All
this had an adverse effect on their organizing efforts of the
past.

The most significant change in organizing potential
lies in the sheer numbers of women in the work force--today
more than half of all adult women between 18 and 64 years
old are employed, compared with little more than 10 percent
in 1900. Increasingly, families depend on two psychecks
(and sometimes three), while growing numbers of women are
single heads of household. The spiraling divorce rate itself
is evidence of women's need for economic independence. It
would be surprising if these circumstances did not translate
themselves into a new awareness of women's need to exercise their collective power to press for dignity and equality
in the work place.

Working Women and Women's Movements: Past and Present

What was the relationship of working women's organizations of the past to other women's organizing efforts of
the time and what can be learned from a look at this relationship? The 20th century brought with it the National
Women's Trade Union League, founded in 1903, which united
working women and middle class "allies" for the first time
in a national organization. The goal of the League was to
help women organize and to break down the barriers to their
entrance into labor unions. As an outgrowth of a reform era
which also gave birth to the social work movement, educated
middle class women offered their energies and organizational
abilities to provide opportunities for working women to develop their own leadership skills. One important outgrowth
was that a number of working women went on to devote their
lives to the labor movement as organizers, educators, and
grievance representatives.

Recognizing the importance of involving government in women's concerns the League also pioneered in lobbying for women's issues and protective labor laws. Among the direct outgrowths of its efforts were the establishment of the Children's Bureau and the Women's Bureau in the U.S. Department of Labor.

Another role that the League played was that of buffer between the suffrage movement and working women's organizations. It saw the need to draw the two together, to help both groups develop their potential strength and cooperate on issues of common concern. However, when the suffragists failed to take sufficient interest in the concerns of women workers or to reach out and include them in the struggle to win the right to vote, the League helped working women form their own suffrage organizations.

Again today, when working woman's organizations have emerged to help their members gain power over their lives as women and workers, they are functioning independently from the "mainstream" of the feminist movement. However, individual leaders of the new organizations, many of whom are college-educated feminists themselves often assume the role that the League once did--that of a buffer or a bridge to feminist organizations. CLUW, for example, is a member of ERAmerica, the coalition of women's organizations formed to work for ratification of the Equal Rights Amendment.

Although many of today's feminist organizations have made overtures to working women, essentially they have not reached them. Ratification of the Equal Rights Amendment is often viewed as a contemporary parallel to the drive to win the right to vote. In the context of the recent problematic history of the ERA, one might well ask: Are bridges between the feminist movement and working women's organizations essential to the survival of both? Could one force continue to grow without the existence of the other? If not, how will those bridges be strengthened?

Kinship to Unionism or Feminism?: A Wide Spectrum

The members of all four organizations share two common denominators: all are workers and all are women. As working women they all have experienced discrimination based on sex, which is what motivated them to become active

in the struggle to combat it.   Beyond those basic similarities
lie a number of differences reflected in the style, structure,
goals and membership bases of the organizations.

It is useful to explore some of these differences in
the context of both unionism and feminism--the two movements
that provided the legislative, political and social foundation
upon which these new organizations were built.   Within this
context, the four new groups fall along a spectrum.   At one
end, the organization most influenced by the labor movement
(CLUW) appears to be the least influenced by the feminist
movement.   At the other end, the organization least directly
influenced by the labor movement (WE), appears to be the
most influenced by the feminist movement.   Union WAGE and
Nine to Five fall between those two, and both play an inter-
facing role between the two movements.

CLUW was organized by a group of nationally recognized women who held key leadership positions--both elected
and appointed--within their international unions.   The national structure they established resembles that of a large union,
with tight organization, an extensive governing body at the
national level which makes policy decisions, and carefully
outlined procedures for many of its activities.   It operates
within the constraints of labor movement policies.

Since all CLUW members must first be union members in order to join, they are already part of formal negotiating bodies which protect their rights as workers and
bargain for them on wages and other economic issues.
CLUW is not, therefore, involved with members' job-related
concerns, but rather with the generic "bread and butter" issues that cross union lines.

CLUW works indirectly on the concerns of unionized
working women by raising issues--ranging from equal pay to
paid maternity leaves and improved health and safety regu-
lations--that may eventually be adopted as bargaining issues
by the individual unions to which CLUW members belong.
The strategy is one of internal pressure applied by members
on their own unions, and public consciousness-raising techniques employed by CLUW to impact upon the labor movement as a whole.

The primary direct function that CLUW serves for
its members is that of a training ground for leadership development, to help women move up in their own unions.

Through membership in local chapters, CLUW members have
an opportunity to develop a variety of skills--public speaking,
lobbying, campaign organizing--which they then utilize in their
own union settings to pursue their own goals.   While there is
no overt effort to do so, the thrust of the organization clearly
serves to move CLUW members toward many of the goals
espoused by the feminist movement--both those that relate to
equal status for women in our society and those that relate
to specific women's issues.

Union WAGE was founded by women trade unionists
who also considered themselves feminists.   Membership,
however, soon expanded to include women workers who were
not unionized, many of whom are more concerned about work
issues than "women's" issues.   By comparison to CLUW, the
structure is highly informal and flexible.   For many years,
the newspaper was the major organizational vehicle, with
chapter formation coming at a later stage.

As an independent group, WAGE often plays the role
of labor movement critic.   It sees itself as an outside pressure group working to give women's concerns and issues a
higher priority within labor unions and to help unorganized
women gain union protection.   It involves itself directly in
such activities as supporting organizing drives and strikes of
women workers; helping WAGE members develop organizing
skills and strategies; and endorsing internal union struggles
for rank and file democracy.

Although it sometimes takes a critical stance, WAGE
has more allegiance to the union movement than to the feminist movement.   Its primary concern lies in protecting the
rights of women workers.   Not long ago it was involved in
a struggle with feminist leaders over the timing of the move
to ratify the California State ERA.   WAGE wanted to insure
that prior to ratification, protective labor laws that benefitted
women would be legally safeguarded, i. e. , not abolished in
the name of equality, but extended to men.   It was unsuccessful in winning feminist groups over to its strategy, and many
of those protective laws were lost.   On the whole, however,
WAGE is more overtly feminist than is CLUW.

As opposed to CLUW and WAGE, Nine to Five was
organized by women, many of whom were avowedly feminist,
but none of whom was a union member.   Its organization is
loosely structured and counts heavily on its newsletter and
leafletting to make itself known.

Since its inception, Nine to Five has offered to its
members a place to come for advice in handling individual
job-related problems, as well as a public voice to bring attention to the shared concerns of Boston's women office
workers. The membership has rotated considerably, since
many women become less active once their own problems
are resolved. Other women are motivated by the feminist
movement both to advance into higher job categories and to
become involved on a longer term basis with the broader
issues of sex discrimination, the rights of office workers,
and working conditions.

As Nine to Five began to succeed in winning reforms
such as equal pay and promotional opportunities for women
in different industries and companies, the creation of a
formal bargaining unit for office workers became a realistic
goal. In 1975, Local 925, affiliated with the Service Employees International Union, was established. The union provides legal protection as well as economic benefits for women
who, in the past, were threatened by the loss of their jobs
if their organizing activities became known to management.

A large number of Nine to Five members choose not
to join the union. For them, the parent organization continues to serve some of the same functions as a union would.
At the same time, Nine to Five is a vital part (along with
Women Employed) of the growing national network of women
office workers groups, whose most recent efforts helped to
protect the U.S. Department of Labor's affirmative action
regulations for women and minority group workers. [2]

Nine to Five also serves as a kind of interface between the world of office workers, the women's movement
and the labor movement. Despite the continued hesitancy of
most women office workers to unionize, Nine to Five's leadership predicts that union interest in organizing them will increase and that growing numbers of women will join. The
unionization of a sizable proportion of women office workers
clearly would have a major impact on both the labor movement and the corporate world.

Of the four organizations discussed here, Women Employed's founding members were the most clearly identified
with the feminist movement. Several were well-known activists in Chicago's major feminist organizations, who decided to devote their energies to the issue of sexism in the
work place, particularly as it affected women office workers.
None of the members belongs to a labor union.

Successful organizing campaigns in downtown banks, insurance companies, law firms and a variety of corporations attracted a growing membership of women who identified with neither the feminist movement nor the labor movement. Relatively few of the members had any organizational affiliation prior to joining WE.

Like Nine to Five, WE helps members with individual problems at the same time that it conducts campaigns against specific corporations or industries, and puts pressure on the government to enforce policy and law.   To that extent it functions much as a union does.   Unlike Nine to Five, WE has not become affiliated with organized labor.   It has a larger and more structured membership than Nine to Five, with task forces in over 100 offices that have made women's collective power felt.   To develop women leaders, WE employs what it calls its secret weapon, an Internal Network known as "IN."   Individual women office workers gather information and develop a core of women to share concerns and put this information to work for them.   Without union protection, however, members are still vulnerable to harassment by employers and the struggle continues for economic and other benefits that might be won more easily through union-negotiated contracts.

Although WE leaders anticipate some form of union affiliation in the future, they have resisted such action thus far for three principal reasons: 1) there is still considerable anti-union sentiment among office workers; 2) there is strong management opposition to unionization; and 3) there is no union whose current leadership is considered by WE sufficiently sensitive to the concerns of women office workers. WE has become powerful enough to win a number of job-related demands.   Before sharing any of its power with a labor union, WE can be expected to negotiate for some of its own demands, many of which relate to the goals of the feminist movement.

As an aside it should be noted that the leaders of all four organizations consider themselves feminists, but are sensitive to the fact that the majority of their members--as well as their enormous untapped potential constituencies-- do not.   This has reinforced the specific focus of all four groups on developing the power to bring about equality and dignity for women in the work place through work-related organizations.   Other feminist concerns, such as those related to changes in the roles of women and men in marriage and family life, have no place on their agendas.

Strategies for Developing Collective Power

The strategies used by all four organizations are
adaptations of techniques used by workers ever since they
first discovered the power inherent in combination. For
each, the employer is still "the enemy" and the penalty for
active involvement in organizing--at least for many members
of the three organizations less closely allied with the labor
movement--can still be job loss. There is general recognition that the employer gains by "keeping women down" and
will oppose improvements for women workers unless pressured into acceptance.

An illustration of employer opposition to women's organizing efforts was reported by Nine to Five. Employers
of women office workers in the Boston area not only work
independently to discourage their employees from joining Nine
to Five, they have also organized themselves into a consortium called the Boston Survey Group. The group meets
regularly to compare notes on wage rates, in an effort (thus
far successful) to keep down the city's pay scale.

Carefully planned and executed strategies thus become
essential in the efforts of each organization to exercise power. The membership must understand that goals are not
easily attained. The leaders must find the means to sustain
enthusiasm and interest in organizing campaigns that may
continue over the course of several years. To accomplish
their goals, each organization uses five key strategies: lobbying and political action; education and leadership training;
direct action organizing; written communications; and publicity.

Lobbying and Political Action

Each organization mobilizes its members in support
of specific federal laws and regulations, just as have trade
unions since the days when they fought for free public education, hours limitation, factory inspection and an end to child
labor. Among the four organizations discussed here, some
current areas of national legislative and policy concern include: full employment legislation, strengthened affirmative
action and health and safety regulations, a higher minimum
wage, national health insurance, pregnancy disability insurance, child care, and the Equal Rights Amendment. At the
state level, the groups have worked to bring attention to--and
in some cases won reforms in--areas of special concern to
women workers such as insurance regulations and extension

of some protective laws to men. On both national and state
levels there is increasing cooperation with other organizations
sharing similar economic concerns. The new coalitions that
are forming enhance the power of each of the participating
groups.

Lobbying involves women workers in visiting elected
officials in state capitals or in Washington, D. C. ; in preparing and delivering testimony before governmental committees; and in organizing letter-writing, telegram and peti-
tion-signing campaigns. The new organizations have begun
to mobilize politically behind candidates who support their
interests. It is not the techniques that are new or different;
the difference lies in the number of working women who are
getting involved in political issues and campaigns, asserting
their right to be heard, supporting women as candidates and
running for office in their own organizations. Ultimately,
the cumulative effect will be felt at all levels of politics,
the government and labor unions.

Education and Leadership Training

The first workers' education "specialist" in labor history was a woman. During early 1840's, mill worker Sarah
Bagley held classes for her fellow workers in her own board-
inghouse room after working hours, preparing for the day
when they would organize the Lowell (Massachusetts) Female
Labor Reform Association. Today, the four groups discussed
here use a wide range of workers' education techniques to inform their members and to build leadership skills. There
is a sense of having to make up for lost time, for a lack of
organizing history (particularly on the part of office workers),
and for a lack of trained and paid staff (particularly in the
case of CLUW which has no paid staff) to move the organization forward.

Among the techniques used by the four organizations
are: conferences and conventions; special training institutes,
workshops and short courses for members through university
labor extension programs; special meetings with guest speakers on issues of concern to members; and discussion groups
that focus on such problems as assessing and maximizing the
power of women workers in a given situation. The step-by-
step planning and running of such education programs is considered as important to the educational and leadership development process as the programs themselves.

As an illustration, WE relies on both formal and informal leadership training. In addition to sending members
to the Midwest Academy (a training institute in Chicago), it
uses such devices as role plays to teach members how to
recruit others, to develop strategy and to negotiate. But in
addition, every meeting and group action is seen as a form
of training for newer leaders. CLUW sees its chapter and
national education programs--whether on specific issues or
on political actions such as lobbying--as key methods for developing leadership and increasing the participation of members in their own labor unions. Through this increased
participation, CLUW seeks to develop a greater awareness
within unions of issues important to women members, often
neglected in the past, and to prepare more women to run for
union offices.

Direct Action Organizing

Direct action organizing is seen by all four groups as
the most effective way to involve members in learning by
doing and to enable them to see the concrete results of their
collective activity. These methods, too, are borrowed from
the past. The Consumers' League of the late 19th and early
20th centuries, for example, promoted boycotts of stores
and the products of firms not supporting fair working conditions and staged street demonstrations to call further attention to their campaigns. In recent times, unions have boy-
cotted Farrah pants and are currently boycotting the products
of the J. P. Stevens Company in support of the right of
Stevens' employees to organize and bargain collectively.

These methods, however, have been honed to a sophisticated edge and fused with others--such as confrontation
techniques that grew out of the civil rights and women's
movements--by organizations such as Women Employed and
Nine to Five. Each of WE's campaigns lasts for a year,
sometimes longer. The first step involves compilation of
individual complaints from office workers in a large, downtown Chicago firm. WE then attempts to meet with management to discuss the workers' grievances. If the results are
unsuccessful it proceeds to file charges with appropriate
government agencies. Simultaneously it launches a publicity
campaign against the company through leaflets, press re-
leases and noontime demonstrations outside the company.

Next it tries to move government agencies to enforcement action through urging area congressional repre-

sentatives to put pressure on these agencies.   Action against
"related targets" such as individual members of the firm's
Board of Directors, industry associations to which the firm
belongs, and large corporate customers of the firm comes
next.   At the same time, WE works from the inside to
strengthen the network of concerned employees and assists
them in organizing meetings with supervisors in efforts to
resolve specific problems.

Action does not stop there.   WE monitors the work
of government agencies and exposes any laxness in enforcement of the equal employment laws.   Where an agency is
seen as "falling down on the job," hearings are organized
and government officials are requested to discuss their
agency's performance and answer questions.   WE prepares
position papers on government inaction or on proposed changes
in regulations that would be detrimental to women workers,
and testifies before congressional committees.   It combines
these actions with mass rallies to promote additional support
for its local campaigns, through letter-writing and petitions.
In many instances it forms coalitions with other women's
and civil rights groups similarly affected.   Politicians are
asked to present their positions in writing prior to an election for the group to review.

Nine to Five, with a similar program, works on a
public, city-wide level as well as on an in-company level,
where members form task forces to monitor their firm's
compliance with the equal opportunity laws and to generate
internal pressure to resolve problems.   If a firm refuses
to cooperate, pressure is put on government officials at all
levels to launch an investigation, while a lawsuit is brought
against the company in question.   Also, says one of the
leaders, "We publicize widely.   A suit against one company
serves as a warning to others."

In the words of a WE leader: "The focus is on defining specific campaigns, developing a strategy which includes analysis of all possible targets and actions to be tak-
en, and working out a timeline."   Not only is the goal to
build the organization and to solve a specific problem, but
also to give women a sense of their own power through experiences demonstrating that it is possible to bring about
change.

Written Communications

Each of the four organizations issues a regular news-

paper or newsletter, which is considered essential for keeping
its members informed about issues and activities. It is also
used to recruit new members, and in some cases to educate
the public about the organizations' goals and activities. In
the case of CLUW, which has both national and local chapter
newsletters, publishing news items on individual chapter activities generates ideas for other chapters at the same time
that it recognizes chapter accomplishments.

Union WAGE is the only one of the four organizations
which publishes a newspaper (as distinct from a newsletter).
It is highly sophisticated and has subscribers throughout the
U. S. and in several foreign countries. Union WAGE is
unique in that it is the only newspaper that devotes its attention solely to issues pertaining to women workers and organized labor. While California-based activity is given the
most prominent coverage, other labor struggles of women
are covered as well. Exposés in WAGE's newspaper have
influenced the actions of California public officials, corporate
managers and labor leaders. Through the newspaper, WAGE
has developed a broader power base than one dependent on its
members alone.

All four organizations supplement their news vehicles
with leaflets and brochures, most of which are published on
the proverbial shoestring with "labor donated." In addition
to their uses as communications and education tools, the publications of all four groups serve as techniques for developing members' skills in areas such as writing, editing, lay-
out and design. These skills are transferable to a variety
of other organizing and political activities.

Publicity

For all four organizations, a major goal is increasing
their membership base. All are quite small in comparison
to their potential constituencies, which they have only just
begun to tap. The use of the public media is central to this
effort, and to the fund-raising efforts on which each organization depends for its existence. Membership dues are low
and membership itself relatively small, so fund raising becomes a critical activity--at least for the time being--for
the support of the new organizations.

Each of the organizations discussed has developed a
power and an influence that far exceeds its numbers. Each

recognizes the importance of cultivating and utilizing the climate of the times to maximum advantage, and of building a
sense of history among the women it seeks to organize. Because the fact that today's working women are organizing is
news and the mass media covers at least certain special
events and activities of these new groups, such coverage is
used to build momentum and strength and present the organizations goals to the outside world.

Conclusion

The four groups discussed here have generated a new
momentum. It is appropriate, in conclusion, to pose some
questions about where this momentum might lead. Can it be
sustained? What could the future hold for these new working
women's organizations, and for others like them that are
emerging? Will it indeed become a movement? Three possible scenarios for the future suggest themselves, and are
presented here tentatively in the hope that they will generate
discussion and further thought.

From Network to Association?

In November of 1976, representatives of Women Employed and Nine to Five--along with those of similar organizations of clerical workers from cities as scattered as San
Francisco, New Haven, Cleveland and New York--met in
Germantown, Ohio to develop plans for a loose-knit but cooperative network to coordinate and strengthen their efforts
at a national level. While each of these groups seems to
eschew formal organizational structures and seeks to preserve
its autonomy locally, the potential impact on federal legislation and policy of such a nationally concerted effort is considerable.

Each group at the Germantown meeting agreed to spon-
sor, during the month of February 1977, a major conference
in its own city to call attention to the dangers to women and
minorities of the proposed weakening of the Equal Employment Opportunities Commission's affirmative action guidelines
--the first major target of the network.

A proposal for foundation support of this nascent network of six office worker groups was funded in the spring of
1977. [3] It is now possible to foresee the emergence of a national association of office workers retaining individual group

autonomy, but joining in efforts to affect both corporate policies and federal legislation concerning equal employment.
Foundation support makes possible the centralized training
of leaders to spearhead new office worker organizations in
other cities, and the launching of sustained national campaigns to highlight issues of concern to office workers--a
massive consciousness-raising effort.

Precedent for the development of such an association
can be found in the National Education Association and the
American Nurses Association, to name just two. While both
these organizations still resist calling themselves labor unions, in almost every respect they function just as do international unions with member chapters. Similarly, as association of office workers might function independently of the
rest of the labor movement, while increasingly taking on
trade union roles. For example, it could deal directly with
the National Labor Relations Board, bargain collectively for
its members, and administer contracts. If it does develop
a formalized structure and financial self-sufficiency, it could
bypass the labor movement and offer an alternative to unionization for office workers.

The Local 925 Model

Because women in the past were excluded from participation in most unions, they formed unions of their own.
However, one of the lessons of American labor history is
that independent organizations of women workers, unaffiliated
with strong national unions, never succeeded. Today, however, as Ed Townsend of the Christian Science Monitor (December 13, 1976) points out, "Organized labor is wooing
women workers." He outlines labor union plans to fight for
such benefits as disability pay for pregnancy-related illness,
even though that fight may involve persuading men in some
unions to trade off contract demands that are in their own
self-interest, and to support this concern of women members
instead.

This is part of a new recognition by labor leaders
that women constitute an increasing proportion both of the
work-force and of unions. In recent times, the over-all
membership of labor unions has been stationary, with membership loss being replaced by newly-organized workers in
teacher, government and hospital unions, many of whose
members are female. These and other white collar and
service occupations have replaced blue collar industrial jobs

as the areas of greatest organizing potential. Not only are
they still largely non-union, but also they include job categories where close to two-thirds of the country's 38 million
working women are employed. Moreover, the Bureau of
Labor Statistics predicts that by 1985 the number of workers
in these occupations will increase by 50 percent.

The potential for new labor union membership is dramatic. There is growing evidence that the labor movement
is well aware of this. As reported in the Wall Street Journal (January 18, 1977):

> Organizing new members gets a boost at the AFL-
> CIO. The labor federation sets up an inter-union
> coordinating committee to promote organizing simi-
> lar in structure to its potent political operations
> committee. Though officials hope organizing activ-
> ity eventually will equal political efforts, the new
> group begins without the money base afforded to
> political action.

If the labor movement should actively finance efforts in this
direction, some questions arise concerning how the movement
itself might undergo change in the process. Some answers
are suggested in the model presented by Local 925 of the
Service Employees International Union, AFL-CIO. Organized
by Nine to Five, whose members have the option of joining
the union, Local 925 has a high degree of autonomy within
SEIU structure and its independent organizing activities are
encouraged and financed. The local enjoys such benefits as
the expertise of the International's staff, and the use of the
resources of a nationwide organization.

Karen Nussbaum, Local 925 organizer, believes this
model offers a viable option. Speaking at a Midwest Academy alumni retreat in August, 1976, she told of Nine to
Five's search for a union that would take its members in.

> We approached 10 different unions and said, "We're
> 9 to 5, an organization of women office workers.
> We represent 200,000 women. We want money and
> we want complete autonomy."

> Well, most of them were polite. They said, "...
> we're just not able to do that within our interna-
> tional constitution." Or, "Do you have any collec-
> tive bargaining agreements?" Or things like that.

Luckily, SEIU, the Service Employees Union, said,
"Sure, okay, we'll give it a go," and gave us a
charter last summer. [4]

She went on to describe the most startling aspect of
the new local's organizing efforts: the discovery of how hard
it was. Getting a majority of workers signed up and winning
a collective bargaining agreement was very different from
Nine to Five's demonstrations and easy newspaper publicity.
But the prior experience with Nine to Five and the contacts
through that organization proved eminently helpful. The new
local needed all the support it could get, for resistance from
employers was far worse than anticipated.

This energetic young leader sees a rising tide of interest on the part of labor unions in office workers, although
she questions whether unions are not waiting for "the groundwork that the women's movement is doing ... and choosing
their own time very carefully so that they don't have to suffer so many of the losses." Her recommendation for office
workers is to begin with Nine to Five type organizations,
altering the line "a little bit more away from the emphasis
on sex discrimination and more towards emphasis on the
right to have a say," which she feels leads more naturally
into collective bargaining and union organization. The possibility exists for acting together "to try to concentrate our
impact within one union," she states, but views the biggest
problem that of maintaining organizational continuity. The
goal must be large scale organization of clerical workers.
"That's what we're struggling for," she affirms.

Direct Outreach as an Approach

The last of the three scenarios focuses on CLUW as
a potential bridge between the labor movement and unorganized women workers. While CLUW is open only to union
members, one of its four major goals is to organize unorganized women workers. At present it lacks the resources to
pursue this goal. However, given the right circumstances,
we can envision a concerted drive to bring unorganized wom-
en into the labor movement, coupling the expertise of active
CLUW members with the financial resources of the labor
movement. Such action is in line with the AFL-CIO's recently established inter-union organizing committee.

With only some 6,000 members, CLUW nonetheless
has effected change in the labor movement. The formation

of local CLUW chapters and CLUW groups in individual local
unions has brought growing visibility to union women's concerns.   More importantly, women unionists have moved into
staff jobs and have been elected to an increasing number of
posts at every level: shop stewards, local presidents and
international executive board members.   Unions have passed
resolutions supporting women's issues.   Their newspapers
have featured news of women members as they rarely did in
the past.   CLUW is credited with the AFL-CIO's reversal of
its anti-ERA stand and its now active support of the Equal
Rights Amendment.   And in AFL-CIO headquarters, where
every department head with the exception of the librarian is
a man, a CLUW member has been named Associate Director
of the Civil Rights Department in charge of Women's Activities, while four union women have been appointed to the
previously all-male Civil Rights Committee.

        Still, only about 7 percent of top union leaders, both
elected and appointed, are female, while some 22 percent of
union membership is, and no woman yet heads a major union
or sits on the AFL-CIO Executive Council (made up of union
presidents).   There is considerable room for change, and
CLUW has begun that process.   But to maintain its momentum, CLUW leaders are aware that women must win more
proportionate representation in policy-making roles.   This is
a realistic possibility only if the labor movement grows and
its composition changes.

        Since the movement's growth depends to a great ex-
tent on organizing women workers--an increasing proportion
of the work-force--one of CLUW's major goals and the interests of the labor movement coincide.   If office workers
were organized, they alone could increase total union membership by 50 percent.   Given the labor movement's growing
interest in women workers and the energies that CLUW might
channel into organizing if provided with union backing and
financial support, it would appear in the best interests of
both groups to put to the test CLUW's hypothesis that women
are best able to organize other women.

        It would require carefully coordinated effort and train-
ing of organizing staff.   The highest degree of tact and diplomacy would be needed, plus long-term funding over a period
of years.   It would mean compromises to cope with jurisdic-
tional problems--perhaps the greatest obstacle to success.
Commitments might be needed to new locals, or even to new
unions organized as a result of such a campaign, that they

could maintain their own identity and modus operandi within a labor union structure. However, strong precedent within the labor movement already exists for union groupings by occupational jurisdictions. There are departments of the AFL-CIO that coordinate the interests of public workers, transportation, and building trades workers in different unions. There is also a special department concerned with clerical and technical workers. As office workers in different industries increasingly seek organization, labor unions will have to work out ways to avoid destructive competition.

This paper has explored a relatively new phenomenon: the development in the 1970's of new working women's organizations that carry with them great potential for change. The authors sense some new directions, but recognize that it is far too soon to predict outcomes. Each of the three scenarios outlined above implies that working women will continue to develop their collective power. If Women Employed, Nine to Five, Union WAGE and CLUW are representative of the new wave of working women, it is clear that that wave has yet to crest.

Even though many working women do not feel entirely comfortable with some aspects of the feminist movement, increasingly they acknowledge their debt to it. In the long run, these new working women's groups can bring a necessary new vitality to the feminist movement. For they are, after all, women's organizations, bringing together working women who seek a pragmatic approach to dealing with their concerns. Women's jobs and their dignity and sense of self depend on them. As one union woman put it: "When you are trying to organize for power, you really know that you need each other." That is the message that has sustained the labor movement, the women's movement and all other successful social movements since the beginning of time.

NOTES

1. For Women Employed: Day Creamer, Executive Director and Jean Hoffenkamp, Chairwoman; for Nine to Five: Ellen Cassedy, Staff Director; for Union WAGE: Joyce Maupin, Founding Member and for many years Executive Secretary and Manya Argue, President; for the Coalition of Labor Union Women: Joyce Miller, National President.
2. In August 1976, the U.S. Department of Labor proposed

to weaken Office of Federal Contract Compliance rules.
Women office worker groups and other civil rights organizations mobilized to defeat these revisions.
3. The six include Women Employed in Boston, Women Office Workers in New York, Nine to Five in Boston,
Cleveland Women Working, Dayton Women Working,
and Women Organized for Employment in San Francisco. In July, 1978, the six, together with the National Commission on Working Women, received funding to set up a program of educational and career
counseling for women in banking, insurance and publishing in their cities.
4. This and other quotations from Nussbaum "Unions and
the Working Women's Movement," is based on a presentation at the Midwest Academy Annual Alumni Retreat, William Bay, Wisconsin August 6-8, 1976.
Chicago, Midwest Academy, December 1976.

Chapter 9

ORGANIZING FOR POLITICAL POWER:
The National Women's Political Caucus

by Rona F. Feit

It has been over eight years since a group of women
leaders announced that women were going to unite to elect
women to public office, to free politics from the domination
of men in smoke filled rooms and to bring a new humanism
into the halls of power. The vehicle for this move for political power was to be a multi-partisan, feminist organization called the National Women's Political Caucus. Now, as
women struggle to get the Equal Rights Amendment ratified,
to keep the right to abortion from being pruned out of shape
by legislation and regulation, to improve the persistently inferior economic position of women, to elect anything like a
proportionate share of women to the House and the Senate,
and to have women appointed to the Supreme Court and the
Cabinet, an appraisal of women's move for political power
and the role of the Caucus seems in order.

That women have more political power today than they
had eight years ago seems undeniable; that they have less
than they hoped for, expected or need is also undeniable.
The status of women's drive for political power cannot be
attributed merely to the effectiveness or lack of effectiveness
of Caucus leadership. Some understanding of the problems
women face in taking and using political power can be gained,
however, from a critical review of the Caucus experience.
Despite many difficulties, the Caucus has survived and grown.
Understanding the reasons for its survival and growth provides some basis for appraising its strengths and weaknesses
and for estimating its future political impact. What follows
is one woman's attempt to make such an analysis and judgment. It is the attempt of someone involved in the Caucus
from the beginning as a member of the Initiating Committee,
the first National Policy Council and then the National Advisory Board. It is based on personal observation, private
records, conversations with others active in the Caucus, and

184

an extensive review of Caucus documents, both internal and public. [1]

The National Women's Political Caucus was founded in July 1971 in a conference of about 300 women leaders that Newsweek magazine called "rowdy" but which, it also noted, produced a "plausible definition and a strategy for a women's political movement where none had existed before. "[2] The Caucus was launched quickly in the public mind as an important new political development by extensive media reporting of its founding and of its subsequent activities. The early attention paid to it probably resulted from the status and celebrity of many of its founders and first leaders and from its potential for influencing the 1972 Presidential nominations and elections. After that, it rapidly became the media's main source of information and comment about women in politics.

The Caucus pledged itself in its initial "statement of purpose" to oppose racism, sexism, institutional violence and poverty through the election and appointment of women to public office, party reform, and the support of women's issues and feminist candidates across party lines. [3] At first, it was a loose umbrella organization coordinating mostly autonomous but like-minded state and local caucuses. National leadership was provided for the first 19 months by a National Policy Council which included among its members: Betty Friedan, originator of the Caucus idea and author of The Feminine Mystique; Bella Abzug, then a Congresswoman and a major moving force in the Caucus; Congresswoman Shirley Chisholm; Gloria Steinem, then a contributing editor of New York magazine; Shana Alexander, then Editor-in-Chief of McCall's magazine; Liz Carpenter, former Press Secretary to Mrs. Lyndon B. Johnson; Virginia Allan, former chairwoman of President Nixon's Task Force on Women's Rights and Responsibilities; LaDonna Harris, Indian rights leader; Myrlie Evers, California civil rights leader; Dorothy Height, President of the National Council of Negro Women; Fannie Lou Hamer, Mississippi civil rights leader; Olga Madar, then vice-president of the United Automobile Workers; Beulah Sanders, then vice-president of the National Welfare Rights Organization; Wilma Scott Heide, then President of the National Organization for Women; Elly Peterson, former vice-chairperson of the Republican National Committee; and Jill Ruckelshaus, then a White House aide to President Nixon. [4]

The Caucus soon began to build a more formal nation-

wide membership organization with member caucuses of varying strengths in most of the states and with provision for national conventions of elected delegates every two years to set
policy and elect officers.   It has gradually evolved into two
basic legal entities: the non-profit membership corporation
known as the National Women's Political Caucus, Inc. and
the political committee known as the National Women's Political Caucus Campaign Committee.   The membership corporation has developed a varied structure of standing committees,   Task Forces,   and special interest caucuses.   It has
spawned related but independent organizations such as Wom-
en's Education for Delegate Selection (WEDS), the National
Women's Education Fund (NWEF) and the N. W. P. C. Equal
Rights Amendment Fund, Inc.   WEDS was created temporarily
in 1972 to be the non-profit funding and organizing vehicle
for the dramatically successful Caucus-backed drive to increase the number of women delegates at the 1972 national
party nominating conventions.   NWEF was created later to
be the permanent non-profit vehicle for other needed research
and education efforts related to women in politics.   The ERA
Fund is the fund-raising vehicle for Caucus efforts to insure
ratification of the equal rights amendment to the Constitution
by electing or defeating key state legislators in unratified
states.

The Caucus network of organizational and individual
supporters and friends now extends its influence beyond the
reach of its formal membership rolls and budget.   Increasingly, it has joined issue coalitions and operated in joint efforts with other women's groups as the political insider and
tactician.   A notable example has been its creation and leadership of the Coalition on Women's Appointments, a group
of more than 50 women's organizations which has had a major role in finding and placing qualified women in high level
Carter administration posts.   Another example was its creation and leadership of the Pro-Plan Caucus at the first National Women's Conference in Houston, Texas in 1977.   The
Pro-Plan Caucus advocated passing all the points of the proposed National Plan of Action essentially without amendment.
The intention was to avoid wrangling and delaying tactics that
might make it impossible to get through the agenda and give
an impression that women were hopelessly divided over issues.   The Caucus was largely responsible for the highly
disciplined and successful floor operation that kept debate
and amendments to a minimum and allowed the conference to
move smoothly through a complex and controversial set of
resolutions.   While the Caucus cooperates with other groups

working for ratification of the Equal Rights Amendment, the
NWPC-ERA Fund, Inc. proceeds with its own highly effective
elective strategy. As one element of a coalition struggle to
preserve abortion rights, the Caucus led an important and
well organized grass roots lobbying campaign against Congressional cutbacks on abortion funding.

The political impact of the Caucus has been widely
acknowledged by the press and politicians. As early as 1972,
in one of the first but certainly not the last of such articles,
the New York Times reported that the Caucus had impressed
New York State politicians who had "shrugged off" such feminist movements "only a year ago," and that "a majority of
male politicians interviewed felt that there would be a very
strong pressure for the nomination of female candidates ...
in the next two years."[5]

Aside from helping to place women in public office or
to win legislative and party fights, the Caucus can justly
claim credit for a much more basic accomplishment, creating women as a political interest group. At the time the
Caucus was born, women as a group were not a political
factor of any importance. The issue of how many women
were serving in political leadership roles had not scratched
the public consciousness. No one, in fact, monitored or
knew how many women there were in public office nationwide.
The representation of women at national party conventions
was of interest only to a small group of reformers, and the
concept of women's issues as a sub-group of political issues
did not exist. There were no national campaign funds for
women candidates and no one was lobbying for the appointment of women to public office. The Caucus was the leader
in changing all of this.

Most observers agree that the Caucus has been particularly effective within the two major parties, in the national capital and in state capitals where there is a strong
state caucus. In Washington, D. C. , the Caucus has gained
a reputation for political professionalism that has given
credibility to its efforts everywhere else. With effectiveness,
the number of its supporters and its financial strength have
increased. Its annual Washington fund-raisers have become
major social events, attended by top government officials including, on occasion, the President. It is already outgrow-
ing its fourth suite of offices. While its leaders, from the
beginning, have been quoted widely in the press, they now
can speak for a far more coherent organization backed by a

larger, more experienced staff and a fund-raising ability that
has grown from raising about $70,000 in its first year to
over $700,000 in 1978.

   The Caucus's growth in strength and influence and
women's emergence as a political interest group have not
meant, however, that women have become a powerful political
force.   Ultimately, political power comes with the ability to
shape major policy and to deliver money and votes to issue
fights and candidacies.   In some cases, nationally and locally,
the Caucus has shown this ability, but it has not been able
to do so consistently.   In general, the Caucus has been sad-
dled with too much to do and neither the funds nor the grass
roots voting strength to do it.   Women are still politically
divided and disorganized.   A women's voting bloc has not
emerged.   What has emerged, directly or indirectly as a result of Caucus efforts, are small groups of politically oriented women strategically placed in more and more institutions and organizations.   They constitute an ever-growing
political base for a women's political movement that has real
focus and power.   The Caucus has only begun to organize
this base.

   Yet, the progress of the Caucus has been remarkable.
Originally, many expected it to be just another election year
phenomenon.   In 1972, after the Caucus's highly publicized
impact on the Republican and Democratic conventions, reporters called the Washington office to ask when the Caucus
was going out of business.   Why should they have thought
otherwise?   The Caucus had no money.   Its staff of five
young women operated out of shabby offices and had not been
paid for months.   Its strongest leaders were mostly celebrity women with other busy careers.   Its state and local
caucuses were new and shaky.   There were no field organizers and infighting was common at every level including the
National Policy Council.   It was natural to think that only
the excitement and agendas of the election year had held the
Caucus together.   Having made some points, it would now
fade away.

   That the Caucus survived and maintained its central
position as the rallying point for the women's political movement is due to several circumstances.   It is a tribute, first,
to the underlying strength of the women's movement which
nourished it.   The basic elements of that strength which existed in 1971 continue to exist now.   While many feminists
take these elements for granted, they are the fruit of long

years of effort. The root of the women's movement is, of
course, the fundamental injustice of women's circumscribed
and inferior status in society and the related problems of
women's lack of equal opportunity and fair treatment in political, educational, economic, religious, social and family
institutions. The women's movement could not exist, however, without large numbers of women being aware of these
issues, without their emancipation from the belief that all is
as it should be. In 1971 large numbers of such women existed, were passionate about the issues, had expertise in organized social action acquired through education and involvement in a variety of organizations for change, and could communicate with each other through women's and feminist organizations and resulting networks of personal acquaintance.
Without these strengths to rely on, the Caucus could never
have survived the organizational disorder that marked its
early years.

The survival and growth of the Caucus was also helped
by a general national consensus on the legitimacy of its cause.
It was, as its founders had the genius to recognize, an idea
whose time had come. Political organizing was greeted
everywhere as a logical next move for women, and often it
was welcomed as a relief from the "sexual politics" of the
women's liberation movement. 6

The interest of the media in the women's movement
and the Caucus also played an important supporting role in
the drama of its survival. Even when the media was critical, it spread information and changed attitudes. News
coverage amplified the effect of everything the Caucus did,
nationally and locally. To an organization which could hardly
afford to print and mail its own newsletters, this was invaluable.

The Caucus's own strengths, finally, determined its
fate. What was needed in 1971 for a women's political
movement to take shape was a political focus, broadly acceptable leadership and an organizing strategy that could
unite large numbers of American women. These the Caucus
provided.

The wave of Caucus organizing that sprang up in almost every state after the Caucus founding was initiated by
an amazing variety of women, many of whom had no previous connection with the organized women's movement. They
responded to the Caucus message and the sense of real pos-

sibility for action and change that is conveyed. The credibility and legitimacy which its well-known leaders gave to the
Caucus was essential to this response.

Though the leadership was heavily Eastern, liberal
and Democratic, there was reassuring representation from
other regions of the country, from the Republican Party,
from minority groups and from a variety of ages and types.
The power and glamour which several of the leaders projected helped to draw women to Caucus meetings and persuaded them that something important could really happen.
Despite differences among the Caucus "superstars" and seemingly endless power struggles in the Policy Council witnessed
by newly elected state representatives, these leaders served
the Caucus faithfully. They traveled and spoke for the Caucus at their own expense, raised money and used their influence generously. For the most part, they responded
gracefully to the wave of anti-elitism which called for new
leadership in 1973 and they relinquished the reins without
withdrawing their support. They were followed by a home-
grown steering committee under the leadership of a political
luminary partly created by the Caucus, Frances "Sissy"
Farenthold of Texas. The Caucus had backed her nomination as Vice-President on the McGovern ticket in 1972 and
she had made a surprisingly strong showing. She was followed as national chairperson in 1975 by a young, unknown
Black Republican woman, Audrey Rowe Colom,[7] and in 1977
by a retired labor leader and former National Democratic
Committeewoman, Mildred Jeffrey. After the strong start
provided by the original founders, the Caucus clearly was
strong enough to be led by talent from within its own ranks
and without dictation from any one political group.

The Caucus's political focus and organizing strategy
attracted broad support from women. Its goals were perceived as fair and attractively humanistic and its method was
perceived as sensible and realistic practical politics. In
most places, Caucus organizers, despite being mostly self-
appointed volunteers, practiced the "politics of inclusion"
recommended by the Caucus. They reached out to all the
women in the community and succeeded in bringing together
feminists, reformers, radicals, political neophytes, political
professionals, issue activists, housewives, career women and
poor and rich women of all ages, races and backgrounds.

Those who responded found that the national caucus
they had heard so much about could give them little practical

help in organizing at the local level. They sought unity and
were overwhelmed by diversity. The Caucus quickly became
heir to the major problem of all coalitions, how to satisfy
diverse interests without compromising conviction, coherence
and force. An examination of the principal threats to Caucus
unity and why they did not succeed helps to explain not only
why the Caucus has survived and grown but also the kind of
coalition it has become.

Avoiding Fragmentation Over Issues

From the beginning, it appeared possible that the
Caucus's attempt to mobilize a broad-based coalition of wom-
en across party, race, cultural, ethnic and class lines would
fail because of differences over specific issues. The fact
that women had not demonstrated agreement upon a political
philosophy or agenda was acknowledged. The belief that unity
could be achieved was, therefore, a leap of faith.

Some of the founders made bigger leaps than others.
The more cautious ones felt that unity could be built around
a core of "women's issues" and the need to end women's
exclusion from political decision making. Others were hopeful that women shared a common perspective based on their
roles outside the power structure as nurturers and consumers or as victims of sex discrimination in education and
employment. They thought women would consequently have
similar views of a broad range of issues, "social" as well
as "women's issues. Some thought consensus would arise
out of women's innate humaneness, an alleged quality which
made them more responsible in relation to power than men.
The assumption that women were by nature more humane
made some of the women uneasy, but since the case for political equality did not depend upon it, it was allowed to pass
largely unexamined. There were also some who felt that the
Caucus should take only one issue stand--that of an equal
voice for women in the political life of the nation--and that
achieving this goal would mean that humane social changes
would automatically occur.

At the organizing conference, these different views
came up most pointedly in relation to two questions: 1) Would
the Caucus support any woman over any man in a political
race? 2) Would the Caucus set forth an issues platform?
The temperament of those who attended the organizing conference was feminist, pragmatic and activist. The answers

that emerged to these key questions left important concepts
ambiguous but succeeded in setting a direction without creating a line item orthodoxy.

The Caucus would not support any woman over any
man. It would "rally national and local support for the campaigns of women candidates--federal, state, and local--who
declare themselves ready to fight for the rights and needs of
women, and of all under-represented groups. "[8] Furthermore,
it would "[g]ive active support only to those candidates for
public or party office, whether male or female, who support
women's issues and employ women in decision-making positions on their administrative and campaign staffs. "[9]

But what was a "women's issue"? The Caucus's 1971
statement of purpose offered only principles and guidelines,
not a platform. Women were to "unite against sexism, racism, institutional violence and poverty. "[10] The list of issues it did offer were offered as "guidelines to the kinds of
concerns ... women must have as women, not as imitators
of the traditional male style and male politic. "[11] The list
made clear that no narrow definition would suffice. It covered more than the traditional concerns of women for equal
treatment, equal pay for equal work, control over women's
reproductive function and child care. It spoke of tax inequities, unemployment insurance, ending the war in Indo-
china, ending the arms race, ending investigative harassment
of those proposing social change, comprehensive health care,
preservation of the natural environment, and many other issues. The statement acknowledged that it advocated "sweep-
ing social change" and called for reordering of the country's
resources "to pay for life instead of death. "[12]

To some at the conference, the guidelines seemed not
merely liberal but radical, but they were adopted overwhelmingly. What made it possible for more conservative women
to stay in or come in was the fact that the principles and
political strategies proposed were acceptable. The issue
guidelines were put forth only for state and local caucuses to
consider and were not binding.

It remained unclear for six years exactly what kinds
of issues a candidate would have to support to be backed by
the Caucus. Formal endorsement criteria varied from caucus
to caucus. Endorsement was often finessed by rating systems
in which candidates were judged acceptable, preferred or not
acceptable. In 1977, when the Caucus finally had some money

to give candidates, national endorsement guidelines were adopted. These guidelines, issued by the Campaign Support Committee, require that the candidate be a feminist, express support for Caucus goals and purposes and specifically for the Equal Rights Amendment, the 1973 Supreme Court decision on abortion and publicly funded child care. A past record of support for these positions is essential and the candidate must be willing to make the Caucus endorsement known to the public. While these guidelines do demand a certain conformity on issues, they are about as broad as they could be and still be considered feminist.

A tolerant approach to local caucus activity around issues has continued since 1971. Local option on issues actually promoted has remained a feature of Caucus organization. Despite the fact that its national conventions do take stands on issues and the national steering committee is bound to implement them within its budget constraints, local and state caucuses are only required to support the Caucus's purpose and goals and not take actions opposed to national stands.

The three bi-annual Caucus conventions that have set policy for the Caucus since 1971 have continued to see "women's issues" broadly. In Houston in 1973, delegates asked for action on a long list of issues including ERA, party reform, pension plan inequities, social security reform, campaign finance disclosure laws, peace and amnesty, women's studies in schools, equality in financial transactions, credit and mortgage loans, equal access of single women to rental housing, prison reform, rape law reform and enforcement, assistance to rape victims, the right to sexual privacy, extension of the coverage of the National Labor Relations Act, welfare benefit improvement, and other issues. [13] A similar breadth of issues received support in Boston in 1975, but for the first time budget impact statements were required to be appended to the resolutions. [14] A sense of the limits of what the Caucus could do had finally appeared. In San Jose, California in 1977, a similarly long list of issue resolutions was passed, but there was also a rather general omnibus "Legislative Resolution" demonstrating a sense that the national leaders could be trusted with a broad mandate. The agenda of issues was by then so familiar and the Caucus's stance so well understood that a blanket authorization to "continue its aggressive lobby and coalition efforts on the following legislative issues" was deemed to be guidance enough. [15] The shorthand list which followed named issue areas, some broad (Civil Rights), some narrow (Battered Women). Almost all

of the areas of concern had been addressed in prior conventions, including the organizing conference.

By stressing its role as a political strategist, teacher
of political skills, supporter of women for public office, and
fighter for an equal voice in decision making for women, the
Caucus's stands on specific issues have become part of a
package and not the only focus of its members attention.
The flexibility on issues that it allows its local and state
caucuses minimizes doctrinal conflict. The fact that its
positions on issues are voted upon by democratically elected
convention delegates neutralizes most feelings that a little
group at the top is speaking only for itself.

The polarizing debate that could have taken place over
what constitutes a "women's issue" and what a "social issue"
has never happened. The Caucus's Legislative Committee
now recognizes some issues as "front line" and some as tar-
geted "for support only."[16] This setting of priorities is
based on an appraisal of which issues have the greatest impact on Caucus members, what Caucus resources are available, and which issues require visible Caucus support either
because the Caucus's lobbying absence would be read by
legislators as lack of support or because other groups are
not making these issues a priority.

Fears that positions on a broad range of issues would
make it impossible for a broad spectrum of political approaches to work together under the Caucus umbrella have
proven to be unfounded. Republican, Democratic and Independent women have shown themselves to be both more eclec-
tic in their political stances and more aware of the need for
a united effort than the conventional wisdom predicted. They
have been willing to stay in to fight for their positions rather
than stay out and divide their forces.

Avoiding a Partisan Split

The Caucus's success in becoming and maintaining itself as a multi-partisan organization has been built on more
than flexibility on issues. This difficult achievement took
conscious effort. Commitment to the Caucus idea by a few
strong Republican women and the conviction of others that
the Republicans must be included if the Caucus was to have
real power led to several concrete steps to overcome early
Democratic domination of the Caucus.

First, additional Republican members were appointed to the elected Policy Council to balance it better. [17] These Republican members then worked patiently to overcome the initial reluctance of Republican women to become involved. In 1973, at the Houston convention, a rule requiring some party balance in electing members at-large to the steering committee was adopted. In 1975, new bylaws established rules which require affirmative action to achieve multi-partisan balance in local caucuses and at the national level. At least one national Vice-Chair must now be a member of a major political party different from that of the Chair.   All national officers are required to "reflect the commitment of this organization to multi-partisan participation."[18] Since member caucuses must adopt bylaws consistent with the by-laws of the Caucus, these requirements extend throughout the Caucus structure.

Perhaps more important than these bylaws changes has been the chance development within the Caucus of Demo-cratic and Republican Task Forces. They have brilliantly answered the need for the Caucus to be effective within both major party structures without sacrificing the leverage party women gain by their unity across party lines. By becoming effective within the parties, they have attracted party women to the Caucus.   They have enabled women with impeccable records of party loyalty and hard work but with a concomi-tant commitment to advancing the cause of women to allay male party official's suspicion of the women's movement. These trusted party women have given party respectability to ideas first associated in party minds with a radical fringe, and they have reduced ideological polarization on women's issues.   The Task Forces have contributed much to the ac-ceptance of women's issues and women candidates as issues of democratic principle.

The seeds of both Task Forces were planted just be-fore the 1972 Presidential Nominating Conventions when a meeting of the Policy Council decided to elect caucus spokes-women from each party to serve as leaders of the Caucus efforts at their respective conventions.   Gloria Steinem was elected for the Democrats, Jill Ruckleshaus for the Repub-licans.   The Democratic Convention came first that year, and the impact of the Caucus efforts to increase the number of women delegates and to mobilize them around credential fights, the abortion issue, and the Vice-Presidential nomination re-ceived heavy press attention.   This emboldened the Republican women.   Facing greater resistance, they concentrated on de-

livering the Caucus message in a soft, unmilitant manner to
a meeting of Republican women delegates.   The reception
was cool at first, but gradually there was increasing responsiveness to the suggestion that Republican women ought to
have more power in the party than they did.   Caucus women
succeeded in getting some movement in this direction with
the adoption of Rule 32, which instructed each state to endeavor to have equal representation of men and women in
convention delegations.

It was not until 1975, however, that efforts to form
a permanent Republican Task Force got underway.   There
was growing concern in both Republican and Democratic
corners that the delegate gains for women would not be maintained at the upcoming 1976 conventions.   The National Wom-
en's Education Fund proposed to step into the role played by
Women's Education for Delegate Selection in the 1972 conventions, educating women for election as delegates and in credential challenge procedures.   Congresswoman Margaret
Heckler of Massachusetts and Rosemary Ginn, then a Republican National Committeewoman and subsequently Ambassador
to Belgium, called a meeting of feminist Republican women
to consider NWEF's proposals for action.   The women attending decided that they needed a vehicle through which they
could communicate and pressure the party to expand the role
of women.   They chose to organize under the umbrella of the
Caucus rather than solely within the party in order to have
more independence.   In January 1975, the establishment of
the Task Force was formally announced at a press conference and Pat Goldman, Director of the liberal Republican
Wednesday Group became its first Chair.

Caucus Democrats developed a Task Force in 1974.
It was formed first as a Democratic Party Reform Task
Force to fight for women's interests at the meeting of the
Democrat's Charter Commission in August 1974.   The battle
over affirmative action that occurred there convinced Caucus
women that the Task Force needed to be reactivated for the
Democrat's mini-convention in Kansas City in December 1974.
Led by Mildred Jeffrey, the Task Force became a permanent
fixture of both Caucus and party activity.

In May 1976, the party Task Forces held a joint press
conference attacking the failure of both parties to attain even
the same number of women delegates they had in 1972.   Republican women credit the widespread coverage this press
conference received with making Republican state party chair-

men balance delegations with more women. The effect on the
Democratic Party was less discernible. At the 1976 conventions, Republicans showed an increase in women delegates,
31. 5 percent up from 29. 5 percent in 1972. Democrats
showed a decrease, from 40 percent to 34 percent.

At the 1976 Democratic Party convention, however,
the Democratic Task Force made a major issue of gathering
support for a minority report urging the party to adopt an
equal division rule to insure equal numbers of men and wom-
en delegates to the 1980 convention. Working with women's
groups within the party, the Task Force forced two negotiating sessions with Jimmy Carter on this issue. It finally accepted a compromise in which President Carter agreed to
campaign for the Equal Rights Amendment and to include
women in significant posts in his campaign and administration in exchange for withdrawal of the minority report. As-
surances were given to the women that there would be equal
division of men and women delegates at the 1978 mid-term
convention. Such equal division did occur in 1978, and, after
several setbacks and struggles, new rules were adopted guaranteeing equal division in 1980.

The fight waged by the women at the Democratic Convention in 1976 was the focus of press attention because all
other issues had been ironed out in advance. The women
themselves had been successful in getting most of what they
wanted into the Democratic Platform, leaving only the delegate issue for the floor. The Task Force operation in 1976
was well organized and well financed, a far cry from the
shoestring operation that the Caucus ran in Miami in 1972.
A similarly well organized effort is planned for 1980. The
Democratic Task Force is working to insure that feminist
women serve as delegates and that the party honor its mid-
term convention commitment to work for the election of wom-
en to 50 seats in Congress and to one-third of the state
legislative seats.

For the first week of the Republican Convention in
1976, the controversial issues were the feminist issues.
The Republican Task Force led a skilled and successful effort to keep support for the Equal Rights Amendment in the
party platform. It also succeeded in passing a minority report on abortion that coincided with the Task Force's position. The difference from the rather timid Caucus efforts
at the 1972 convention was electrifying. Since then, the Republican Task Force has continued to grow in strength, pub-

lishing a newsletter, collecting dues, attracting many new
members and providing an important progressive force within
the Republican Party.

The evolution of the party Task Forces within the Caucus has strengthened the Caucus's credibility as the leader
of a broad new political force.   Relations between Republican
and Democratic Caucus women are more comfortable and cooperative than ever before.   There is no longer evidence of
the strain between Democrats and Republicans evident at the
1973 Houston convention when Nixon was in the White House
and the war in Viet Nam continued.   At that convention a
Bella Abzug speech attacking Nixon threatened to rupture bi-
partisan relations.   At the 1977 Caucus convention in San
Jose, it was the Republican's turn to offer criticism of a
Democratic President and they did it gracefully.   Said Mary
Louise Smith, past Chair of the Republican National Com-
mittee, "I'm pleased to be here as a Republican feminist.
I know some people consider that a contradiction in terms.
But Republican feminists are no more responsible for Phyl-
lis Schlafly than Democratic feminists are responsible for
Jimmy Carter's position on abortion."[19]

Avoiding Factionalism

The Caucus's insistence on the inclusion of all kinds
of women in its membership came originally from its founders and was a matter of democratic principle, feminist sisterhood and a conscious strategic gamble.   The strategy was
that only such inclusiveness would keep the Caucus from
being dismissed as either fringe or elitist.   The gamble was
that such a diverse group might split into warring factions
and distort, disrupt or destroy all hope of a women's political movement.

In some local caucuses, factionalism did paralyze the
ability to function.   In others, factions dropped out and inclusiveness was lost.   In some, inclusiveness was never
practiced and small power groups used the caucus for their
own ends.   Without field organizers, there was little the national leadership could do to assist with these problems or
to control them.   Affirmative action plans became a pre-
requisite for member caucuses to have voting privileges at
national conventions, but with rare exceptions the Caucus has
not had the enforcement capability necessary to force compliance.   Despite such problems, the Caucus has managed to

attract and keep an exceptionally diverse membership without
bogging down in internecine warfare.

The Caucus's commitment to sharing power with
legitimate special interest groups is probably the main reason that it has not been destroyed by them. Early sensitivity to the need to recognize and respond to such groups
was evident in the make-up of Caucus convenors. Minority
women in particular were sought for participation in the Caucus founding. Special interest caucuses of Blacks, Radical
Women and Young Professional Women emerged in a rudi-
mentary form at the organizing conference, and their resolutions were adopted.

When special interest caucuses emerged again in
Houston in 1973, rules were adopted for recognizing them
and giving them votes on the steering committee. In Boston
in 1975, additional special interest caucuses were recognized
and made part of the Caucus structure.

The Caucus approach to defining a legitimate special
interest group seemed to evolve naturally out of pragmatic
political instincts. The Caucus took note of historically underrepresented minority groups and its goal of ending racism
and decided on guaranteed representation for such groups in
its leadership. It recognized that the issue of sexual preference had a major constituency within the women's movement
and moved to guarantee Lesbian women a place among its
leaders. It noted the unique political potential of feminist
female staffers on Capitol Hill and elected to give them leadership representation. Then it acknowledged that any group
with the support of 10 percent of its convention delegates
was significant enough to require a leadership voice. By
providing a mechanism for recognizing and responding to
such groups, the Caucus demonstrated its commitment to inclusiveness in unmistakable terms and freed these groups
from having to struggle for dignity and power.

The Caucus now gives voting representation on its
steering committee to special interest groups in two ways.
Blacks, Chicanas, Puerto Ricans, Native Americans, Asians,
Lesbians and the Capitol Hill Caucus have been recognized
as permanent special interest caucuses. They each have one
steering committee representative except for Blacks and Lesbians who have two each. The minority caucuses are also
assured that they may elect additional representatives if the
steering committee does not reflect the percentage of ethnic
minorities in the population at large.

The Caucus also gives voting representation to special interest caucuses which spring up at national conventions. These must supply a statement defining their special interest along with signatures of 10 percent of the delegates with credentials at the convention. Signers must subscribe to a statement that they are members of that special interest group. No delegate may belong to more than one such caucus. These special convention caucuses only exist between conventions, but each has steering committee representation during that period. At San Jose in 1977, delegates formed an Older Women's Caucus, a Labor Caucus and a Legal Support Caucus. The Legal Support Caucus has been particularly effective, sparking the Caucus's Judicial Appointments Project, a concerted campaign to get more women appointed to the Federal bench.

There is some Caucus feeling, particularly among the ethnic minorities, that the convention caucuses should not be given voting representation but should, instead, be issue Task Forces. They believe that representation for special interest caucuses is justified as affirmative action for historically underrepresented groups, but see no need for special provision for others. Many Caucus members agree, and bylaws changes may be made.

Some Caucus members feared that special interest caucuses would perpetuate unfortunate divisions already existing in society and fragment the Caucus. They hoped for dialogue and interchange at the local level, not separatism. What has happened is not that dialogue has been eliminated, but that it tends to take place rather formally through resolutions and representatives.

At the same time, much has been gained. Intense disagreements and power struggles within special interest groups have been played out at their meetings and have not unnecessarily engaged the energies of others. These groups have had a vehicle for developing their own positions and leadership in a coherent way. They have not had to obstruct other agendas to be heard. Their position within the larger Caucus has enhanced their power both in the Caucus and outside it.

Several of the special interest groups have not taken full advantage of the recognition and power offered to them by the Caucus. Others have. Recently, and for the first time, the Caucus has been able to allocate some money for special interest caucus projects. This may spur the development of these caucuses.

The importance of these caucuses to the Caucus has been in their concrete demonstration of Caucus willingness to share power with the less powerful, as much as in the contributions of their membership to Caucus policies and programs. Ethnic minority groups especially have been gratified by the existence of these caucuses and by the Caucus requirement that at least three of the six highest Caucus officials be members of ethnic minority groups. A basis for mutual trust and respect exists within the Caucus. With such a basis, factionalism has not had a reason to grow.

The Future

The foregoing analysis of how the Caucus has survived and grown and of what it has become provides some assistance in estimating its future political impact. The main supports of its success thus far--the strength of the women's movement, the public perception of the legitimacy of its cause, media interest and the Caucus's own political sophistication, credibility, resources, inclusiveness and flexibility--show no signs of diminishing. If anything, there is evidence that the gains it has already made will now allow it to move ahead more effectively.

Yet, the difficulties it faces have also grown. The opposition is better organized. The issues raised by the women's movement and the Caucus are increasingly recognized as fundamental and, therefore, threatening to vested interests. Whatever political magic the emergence of women as a political interest group first had is largely gone. Much hard organizing work remains.

Even the political climate has worsened. Suspicion of government is great and of politicians even greater. Economic uncertainty, persistent unemployment and inflation are crippling standard political approaches to social problems. Equal opportunity through affirmative action is under re-examination and attack by court challenges alleging reverse discrimination. There is an increasing sense that America's ills are so interconnected that cause and effect relationships can neither be identified nor controlled.

The Caucus cannot be unaffected by these problems of

political opposition, confusion and alienation. It has internal
problems as well. For all its strengths, it has always been
and remains overextended, undermanaged, underorganized
and underfunded.

It has taken on much of the shape if not the precise
mission of a national political party, and it has all the problems of such parties. The parallels are obvious. Like the
parties, it is an amalgam of diverse members and ideas
under a banner of social change through the existing political
system. It aims at the election and appointment of its adherents in every political arena. Like the political parties
it provides visibility and support for its candidates and leaders and is a source of job referrals. It must depend on
volunteer labor, volunteer organizing ability and voluntary
financial support for almost all that it does. Concerned with
practical political action, it suffers from the same piece-
meal approach to problems and the same policy making weaknesses from which the major parties suffer. Like them, it
mainly depends on other groups--in the case of the Caucus,
groups such as the National Organization for Women, other
feminist organizations and social action groups--to address
problems in detail and to frame the social issues then urged
politically by the Caucus.

At a time when the country seems to be seeking a
new vision, the Caucus offers, like the parties, mainly the
standard liberal vision of the future and of politics. It adds
to the picture the insights of the women's movement and the
conviction that the full political partnership of women and
men will bring new perspectives and new solutions.

Caucus leaders make no apology for this approach.
They are convinced of its value and are concerned mainly
with improving it. They freely admit Caucus failings but
see them as largely organizational. The list of necessary
improvements includes more grass roots organizing, better
communication between national, state and local levels, a
less cumbersome structure, leadership training, better
planning and budgeting, more professional fundraising, more
outreach to neglected groups of women, clearer objectives
and greater accountability. There is wide agreement that
the worst is over for the Caucus as an organization and that
its best years are ahead.

This confidence in the survival and continued improvement of the organization is not paralleled by equal confidence

that the Caucus will be able to lead a dramatic new advance in the struggle for a non-sexist, non-racist, non-agist, non-violent, non-poor society. The expectation is for a long, slow, uphill climb, fighting rear guard actions all of the way. New surges forward may erupt out of anger over specific issue setbacks or other crises, but the Caucus women expect that there will be a continuing need for the Caucus's knowledge of the political power system and the detailed organizing and strategizing that turns anger into agendas and agendas into action.

Those with more radical visions of politics have complained that the Caucus's emphasis on pragmatic political reality is a form of "selling out" to the system it is supposed to reconstruct. Many have left the Caucus because they felt it offered unimaginative and ineffective political alternatives. Others with radical viewpoints have become persuaded that incrementalism is the main method of American politics and that to eschew it is to abandon the field to the enemy.

Criticism that the Caucus is too caught up in the power game and has lost sight of feminist values of cooperation and community has not been uncommon and has sometimes been merited. Power politics at all levels of the Caucus has frequently been indistinguishable from the masculine variety. Awareness of this has led the Caucus to an increasing focus on leadership training in which questions of the proper use of power and the need to set norms of organizational behavior have been getting fresh attention.

Feminist criticism of the Caucus has been useful. It has reminded Caucus leaders of the need to respond to the deepest concerns of feminist thinkers at the same time that they deal with old time politicians and seek to organize housewives, businesswomen and other relatively unorganized groups of women who have little background in feminist critiques of society. The Caucus needs the interplay of feminist vision with the life experience of all kinds of women. Only such an interplay can insure that Caucus activity rises above mere interest group politics. While a fair share of power and resources for women is a necessary and legitimate Caucus aim, the life-giving impulse of the Caucus has always been humanist and feminist in a way that goes beyond the politics of who gets what, where and when. Neglect of this impulse could destroy the Caucus.

As the Caucus enters the 1980's, it will have to contend with the impact of two future-shaping events for which
it has helped to set the stage. The first will be the 1980
Democratic National Convention. For the first time, half of
the delegates will be women. If the Caucus succeeds in
mobilizing the women delegates, women could control the
convention. Whether or not women play such a role, they
will inevitably be a major power group, not to be ignored
with impunity either in 1980 or in the following years. The
second event will be the success or failure of the effort to
ratify the Equal Rights Amendment by 1982. If the battle
is won, there will be a new surge of activity as the resources poured into that fight are redirected into other battles. If it is lost, it seems likely that the outrage of American women will galvanize the entire women's political movement. The Caucus is bound to play a central role in whatever happens.

The Caucus will also be contending with the continual-
ly growing impact of women's increasing presence in the
work force. A new women's consciousness of economic issues is already emerging as a result of this major demographic shift. The national budget, trade, tax, business,
labor and social welfare policy are fast becoming women's
issues for a rapidly expanding constituency of working wom-
en. The Caucus has never been primarily an issue-focused
organization. The election and appointment of women to public office has been and will probably continue to be its principal activity. But the issue of putting women into decision-
making political roles cannot be promoted effectively without
vigorous debate over other women's issues, both narrowly
and broadly defined. This debate is growing, not diminishing, as women move into new economic roles. If the Caucus organizes properly, it should be able to use this debate
to recruit new members and supporters and build its strength.

Implicit in this analysis of the Caucus's future is a
sense that the politicization of women is proceeding rapidly.
There is much evidence that this is true. Traditional "white
glove" women's organizations are dying out, while activist
groups are proliferating. Women in all occupations increasingly are aware of power relationships, want power, and
are confident that they can get it. They have seen the
changes a few years and a little militance have brought.
The system has responded. Therefore, it can be made to
respond more. While political alienation is evident in low
voter turnouts of both men and women, the number of women

voters is an increasing proportion of those who do vote, and
working women are the fastest growing group of voters in
the electorate.   A recent analysis of who votes and who does
not concluded that voters differ from non-voters only in believing that, as individuals, they can control what happens
to them in the future.   Women are full of a new sense of
their own possibilities and more women are voting than ever
before.

       In a 1977 book entitled The Fall of Public Man,
Richard Sennett lamented what he took to be a national retreat from a vigorous public life into a primary concern for
our private lives which was destructive to a rational understanding of society and to active and intelligent participation
in the resolution of public issues. 20   What is surprising in
this historically grounded and sensitive analysis is Sennett's
failure to note the new political engagement represented by
the women's movement.   In tracing the survival and growth
of the National Women's Political Caucus, one sees not the
fall of public man but the rise of public woman.   The Caucus experience and the experience of the women's movement
in general show more and more women freeing themselves
from the trap of social isolation, of an overemphasis on private lives and derived status and finding self discovery and
realization through public communication, public accomplishment and public roles.

       While Sennett worries that the American fashion of
exchanging personal intimacies easily and readily has de-
generated into a politics of personality and a failure to go
beyond such intimacies for understanding and meaning, American women have been using the sharing of personal intimacies to discover their objective condition and the causes and
effects of their depression and powerlessness.   Feminist
women, after all, announced that the personal is the political,
that there is an intimate connection between the quality of
women's personal lives and public power structures and
norms.   Feminists showed women that much of what they
blamed themselves for as due to character or personality defects was the result of societal conditioning and structures.
The women's movement is based on the famous "click" of
perception that something happening to an individual woman
has to do with her being a woman and not with her individual
being.   Women have been politicized by the sudden understanding that their private problems are often really public
problems and demand public, not private, solutions.

The National Women's Political Caucus is an important expression of women's emergence from privatism into
new public roles, from second-class citizenship into a demand
for all the privileges and immunities heretofore reserved for
men.   For the first time in American history, women in
large numbers are seeking change through direct participation in the central political and economic power structures
of the country.   They are doing this without apologies for
being women, but with an ever-growing sense that whatever
may be distinctive about women's experience or nature must
be taken into account if there are to be sane public policies.

As the nation seeks answers for new or persistent political problems, the rise of public woman is one of the more
hopeful signs that answers may be found.   How quickly and
effectively this new public woman rises will depend partly on
the organizing efforts of groups like the Caucus.   Its survival
and growth, and the continued strength of the women's movement in general, show that women are not only making new
demands on old systems but are willing to do the kind of
work that makes systems respond.   The progress of the Caucus is evidence once again that the desire for social change
in a democratic system can be translated into concrete results at an accelerated pace by imaginative political leadership and organizing strategies.

NOTES

1.   At various times in recent years, I have discussed the
     Caucus experience and its future with present and
     former staff members, officers, steering committee
     members and consultants hired by the Caucus.   The
     following people have been especially helpful.   They
     bear no responsibility, however, for my analysis and
     conclusions.   My thanks to Denise Cavanaugh, Rox-
     anne Barton Conlin, Dolores Delahanty, Angie Flores,
     Sharon Flynn, Pat Goldman, Joanne Howes, Mildred
     Jeffrey, Marlene Johnson, Ann Kolker, Debbie Leff,
     Jane Pierson McMichael, Anne Monnig, Lael Stegall
     and Fredrica Wechsler.
2.   Newsweek, July 26, 1971.
3.   Statement of Purpose of the National Women's Political
     Caucus, July 11, 1971, National Women's Political
     Caucus, Washington, D. C.   These goals are restated
     in the current Caucus by-laws.   The eradication of
     ageism has been added as a goal.

4. The other members of the National Policy Council and their backgrounds or other roles at that time were Lupe Anguiano, a Chicana activist; Nikki Beare, a member of the Dade County (Florida) Commission on the Status of Women and a NOW chapter president; Lorraine Beebe, a Republican member of the Michigan State Senate; Joan Cashin, an organizer of the National Democratic Party of Alabama; Mary Clarke, a leader of California Women's Strike for Peace; Pam Curtis, a national staff member of Common Cause and former assistant to Elly Peterson at the Republican National Committee; Brenda Feigen Fasteau, New York lawyer and national vice-president of NOW for legislation; Rona F. ("Ronnie") Feit, coordinator of the Caucus's founding conference and a Columbia University law student; JoAnne Evans Gardner, a national board member of NOW and Republican nominee for the Pittsburgh (Pennsylvania) City Council; Elinor Guggenheimer, a national leader of the day care movement, former member of the New York City Planning Commission and Chairwoman of the New York City Democratic Advisory Council; Margaret Laurence, a Washington, D. C. lawyer and President of Women United; Vivian Carter Mason, Second National President of the National Council of Negro Women and a leader of Norfolk, Virginia's Women for Political Action; Midge Miller, a Democratic member of the Wisconsin legislature; Paula Page, Director of the Women's Center, U. S. National Student Association (who later resigned) and Carole Ann Taylor, a staff member of the New York State Women's Unit in the office of Governor Rockefeller. Cecelia Suarez, a West Coast Chicana leader, Evelina Antonetty, a Bronx, New York, Puerto Rican activist, and Mia Adjali, a leading national staff member of the Methodist Church were appointed to the Council during the first year but were never visibly active. During the first 19 months, elected representatives of recognized state caucuses also joined the Council, expanding it by over 40 members.

5. New York Times, March 3, 1972, p. 31. The New York State Women's Political Caucus, initially one of the strongest in the nation, has since fragmented and needs reorganization. The National Caucus, however, continues to find strong support and to have influence in New York.

6. See, for example, the essay, "Women's Lib: Beyond Sexual Politics," Time, July 26, 1971.

7. Now known as Audrey Rowe.
8. Statement of Purpose.
9. Ibid.
10. Ibid.
11. Ibid.
12. Ibid.
13. Resolutions: Houston Convention, 1973, National Women's Political Caucus, Washington, D. C.
14. Resolutions: Boston Convention, 1975, National Women's Political Caucus, Washington, D. C.
15. Resolutions: San Jose Convention, 1977, National Women's Political Caucus, Washington, D. C.
16. Quarterly Report, Spring 1977, National Women's Political Caucus, Washington, D. C.
17. These appointed Republicans were Lorraine Beebe, Pam Curtis, Barbara Kilberg and Elly Peterson.
18. National Women's Political Caucus, Inc. --By-Laws, National Women's Political Caucus, Washington, D. C.
19. Quarterly Report, Fall 1977, National Women's Political Caucus, Washington, D. C.
20. Richard Sennett, The Fall of Public Man (New York: Alfred A. Knopf, Inc. , 1977).

PART IV

ORGANIZING FOR ECONOMIC STRENGTH

INTRODUCTION

It is difficult these days to find anyone who thinks of economic discrimination as fair practice. The next two essays discuss the economic problems that face women who are not financially independent, whose incomes are low and who are divorced, widowed or otherwise single. Inherent in both papers is the caveat that women should learn how to protect themselves economically.

In Chapter 10, Yvonne Braithwaite Burke comprehensively defines significant legislation that affects the economic status of women. Examining contemporary legislation, Burke gives it an historical perspective. She also makes it quite clear that equality will be gained only if women organize.

Lucy Mallan's important essay focuses on the problems facing women as workers and dependents. As an economist, Mallan is concerned about the earning's gap, and the economics of the single and married woman. She presents the reader with an in-depth analysis of women's income-related problems.

The focus is on the present practices of the institutions affecting women's income and support. Mallan's discussion of what individual and group action can do to prevent future discrimination is an informative, long range plan for developing economic equality.

Chapter 10

ECONOMIC STRENGTH IS WHAT COUNTS

by Yvonne Braithwaite Burke

In 1776, Abigail Adams, the wife of our second President, pointed out to her husband, John, the parallel between British oppression of the colonies and the social system which gave man unlimited power over their wives and daughters.

She wrote: "In the new code of laws which I suppose it will be necessary for you to make, I desire you would remember the ladies and be more generous and favorable to them than your ancestors. Do not put such unlimited power in the hands of husbands. Remember, all men would be tyrants if they could. If particular care and attention is not paid to the ladies, we are determined to foment a rebellion, and will not hold ourselves bound by any laws in which we have no voice or representation."

John's answer was significant and prophetic. Although he relied heavily on his wife's political judgment and advice throughout their married lives, he would not take seriously her plea for women's legal and social equality.

He answered: "As to your extraordinary code of laws, I cannot but laugh. We have been told that our struggle has lessened the bonds of government everywhere; that children and apprentices were disobedient; that schools and colleges were grown turbulent; that Indians slighted their guardians, and servants grow insolent to their masters. But your letter was the first intimation that another tribe, more numerous and powerful than all the rest were grown discontented...."

"Depend on it, we know better than to repeal our masculine systems," John Adams concluded.

John was right. Women have struggled to open the "masculine system" for more than one hundred and fifty years.

We labor under a system devised for our exclusion. Each
success we experience is hard fought and only brings into
view the other obstacles in our path.   We have not yet
achieved the dignity of being accepted on our own merits as
human beings.   This will come only with the power to participate fully in the forces which shape our lives.

In the struggle against political and economic powerlessness, a careful assessment of conditions today combined
with strength drawn from our rich feminist heritage can provide the confidence and positive sense of direction women
need.   In assessing the condition of women, we must recognize the symbiotic nature of politics and economics.   Political
and economic forces do not operate in a vacuum.   Understanding this, women will be equipped with the perspective
and wisdom to break through the encrustations of tradition
and to dispel the anxieties of those who are threatened by
equal rights.

Many of us have forgotten the determination and conviction of the women who brought about the Nineteenth Amendment and the right to vote.   Many of us are ignorant of the
debt we owe to Carrie Chapman Catt whose skills as an organizer and clear vision were devoted to leadership of the
women's suffrage movement for twenty-five years.   Mrs.
Catt was a strategist.   In 1916, she formulated what was
called a "Winning Plan" which remained a secret even though
it plotted out in detail a six-year campaign for suffrage by
Federal amendment and was signed by officers of more than
thirty-six state suffrage associations.

In explaining the plan, Mrs. Catt said: "It will require, however, a constructive program of hard, aggressive
work for six years, money to support it, and the cooperation
of all suffragists.   It will demand the elimination of the spirit of criticism, backbiting and narrowminded clashing of personalities which is always common to a stagnant town, society or movement, and which is beginning to show itself in
our midst.   Success will depend less on the money we are
able to command, than upon our combined ability to lift the
campaign above this sordidness of mind, and to elevate it to
the position of a crusade for human freedom. " Mrs. Catt
always had her eye on the goal and her votes counted.

As it happened, the unforeseen circumstances of
World War I worked to accelerate the Plan.   Women were
doing war work in factories, post offices, and munition plants.

They also stepped up their campaign for the vote. Moreover, the American Woman Suffrage Association refused to allow womens' participation in the war effort to go unnoticed by Congressmen or state legislators. The Nineteenth Amendment was accomplished two years earlier than Mrs. Catt had planned. The determination and administrative skills demonstrated by feminist leaders then, stands as a model for us today.

The present protracted struggle to ratify the Equal Rights Amendment appears almost as a duplicate of the earlier Woman's Suffrage Amendment. It guarantees equal treatment to women under the law and was introduced in Congress first in 1923. It has been introduced each subsequent session and, each time, it languished and died in committee.

Finally in 1972, ERA was passed by Congress and was sent to the state legislatures for ratification. Of the required thirty-eight votes needed to ratify the amendment, thirty-five states have voted for it. Today, however, hopes look dim for ratification by three more states by the March 22, 1979, deadline. How is it possible that women, who number more than half the population, can still be denied equal rights under the law?

The frustrations of powerlessness are not new. It was in London in 1840 that Elizabeth Cady Stanton and Lucretia Mott met at the World Anti-Slavery convention and were barred from attendance because they were women. They retreated in humiliation, and out of their subsequent conversations was born the movement that gave women the vote.

In 1850 at Worcester, Massachusetts, women held one of their first conventions with delegates from nine states. Sojourner Truth, new to the realization that white women were denied human rights, spoke to the group and asked a question. She said, "Sisters, I aren't clear what ye'd be after. If women want any rights more than they got, why don't they just take 'em and not be talking about it?" The answer to Sojourner's question still puzzles many of us today.

Sojourner Truth was a remarkable emancipated slave who was born and raised in New York state. She never learned to read or write but she did learn how to phrase the basic questions. Though she makes it clear that she saw no reason why women should not get the vote when Blacks did,

her opinion was not to prevail. She said, "There is a great
stir about colored men getting their rights, but not a word
about the colored women theirs, you see the colored men
will be masters over the women, and it will be just as bad
as it was before. So I am keeping the thing going while
things are stirring; because if we wait till it is still, it will
take a great while to get it going again. "

Sojourner's comments were prophetic. The legal
right of Black men to vote was established by the ratification of the Fifteenth Amendment in 1870. But the right of
women of any color to vote took another fifty-two years.

The Civil War brought all activity for women's rights
to a standstill. Elizabeth Cady Stanton and Susan Anthony
put aside the women's issue to collect a million signatures
to a petition asking Congress to pass the Thirteenth Amendment banning slavery forever. Though the one million signatures was an impossible goal, 400,000 signatures were
presented to Congress in 1864. The women were confident
they would be rewarded with the franchise at the end of the
war by a grateful Republican Party.

The extent of the struggle ahead was made evident in
1865 when a vote taken in the U.S. Senate to decide whether
to extend the right to vote to women in the District of Columbia resulted with nine votes in favor and thirty-seven opposed.

Congressman Frelinghuysen of New Jersey expressed the
fears of many and stated the argument used against granting
rights for women for the next fifty years:

> It seems to me as if the God of our race has
> stamped upon [the women of America] a milder,
> gentler nature, which not only makes them shrink
> from, but disqualifies them for the turmoil and bat-
> tle of public life. They have a higher and holier
> mission. ... Their mission is at home, by their
> blandishments and their love to assuage the pas-
> sions of men as they come in from the battle of
> life, and not themselves by joining in the contest
> to add fuel to the very flames. ... It will be a
> sorry day for this country when those vestal fires
> of love and piety are put out.

Sojourner Truth had the answer for that one too. She
said:

That man over there say that women needs to be
helped into carriages and lifted over ditches, and
to have the best place everywhere.   Nobody ever
helps me into carriages, or over mud puddles, or
gives me any best place.   And aren't I a woman?

Look at me!   Look at my arm!   I've plowed and
planted and gathered into bards, and no man could
head me.   And aren't I a woman?

I could work as much as a man and eat as much,
when I could get it, and bear the lash as well.
And aren't I a woman?

Sojourner speaks for more and more women every
day.

If our elected representatives in 1865 did fairly represent their wives, they certainly did not speak for the single
women, whether widowed, divorced or unmarried, who lacked
the services of protectors to shield their "milder, gentler
nature" and who out of necessity had to look out for their
own interests.

The number of women today who are looking out for
their own interests, either by choice or necessity is on the
rise.   Five out of every ten women have outside jobs and
women make up 40 percent of the nation's work force.

No one was able to predict the phenomenal rate of
women entering the labor market in the early 1970's.   In
1974, the Bureau of Labor Statistics estimated that by 1980
about 37 million women would be working or seeking jobs.
But that prediction was surpassed in 1976.

Naturally, the economic position of women could be
substantially improved through employment.   Unfortunately,
women have been traditionally the last hired and the first
fired.   Today, women earn on an average of $.59 for every
$1 men earn for their work.   Twenty years ago, women
earned $.63 for each $1 men earned.   Because most women
moving into the work force still get the low-paying jobs,
their average income is actually decreasing in comparison
with men's.   For example, in 1974 women accounted for
63 percent of workers earning between $3,000 and $4,999.

Obviously, earning a paycheck is not enough.   Women

must be able to advance to higher paying jobs in policy making and managerial positions. Laws prohibiting discrimination on the basis of sex have helped open up positions, and
even more progress has been made in the courts. However,
both the legislative and judicial processes are very slow.

Pacific Telephone is an example. There has been a
change in policy which eliminates the designations "male jobs"
and "female jobs." The percentage of women in traditionally
male jobs has risen from 3.9 percent in 1973 to 10 percent
today. Nonetheless, little has changed at the top. Even
though 54 percent of all phone company workers are women,
only 34 or 2.5 percent of the 1,356 top supervisory positions
are women.

Frederick Douglass, famous Black abolitionist, said:

> When I ran away from slavery, it was for myself;
> when I advocated emancipation, it was for my peo-
> ple; but when I stood up for the rights of women,
> self was out of the question, and I found a certain
> nobility in the act.

Nobility was a strong motivation for Frederick Douglass. It is not, however, for those who sit in our state
legislatures. Once again, we are reminded that 91 percent
of state legislators, nationwide, are men. Women in state
legislatures have risen from 6 percent in 1972 to 9 percent
in 1977. Though 50 percent higher than five years ago, today's 9 percent is hardly a figure in which we can take pride.
Power comes from political representation, and women are
still largely excluded.

The obvious solution to the nobility versus self-interest
conflict is to see more women in elected and appointed public
office. Again, the record is discouraging.

No one needs to be reminded that there has never
been a woman President or Justice of the U.S. Supreme
Court. There had been only two women Cabinet members before President Ford appointed Carla Hills to HUD in 1975.
In 188 years, there have been four women elected and seven
women appointed to the U.S. Senate. During that time,
eighty women have served in the House of Representatives.

In my home state of California, 1925 was the biggest
year for women in politics in our history. Florence Kahn of

San Francisco and Mrs. Ella Mae Nolan served in the California delegation to the U.S. House of Representatives.

Only once since that time have we had two women from California concurrently serving in Congress. Today, Representative Shirley Pettis and I are members of the California delegation in the House.

It was also in 1925 that the United States had two women governors--Nellie Tayloe Ross of Wyoming and Ma Ferguson of Texas. Only when Dixy Lee Ray was elected Governor of Washington last November, were we able to match 1925. She joined Ella Grasso, Governor of Connecticut, to make, again, a total of two women governors.

Discouraging as it is, the revolution predicted by Abigail Adams is underway. Not only in the job market and the halls of state legislatures but also in the courts. Women have won major court cases, several before the Supreme Court.

In Reed v. Reed (1971), for the first time, the Court extended limited Fourteenth Amendment protection to women. This amendment, originally enacted in 1868 to extend equal protection of the laws to emancipated slaves, was now said to apply to women in limited instances. The court declared the Idaho statute unconstitutional which provided that when two persons equally entitled to appointment as an administrator of an estate, the male applicant must be preferred over the female. The Court ruled that discrimination on the basis of sex in the job classification of individuals administering intestate estates was a violation of the Equal Protection Clause of the Fourteenth Amendment. This ruling opened the door for subsequent decisions strengthening the economic independence of women.

An important economic victory was the case of Frontiero v. Richardson (1973). Here the Court ruled that a congressional statute that required a female member of the armed services seeking housing and medical benefits for her husband to prove his financial dependence on her but did not impose a similar burden on a man seeking the same benefits for his wife. This case is significant for at least two reasons. First, it recognizes that women are potential "breadwinners." Second of all, it placed a sizable dent in the dual system that has been with us for centuries. Two years later, striking another blow to the dual system, the

Court extended to the husbands and families of women workers the same social security benefits granted to the wives
and families of men workers.

Since the early 1960's women have steadily made gains
politically.   Several major pieces of legislation have enabled
women to strike critical blows at the edifice of sexual discrimination.   Among the most important laws passed recently are: Title VII of the Civil Rights Act of 1964 and Title
IX of the Education Amendments of 1972.

The Civil Rights Act of 1964 is landmark legislation
in the field of race relations.   Also significant is what the
Act did to further employment rights for women.   Title VII
states that it "shall be an unlawful employment practice" for
a covered employer, because of race, color, religion, sex,
or national origin: 1) to fail or refuse to hire or to dis-
charge any individual with respect to his compensation, terms,
conditions or privileges or employment, or 2) to limit, seg-
regate, or classify his employees in any way which would deprive any individual or employment opportunities or otherwise
adversely affect (his) status as an employee....

Although employment discrimination was outlawed in
1964, it was not until 1972 that sex discrimination was legally banned.   Title IX of the Education Amendments of 1972
prohibits discrimination in federally assisted education programs.   The Office of Civil Rights in the Department of
Health, Education and Welfare has issued comprehensive
guidelines for high schools, colleges, and universities defining sex discrimination under Title IX.   The H. E. W. guidelines apply to admission policies, recruitment, course of-
ferings, scholarship aid and athletics.

Women are in the process of claiming their places as
equal.   Presently before Congress are three bills which have
risen out of women's current needs.

First is the Displaced Homemakers Act[1] which I have
introduced.   This bill recognizes the problem faced by the
increasing number of women who find they must enter the
job market after having spent the major portion of their lives
as homemakers.   This legislation would establish Multipurpose Service Centers to help these women become self-
sufficient, productive members of the labor force.

Statistics on women in the middle years are dramatic.

In 1973 there were almost 9 million widows and 3 1/4 million divorced women, a 41 percent increase in widows since 1950 and 166 percent increase in divorces since 1950.

Between the ages of 40 and 54, the number of widows increases more than five times and the number of divorces doubled. Thirty percent of the unemployed women looking for part-time jobs are 55 years old and over.

It has been demonstrated in a pilot project called the Alliance For Displaced Homemakers, located in Oakland, that women who have sought counseling are, most often, easily helped. They need the support and perspective of those who can view their situation dispassionately. Often they are able to adapt the skills they developed as homemakers into wage paying jobs.

The second bill would provide for part-time working opportunities in federal civil service. The Part-time Career Opportunity Act will enable married women with children, many of whom hold impressive professional credentials to qualify for federal employment. The bill is needed because the present regulations effectively discourage Federal agencies from offering job opportunities to the millions of Americans who cannot work a full 40-hour week. Also, many highly experienced older workers and people continuing their education would be available on this basis.

Yet this legislation has languished in Congress for some time. Legislators should understand how important it is for hours to be flexible. Without such flexibility, the government is denied access to a significant source of talent. A major New York placement agency reported that it receives, "five times as many responses for a part-time job as for a comparable full-time job," and that, "for many jobs, the best people on the market are people who want to work part-time." If women were adequately represented in Congress, this legislation would have passed long ago.

The third important piece of legislation is a revision to create an equity for women in the Social Security Act. The impact of these revisions will be very significant for older women.

In 1935 when the Social Security Act became law, few women worked outside the home and divorce was not as common as today. Today, women are 40 percent of the work

force.   And divorces in 1975 passed the one million mark
for the first time.

As the law now stands, if a woman divorces before
20 years of marriage, she loses all access to social security
benefits through her husband's wage record.   A woman becomes aware of this tragic injustice after having spent her
many years working in her home, unaware that her later
years are unprovided for under Social Security unless her
marriage lasts over twenty years.

The Fraser Bill as the Equity in Social Security for
Individuals and Families Act provides for the maintenance of
individual social security records.   It will eventually eliminate benefits received through the wage record of another.
It will assume that work in the home has economic value and
that the spouse working in employment not covered by Social
Security will be credited for a share of the family income
earned in covered employment.

There is a provision that a husband and wife can split
their combined credits 50/50.   This would be equitable if
they earned close to the same amount each year.   If one of
their salaries is significantly higher, or if only one of the
couple is in covered employment, the law could allow each
to take 75 percent of the credit of the highest salary.

This system will give each partner his or her own
social security record, computed annually.   The proposal
creates portability in social security records.   Partners may
marry, be widowed, divorce or remarry without losing benefits.   Their personal records follow them throughout their
lives.

There are also provisions under this Act for widow's
benefits for women between 50 and 60 years of age who are
left with no income.   It will provide a minimum income to
the newly widowed homemaker to sustain her during the
period she is adjusting to her new life situation.   The benefits are phased out as the widow is able to join the labor
market.

The tie of the widow's benefit with the services of the
Displaced Homemakers Centers is obvious and natural.
These provisions should have been law long ago.

Even with the enactment of legislation such as this,

there remains a struggle.   When I think of the road before us, a quote from Reverend Martin Luther King, Jr. comes to my mind:

> A solution of the present crisis would not take place unless men and women work for it.   Human progress is neither automatic nor inevitable.   Even a superficial look at history reveals that no social advances rolled in on the wheels of inevitability. This is no time for apathy or complacency.   This is a time for vigorous and positive action.

Women today would do well to heed Reverend King's admonition.   Unless we do, we will struggle endlessly.

NOTE

1.   Since this essay was written, the Displaced Homemakers Act has become a federally funded program, subsumed under CETA (Comprehensive Employment Training Act) and the Vocational Education Act.   Additionally, several states have passed their own Displaced Homemakers Act, and there are about seventy state Multipurpose Service Centers throughout the country.

Chapter 11

WOMEN'S INCOMES AS WORKERS AND DEPENDENTS

by Lucy Mallan

This chapter discusses incomes of women who have been married. Their surest and largest income source is what they earn themselves, but women's earnings have never been high. While married, most earn less than their husbands, if they work at all. When their marriage terminates, incomes of each spouse drop to what they can earn individually, plus whatever supplements are available. This is not generally a hardship for men but amounts to small incomes, on average, for women on their own, because women's earnings are low, and supplements lower.

The low incomes of ex-dependent women form the major focus of this chapter. Here are the facts:

Sex and family status	Median income, 1975[1]	Percent poor, 1975[2]
Women who live alone	$ 3,978	29%
Men who live alone	6,612	20
Families headed by women	6,844	33
Families headed by men[3]	16,122	6

The mainstay of these women's support is their earnings. Other sources, such as public assistance, alimony or child support (if divorced), social security (if widowed with young children), income from savings, and the like, cannot themselves support a family. For example, in 1975, for families with a female head, earnings were crucial to their chance of staying out of poverty. [4]

Source of income	Percent who were poor
No wages or salaries	64%
Wages or salaries only	24
Wages and salary and supplement	20

221

Obviously, it is better to work than not to work from the point of view of income. Nevertheless, work is no guarantee of riches, nor does it even provide an overwhelming chance of avoiding poverty.

Though there are high earning women, on the average they earn about three-fifths of what men do. [5] This situation has remained virtually unchanged for at least twenty-five years, varying within at most a few percentage points. In fact, earnings of full year, full-time women workers are, if anything, smaller percentage of men's than they were a quarter century ago.

Analysis of the earnings gap forms the bulk of this chapter. A very brief discussion of the inadequate available supplements follows, to demonstrate the devastating impact of these low wage and salary levels on women's incomes. Finally, a few implications for action, on the individual and group levels, conclude the discussion.

I.   EARNINGS

In 1974, women's median earnings were 57.2 percent of men's, for full-year, full-time workers. [6] What accounts for this difference? Two main explanations are offered: women's qualifications and women's opportunities.

More scientifically phrased, some observers stress investment in the human capital of workers--time and money spent in education, training, or continuous on-the-job experience. They believe that women do not invest in themselves to the extent men do. Decisions not to do so are sometimes encouraged by women's families, by counselors, and others.

Other observers emphasize institutional factors, such as discrimination of various kinds, which keep women from realizing the same return on their "investments" as men do. Women with the same education, training, and work experience as men do not as easily translate them into lucrative occupations with promotion paths, or, ultimately, into equivalent rates of pay. In many cases access to certain jobs, assignments, or promotions is denied to some workers simply because they are women. Women are also probably reluctant to advance themselves, both because they have traditionally been socialized to be "feminine" and because they expect discontinuity in their careers.

Studies have found that the human capital explanation accounts for much of the earnings differential, but education and experience cannot explain all of the gap. Occasionally, wage differentials between men and women are absent in these studies, but only in special situations where not only these human capital factors are controlled, but also the job descriptions are defined to be identical [for men and women]. More often a differential remains, even when education and experience are held constant, reflecting differences not in human capital, but in opportunity, or return to human capital investment. The following sections explore the various components of the earnings difference.

Education

The median number of years of school is about the same for women as for men (12.3 years in 1975). [7] A slightly greater percentage of men, however, complete college and go on to professional school than do women. In 1974, for example, the situation[8] was:

	Women	Men
Completed 4 years of college	6%	7.9%
Completed first postgraduate year	2.7%	6.2%

The main ways education influences pay are indirect. First, the more educated a woman is the more likely she is to work at any age. Thus education influences the amount of lifetime work experience, which has a direct influence on wage level.

Second, formal education is important in determining one's first job, a recent study has found. [9] After that, job history becomes more important. Education can thus be said to be necessary for, but no guarantee of, a job with high prestige. Accordingly, women with high levels of education are more likely to be in jobs with mid-level prestige than are men, though this differential is closing.

Because of the indirect influence of education on earnings, and because of the near equality of women's and men's education at the median, and the small proportion of men and women at very high levels, studies have shown that even if the amounts of education were equal, earnings differentials between men and women would not decrease by much. [10]

Work Experience

 Unlike education, average time on the job, or just
time in the work force during adult years, is very different
for men and women. Even though about 85 percent of wom-
en work at some time or other, [11] and 43 percent of women
age 16 or over are in the labor force at a given time, [12]
most women, at least most married women, take a number
of years out of the labor force for childbearing or other
homemaking activities. For example, women and men who
worked at all in the years 1961-70 had very different work
histories for that period. [13]

| | Years worked 1961-70 | |
| | Women | Men |
Age in 1971		
30	5. 7	9. 2
40	5. 8	9. 4
50	6. 8	9. 4
60	7. 0	9. 5

 Experience differences contribute a sizable portion of
the difference in earnings. First, learning takes place on
the job, which supplements formal learning acquired at
school, though not all jobs require the same amount of learning. Some can be learned in a few hours, such as elevator
operator, and some take years, for example a college professor. In a recent study, [14] it was found that experience
of more than six years did not affect earnings much in relatively unskilled jobs, but did in jobs with high or medium
skill ratings. The kinds of jobs women take, then, affect
the importance of work experience, and, conversely, the expectation of the continuity of their careers and gaps in their
experience may affect the kinds of jobs they take.

 Experience may affect earnings also by way of the
general sorts of learning which take place simply by being
in the work force. The exact sort of learning which takes
place in this general way is difficult to quantify, but it seems
clear that there is some effect.

 Finally, gaps in experience may affect earnings negatively, not simply because job learning does not take place
during these periods. To the extent that time out of the labor force is spent not in school but at home, there may be
an atrophy of skills during these periods. It is probable that

this negative effect would be felt more by highly educated
people than by those less educated, for the skills in the jobs
they have left will take more time to relearn.

The influence of experience on earnings has also been
tested by Mincer and Polachek in an important study.[15] It
was found that if the amount of experience of women were assumed to be the same as for men, 45 percent of the wage
gap between married men and women would be explained.
Moreover, time spent at home had a measurable cost, more
for highly educated than for less educated people.

Though experience is important for both men and wom-
en, it does not have as high a payoff for women as for men.
If men and women of the same age, say 45, who earned the
same amount in their first job, are compared, an extra three
months of experience accounts for $33 of current earnings
for a man, but only $21 for a woman.[16] The inequality of
returns to experience has to do with the kinds of occupations
women are in, the kinds of promotion paths they are able to
pursue, and discrimination, among other things.

The prospect is that women's work experience will
lengthen, as it has over the past twenty years. Recently
women have been working for longer periods throughout their
lives. Women of corresponding ages worked more quarters
in the 5-year (twenty quarter) period 1965-70 than from 1951-
54.[17] Because of the low payoff of experience to women,
this trend cannot be expected to close the earnings gap. In
fact, apparently because other factors have been working
against women, the gap has widened slightly over the past 25
years, the very period over which experience has been
lengthening.

Occupations and Women's Roles

It is well known that men and women are in different
jobs. Three-fourths of clerical workers are women, and 70
percent of all elementary and secondary school teachers.[18]
It is easy to think of the jobs that are predominantly female,
ranging from chambermaid to librarian.

The index of dissimilarity, calculated by the Council
of Economic Advisors, showed that occupations were 60 percent "dissimilar" in 1970 and 63 percent in 1960.[19] This
means that about the same proportion of women were in

feminine jobs at the beginning of the decade as at the end.
In other words, occupational segregation has not changed
much, for the better or the worse. The same observation
can be made for the decade of the fifties.

The causes of occupational segregation are difficult
to assess. Part of it is tradition, and its effect on women
and men. It takes a brave woman to sell cars, and a brave
man to teach sewing. Preparation for these roles starts at
a very early age. It is certain that different courses are
taken at school. Women in vocational education are overwhelmingly in clerical or food-related fields, men in such
fields as auto mechanics. As for college majors, women
are in languages and education, but the scientists are overwhelmingly men. In professional school, these proportions
are changing, particularly in law: up from under 10 percent
to about one-third in the last few years which implies that
the future will be different. At lower levels, traditional
choices still prevail. The parts played in these choices by
high school and college counselors and by other influences
that shape women's lives are difficult to trace.

In part, sex segregation in occupations persists because of employers' practices, according to their own views
of traditional roles and jobs for women. It is partly because of expectations about turnover and absenteeism, resulting in statistical discrimination--assigning to an individual
the characteristics of a group. In part it may be "tastes"--
a dislike of seeing women in certain jobs. When segregation
of occupations persists because of employers' reluctance to
hire or promote women in non-traditional jobs, it is referred
to in the literature as "crowding. "[20]

Given that occupational segregation or crowding exists,
what are the effects on pay? Some important studies can be
mentioned. First, one study showed an overall effect of about
20 percent of the pay differential between married white men
and women attributable to occupational segregation. [21] Another study already mentioned, [22] which divided 295 occupations into skill groups, also analyzed the effect of predominantly female occupations. For low skill and medium skill
occupations, the amount of segregation was important in explaining low earnings of women. For higher skill occupations,
the amount of preparation necessary and the number of years
of experience were more important than whether the occupation was sex segregated within these groupings. A third
study looked at industry, rather than occupational groupings.

It was found that women's wages were less depressed relative
to men's in predominantly male industries. This finding
simply confirms the idea that women in traditional women's
roles are paid less than when they transfer into jobs not generally thought of as feminine preserves. The same study
found that women's jobs paid relatively better in government
than in private industry. The precise reason is not clear;
whether promotion paths are more open or wage discrimination in the same job is less common but the effect was significant and has been confirmed in at least one other recent
study. [23]

Women are still grouped by and large in traditional
occupations, embodying traditional roles though some American women are entering traditionally male preserves. Job
crowding and segregation along with traditional role preparation remain prime candidates as causes of much of the earnings gap.

Discrimination

Discrimination exists in many guises. As suggested,
it involves promotion paths, access to training programs,
counselling while in school, and many other more subtle
pressures. In this section wage discrimination, and some of
the less subtle forms of employment discrimination will be
emphasized.

Differential pay for the same work is now illegal.
However, a large and unknown amount still goes on, and has
been documented in certain blue collar situations. [24] Discrimination against blue collar women takes many forms.
First, jobs requiring the same amount of skill are graded differently, depending on whether they are performed by a man
or a woman. Then they are paid according to grade. Second, evaluations are sex biased. Third, some plants are
sex segregated, with different pay scales applying. Fourth,
discriminatory assignments to low classifications have led to
discriminatory layoffs.

Though unions are often to blame for allowing this
situation to persist, some unions have been aggressively
fighting for equality, sometimes over the objections of wom-
en themselves who did not fully understand the consequences
of common practices.

One union encountered plants and jobs so thoroughly segregated that even the women did not know they were equivalent. Other plants show hiring policies which are clearly discriminatory, for example, sex differences in grades for which workers with no experience are hired.

Professional women also suffer discrimination, as, for example, was shown in a study of professionals in Corporation "X" in Princeton, New Jersey,[25] and in various studies of the academe world. The discrimination comes in promotion policy and in more subtle ways.

One remedy for discrimination is action in the courts. Many suits have already been filed. One of the more spectacular was the AT&T suit, wherein the consent degree of January 1973 was the largest back pay settlement ever made. The case dealt with every aspect of employment discrimination: equal pay, seniority, upgrading and transfer, affirmative action goals and timetables, back pay, and pay adjustments. Strategies for resolution worked out by the Federal compliance agencies were as varied as the issues dealt with.[26]

Another remedy besides legal action is negotiated settlement, which sometimes, to be sure, is performed under threat of court sanctions. Often restructuring of jobs and even machines, or redefinition of goals which seem to be in conflict with non-discrimination can be accomplished. For example, if seniority is defined to be plant-wide, rather than job-wide, both the principle of seniority and the principle of nondiscriminatory layoffs are protected.

"Old-Boy" hiring networks which exist in some professions have been attacked with persuasion of varying mildness, and with varying success. Most of the learned professions have committees on the status of women. They perform important services, for example, publication of job rosters and of statistics of women at different ranks in universities. This sort of action is extremely important when hiring is done through friends and contacts. The combination of the law, plus available lists of "old-girls" forces employers to be more inclusive in their hiring.

The Economics of Marriage and the Earnings Gap

To a large extent, it has been shown, the earnings

gap is the responsibility of discrimination from employers
and coworkers, and other forces which shift women into occupations reflecting women's traditional roles. To some extent, however, it is the economics of marriage which provides disincentives for investment in the careers of women.

When couples marry, traditionally the wife specializes
in work at home and the husband in work outside the home,
at least to some degree. This specialization is based on the
assumption that the marriage will endure and that the couple
will pool their income--money and nonmoney--indefinitely.
If this proves not to be the case, the woman bears most of
the economic penalty.

It is common for deliberate disinvestment in the career
of the woman to take place. It would be irrational from the
point of view of family income in most cases for the woman
to go back to work as soon as her children are born, and the
man to stay home. Given the pay levels of men and women,
it is more important for his career to be continuous than for
hers. For the same reason, it is rational for him to finish
his schooling as fast as possible, at the sacrifice of hers if
a choice must be made. An example of this deliberate policy
is the frequent case of family migration. A recent study has
shown that this has a negative effect on women's earnings,
but this is presumably more than compensated by the growth
in his. [27]

Another example is the choice of work close to home,
when she does work. Another study has shown that distance
to work is an important variable in the earnings gap, and
that when this is held constant the gap decreased. [28]

After the children are in school, or in high school,
and expenses and free time begin to mount, their mother
often returns to the labor force and continues to work full
time until retirement age. Though her pay never reaches
what it would have been, had she not taken time out, she
makes enough to enhance the income of the couple; at the
median wives contribute about one-fourth of husband-wife income when they work. [29] In these twenty to twenty-five
years before retirement, the husband is at the peak of his
earning power. As a result, incomes of couples in these
age brackets are high, though the high expenses that occur at
this period of life make it difficult to make ends meet notwithstanding.

In effect, through this deliberate strategy, the family maximizes money plus non-money income over its life cycle. If the marriage terminates, however, the woman will be less equipped to make her living than the man. In effect she has incurred costs measured in her own earning power, and perhaps even transferred resources to his career, while she specialized in work inside the home. She should be compensated for the costs incurred to maximize the joint income of the couple. This compensation is alimony, of course. Judges often do not understand this and confuse the ability of a woman to work, with the ability to earn adequate amounts. It is easy to neglect the cost she has incurred over the course of the marriage, measured in her potential earnings.

Thus the process is self-reinforcing. The low wages of women workers make it efficient for women to specialize in the home, which is one of the forces keeping women in certain traditional occupations. For the individual, the wage structure is a given, providing an incentive to act in such a fashion that the sum of individual decisions is to perpetuate the process by which women's wages stay low. This process which goes on in millions of families both is a major force keeping women's wages low and a major reason why women usually bear the costs of marriage termination.

Men are caught in this vicious circle as much as women--though they do not pay the same penalty. They too are faced with the wage differential which makes it rational for their own careers to take preference over those of their wives.

This brief review has shown how deep and diverse are the causes of the wage gap. Evidently the battle against it must be fought on several fronts simultaneously, by many people, using several strategies, from consciousness raising among counselors and employers, to Federal and state enforcement and compliance of anti-discrimination laws and court decisions, to education of women themselves at every level.

II.   EARNINGS AND INCOMES OF WOMEN ALONE

What are the implications of women's earnings for women's incomes? The earnings gap affects both married and nonmarried women. Married women are not dependent on their own earnings, however; as was pointed out at the

very beginning of this chapter, there is almost invariably another source of income available. Divorced, separated, and
widowed women do look on their own earnings as the main-
stays of their modest incomes. Supplements are small by
comparison.

Supplements to Earnings for Younger Women

What are the supplements to earnings that are available for widows and divorced and separated women? First,
alimony and child support are not available to all, and the
payments are often small. Awards are often inadequate--
and the trend does not show improvement. A recent study of
a national sample of families found 424 households of mother
and children where the mother was eligible to receive child
support or alimony payments. Sixty percent of those eligible
received payments some time over the five year period 1968-
73, and of those, about two-thirds, or 40 percent of the
total, received payments in a given year. The average
amount received was about $2,000 per year per family. [30]
Second, though about one-third of divorced and separated
women with children receive public assistance, 69 percent of
those receiving in 1975 were poor. [31] The purpose of public
assistance, after all, is to alleviate only the worst hardship,
so this is not surprising. Third, widows with children (but
not widows under 60 without children) are eligible for social
security benefits. Almost two-thirds of the widows with
children receive this source of income. In 1974, 16 percent
were poor. [32]

Supplements and Replacements for Earnings for Older Women

Because earnings are less common as a person ages,
older women must depend even more on supplements to and
replacements for earnings than younger women. These are
based on the woman's former earnings or on her former husband's earnings. Median incomes of these divorced, widowed,
and separated women decline as they get older; for those 62-
64 years, the median in 1974 was almost $4,000, for those
65-72, just under $3,000 and for those 73 and older, closer
to $2,000. [33] About one-fourth of widows and divorcees 65
and older and living alone were poor in 1975. [34] The reasons are familiar ones; private pension income usually goes
to those who have had long unbroken careers in highly in-
dustrialized industries, not very frequently to women. Social

security income based on one's own record tends to be low
if the record contains low wages and/or a relatively short
working span. Widows have been, since 1972, eligible for
100 percent of their husband's benefit but the percentage goes
down if the claim is made before age 65. Divorcees are
eligible for a maximum of one-half of their ex-husband's benefit, and then only if the marriage endured for at least twenty
years. This brief sketch of the problems of older women
shows that their low earnings follow them throughout life. [35]

Reforms of the institutions affecting older women,
particularly social security, are the subjects of vigorous discussion in government and out. The problem is by no means
simple because the interests of one earner and two earner
couples, of divorced women and widows and of disabled workers and homemakers must all be protected, within the general
framework of a non-means tested social insurance program.
In spite of the complications, some promising approaches
have been discovered.

CONCLUSION

What Society Says to Women

Apparently women, then, receive mixed messages
from society at large. Though it is more and more the
norm for women to work outside the home, primacy of the
husband's career is still close to universal when choices
must be made, such as which spouse is to leave a job and
move with the other, which is to stay home with the young
children, and which is to help with the education of the other.
The message here is that women's work is not as serious as
men's. On the other hand, if the marriage is over, the
woman is expected to stand on her own feet, ill prepared
though she may be. Transfer payments, public and private,
in no way compensate women for their lower earnings, even
if they have custody of the children of the couple. Women
are told, do not bother to build up your human capital, but
that is all you will have if you are in trouble. Women must,
however, rely on their own earnings, and, as has been seen,
earnings do not support them at a very high level.

Recommendations

Recommendations are here divided into three compart-

ments: cautions and advice for young women in formulating
their own life plan, social goals to strive for, and areas
where study is needed.

Advice for individuals.   Clearly, marriage does not
provide the financial security it did once.   The probability of
escaping divorce, desertion, widowhood, and low income is
too small to bank on with certainty.   We all routinely hedge
much smaller risks.   We insure against fire and other catas-
trophes.   Why then do so many women have unhedged life
plans?   A trade or profession is important (and fields not
traditionally female preserves should be considered), and occasional experience or practice is important, to maintain
skills and contacts.

Social goals.   These recommendations have to be
aimed both at the earnings gap and at the inadequacy of the
supplements.   Some recommendations are short term and
tangible, some are clearly long term.   A short list might
contain the following:

1.   Anti-discrimination action might have a bigger payoff than is generally assumed.   It would be unjustified
complacency to believe the battle has been won.   Action
would include:
    a) Lobbying to fund EEOC at a higher level.
    b) Pressure on unions and others to bring suits sim-
        ilar to the IUE actions, which involve classifica-
        tion of jobs.
    c) Study of the AT&T case to identify subtle methods
        discrimination.   Then bringing cases in the courts.
    d) Persuasion, discussion, and if necessary, threats
        to obtain out of court relief from employers.

2.   Support for better protection for wives in divorce
proceedings and after is important: better search for
delinquent fathers and husbands, right to a lawyer, support for adequate awards, and adequate enforcement.

3.   Support of displaced homemakers legislation, to help
divorced and separated women raise their sights and
their earnings.

Areas for study.   1) Investigation of training, counseling and education which track women into women's occupations; 2) study of proposals for reform of institutions which
affect the elderly so that the interests of different groups are
protected; and 3) study of welfare reform.

In general, this chapter has demonstrated a circular
process--by which earnings of women married or not are
depressed--and incomes of women, including earnings and
everything else, are low.   The main exceptions are married
women supported by their husbands and the small percentage
of women who earn above the median for men.

Individual men cannot be expected to spring from the
trap, any more than individual women.   We all wander
around in the same circles, though some are victimized more
than others.   Women who believe they will never have to earn
a serious living and parents and counselors who encourage
them in this belief--employers who are afraid to hire for non-
traditional jobs, or promote to non-traditional levels, because
they fear reactions of coworkers or those supervised or because the thought does not occur, husbands and wives who
do not make contingency plans, the public who do not insist
on adequate enforcement of existing legislation on discrimination or protection for divorced women--all contribute to the
problem.   The ways to break out of the process are many
and the more who become aware of the fact and are willing
to apply pressure, the weaker the bonds will be.

NOTES*

1. See reference 21, Table 21.
2. See reference 19, Tables 27 and 28.
3. See reference 19, Table 27.   Since female-headed families in general have only one earner, two-earner
   husband-wife families are excluded from this calcula-
   tion.
4. See reference 19, Table 37.
5. See reference 27.
6. See reference 25.
7. See reference 23, Table B.
8. See reference 23, Table B.
9. See reference 16.
10. See reference, 4, and many of the studies cited in 10.
11. See reference 18, Table 1.
12. See reference 23, Table B.
13. See reference 12.
14. See reference 8.
15. See reference 14.

*References begin on page 235.

16. See reference 12.
17. See reference 12.
18. See reference 27.
19. See reference 26, appendix to chapter 4.
20. Barbara Bergmann is usually credited with articulation
     of the "crowding" hypothesis. See reference 1.
21. See reference 3.
22. See reference 8.
23. See references 4 and 2.
24. See reference 15.
25. See reference 11.
26. See reference 28.
27. See reference 17.
28. See reference 4.
29. See reference 24, Table P.
30. See reference 7.
31. See reference 19, Table 38.
32. See reference 20, Table 54.
33. See reference 19, Table 15.
34. The Social Security Administration has produced ex-
     tensive reports on the income and sources of income
     of the aged. See particularly references 6 and 21.

REFERENCES

1. Bergmann, Barbara R., "Occupational Segregation,
    Wages and Profits Wages and Profits When Employers
    Discriminate by Race or Sex," Eastern Economic
    Journal, April-July 1974, pp. 103-110.
2. Brown, Gary, "How Type of Employment Affects Earn-
    ings Differences by Sex," Monthly Labor Review, July
    1976, pp. 25-30.
3. Chiswick, Barry R., June A. O'Neill, James S. Facker,
    and Solomon W. Polachek, "The Effect of Occupation
    on Race and Sex Differences in Hourly Earnings,"
    Proceedings of the American Statistical Association,
    1974, Business and Economics Statistics Section, pp.
    219-228.
4. Fuchs, Victor R., "Differences in Hourly Earnings Be-
    tween Men and Women," Monthly Labor Review, May
    1971, pp. 9-15.
5. _____, "Women's Earnings: Recent Trends and
    Long-Run Prospects," Monthly Labor Review, May
    1974, pp. 23-26.
6. Grad, Susan, Income of the Population Aged 60 and
    Older, 1971, U.S. Department of Health, Education,

and Welfare, Social Security Administration, Office
of Research and Statistics, Staff Paper No. 26, Washington, D.C., 1976.

7. Jones, Carol Adaire, Nancy M. Gordon, and Isabel V.
    Sawhill, Child Support Payments in the United States,
    Working Paper 992-03, The Urban Institute, Washing-
    ton, D.C., October 1976.

8. Jusenius, Carol L., "The Influence of Work Experience
    and Typicality of Occupational Assignment on Women's
    Earnings" Chapter IV in Parnes, et al., Dual Careers:
    A Longitudinal Analysis of the Labor Market Experi-
    ence of Women, Vol. IV, Center for Human Resource
    Research, Ohio State University, Columbus, Ohio,
    1975.

9. Kahne, Hilde, "Economic Perspectives on the Roles of
    Women in the American Economy," Journal of Econom-
    ic Literature, December 1975, pp. 1249-1292.

10. Kohen, Andre I., with Susan C. Breinich, and Patricia
    Shields, Women and the Economy: A Bibliography and
    Review of the Literature on Sex Differentiation in the
    Labor Market, Center for Human Resource Research,
    Ohio State University, Columbus, Ohio, March 1975.

11. Malkiel, B. G. and J. A. Malkiel, "Male-Female Pay
    Differentials in Professional Employment," American
    Economic Review, September 1973, pp. 693-705.

12. Mallan, Lucy B. "Work Experience and Women's Earn-
    ings, 1951-71," Paper at panel of Washington Statis-
    tical Society, May 1976.

13. _____, "Young Widows and Their Children: A Com-
    parative Report," Social Security Bulletin, May 1975,
    pp. 3-21.

14. Mincer, Jacob and Solomon W. Polachek, "Family In-
    vestments in Human Capital: Earnings of Women,"
    Journal of Political Economy, Part II, March/April
    1974, pp. S76-S108.

15. Newman, Winn. "Presentation III" for Panel Discussion
    on policy issues in Blaxall, Martha, and Barbara Rea-
    gan (eds.), Women and the Workplace: The Implica-
    tions of Occupational Segregation, The University of
    Chicago Press, Chicago 1976.

16. Parnes, Herbert S. and Gilbert Nestel, "Factors in
    Career Orientation and Occupational Status," Chapter
    III in Dual Careers: A Longitudinal Analysis of the
    Labor Market Experience of Women, Vol. IV, Center
    for Human Resource Research, Ohio State University,
    Columbus, Ohio, 1975.

17. Sandell, Steven H. "The Economics of Family Migra-

tion" Chapter VI in Parnes, et al., Dual Careers: A Longitudinal Analysis of the Labor Market Experience of Women, Vol. IV, Center for Human Resource Research, Ohio State University, Columbus, Ohio, 1975.

18. U. S. Department of Commerce, Bureau of the Census, Census of Population: 1970, Subject Reports, Final Report PC-(2)-6B, "Persons Not Employed," Washington, D. C. 1973.

19. _____, "Characteristics of the Population Below the Poverty Level, 1974," Current Population Reports, Consumer Income, P-60, No. 102, Washington, January 1976.

20. _____, "Money Income in 1974 of Families and Persons in the United States," Current Population Reports, Consumer Income, Series P-60, No. 101, Washington, D. C., January 1976.

21. _____, "Money Income in 1975 of Families and Persons in the United States," Current Population Reports, Consumer Income, Series P-60, No. 105, Washington, D. C., January 1977.

22. U. S. Department of Health, Education, and Welfare, Social Security Administration, Office of Research and Statistics, Reaching Retirement Age: Findings From A Survey of Newly Entitled Workers, 1968-70, Research Report No. 47, Washington, D. C., 1976.

23. U. S. Department of Labor, Bureau of Labor Statistics, "Educational Attainment of Workers, March 1974," Special Labor Force Report, No. 175, Washington, D. C.

24. _____, "Marital and Family Characteristics of the Labor Force, March 1975," Special Labor Force Report, No. 183, Washington, D. C.

25. U. S. Department of Labor, Women's Bureau, The Earnings Gap Between Women and Men, Washington, D. C., 1976.

26. U. S. President, Economic Report and Annual Report of the U. S. Council of Economic Advisors, 1973, Washington, D. C., 1973.

27. Waldman, Elizabeth, "Are Women Getting Paid What They're Worth, or Are They Worth What They're Getting?" Paper prepared for panel meeting of Washington Statistical Society, May 1976 (mimeographed).

28. Wallace, Phyllis A., "Impact of Equal Employment Opportunity Laws," Chapter 6 in Kreps, Juanita M., ed., Women and the American Economy: A Look to the 1980's, The American Assembly, Columbia University, Prentice-Hall, Englewood, N. J., 1976.

PART V

WOMEN AND POLITICS

INTRODUCTION

The next four authors have written essays that contribute significantly to our understanding of equality, power and how to obtain both.   These essays have as their focus, the developmental stages of the political woman.

Irene Diamond analyzes the relationship of female political candidates, the women's movement, and the National Women's Political Caucus.   Studying trends in the political life of women in the United States, Diamond lays the groundwork for further research concerning the future of women in politics.

Maureen Fiedler's study focuses on the ambition of certain women to hold high political office in the United States Congress.   Who seeks much responsibility and power, what are the differences between male and female congressional aspirants and what are the influences or constraints of education, family, and self-perception?   These are some of the questions Fiedler analyzes, documenting her work with considerable data.

In M. Margaret Conway's analysis of women as voluntary political activists, a broader understanding of the complexities of the political woman begins to emerge.   We see patterns of political participation and characteristics of women in political leadership roles as well as the influences to which political women respond.

The last essay in this section, by Sarah Liebschutz, crystalizes the relationship between the role of politically in-

volved women and the future of the Republican Party.   In
this study, Liebschutz analyzes the significance of women's
increased participation in the party, including women's motives for becoming involved and their attitudes toward other
women in politics.

Chapter 12

EXPLORING THE RELATIONSHIP BETWEEN FEMALE CANDIDACIES AND THE WOMEN'S MOVEMENT

by Irene Diamond

In the 1972 general elections thirty-two women were major party candidates for the U.S. House of Representatives, and 842 women were major party candidates for seats in state legislatures. In 1974 forty-one women were major party candidates for the U.S. House, and 1,126 were major party candidates for the state legislature. These figures suggest that we may be witnessing the beginning of a new trend in female participation in campaigns for public office. Normally I would not dare to use the term "trend" on the basis of such limited data, but the recognition by friend and foe alike of the emergence of a women's movement in the early 1970's gives me cause to believe that I am not being foolishly daring. The critical question is, what is the relationship between this apparent trend in female political participation and the women's movement? If data were available on the careers and motivations of female candidates both in 1974 and earlier periods, one might systematically investigate this question, but such data are not available to me or any other researcher I know of. What I do have available are the results of a survey administered by the National Women's Political Caucus as part of its "Win With Women '74" project. This survey was designed by the NWPC to make available to the press, public, political parties, and female candidates themselves descriptive information on women in politics in 1974. Though the questionnaire differs somewhat from one designed solely for research purposes, given the total absence of systematic information about female candidates these data provide valuable insights for both the political organizer and scholar.

This paper will delineate basic descriptive information on female candidates and their campaigns--who were the candidates?; where did their support come from?; was their sex a disadvantage in campaigning? And finally the typical goal of political campaigns--victory at the polls--will be addressed.

241

What were the factors contributing to female success in the
1974 primaries? As my main interest in these data is in
insights they afford about possible futures for women in politics, particular note will be taken of changing patterns of
mobilization, organizational developments, and changing life
styles.

Methodology

The questionnaire was designed and administered by
the staff of the NWPC. The goal was to distribute the questionnaire to all female candidates for state and Congressional
office in the 1974 primaries. The NWPC obtained the names
and addresses of such candidates by obtaining primary filing
lists from secretaries of states. In states where these lists
were either unavailable or unreliable names were verified by
checking with other available sources--The Women's Division
of the Republican and Democratic National Committees, state
Republican and Democratic headquarters, Congressional offices, or local NWPC affiliates. [1]

Because of the difficulties of obtaining complete lists
of primary candidates and the variability of primary election
dates, in twenty-two states the questionnaires were mailed
after the state's primary election had already been held. [2]
One result of the pre- and post-primary mailings is that
primary winners are probably somewhat over-represented in
this sample. Sixty-nine percent of the pre-primary respondents were winners, while 82 percent of the post-primary
respondents were winners. (Why bother to fill out a questionnaire if you have already lost?) In order to avoid the effects of this bias, only pre-primary responses will be used
when analyzing primary outcomes.

The questionnaire was mailed to a total of 1,550 candidates, and usable responses were received from a total of
625 candidates for an over-all response rate of 40 percent.
The response rate for Democrats was somewhat higher than
the rate for Republicans (44 percent Dem., 35 percent Rep.),
which means that Democratic candidates are somewhat over-
represented in the sample. This party difference in response
rate is not surprising when we consider that the questionnaire
was distributed by the NWPC, an organization which tends to
be heavily Democratic in membership and occasionally is even
misperceived as a front for the Democratic party. [3] Another
factor which may have contributed to the differing response

rates is that in the actual candidate population Republicans
are more highly represented among incumbents than among
non-incumbents. Incumbents very likely have been the re-
cipients of previous questionnaires and may be somewhat less
than excited about responding to yet another questionnaire.
Since Republicans were not markedly under-represented in
the sample and there is no certainty about the nature of the
Republican respondent/non-respondent differences, party
weighting procedures were not used in the analysis.

Analysis of Findings

        The respondents in this survey were candidates for a
variety of state and national offices; 6 were candidates for
the U. S. Senate, 59 for the U. S. House, 107 for the State
Senate, 398 for the State Assembly, 7 for Secretary of State,
and 29 for other state-wide offices (Governor, Commissioner
of Education, etc.) A typical female candidate in 1974 might
be married, college educated, white, between 45 and 54
years of age, and the mother of two children, only one of
whom still lives at home. She is not currently employed
but has been previously employed for an extended period as
a teacher. She has never run for public office before but has
held party office in her local community and has given a considerable amount of time during the last few years to the local Heart Fund drive. She is not a member of the National
Women's Political Caucus, nor has she had any previous contact with the Caucus. She feels that inflation is the most
important problem facing the country and, not surprisingly,
she sees inflation as the most important issue in her campaign. This typical candidate in 1974 is remarkably similar
to the typical female office-holder described in earlier
studies. [4] Her views about the most important problems facing the nation reflect the concerns of the American public--
both men and women--in the last summer and early fall of
1974. [5] Has nothing changed? This was the year of "Win
With Women '74," and the political arm of the women's
movement had now been in operation for three full years;
where was the "new" political woman we expected? A new
political woman does not emerge from these data, but then
the typical female candidate is not every candidate: this is
a large sample and there is considerable variation in the
data.

        As stated above, the typical female candidate had nev-
er run for public office before. More precisely 50 percent

of these candidates have never run either for nomination in
a primary or for public office in a general election. Do the
1974 newcomers differ appreciably from candidates of previous years?

A significant difference of the 1974 newcomers is
their age. They are younger. Twenty-eight percent of the
newcomers are under 35 years of age, while only 14 percent
of those who have run before are this young. Perhaps what
is most interesting about the age distributions is that there
is still a good proportion of women beginning their careers
at relatively advanced ages. One candidate for the state
senate who was a grandmother of 16 grandchildren felt it
necessary to explain her candidacy!

> I married at age 55, after a 5-1/2-year honeymoon
> as a second wife, my husband died leaving me a
> millionaire. Unless I tell you this you'll never
> understand my decision to run at my age. (ERA!)

But in fact this candidate is not as unusual as she thinks.
Freed from the responsibilities of childrearing many a grandmother has begun her career in the state legislature. On
the other hand there is some suggestion in these data that
the overall age distribution among female activists may be
shifting toward the male pattern: 21 percent of all these
women candidates are below 35 years of age. In a nationwide survey of women state legislators elected in 1970 only
12 percent of the women were under forty years of age. [6]
These earlier data are for elected officials, not candidates,
but as the present study does not indicate that voters systematically discriminate against younger women it seems
reasonable to infer that the average age of women running
for public office has declined in the last four years.

More younger women may be choosing to run for public office but they are also making some other choices which
may be of profound significance. Forty-nine percent of the
women 25-35 years of age do not have children. These wom-
en do not simply reflect the declining birth rate in the population at large, for nationally only 25 percent of the women
in this age cohort do not have children. [7] Clearly holding
public office and caring for children are still seen as incompatible roles among young women who opt for a political
life.

Marcia M. Lee in a study comparing female and male

activists in Westchester County, N.Y., in 1972 found that the big break between the sexes was not in time devoted to political activities but in willingness to run for political office and that for women the latter was markedly affected by having children at home. Comparing the inhibiting consequences of child care responsibilities with female perceptions about the propriety of women in politics and fear of sex discrimination, Lee concludes, "The factor least likely to change, and, therefore, most likely to continue to restrict women from fully participating in politics in the future, is child care."[8] The data here provide no grounds for differing with this depressing conclusion. As the option not to have children becomes more socially viable it will perhaps be easier for young women who choose this course to enter the public arena (single and childless women often have to justify their status to the public). This would enlarge the female recruitment base somewhat, but it is unlikely that this new mode of entrance would become frequent enough to put women on an even footing with men. (Moreover, I would argue that it would be retrogressive rather than progressive if large numbers of women were to choose this option. Choosing the "freedom" of childlessness can be viewed as an essentially adaptive act within the present sexual division of labor.)

Aside from age, the social background (education, employment, marital status and number of children) of newcomers is not noticeably different from that of non-newcomers. The same applies with respect to political careers: there are no marked differences either in prior party offices or prior appointive offices. Newcomers have held fewer such offices, but the differences are not of such a magnitude as to indicate a substantial change in recruitment patterns. Expectedly a greater proportion of the candidates at the state level are newcomers than at the Congressional level. But it is noteworthy that newcomers constitute 40 percent of the Congressional candidates. Perhaps women are beginning to shoot for the top without first climbing the ladder.

The similarities between newcomers and non-newcomers have been stressed, but there are slight differences in party affiliation and Caucus membership worth noting. Republicans are more highly represented among non-newcomers than among newcomers, whereas Democrats are stronger among newcomers. Since most of the third-party candidates are from parties on the Left (e.g., Peace and Freedom party in California and Liberty Union in Vermont) this increase is likely due to ideological commitment and a consequent effort

at recruitment rather than a pragmatic decision to make wom-
en sacrificial candidates. The explanation for what may be
happening in the two major parties is not so readily apparent.

Table 1. Newcomers Compared to
Candidates Who Have Run Before

	% of Newcomers		% of Non-newcomers
Under age 34	29		14
Republican	28	(-9%)	37
Democrat	64	(+5%)	59
Third party	8	(+4%)	4
Member NWPC	30		34

Are local Democratic party organizations making a more active effort to recruit women? Or does this represent a shift
in party affiliation among activists, reflective of the changes
taking place in the general population?[9] The matter is in
need of further investigation.

With respect to Caucus membership newcomers are
somewhat less likely to be members of the NWPC (see Table
1). The actual percentage difference is so slight as to be
negligible, but since one might have expected a greater proportion of Caucus members among newcomers rather than the
reverse the finding is worth exploring. Clearly newcomers
are not being mobilized via membership in the Caucus.[10]
This newcomer/non-newcomer difference is particularly striking with respect to the incidence of contact with the Caucus:
among candidates who are not NWPC members 65 percent of
the newcomers indicated they had had no previous contact
with the Caucus (prior to the questionnaire itself) whereas
43 percent of the non-newcomers have had no contact. It
would appear that the unprecedented participation by newcomers in 1974 cannot be directly attributed to the activities
of the NWPC. The impact of the Caucus on participation is
probably of a more indirect nature and thus is not being
tapped by the measures used here. What is indicated is that
Caucus affiliation is more common among established candidates than among those who are making their first ventures
into electoral politics. In fact electoral success may often
be the incentive for pursuing membership. One newcomer
who successfully weathered the primary responded to the
question about Caucus membership with, "No I'm not but I
plan to join now." This response could explain why incum-

bents are much more likely to be Caucus members (47 percent) than non-incumbents (29 percent).

On the whole newcomers do not differ appreciably
from candidates who have run before. There is one extremely interesting variation, however, which may be of significance
in looking towards the future. Only 20 women (3 percent)
mentioned women's rights issues as an important issue in
their campaign (this is discouraging if one recalls from the
NWPC Statement of Purpose "We shall raise women's issues
in every election") and these women were disproportionately
newcomers (17 of the 20). [11] The numbers involved here are
so small (clearly the most important observation to make
is that women candidates are not stressing women's issues
in their campaigns) that it would be unwise to develop a profile of such candidates or make any firm predictions about
the frequency of such issues in the future campaigns, but
there is a suggestion that newcomers are more likely to raise
women's rights issues. The use of a campaign as a vehicle
for raising issues and affecting consciousness can be viewed
as a rational goal in and of itself, but in our political system campaign strategies tend to be assessed in terms of
their immediate payoff at the polls: of the candidates who
raised women's rights issues only five survived through the
general election. Considering the nature of the data (so few
cases and the lack of any qualitative information on the campaigns) it would be inappropriate to make any casual connections, but I would stress the importance of further research on this matter.

It is difficult to discern the impact of the current
women's movement by looking only at who the candidates
were, but if support in the actual campaigns is examined
noticeable patterns begin to emerge. The candidates were
asked to indicate both the major groups or organizations that
supported their candidacies and the type of support received.
Not surprisingly party organizations emerged as the most
frequently mentioned source of support. Labor and professional organizations were next, and it is these three that are
the most important source of that critical campaign resource
--money. However, at the local level women's political
Caucus groups ranked just third behind party organizations
and labor. Though they were not a major source of support,
women's rights groups also emerged. As might be expected
women's Caucus and women's rights groups typically supply
endorsements and workers rather than money. Although
there was no direct test of the motivations of these candidates,

it does seem likely that the unprecedented number of female
candidates in 1974 was in part attributable to ambitions
kindled by these new support groups for women. Women's
minimal participation in elective office has often been attributed to their lack of political ambition, but as ambition
is partly a response to opportunities, women's traditionally
low political ambition can be attributed to their realistic
assessment of opportunities open to them. The presence in
the political environment of positive supports for women may
change such assessments.

As new sources of political support begin to emerge
for women, we would expect an increase in ambition among
some women. This process is not likely to be a one-way
street: organizational support for women is likely to generate organized opposition. Ten percent of these candidates
faced opposition from groups identified with anti-women's
rights issues. The recent defeat of state E. R. A. amendments in N. Y. and N. J. suggests that the opposition is becoming both better organized and more influential.

We can also see some impact of the women's movement in the candidates' assessments of the advantages and
disadvantages experienced as a woman candidate. The most
frequently mentioned advantage referred to the "high visibility" of women in politics, while the typical disadvantage referred to the "general prejudice against women in politics."
These may be viewed as "traditional" advantages and disadvantages, for they have been noted in earlier studies. However, such comments as, on the one hand, "women themselves are becoming cognizant of the fact that they need
spokeswomen" or "some women will vote for any woman"
and, on the other hand, "people assume I'm a radical militant and radical women's libber" or "automatically termed
women's libber" suggest that the sheer existence of feminist
activity in the land has in itself added a new dimension to
the relationship between female candidates and constituents.

If female candidates traditionally have been more visible simply because they stood out in a field of male candidates, they have become even more so today because each
such candidacy has become something of an emotionally
charged symbol irrespective of the ideology of a particular
candidate. Perhaps the most striking finding is that the advantages of being a female candidate were just as frequently
mentioned as disadvantages: 60 percent of the candidates perceived advantages while 58 percent perceived disadvantages.

Moreover, these perceptions are not mutually exclusive of each other; candidates who perceive advantages also tend to perceive disadvantages. [12] The strength of this relationship may be somewhat exaggerated by response set (respondents who took time with the questionnaire may be more inclined to give some response to both questions while those who did not may be inclined to simply write "none"), but arguing against the dismissal of this relationship as a methodological artifact is the additional finding that both younger women and NWPC members have a higher awareness of advantages and disadvantages than others.   The relationship is undoubtedly a product of particular socialization experience.   Though the media may often associate raised consciousness with angry women who see only the negative aspects of their sex status, social psychological theory would in fact predict the findings here.   Heightened consciousness creates the ability to perceive patterns which were previously unobserved: therefore an increased awareness of the salience of sex roles in social relationships should lead to the recognition that such roles have multitudinous ramifications, both positive and negative.

Though the over-all relationship between the perception of campaign advantages and disadvantages is best explained by pre-campaign socialization experiences, there is evidence that the perception of the campaign experience is also influenced by the campaign outcome.   Among the candidates who received the questionnaire after they had already completed their primary those who had been successful were more sanguine about the influence of sex.   Sixty-seven percent of the winners indicated that they had experienced advantages as a woman candidate, and 57 percent indicated disadvantages, while 55 percent of the losers indicated advantages, and 74 percent indicated disadvantages.   This "outcome bias" attests to the presence of some degree of subjectivity in these evaluations, but I would still argue that over-all patterns indicate that the candidate's sex status has discernible objective consequences.   The statements concerning the disadvantages or advantages of being a woman candidate cannot be dismissed as mere subjective reflection.

The final question which may be addressed is the matter of campaign success--what were the factors that contributed to victories by women in the 1974 primaries?   Not surprisingly, the single most critical one is incumbency.   All the incumbents in this sample were successful.   Among non-incumbents party support was crucial: 42 percent of those who did not have party support lost their primaries, while

among those who did have party support only 21 percent lost.
Interestingly, candidacy in previous primaries or experience
in local, party, or appointive office is of no consequence for
victories.   Money, however, is not irrelevant.   Of those
candidates who did not mention money as a type of support
that they received during the campaign 38 percent lost, while
among those who did mention money only 19 percent lost.
This difference, however, is probably somewhat exaggerated
by the fact that incumbents tend to receive more money.
The candidates were also asked how much money they thought
their major opponent would spend.   Such measures are obviously not reliable measures of the actual amounts of money
raised, but if we compare the relative differences, it would
appear that as relative disadvantages decrease the chance of
winning increases.   Among non-incumbent candidates for
state assembly seats those who were successful averaged
$1,920 more than their opponents while those who were un-
successful averaged $5,105 less than their opponents.   Sim-
ply put, money invested in women candidates is not wasted.

        Judgments as to the relevance of other factors was
inconclusive.   Of particular interest is the question of wom-
en's Caucus support.   If in fact more women became candidates because of the emergence of new support groups for
women, do women who receive direct support from such
groups during the campaign fare better or worse than those
who do not?   Because there were so few women in the pre-
primary states who indicated such support it is impossible
to make any firm judgments.   Forty-eight women indicated
women's Caucus support, and 40 percent of them lost the
primary, while among those who did not indicate support 29
percent lost.   This difference is not explained by party support or incumbency (i. e. , candidates who received Caucus
support were not less likely to be incumbents or not have
party support), but it is certainly not substantial enough to
indicate that Caucus support is a hinderance.   Caution is also
advised by the fact that we are dealing with averages derived
from races in a variety of states.   Caucus support is very
probably considerably more valuable in certain districts than
in others.   A candidate in Florida who did not receive Caucus support and won her race responded to the question, "How
can the Caucus help you?" with, "By not insisting that I state
my views on E. R. A. , many here are opposed."   The information in this particular case is much too scanty to permit
any causal inferences, but the data from this questionnaire
and my own observations of Caucus procedures for endorsing
candidates make quite clear that the Caucus goals of reform-

ism--getting more women elected to public office--and lib-
eralism--gaining public acceptance of feminist issues--may
not always be compatible. [13]

Undeniably from a policy point of view it is important
to determine those conditions which allow for both goals, and
to develop the necessary strategies which would maximize
such conditions. But caution should be exercised. Because
of the dominance in American politics of non-ideological
parties, whose primary purpose is the winning of elections,
neither the practitioner nor the scholar possesses concepts
for effectively evaluating political campaigns. The typical
criterion--success on election day--is surely inadequate for
assessing the impact of organizations which have complex
ideological goals. As suggested earlier, it is possible to
conceive of a campaign as a vehicle for effecting consciousness, and if this approach were to become part of the conceptual apparatus then it might even be possible to develop
new measures for evaluating campaigns. Would it be too
much to hope for that in the process of changing American
politics the women's movement will force a reconsideration
of the very way we study politics?

NOTES

1. Official filing lists were unavailable for Alabama, Iowa,
   Massachusetts, Nevada, New Hampshire, New York,
   North Dakota, Oklahoma, Rhode Island and Vermont.
2. These states were: Alaska, Arkansas, Indiana, Iowa,
   Kentucky, Louisiana, Maryland, Massachusetts, Mon-
   tana, Nevada, New Hampshire, New Jersey, North
   Carolina, North Dakota, Oregon, Rhode Island, South
   Carolina, South Dakota, Texas, Utah, Vermont, West
   Virginia. All other states will be referred to as the
   "pre-primary states."
3. For instance at the NWPC national convention in Houston (1972) a survey indicated that only 13 percent of
   the delegates identified with the Republican Party.
   Mike Kagay, "Feminist Leaders and Followers Project," (Princeton University, unpublished paper).
4. Jeane Kirkpatrick, Political Woman (N.Y.: Basic
   Books, 1974); Irene Diamond, Sex Roles in the State
   House (New Haven: Yale University Press, 1977),
   p. 177.
5. Gallup Opinion Index, September 1974, Report No. 111.
6. Diamond, op. cit., p. 275.

7.   National Center for Health Statistics, 1973 <u>Natality Vol-</u>
     <u>ume</u> Table 117 (to be published).
8.   Marcia M. Lee, "Why Few Women Hold Public Office:
     The Incompatibility of Democracy and Traditional Sex-
     ual Role Assignments," <u>Political Science Quarterly</u>,
     91. (Summer 1976), 31<u>3.</u>
9.   Gallup Opinion Index, June 1975, Report No. 120, p. 22.
10. The newcomer/non-newcomer difference held for both
     paper membership ("Are you a member of the National
     Women's Political Caucus?") and active membership
     ("What voluntary organization (other than party) have
     you given time to during the last five years?").
11. "Statement of Purpose Adopted by the National Women's
     Political Caucus," (mimeographed, July 1971).
12. Gamma Correlation equals . 67--scoring advantages 1
     and disadvantages 1.
13. For example in California local Caucuses decided on
     endorsements through a screening process in which
     the criteria were the candidate's viability and stand
     on feminist issues. Susan Carroll suggests this
     formulation of Caucus goals in "Women's Rights and
     Political Parties: Issue Development, the 1972 Con-
     ventions, and the National Women's Political Caucus"
     (unpublished M. A. thesis, Indiana University, Bloom-
     ington, Indiana, 1975).

Chapter 14

THE CONGRESSIONAL AMBITIONS OF
FEMALE POLITICAL ELITES

by Maureen Fiedler

The Basic Problem

A recent poster printed by the National Organization for Women reads: "A woman's place is in the House and in the Senate." However valuable this may be as advice for the future, it is anything but a description of the past or present status of the American woman in Congress. Only 91 women have ever served in the U. S. House of Representatives, and only 11 have ever been United States Senators. 1 In 1975, only 19 women (4. 4 percent) of the 435 Representatives are women, and no women presently serve in the U. S. Senate.

Furthermore, women do not often seek congressional office. In 1974, which the National Women's Political Caucus proclaimed as a year to "Win with women," only 44 women sought House seats, and only 3 women won major party nominations for the U. S. Senate. 2

The central question which faces those interested in the relations between sex and power is simply "why?" Why have so few women achieved political power in Congress (and other public offices) 56 years after their political rights were guaranteed by the Nineteenth Amendment to the Constitution? Why have so few women sought congressional office or entertained serious ambitions for public office generally? Power, as the axiom says, goes to those who seek it.

This question is, of course, part of a larger concern of political scientists: why does anyone--male or female-- aspire to public office? What systemic factors or individual political, socio-economic, or psychological characteristics "enable" a citizen to consider a political career?3 What individual or political-system factors constrain ambition?

Since the publication of Joseph Schlesinger's Ambition

and Politics,[4] a number of studies have explored various aspects of "ambition theory." Some have focused, as did
Schlesinger himself, on the "opportunity structures" provided
for potential candidates by various offices or political sub-
systems.[5] Others have analyzed the consequences of ambition for higher office for the behavior of lower-level legislators.[6] A third group has dealt with questions more directly related to this study: the relationship between political
ambition and individual socio-economic, psychological, or
demographic characteristics.[7]

None of these studies deals directly with the relation
between sex identifications and ambition;[8] indeed, none of
those who used survey analysis in their studies gave any hint
of having women in their samples. But these analyses do
provide valuable clues to characteristics which might be expected to "enable" anyone to seek high public office. For
example, some studies reveal that those aspiring to higher
office tend to be younger and better educated than those with
no desire to advance.[9] Other studies describe the "ambitious" as having strong egos or well-developed achievement
orientations.[10] Logically, such differences would be expected to hold for both sex groups.

If we are to discover what enables or constrains wom-
en in seeking congressional office, we must also understand
what enables or constrains men in seeking that office. Without such comparative analysis, we risk attributing to one
sex ambition-related characteristics that may well be characteristics of the "ambitious" in both sexes.

But women are clearly a special category among the
"non-ambitious" in politics, and recent studies have focused
directly on theories linking sex to the quest for political
power. In Political Woman,[11] Kirkpatrick discusses four
"hypothetical constraints" which various political and social
analysts have suggested restrain women from seeking elite
political status:

> 1) physiological constraints--or the familiar
> "biology is destiny" theme which asserts that fe-
> male physiology is "naturally and universally" un-
> suited for the exercise of political power;
> 2) cultural constraints--the belief that sex-
> related cultural norms have categorized politics as
> an "improper" arena of female activity, and that
> the strength of such norms (shared by both sexes),

and penalties for their violation, have restrained
all but a few non-conformist women from seeking
positions of political influence;

　　　3) role constraints--the notion that family-
centered female roles are incompatible with the
time and energy requirements of high public office;
and

　　　4) male conspiracy--the belief that men are
oppressor-culprits who maintain a rigid sex-based
caste system which excludes women from any real
share in political power. [12]

　　Because some women have been notably successful in
winning and exercising power, and because democratic politics does not require physical force for the acquisition of
power, Kirkpatrick found little credence in the first theory.
She found some evidence of male desire (not actual "conspiracy") to keep women from inner political circles in state
legislatures, but in the epilogue to her study, she emphasized the centrality of role constraints and cultural norms
(pieces of one social whole) in restraining women from
achieving elite political status.　The changes she believes
are necessary if women are to become the political equals
of men spell out the meaning of these constraints:

　　　... it would be necessary to abandon the notion
　　　... that men are the natural governors of society
　　　... that femininity is inexorably associated with sub-
　　　missiveness of female to male, that, in a woman,
　　　the desire for power is a signal of alienation from
　　　her true identity....
　　　What must also go is the expectation that the
　　　male will have prime responsibility for the finan-
　　　cial support of the family and the female for its
　　　nurturance ... if wives are to reach the top in
　　　politics, then husbands must be willing to take on
　　　substantial responsibility for home and family. [13]

　　She asserts that cultural beliefs and role conceptions
and practices are related strongly to political ambition and
political success for women.　Presumably, women who have
abandoned constraining cultural norms, acquired professional
skills, and developed a lifestyle (in or out of marriage)
which leaves time for full-time political pursuits would be
most likely to entertain ambitions for high public office--and
most specific for our purposes here--congressional office.

Role-flexibility would seem especially important for
the female Congressional aspirant. Not only are congressional campaigns usually full-time, energy-consuming enter-
prises, the resulting position, if secured, is more than a
full-time job.[14] It requires establishing a year-long residence in Washington as well as the home district, frequent
travel from one to the other, and unpredictable hours crowded
with committee hearings, staff co-ordination, constituent
visits, speech-making, and sometimes late night sessions on
the floor of the House or Senate. Any woman seriously contemplating such a life would certainly have to adopt a life-
style compatible with the requirements of office, especially
if she is married and has young children at home. If she
is married and hoped to sustain her marriage, her husband
would almost certainly have to acquiesce in her preferences
and assume considerable responsibility at home.

Psychologically, the female congressional aspirant
would be expected to have developed beliefs about her sex
identifications which reflect a "political feminist consciousness": beliefs that women as well as men can be successful at the pinnacle of political power, and that femininity,
marriage and motherhood are compatible with a political
career. The rejection of "cultural constraints" would seem
a necessary pre-requisite to any quest for Congressional
office.

These are traits the would-be female Representative
or Senator would have to acquire in addition to characteristics generally associated with "gladiatorial" political activity:[15] middle to high socio-economic status,[16] a strong
sense of personal efficacy,[17] a firm sense of self-esteem
and a need for achievement,[18] and a sense of the importance of politics for the self.[19]

Naturally, a woman could adopt a life-style with great
role flexibility and believe firmly that women belong in public office without having a shred of interest in a political
career for herself. Many men with strong egos and high
achievement orientations--even those with a real interest in
politics--channel their energies into the business world or
the professions rather than public service. Complex value-
preferences factor into the "ambition calculus" for both
sexes. But a woman who does aspire to a non-conventional
role for her sex--such as a seat in the Congress--would
certainly be expected to have freed herself from the cultural
and role constraints which keep other women from even considering the option.

Some Hypotheses

These preliminary considerations suggest several hypotheses relating congressional ambition to sex identifications.
First, it is necessary to determine whether and/or to what
extent female political elites--in this instance, the women
who were delegates to the Democratic and Republican National Conventions in 1972[20]--had less ambition for Congress
than male elites. It is also important to determine how expectations of success in achieving congressional office dif-
fered for each sex:

> Hypothesis #1: a) Female political elites are less
> likely than male elites to entertain ambitions for
> Congressional office, and b) women who claim such
> ambitions are less likely than male aspirants to be-
> lieve they can achieve their goal.

If this hypothesis proves valid, two questions follow:
What characteristics are related to ambition regardless of
sex? What characteristics are related to ambition for wom-
en? Only by comparing the congressionally ambitious and
non-ambitious within each sex-group is it possible to distinguish these two sets of characteristics, and discover
whether there are any traits related to female congressional
ambition that are not related to male congressional ambition.
With this basic query, we move into relatively unexplored
territory.

Although recent studies comparing female and male
political elites report some differences between the two in
occupational background, socio-economic status, position in
the life cycle, ideology, and socialization,[21] none deals directly with the question of comparative ambition for high
public office. "Ambition literature," on the other hand, does
not deal directly with the sex variable. We would expect
the "ambitious" of either gender to differ from the "non-
ambitious" in a number of ways, but nothing in contemporary
political science gives any clues as to how "ambitious" wom-
en might differ from "ambitious" men, when both have already established some claim to status as political elites.

We need to test the data first for characteristics
which are functions of Congressional ambition, and not sex
identifications:

> Hypothesis #2: Within each sex group, Congres-

sional aspirants are significantly different from the
non-ambitious in: a) life-cycle position; b) educational attainment; c) family socialization to politics; d) achievement orientations; e) self-image;
f) the perceived importance of politics for self.

These characteristics are drawn from much of the literature on political participation and political ambition previously cited. [22] Based on this same literature, there is no
reason to conclude that ambition is a function of demographic
factors such as racial, ethnic, regional, or religious identifications; civic affiliations; political style; or ideological
identifications:

Hypothesis #3: Congressional aspirants in either
sex group are not significantly different from the
non-ambitious in a) racial, ethnic, regional, or
religious identifications; b) civic affiliations;
c) political incentives; or d) ideological identifications. [23]

Our earlier discussion of feminine roles and cultural
norms would lead us to believe that ambitious women differ
most significantly from non-ambitious women on measures of
"political feminist consciousness" and role-flexibility. Of
course, it is not possible to test these variables for both
sexes. Male conceptions of "male role" have never been
defined as major barriers to political ambition; it is femininity that has been associated with submissiveness, and
auxiliary rather than leadership functions in political life.
But congressionally ambitious women can be compared with
non-ambitious women on cultural and role dimensions of female existence to determing their relationship to political
aspirations for high office.

Any woman who seeks high office is an anomaly on
the American political landscape. The higher the office to
which she aspires, the less likely she is to have female colleagues, and the more likely she is to stand out as one of a
small band of non-conventional women. Consequently, the
fourth hypothesis anticipates not only a relation between ambition and "feminist consciousness," but between levels of
ambition and such "consciousness":

Hypothesis #4: The level of political ambition
among female elites is significantly related to
"feminist consciousness" as defined in these sub-
hypotheses:

a) The higher the office to which female elites
aspire, the lower their perception of non-biological
sex differences as innate or natural, and the lower
their inclination to believe that the political order
is the "natural" domain of men.

b) The higher the office to which female elites
aspire, the lower their perception of conflict between femininity and professional or political roles.

c) The higher the office to which female elites
aspire, the less likely they are to be satisfied with
the "influence" (or "power behind the throne") commonly associated with auxiliary female roles in
politics. [24]

This hypothesis anticipates that female aspirations for
congressional office are strongly and significantly related to
the rejection of sex-related culturally-constraining norms.
We expect that a partial answer to the question: "why have
so few women (compared to men) sought congressional office?"--will be that women have been restrained by the acceptance of sex-role norms that have defined them out of
influential power processes.

Finally, previous discussion would lead us to expect
that female congressional hopefuls, when compared with wom-
en not ambitious for public office, would have developed--
or would at least anticipate--a life-style compatible with the
time and energy requirements of legislative office.   Such a
life-style might mean single rather than married status, marriage without children--or at least without young children, or
an anticipated "work pattern" that would permit freedom from
full-time homemaking responsibilities.   The final hypothesis
provides a test of this assumption in relation to both present
and anticipated feminine roles:

Hypothesis #5: a) Female congressional aspirants,
when compared with women not ambitious for public office, are significantly more likely to have developed a life-style compatible with a congressional
role. b) Alternatively, congressional aspirants
among female elites are more likely than women not
politically ambitious to desire such a life-style. [25]

The preliminary discussion of problems facing women
in politics leads us to expect that the fourth and fifth hypotheses will be most significant in delineating sex-differences
in congressional ambition.

The Data

 All of these hypotheses will be tested on a sample survey of male and female political elites who might be expected to entertain congressional--or other public office-- ambitions: delegates to the 1972 Democratic and Republican National Conventions. [26]

 Two data sets were used: a specially drawn quota sample of 1336 face-to-face interviews designed to include equal numbers of men and women, and a mail questionnaire sample of 2449 delegates which yielded a 51 percent response rate for Democrats and a 63 percent response rate for Republicans. An "intersect" sample of delegates was personally interviewed and returned mail questionnaires. Careful cross-checking of these three data segments indicates a very high degree of comparability across samples, and the structure and size of the sample of women support a high level of confidence in the findings presented here.

Findings

 What we are exploring here is in Schlesinger's terminology, "progressive ambition"--aspiring to attain an office more important than the one presently sought or held. [27] All of the elites in our sample have attained the status of national convention delegates, and most reported having held some other party office. [28] Experience in public office-holding was low at both conventions, and very few members of Congress are included in the sample.

 Delegates were asked this question: "Thinking of all the possible offices and positions in politics, from local to national ... which of the following would you most like to be if you could have your personal choice? Consider public office." This was followed by a list of specific public offices at local, state and national levels, as well as a "not interested" category.

 A positive response required no delegate commitment to run for office, no public statement of candidacy, no investment of time or money. It meant only that the delegate had considered the possibility of public office, and privately wished to attain it. On the basis of this criterion, how do the sexes fare comparatively in their ambitions for public office, and especially congressional office? Are the expectations stated in hypothesis #1 correct?

TABLE 1

1972 Convention Delegates: Ambitions for Public Office; by Sex and Party by Sex (%)*

Public Office Ambition**	All Delegates	All Male Delegates	All Female Delegates	Democrats Males	Democrats Females	Republicans Males	Republicans Females
President-VP	7	11	2	12	3	7	0
U.S. Senator	22	28	14	28	17	27	6
U.S. Representative	9	11	6	11	7	11	3
Appointed National Office[1]	11	12	11	12	11	12	10
Governor	5	7	1	5	1	9	1
Other State Office[2]	14	11	19	10	16	12	24
Mayor	1	1	1	1	1	1	2
Other Local Office[3]	4	3	7	3	7	2	5
No Ambition for Public Office	26	18	39	17	35	19	49
N=	2449	1452	996	913	687	539	309

*These data are taken from the Mail Questionnaire sample of the 1972 Convention Delegate study. Percentages do not necessarily add to 100% due to rounding.

1. "Appointed National Office" includes: Cabinet Member, Ambassador, Federal Judge, Federal Prosecutor, or "other" national office.

2. "Other State Office" includes: Lieutenant Governor, State Judge, State Administrative Posts, State Senator, State Representative, or "other" state office.

3. "Other Local Office" includes: Council Member or "other" local office.

**The question on which this table is based is the following:
"Thinking of all the possible offices and positions in politics, from local to national . . . which of the following would you most like to be if you could have your personal choice? Consider public office." (The question was accompanied by a specific list of offices which included those mentioned above, as well as a "no interest" category).

TABLE 2

Congressional Ambitions by Candidate Preference and Sex**
(%)

	McGovern	Humphrey	Wallace	Jackson	Muskie	Kennedy	Chisholm	Other Dems.	Nixon	Other Reps.
Congressional Ambitions:										
% Women	29	10	4	15	22	24	40	8*	9	8*
% Men	46	36	22	28	38	32	56*	33	37	50*
No Public Office Ambition:										
% Women	36	43	35	30	37	28	5	39*	49	50*
% Men	15	18	29	25	10	20	11*	23	19	19*
N for Women=	445	58	23	27	59	25	20	13*	296	12*
N for Men=	445	144	45	53	81	79	9*	30	518	16*

**These data are taken from the mail questionnaire sample. They describe each candidate preference group according to the percentages of men and women with congressional ambitions (for either the House or Senate), and the percentages of men and women with no ambition for public office. These "candidate preference groups" represent the personal choices of delegates irrespective of how some may have been "bound" to cast a vote on the floor of the convention. Percentages do not add to 100 percent because other levels of ambition have been omitted.

*N's in these cases are too small for real comparisons or conclusions.

Table 1 shows that they are. In both parties, women
are significantly less likely than men to have any interest
in public office whatsoever, at a ratio of 1:2. Those women
who aspire to public service generally yearn for something
less than the Congress. Compared to men, women show low
interest in any elective national office, and almost no interest in state governorships. Only at local and state levels
(excluding governorships) do women's ambitions equal or exceed those of males.

Aspirations for congressional office are a piece of the
larger pattern. Men are twice as likely as women to seek a
Senate seat, and almost twice as likely to think a seat in the
House desirable. The sex-pattern holds for both parties, although Republican women are much less congressionally ambitious than are Democratic.

Table 2 indicates that sex differentials in political ambitions hold for every candidate preference group, except for
Chisholm supporters, and here the results are different by
two factors: the N's are so small, especially for the Chisholm men, as to make the resulting comparison questionable;
and at least 15 percent of the Chisholm women expressed a
desire to be President--a large enough percentage of a small
group to skew the resulting Congressional ambitions of these
women. Suffice to say here that the Chisholm women equal
the Chisholm men in ambition for high national office, and
their Congressional ambitions exceed those of males in almost all other candidate preference groups. The same is
not true of McGovern women. Like other women (except
the Chisholm supporters) they are less likely than their male
counterparts to consider congressional office, and more likely to have no public ambitions whatsoever. This trend is
especially pronounced with the Wallace women, Nixon women,
and Humphrey women, but generally present "across the
board."

It is not surprising that the Chisholm women were
the most likely to entertain non-conventional congressional
ambitions. They had after all, smashed personal (if not political) barriers between femininity and high public office by
supporting a female candidate for the Presidency--the office
at the pinnacle of political power that has been completely a
male domain up to the present time. McGovern women, on
the other hand, while generally not out of sympathy with
Shirley Chisholm on the issues of 1972, chose the more conventional presidential candidate: a man.

But what of the expectations of congressional aspirants in each sex group? Are women less likely than men to believe they can achieve their political goals? Delegates were asked a specific question dealing with such expectations: "Now, all things considered, which of all these positions do you think you are most likely to hold at the top of your career in politics?" This was followed by the same list of specific offices used to ask delegates about their ambitions.

The second part of our first hypothesis is confirmed, as shown in Table 3. In each party, women who aspired to Congress were far less likely than male aspirants to believe they could win a seat in the House or Senate. Generally, delegates recognized the "structure of opportunities" Schlesinger analyzes;[29] they knew that their chances were better in the House where more seats are available. But in both categories, women had lower expectations of political success than men. Most striking of all is the fact that none of the Republican women who aspire to the House actually expected to achieve it.

TABLE 3

Those Aspiring to Congressional Offices Who Believe
They Can Achieve Them (%)*

Congressional Office	All Dels.	All Male Dels.	All Female Dels.	Democrats		Republicans	
				M	F	M	F
U.S. Senate	19% (N=96)	22% (N=84)	9% (N=12)	18% (N=43)	8% (N=9)	29% (N=41)	17% (N=3)
U.S. House of Reps.	32% (N=68)	39% (N=60)	14% (N=8)	40% (N=40)	16% (N=8)	36% (N=20)	0% (N=0)

*This table is based on data from the mail questionnaire sample. It describes those men and women in each party who both aspire to congressional office and expect to achieve their goal. The question on which "expectations" were based is the following:
"Now, all things considered, which of all of these positions do you think you are most likely to hold at the top of your career in politics?" (This was followed by the same specific list of public offices used to ask delegates about their ambitions).

N.B. Only a handful of delegates who aspired to congressional offices believed they could actually win the Presidency or Vice-Presidency. All of these were men. No female aspirants for congressional office expected to achieve more than they sought.

The first hypothesis then is valid for this body of
data: female political elites are less congressionally ambitious than male elites, and those aspiring to Congress are
less likely to believe they can attain it.

Ambition and the Life Cycle

The second hypothesis anticipates that a number of
characteristics will be associated with congressional ambition, but not sex identifications. First, the age distribution
of the congressionally ambitious should be younger than that
of those not ambitious for public office. Schlesinger, for
example, places the model age of entrance into the House at
35-39, and the Senate at 50-54. [30] After age 54, there is a
steady and sharp decline in numbers of legislators serving
a first term. Of course, achieving a House or Senate seat
is one thing; wanting it is quite another. But one would
logically expect that those who desire such positions generally
have sufficient years in life ahead of them in which to achieve
their goal--and serve a sufficient number of years to gain influence with legislative colleagues.

Political women, however, often fill childbearing and
nurturing roles in the family before seeking public office.
Consequently, women who are newcomers to legislatures tend
to be older than their male counterparts. [31] The question
here is: do women's aspirations for legislative office come
later in life too?

The answer is no. Congressionally ambitious women
are as young as male aspirants, when compared to those
without desire for public office. Among 1972 Convention delegates in both parties, the vast majority of male and female
congressional hopefuls were under 50, and almost none were
over 65.

But looked at from another perspective, women in
every age group in both parties were significantly less ambitious than their male counterparts. Even among those under 30, only 32 percent of the women, compared to 49 percent of the men, had congressional ambitions, and 24 percent of the women, compared to only 7 percent of the men,
had no political ambition at all. When women entertain
ambitions for Congress, they are as young as men; it is just
that there are significantly fewer ambitious women--even
among the young.

These data are not very heartening for those who

place their hopes for the future of women in politics on younger generations of women. But there is some evidence of generational change. Among congressional aspirants under 30, the ratio of men to women is closer (10:6.5) than among older age groups where the ratio is generally about 10:4.8. This pattern holds for both parties, although the change in ratios is more pronounced among Republicans than Democrats. But in neither party at any age does the "ambition gap" close completely; if equality in ambition is the goal, it may have to await the next generation.

For the purposes of the second hypothesis, the expected relationship holds: ambition is partly a function of youth for both men and women. A congressionally ambitious woman is as likely to be young as a congressionally ambitious man, when compared to elites with no public office ambitions.

Those women who actually win congressional seats may not be any younger than present female legislators when they first take the oath of office. These data tell us only that female elites dream their dreams at as young an age as male elites.

Ambition and Education

Not only are the ambitious young, they are generally better educated than the non-ambitious--at least as far as exposure to college is concerned. In both parties, male and female congressional aspirants are much more likely than the non-ambitious to have gone beyond high school, and they are somewhat more likely to have attained a college degree. These findings generally confirm those of Steed and Baker and Soule;[32] if personal characteristics are any indication, elites generally perceive congressional office as requiring at least a college education.

Once again, sex differences are not great--with one notable exception. Very few women hold doctorates or their equivalent. Since this category includes the LL.B. degree, however, the sex differences here largely reflect the much greater proportion of lawyers among male delegates (19 percent) than among female delegates (4 percent). These data underline one of the many problems faced by women in contemporary American politics: the scarcity of female attorneys in a polity where the law degree is a common route to political office, and especially congressional office. [33]

Hypothesis #2 is partly confirmed in regard to education. Compared to elites with no public office aspirations, both men and women who aspire to Congress are better educated. Female congressional hopefuls, are less likely than their male counterparts to bring a law degree (or other doctorate) along with their hopes.

Ambition and Family Political Socialization

Soule found a moderate positive relationship between ambition and early, family-centered socialization to politics in his study of state legislators. [34] In these data, the relationship is minimal at best. Using parental activity in politics as a measure of family socialization, we find the ambitious are only slightly more likely than the non-ambitious to have had the benefit of a "political role-model" in one or both parents.

But women, more so than men, may be somewhat influenced by the political activity of their mothers. Where only one parent was active in politics, women's ambition was affected only if that parent was the mother. The percentages of women claiming maternal political activity were too small for any definite conclusions, but the notion that a female political role-model might influence the ambitions of women is an idea that bears further investigation.

The relationship between ambition and family socialization is not sufficiently strong to meet our expectations. But neither can we say that this portion of hypothesis #2 is disconfirmed. Other tests for socialization effects are necessary before conclusions are definitive.

Ambition, Self-Image, and Achievement Orientations

Research linking personality to politics has long confirmed a relationship between positive self-image and political elite status. [35] Recent "ambition literature" has reported associations between ambition, positive self-image, and achievement orientations. [36]

These data deal with political elites: men and women with strong egos. At least 95 percent of the delegates in both parties and sex-groups were inclined to see themselves as "rational, confident, and decisive" personalities.

"Self-image" can refer to a variety of perceptions.

Attitudes of women about women, for example, are self-
images that are sex-specific. Here, a non-sex-specific
measure was used in an effort to discover whether there
were any general relationships between self-image and ambition. (At least, this measure looked non-sex-specific at
first glance.)

One would expect elites with congressional ambitions
to describe themselves as "competitive and ambitious" more
frequently than elites with no public office ambitions. In the
face-to-face interview, delegates were asked to scale themselves on these qualities.

Congressional hopefuls were more likely to perceive
themselves as competitive, ambitious personalities, and this
pattern held for both sex groups, when would-be Senators
and Representatives were compared to those with no aspirations for public service. [37] Nevertheless, women in either
category were not as likely as their male counterparts to
find these adjectives satisfactory. This may be due to the
fact that such designations have not usually been considered
"ladylike" or appropriate for women. In fact, they are the
opposite of such qualities as dependence, passivity, and non-
aggression normally associated with the traditional socialization of women. [38]

This section of hypothesis #2 was then only partly
confirmed: there was a relation between ambition and self-
image but an unanticipated sex difference was also present.
It may be that the particular adjectives used here are too
rooted in sex-stereotyped socialization in the United States
to form a good measure of self-image as anticipated by our
hypothesis.

Ambition literature has linked achievement-orientations
to the quest for office. [39] Those desiring public office are
usually determined people willing to work hard in pursuit of
their goals.

In the mail questionnaire, delegates who aspired to
some public office were asked a question related to achievement and effort: "If there were a real chance to hold the
position you think is most desirable, how much effort would
you be willing to make to get that position?" This was followed by four options describing various degrees of effort.

This question, however, was answered only by those

delegates with <u>some</u> aspirations for public office.   Therefore,
it was not possible to compare congressional aspirants with
the totally non-ambitious.   It was necessary to select the
delegate-group with lowest ambitions for comparative purposes: those who aspired to hold local offices (not including
mayor).

Even with this qualification, striking differences appeared in the degree to which a desire for achievement was
voiced by Congressional aspirants when compared to local office hopefuls.   In both parties, and in both sex groups, the
relationship between ambition and achievement was strong
and positive.   Women with congressional ambitions were
every bit as strong as their male counterparts on this measure.   The expected relationship was confirmed without qualification.

Ambition and the Salience of Politics

As Fishel argued in his study of Congressional challengers, [40] those who entertain aspirations for high office
should have a high commitment to politics and a sense of its
salience in their lives.   Those who anticipate a possible career in Congress with all its time and energy requirements
should certainly give higher priority to politics than those
not considering such a future.

Congressional aspirants in both sex groups and parties were more likely than those without political ambitions
to consider their political activity more important than their
work with any other civil group.   The relationship, however,
was not as strong for women as for men.   There were many
women who regarded politics as more important than other
activities--but who had not considered running for office.
Perhaps many of them have performed the "auxiliary" political functions long expected of women and perhaps they
had come to see this as the "most proper" outlet for their
political interests.   It is impossible to say for sure from
these data.   There is indirect evidence that "something" is
constraining the ambitions of women who regard politics as
highly salient--"something" that is not constraining men.
This section of hypothesis #2 is confirmed then--for men,
but not for women.

Ambition and Demographic Characteristics

The third hypothesis anticipated no significant differ-

ences between the congressionally ambitious and those not
ambitious for public office on a number of demographic characteristics. This assumption held for both parties and both
sexes. Ambition had no relation to race, religious affiliations, the region of the country in which elites resided, [41] or
the type of community in which they were reared. [42] Hypothesis #3 was confirmed in relation to demographic characteristics.

<u>Ambition, Civic Affiliations, Political Incentives,
and Ideology</u>

Hypothesis #3 also suggested that no relationship
would be found between ambition and civic affiliations. Since
we are dealing with political elites, we are examining an active population where only 20 percent of the male delegates,
and 14 percent of the female delegates report no civic affiliations. In such a group, the number of active civic group
memberships had no discernible effect on ambition. This
segment of hypothesis #3 was confirmed for both sexes and
political parties.

Incentives or motives for political activity vary a
great deal. This analysis distinguished two basic "incentive
groups" among elites: those with political motives which
emphasized organizational maintenance--what James Q. Wilson called "solidary" incentives;[43] and those motivated by
political issues or party reforms[44]--what Wilson labelled
"purposive" incentives. [45]

In the questionnaire, delegates were asked to rank-
order various functions of a convention from "most important"
to "least important. " It was assumed here that those who
gave high priority to "party unity" and the "selection of a
winning team for November" emphasized "solidary" or organizational incentives in their political dealings, and those who
gave a high rating to "party reform" or the "adoption of correct positions on national issues" emphasized "purposive" incentives in their style. Ambition had no relation whatsoever
to political incentives as defined here. Only Republican men
showed some inclination to associate ambition with "party
reform"--but the meaning of "reform" in the 1972 Republican
Party was far from clear. [46] The segment of hypothesis #3
which deals with incentives is confirmed.

Delegates were also asked to rate themselves on a
"left-right" scale ranging from "radical" to "reactionary. "

Hypothesis #3 assumed that ambition would have no relation to these ideological identifications. For men, both Republican and Democratic, it had a slight relationship--in the "liberal" direction. But for women as a whole, and Democratic women in particular, the relationship was substantial. Over 50 percent of all women, and over 70 percent of the Democratic women, who aspired to Congress described themselves as either "radical" or "very liberal."[47]

Most Democratic women with their eyes on Congress were young McGovern or Chisholm delegates who tended to accept "liberal" or "radical" labels easily, and to associate feminist views with general ideology. The part of hypothesis #3 dealing with ideology can be confirmed only for men and Republican women.

Ambition: An Interim Summary

Thus far, we have not confronted the real question posed in the beginning: what influences the ambitions of women? We know what influences ambition for both sexes to some degree: youth, education, achievement orientations, and self-image. We know that demographic identifications, civic affiliations, and political incentives have no effect on anyone's ambitions for Congress, and we have some clue that Democratic women relate "ambition" to general ideology. Finally, we know that the "salience of politics" affects the congressional ambitions of male elites, but not female elites.

In other words, we know what does not affect the ambitions of women because they are women, and we have two indications that special factors are working in the case of feminine ambitions: 1) many women who give high priority to politics in their lives do not consider congressional office as a possible expression of that interest; and 2) ambition is associated with ideology among Democratic women--a fact which may indicate that their views about women (which are related to their ideology) will also relate to their congressional aspirations.

With these clues in mind, we can begin to explore the hypotheses dealing directly with female congressional ambitions.

Female Congressional Ambitions and "Political Feminist Consciousness"

The fourth hypothesis proposes a test of three culture-

TABLE 4

The Relationship Between Levels of Political Ambition and "Feminist Consciousness" by Party (Z-scores)

(A)
Perception of Sex Differences as "Innate" at Various Levels of Political Ambition[1]

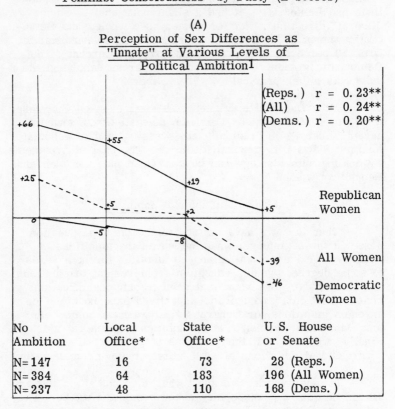

(Reps.)   r = 0.23**
(All)   r = 0.24**
(Dems.)   r = 0.20**

Republican Women

All Women

Democratic Women

	No Ambition	Local Office*	State Office*	U.S. House or Senate	
	N= 147	16	73	28	(Reps.)
	N= 384	64	183	196	(All Women)
	N= 237	48	110	168	(Dems.)

1. The measure of "innate sex differences" was based on responses to the following:
   - --Most men are better suited emotionally for politics than are most women.
   - --Women in public office can be just as logical and rational as men.
   - --Women are emotionally less well-suited than men for business and professional careers.

   (All responses were coded so that a perception of "innate" sex differences received the highest score).

   *For the offices included in these categories, see footnotes 2 and 3 for Table 1.
   **These statistics are Pearson's r's. All are significant at p ≤ .001.

TABLE 4 (cont'd)

(B)
Perception of Female Role Conflicts
at Various Levels of Political
Ambition[2]

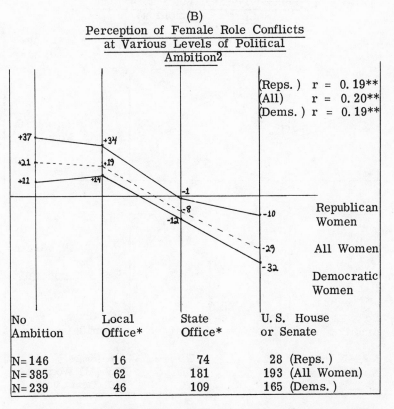

(Reps.) r = 0. 19**
(All)   r = 0. 20**
(Dems.) r = 0. 19**

Republican Women

All Women

Democratic Women

No Ambition	Local Office*	State Office*	U. S. House or Senate	
N= 146	16	74	28	(Reps.)
N= 385	62	181	193	(All Women)
N= 239	46	109	165	(Dems.)

2. This measure of "role conflict" was based on responses
    to the following:
    --It is almost impossible to be a good wife and moth-
    er and hold public office too.
    --Women who succeed in politics usually have to sacri-
    fice their femininity to get there.
    --Children of working mothers tend to be less well-
    adjusted than children of women who stay at home.
    (All responses were coded so that a perception of
    role conflict received the highest score).

TABLE 4 (cont'd)

(C)

Perceptions of Satisfaction with Auxiliary
Female Political Roles at Various
Levels of Ambition[3]

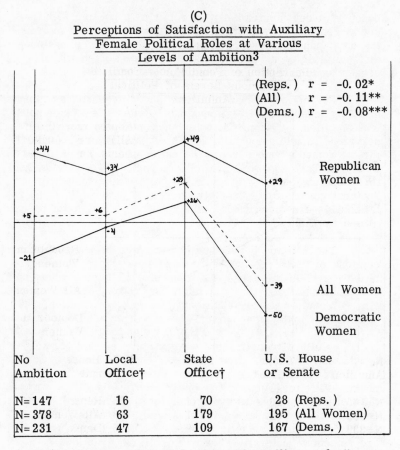

	(Reps.)	r =	-0.02*
	(All)	r =	-0.11**
	(Dems.)	r =	-0.08***

Republican Women

All Women

Democratic Women

No Ambition	Local Office†	State Office†	U.S. House or Senate	
N = 147	16	70	28	(Reps.)
N = 378	63	179	195	(All Women)
N = 231	47	109	167	(Dems.)

3. This measure of "satisfaction with auxiliary roles" was based on responses to the following:
  --While women hold few public offices, they work behind the scenes and really have more influence than they're given credit for.
  --Feminine charm and diplomacy can be a woman's greatest asset in getting ahead in politics.
  --Although not always recognized, women have more real power than men.

†For the offices included in these categories, see footnotes 2 and 3 for Table 1.
*Not significant.
**Significant at $p \leq .001$.
***Significant at $p \leq .05$.

based attitudes about women in relation to politics and society in general. Furthermore, it imposes a stiffer test on the data than those we have employed thus far: it assumes that culturally constraining attitudes about women will decrease as female levels of ambition increase. [48]

Perception of non-biological sex differences as "innate" has an almost linear relationship to women's levels of political ambition. Although Republican women are more "conservative" than Democratic women on this measure (and all three "women's" measures), the pattern holds for them as well (see Table 4A). [49] As the importance of offices desired increases, women's willingness to believe that men are the "natural governors" of society decreases noticeably. All relationships are significantly different from what would be expected by chance. [50]

The relation between feminine ambition-levels and perceptions of "role conflict" is not quite as strong, but the relationship is in the expected direction: the higher a woman's political ambitions, the less likely she is to believe that marriage, motherhood, or traditional "femininity" conflict with politics or employment outside the home (see Table 4B).

"Cultural constraints" were highly relevant for this population of women, even when the women were only thinking about being non-conventional. Serious consideration of public office for women, especially high public office such as the Congress, demands that women shed the cultural preconceptions about themselves that have long pervaded American society (and other societies), particularly any notion that men are somehow "naturally suited" to politics, positions of authority, or the professions.

The third segment of the fourth hypothesis, however, does not hold up under scrutiny. Women who seek high political office are not necessarily dissatisfied with conventional auxiliary female roles, nor are they willing to believe that they have not exercised some influence in these roles in the past (see Table 4C). This is especially true of Republican women, and they differ from the Democratic women in a way that may be especially relevant to this index. Over 60 percent of the Republican women who aspire to congressional office have held three or more party offices; only 29 percent of the Democratic female congressional aspirants fall in this category. Generally, experience in party office was much higher among the Republican women of 1972 than among the

Democratic women. It is certainly possible that many of
these Republican women had exercised real influence in party
circles--whether behind the scenes or not. In contrast, the
Democratic party's 1972 reform rules brought to the fore
many women without long party experience, women less likely
to have exercised political power. Whatever the reason for
partisan differences, this section of hypothesis #4 is not confirmed. The cultural attitudes most clearly relevant to feminine political ambitions are those relating to innate sex differences and role conflict, not the prior political functions of
women.

Ambition and Role-Flexibility for Women

The final hypothesis anticipates that women aspiring
to Congress will either have achieved the "role-flexibility"
necessary for the time and energy requirements of the office,
or that they anticipate a life-style that would permit fulfill-
ment of their political ambitions.

What constitutes present "role-flexibility"? Since the
social role most often associated with career-conflict among
women is that of marriage and motherhood, a woman's ability to eliminate this "conflict" would constitute evidence of
"role-flexibility." Evidence that she has achieved this status
at present might be observable in one or more ways:

1)   She could simply be unmarried, or--if married--
     without the major domestic responsibility of women:
     children.

2)   She could be both married and a mother, but have
     grown children past the age where they need full-
     time care and nurturance.

3)   She might already have full-time employment outside
     the home: proof that she has already found a way to
     combine outside activities with family life (if mar-
     ried). (This is not necessarily evidence, however,
     that she would be able to juggle family life with con-
     gressional responsibilities.)

4)   Normally, she would be expected to have the approval
     of her spouse and she probably should perceive little
     conflict between politics and family responsibilities.

If none of these conditions is present, we would expect that she at least hopes for a life style that would permit congressional office as a major priority in life.

As Table 5 indicates, female congressional aspirants in both parties are less likely to be married than are non-ambitious women.   But so are men with congressional aspirations.   Further analysis of the data showed that single status was simply a function of the youth of congressional hopefuls.

Women who aspire to Congress evidently hope to combine motherhood with a political career.   At least 59 percent of the women with congressional ambitions have children under 12 years of age (see Table 5).   This was also a function of the youth of female congressional aspirants.   Many -- the majority, in fact--were young married women with either no children at all or fairly young children still in their formative years.   Congressional aspirations were entertained by many women not free from conventional female domestic responsibilities.

But a very important role-difference is apparent between women who aspire to Congress and those who do not: female congressional aspirants were much more likely to be employed outside the home.   Women without political ambition were much more likely to be housewives (see Table 5). It is possible that employment convinced many congressionally ambitious women that they could operate successfully outside the home and that family life and careers were compatible.   Or it may be that common factors such as higher education, a desire for personal achievement, or the shedding of sex-related stereotypes influenced both present employment and hopes for Congress.   Whatever the case, the relationship is significant. 51

Alternatively, what do these two groups of women see as a desirable work pattern?   The differences are striking, and they explain some of the questions raised by the analysis of the marital status of ambitious women.   First, it is clear that women who seek congressional careers do not want to abandon their families in the process.   But neither do they want employment to cease with marriage, and very few of them (only 7 percent) consider "no employment outside the home" an ideal.   In contrast, women not ambitious for office are more likely to be satisfied with the homemaking role alone; at least 30 percent of them (compared to only 15 percent of the congressionally ambitious) want employment only

TABLE 5

Ambition for Congress Among Women: Relation to
Present and Anticipated Role Status (%)*

Role Variables	All Female Dels. Congress. Ambition	No Ambit.	Democratic Women Congress. Ambition	No Ambit.	Republican Women Congress. Ambition	No Ambit.
Marital Status:1						
Married with children	63	81	63	79	67	83
Married: no children	13	8	14	7	8	10
Not married	23	11	23	13	25	7
N=	172	334	148	209	24	125
For Those Married: Age of Youngest Child:1						
1-5	25	14	27	19	11	5
6-12	34	26	35	30	32	20
13-18	16	25	16	25	16	25
Over 18	25	36	22	27	42	50
N=	129	306	110	190	19	116
Current Employment Status:2						
Working Now	64	43	64	45	67	40
Housewife Only	24	52	24	49	25	59
Student	8	1	9	2	0	0
Retired, Unemployed, Looking for Work	4	3	3	4	8	1
N=	202	422	178	262	24	160
To what extent do you feel your political activities interfere with your family life?2						
A Great Deal	4	10	5	10	11	8
Somewhat	27	25	30	27	0	21
Not Very Much	41	20	39	20	22	21
Not At All	28	45	27	43	67	49
N=	150	336	134	214	18	122
What is your spouse's attitude toward your political activity?2						
Very much or somewhat in favor of it	95	91	94	87	100	98
Mixed feelings	2	3	3	4	0	2
Very much or somewhat opposed	3	6	3	9	0	0
N=	150	336	134	214	18	122

*This table describes women who seek congressional office, and women with
no ambitions according to present and anticipated role-status. Percentages do not necessarily add to 100 percent due to rounding.
1. These data are from the mail questionnaire sample.
2. These data are from the interview sample.

TABLE 5 (cont'd)

Role Variables	All Female Dels.		Democratic Women		Republican Women	
	Congress. Ambition	No Ambit.	Congress. Ambition	No Ambit.	Congress. Ambition	No Ambit.
Present Work Pattern:[2]						
Outside--no family	7	5	7	6	8	4
Help at home	4	2	5	1	0	3
Combined with homemaking thruout adult life	28	20	27	21	33	18
Interruptions for child-raising	17	8	19	9	0	5
No regular pattern	23	21	24	22	17	19
Only before marriage	5	15	6	14	0	17
None outside the home	12	27	8	23	42	33
Part-time--help at home	4	3	5	4	0	1
N=	194	412	170	256	32	156
What would be your ideal work pattern, the one you would most like to follow if you could?[2]						
Outside--no family	2	3	2	5	0	1
Help at home	24	14	24	18	17	8
Combined with homemaking thruout adult life	35	16	34	15	42	18
Interruptions for child-raising	13	6	15	7	0	5
No regular pattern	15	30	16	30	8	31
Only before marriage	0	5	0	5	0	5
None outside the home	7	21	4	17	33	27
Part-time--help at home	4	5	5	4	0	5
N=	416	196	172	260	24	156

Ambition Relationships:	All Women	Dem. Women	Repub. Women
Marital Status (gamma)	-0.40	-0.36	-0.44
Age youngest child (gamma)	-0.28	-0.19	-0.22
Employment status (V's)	0.30	0.29	0.34
Politics-family life (gamma)	+0.11	+0.09	+0.10
Spouse approve? (gamma)	+0.12	+0.12	+1.00
Present work pattern (V's)	0.27	0.29	0.24
Ideal work pattern (V's)	0.34	0.37	0.29

when desired or needed (see Table 5).   If these women who
aspire to Congress are successful, we may see less of the
"homemaker to lawmaker" route for women in politics. [53]

Finally, how do these women see the relation of politics and family life, and what is the attitude of their husbands?   There is little relationship between perceptions of
family-politics conflict and ambition; almost all the husbands
of all these women approve of their wives' political activities.
Republican congressional hopefuls report very little role-
conflict (37 percent report none at all), and among these wom-
en, all husbands have very favorable attitudes toward the political activities of their wives (see Table 5).

But while almost all women with congressional ambitions report having approving spouses, the same is less true
for men.   The latter do not have wide disapproval from their
wives, to be sure, but those who do are more likely than are
women to consider congressional careers anyway.   Male congressional aspirants are more likely to consider the heavy
responsibilities of the House or Senate in spite of the fact
that they already perceive some family-politics conflict in
their lives (see Table 6).   This analysis of convention delegates tends to confirm other findings which show that men
are more likely than women to move into political roles without the approval of their marriage partners. [54]   Indeed, these
data suggest that, unlike men, women are generally deterred
by family responsibilities and a few are also deterred by dis-
approving spouses.

Hypothesis #5 is certainly confirmed.   Women with
congressional ambitions give evidence of "role-flexibility" in
present employment patterns, if not in marital status.   Compared to women without political ambition, they are much
more likely to desire life styles that offer at least potential
compatibility with congressional office.

Conclusions

In answer to the question: "what constrains the congressional ambitions of women as women?" this analysis has
provided two answers: cultural attitudes that reinforce notions of female submissiveness to males and "innate" differences between the sexes, and real-life role-conflicts that
generate great difficulties for women who desire both a family and a career in politics.

TABLE 6

The Congressionally Ambitious: Men and Women Compared (%)*

Role Status Variables	All Congressionally Ambitious Delegates		Democrats with Congressional Ambitions		Republicans with Congressional Ambitions	
	Men	Women	Men	Women	Men	Women
Marital Status[1]						
Married with children	72	63	69	63	79	67
Married--no children	8	13	9	14	6	8
Not married	20	23	23	23	15	25
N=	525	172	337	148	188	24
To what extent do you feel your political activities interfere with your family life?[2]						
A great deal	20	4	18	5	24	0
Somewhat	46	27	52	30	37	0
Not very much	20	41	15	39	29	63
Not at all	14	28	15	27	11	37
N=	406	150	254	134	152	16
What is your spouse's attitude toward your political activity?[2]						
Very much in favor	52	75	56	72	43	100
Somewhat in favor	34	20	33	22	35	0
Mixed feelings	6	1	5	2	8	0
Somewhat opposed	6	3	5	3	8	0
Very much opposed	1	0	0	0	3	0
N=	402	150	254	134	148	16

Relationships of Congressional ambition with: (all gammas)	All Women	All Men	Dem. Women	Dem. Men	Rep. Women	Rep. Men
Marital Status	-0.40	-0.53	-0.36	-0.48	-0.44	-0.62
No. of children	+0.02	-0.01	-0.04	-0.04	+0.32	+0.04
Age yngst. chld.	-0.28	-0.39	-0.19	-0.39	-0.22	-0.33
Politics-family life	+0.11	+0.31	+0.09	+0.39	+0.10	+0.13
Spouse approval	+0.12	+0.19	+0.12	+0.29	+1.00	+0.04

*This table compares congressionally ambitious men and women; relationships describe the relation of ambition to role for each sex and party group.   Percentages do not necessarily add to 100 percent due to rounding.
1.   These data are from the mail questionnaire sample.
2.   These data are from the interview sample.

Further and more detailed research is needed to separate and scale the relative effects of these variables on
feminine political ambitions. 55

But with our present base of evidence on women's political ambitions for Congress, it seems evident that women
will assume a substantially greater share of power on the
Hill only if they themselves (and their husbands) shed power-
fully ingrained cultural attitudes toward sex roles which have
historically defined American women out of high political office.   And women will assume a greater share of congressional power only if they (and their husbands) develop styles
of married life that share domestic responsibilities and free
women from full-time homemaking tasks.   These changes are
substantial; they involve attitudes ingrained from the time
children first hear what "little girls and boys are made of. "
But the ambitions of some women who aspire to become this
nation's lawmakers, and the attitudes and styles of life they
bring with those ambitions prove that change is both possible
and already in progress.

NOTES

1.   Data on women in the U. S. Senate (which have not
     changed since the 1972 election) may be found in:
     Hope Chamberlin, A Minority of Members: Women
     in the U. S. Congress (New York: New American Li-
     brary, 1973), p. 1.   Data on women in the House are
     courtesy of the National Women's Political Caucus.
2.   The female House candidates were also major party
     contenders in the 1973 general election.   Data from
     the National Women's Political Caucus.
3.   The word "enabling" rather than "determining" is used
     throughout this study because all citizens with the
     characteristics of elites do not, in fact, choose polit-
     ical life as a channel for their talents.   Most socio-
     economic, political and psychological characteristics
     free potential office-holders from common "restraints"
     on elite status; they do not "determine" elite status.
     Thus "enabling" seems to be the more accurate word.
4.   Joseph A. Schlesinger, Ambition and Politics (Chicago:
     Rand McNally and Company, 1966).   Hereafter cited
     as Ambition.
5.   See, for example: Michael L. Mezey, "Ambition Theory
     and the Office of Congressmen, " Journal of Politics
     32 (August, 1970): 563-579; Gordon S. Black, "A

Theory of Political Ambition: Career Choices and the Role of Structural Incentives, " American Political Science Review 56 (March, 1972): 144-159; Leo M. Snowiss, "Congressional Recruitment and Representation, " American Political Science Review 59 (September, 1966): 627-639.

6.   See: John W. Soule, "Future Political Ambitions and the Behavior of Incumbent State Legislators, " Midwest Journal of Political Science 13 (August, 1969): 439-454; Kenneth Prewitt and William Nowlin, "Political Ambitions and the Behavior of Incumbent Politicians, " Western Political Quarterly 22 (June, 1969): 298-308.

7.   This type of analysis is included to some degree in the following: Rufus Browning, "The Interaction of Personality and Political System in Decisions to Run for Office: Some Data and a Simulation Technique, " Journal of Social Issues 24 (July, 1968): 93-109; Kenneth Prewitt, "Political Ambitions, Volunteerism, and Electoral Accountability, " American Political Science Review 64 (March, 1970): 5-17; Jeff Fishel, "Ambition and the Political Vocation: Congressional Challengers in American Politics, " Journal of Politics 33 (February, 1971): 25-56; John D. Parker, "Classification of Candidates' Motivations for First Seeking Office, " Journal of Politics 34 (February, 1972): 268-271; Robert P. Steed and Tod A. Baker, "Ambition and Program Orientations of County Chairmen in the Deep and Border South, " Paper presented at the Annual Meeting of the Southwestern Political Science Association, San Antonio, Texas, March 27-29, 1975 (unpublished); and Soule, op. cit.

8.   In fairness, Joseph Schlesinger, Ambition, does mention "opportunity structures" for women, pp. 172-173. He states there that women's opportunities at a national level are most realistically directed at the House of Representatives, secondarily at the Senate.

9.   See: Schlesinger, Ambition, Chapter 9; Steed and Baker, op. cit. ; Fishel, op. cit. ; Soule, op. cit.

10.   Browing, op. cit. ; Soule, op. cit.

11.   Jeane J. Kirkpatrick, Political Woman (New York: Basic Books, 1974).

12.   Ibid. , pp. 8-23 and pp. 221-240. See also: Jeane J. Kirkpatrick, "Women in Power Processes: A Preliminary Examination of Four Hypothetical Constraints Affecting Women's Political Participation, " Paper presented at the Annual Meeting of the Southern Political Science Association, New Orleans, Louisiana, November 7-9, 1974.

13. Kirkpatrick, Political Woman, pp. 244-245.
14. Donald G. Tacheron and Morris K. Udall in The Job of
    the Congressman, 2nd. ed. (New York: Bobbs-Merrill
    Company, Inc., 1970), p. 303, estimate that the aver-
    age Congressional work-week is approximately 60
    hours.
15. The word "gladiatorial" is, of course, Lester Milbrath's.
    See his: Political Participation (Chicago: Rand, Mc-
    Nally and Company, 1965), p. 18 especially.
16. For a summary of early works relating "gladiatorial"
    political activity to SES, see Milbrath, op. cit., Chap-
    ter 5. The relationship between SES and active po-
    litical participation has been documented most recently
    by Sidney Verba and Norman H. Nie in Participation
    in America (New York: Harper & Row, 1972), Chapter
    8 especially.
17. Milbrath, op. cit., pp. 56-57 summarizes these findings.
18. Browning, op. cit.; Robert Lane, Political Life (Glen-
    coe: The Free Press, 1959), Chapter 11; Lester Mil-
    brath and Walter W. Klein, "Personality Correlates of
    Political Participation," in Gordon Di Renzo, Person-
    ality and Politics (Garden City, New York: Anchor/
    Doubleday, 1974), 109-125.
19. Lane, op. cit., Chapter 12; Fishel, op. cit.
20. CPS 1972 Convention Delegate Study, Center for Political
    Studies, University of Michigan, August, 1973.
21. See: M. Kent Jennings and Norman Thomas, "Men and
    Women in Party Elites: Social Roles and Political Re-
    sources," Midwest Journal of Political Science 12 (No-
    vember, 1968), 469-492; Edmond Constantini and Ken-
    neth H. Craik, "The Social Background, Personality
    and Political Careers of Female Party Leaders,"
    Journal of Social Issues 28 (2: 1972), 217-236; Wilma
    E. McGrath and John W. Soule, "Rocking the Cradle
    or Rocking the Boat: Women at the 1972 Democratic
    National Convention," Social Science Quarterly 55
    (June, 1974), 141-150; Lynne B. Iglitzin, "The Making
    of Apolitical Woman: Femininity and Sex-Stereotyping
    in Girls," in Jane Jacquette, Women in Politics (New
    York: John Wiley and Sons, 1974), pp. 25-36.
        The findings of Soule and McGrath disagree with
    other findings on the relationship of sex to ideology.
    Most studies show a negligible relationship between the
    two. See Jeane J. Kirkpatrick, "Representation in the
    American National Conventions: The Case of 1972,"
    British Journal of Political Science 5 (July, 1975),
    165-322, p. 315 especially.

22. Schlesinger, op. cit., Chapter 9, and Fishel, op. cit. both relate ambition to youth. Steed and Baker, op. cit. and Soule, op. cit. both find the ambitious better educated than the non-ambitious. Soule also found a significant relationship between ambition and early family socialization to politics. Browning, op. cit. found the ambitious strong in self-image, especially in achievement orientations; and Fishel, op. cit. argues that congressional challengers specifically saw politics as a "way of life."

23. In this hypothesis, "political incentives" refer specifically to variations in attitudes toward the political party as an organization. Ideological identifications are measured on a scale ranging from "radical" to "very conservative."

24. This is another way of saying they would rather "make policy, not coffee."

25. This hypothesis will examine: marital status, number of children, age of youngest child, attitude of spouse toward political activity, perceptions of if and how politics interferes with family life, present employment status, and ideal work pattern for the future.

26. National Convention Delegates are certainly "elites" in the American political system. They are charged with important party tasks at a national level: the nomination of Presidential and Vice-Presidential candidates, the writing of party platforms, and determination of party rules for the next four years.

27. Schlesinger, op. cit., p. 10.

28. Contrary to some press reporting at the time of the convention, even McGovern delegates generally had office-holding experience within the Democratic party. Only 28 percent of the McGovern men and 35 percent of the McGovern women reported never having held party office.

29. Schlesinger, op. cit., Chapters 2 and 3 especially.

30. Schlesinger, op. cit., p. 175.

31. Kirkpatrick, Political Woman, op. cit., p. 221.

32. Steed and Baker, op. cit.; Soule, op. cit.

33. As just one citation of evidence on the prevalence of lawyers in American legislatures, see: Malcolm E. Jewell and Samuel C. Patterson, The Legislative Process in the United States, 2nd ed. (New York: Random House, 1973), pp. 74-75.

34. Soule, op. cit. His measure, however, is different than the one used in this analysis.

35. Among others, see: Lane, op. cit., Chapter 11; Milbrath, op. cit., Chapter 3.

36. Soule, op. cit., and Browning, op. cit. Their meas-
    ures of self-image are different from the one used
    here.

37. This does not hold true for Republican men. Perhaps
    many of the non-ambitious males in this category ex-
    ercise their competitive-ambitious self-images else-
    where: in the professions or the business world, for
    example.

38. For an excellent analysis of this traditional socialization,
    see: Judith M. Bardwick and Elizabeth Douvan, "Am-
    bivalence: The Socialization of Women," in Vivian
    Gornick and Barbara K. Moran, eds., Woman in Sex-
    ist Society (New York: Basic Books, 1971), pp. 225-
    241.

39. Soule, op. cit.

40. Fishel, op. cit.

41. Region was divided into: New England and Middle At-
    lantic States, Midwest, South and Border States, and
    Far West.

42. Type of community included: rural area, small town,
    small city, large city, suburb. For Republicans only,
    there was some relationship between congressional
    hopes and ethnic identification. A close examination
    of the data revealed that this was due largely to the
    less ethnically-diverse character of the Republican
    party. The few Republicans who were not English,
    Scottish or Welsh tended to fall completely into either
    the "ambitious" or "non-ambitious" category, leaving
    several cells with zeros.

43. James Q. Wilson, The Amateur Democrat (Chicago:
    University of Chicago Press, Phoenix Books, 1962).
    His latest work on incentives to politics, Political
    Organizations (New York: Basic Books, 1974), is es-
    pecially valuable. Chapter 3 in the latter work is
    particularly relevant to the discussion here.

44. Although delegates in both parties were asked about
    "party reform," its meaning is clear and relevant
    only in the case of Democrats.

45. Wilson, Political Organizations, op. cit., p. 45 ff.

46. It may have had something to do with Rule 30, but it
    is difficult to say.

47. Only 4 percent of Republican female congressional hope-
    fuls consider themselves "very liberal" and none think
    of themselves as "radical." This relationship does
    not hold for Republican women.

48. In order to test this hypothesis, a four-point ordinal
    measure of ambition was constructed, with congres-

sional ambition receiving the highest "ambition-value."
All offices for which there were few female aspirants
(e. g., President and Vice-President), and all offices
not clearly less important than a House or Senate seat
were removed from the data. (It is not clear, for example, that a cabinet post, governorship, or even a
mayorality of a large metropolitan area is less important in the American political system than is a seat
in Congress.) The final measure of "ambition" thus
moved from "no ambition" to "local office ambition"
(excluding mayoralities) to "state office ambition" (excluding governorships) to "congressional ambition."

Three indices measuring the opinions anticipated
by hypothesis #4 were constructed, and transformed
into Z-scores so that the data might be comparable.
Footnote #50 presents the graphed (and "graphic") results flowing from the test of this hypothesis. (These
indices were developed by Jeane Kirkpatrick for use in
her forthcoming work, The Presidential Elite. They
were based on a factor analysis of several questions
relating to women. I want to thank her for permission
to use them here.)

49. As the Pearson r's indicate in Table 4, not much of the
variance is explained. This is not surprising. There
are many reasons that a woman, ambitious for public
office, might choose local or state politics over national lawmaking roles. As is the case with men, she
may simply prefer to deal with local or state problems; these may be her focus of political interest.
What is important here is that the relationship is significantly different than what would be expected by
chance--at $p \leq .001$.

50. If congressional ambition alone is related to this measure of "innate sex differences"--comparing women not
politically ambitious with congressional hopefuls--a
gamma of -0.57 for all women results; -0.49 for Democratic women; and -0.43 for Republican women. With
the exception of achievement orientations (and "youth"
for Republican women), these are the strongest associations evident thus far in the analysis.

51. The second section of Table 5 tells the story even more
clearly. Only 12 percent of the women considering
Congress have never been employed outside the home,
compared to 27 percent of non-ambitious women. At
least 49 percent of the potential female Members of
Congress have already juggled family life with a job--
either by combining the homemaking role and employ-

ment themselves, with household help, or by inter-
rupting employment only for child-raising purposes.
Only 30 percent of the women not ambitious for office
fall in this category.

52. At least 35 percent want to combine employment with
homemaking responsibilities, and another 13 percent
are willing to interrupt some job in order to raise
their children.   At least 24 percent of these women
see a need for household help in pursuing their goals--
not a bad idea for women with congressional responsibilities.

53. Kirkpatrick, Political Woman, p. 61 ff.

54. Kirkpatrick, Political Woman, p. 231.

55. Multiple regression analyses of the entire female sample
indicate that both "feminist consciousness" and "role-
freedom" (and a willingness to accept the traditionally
non-feminine labels of self as competitive and ambitious) are more important than any other variables in
explaining female ambition levels.   No matter what
variables are included in the regression equation (including those that are associated with masculine ambition as well as feminine ambition such as political
salience, youth and education) feminist consciousness,
employment outside the home, and perceptions of non-
conflict between family and politics remain the most
explanatory variables for female ambitions.

Chapter 14

WOMEN AS VOLUNTARY POLITICAL ACTIVISTS:
A Review of Recent Empirical Research

by M. Margaret Conway

The focus of this paper is on women as voluntary political activists in political party and campaign activities.
Elections are still in the United States the principal avenue
to holding formal political power, and political party organizations and personal campaign organizations are the major
vehicles for making nominations and winning elections, especially in many local and congressional districts where
media campaigns are too expensive to be used. Furthermore, those who seek elected public office in the United
States are highly likely to come from the ranks of those
previously active in party and campaign organizations or
from those who have also been active in civic organizations. [1]

Several questions relevant to the role of women as
voluntary political activists should be raised. These include:
1) To what extent are women active in campaign and political party work as voluntary activists? 2) What are the
characteristics of women who are active? 3) What factors
can explain the levels and types of voluntary political activism by women? 4) What strategies can be used to get more
women involved in political party and campaign work and assigned more important roles in such work?

In this article, research findings from a number of
studies are examined in order to provide answers of at least
a preliminary nature to the questions raised above. Some
previously unreported findings from the author's own research
which relate to these questions are also incorporated into the
discussion.

Level of Voluntary Political Activity and
Characteristics of Women Volunteer Activists

The activities of women in political volunteer work

can be examined from two perspectives. One is derived
from the reported political activity of women surveyed in national surveys of the American electorate. The other is obtained from studies of women engaged in what we might call
political elite activity; this includes participation in political
party and political campaign organizations, as well as convention delegates and specialized interest group activity. Excluded from this analysis is a consideration of elected political leaders or appointments to community boards and commissions.

Voluntary Activism: Surveys of Women
in the Electorate

        Conclusions about the level and pattern of women's
political participation have tended to vary with the procedure
used to measure participation. One measurement procedure
used is the creation of composite indices, either through
simple additive procedures or through factor analysis. The
second is to evaluate each type of political activity separately.

        One analysis, using data from surveys conducted dur-
ing the past six presidential elections, indicates that substantial changes have occurred in political participation patterns among women in the electorate. This conclusion is
based on an examination of summed campaign participation
scores, which were calculated from responses to questions
about six types of election related political activity. These
six are attempting to influence someone else's vote, working
for a political party, attending a political meeting, working
in a non-party political organization, displaying a campaign
sticker or button, and making a financial contribution to a
political campaign. Traditionally, women who participated
most in political campaigns tended to be disproportionately
drawn from the more educated groups, from the middle or
upper middle class, and from older age groups. Beginning
in 1960, an increase in campaign participation among professional and white collar employed women occurred. Further changes in patterns of political participation among wom-
en have occurred since 1970; younger women are more likely
to be politically active than in the past. Furthermore, wom-
en who work for pay are more like men than like housewives
in their sense of political efficacy and level of political participation. Another significant change is the increased level
of political participation among women employed in blue collar jobs. [2]

TABLE 1

Political Participation in Three Presidential Elections, By Sex*

	1964 Male	1964 Female	1968 Male	1968 Female	1972 Male	1972 Female
Member of a Political Organization	4.0%	4.1%	3.4%	3.5%	2.1%	3.8%
	NS		NS		p < .01	
Attendance at Political Functions	9.4	7.7	9.8	8.7	9.8	8.2
	p < .04		NS		NS	
Made a Political Contribution of Money	11.8	8.0	8.9	6.5	12.0	9.2
	p < .001		p < .02		p < .05	
Displayed Political Insignia	17.3	16.3	9.6	9.2	14.0	14.1
	NS		NS		NS	
Tried to Influence Others	37.4	28.2	39.8	26.2	36.8	27.7
	p < .001		p < .001		p < .001	
Interest in the Campaign:						
Very Interested	43.4	40.3	43.5	35.2	37.4	27.0
Somewhat Interested	51.9	54.2	37.6	42.0	39.3	42.5
	NS		NS		p < .001	
Voted	80.9	76.2	78.0	74.0	76.4	70.1
	p < .001		p < .02		p < .001	

*Adapted from Table 1, Political Participation by Sex, p. 43-44, in Elizabethanne O'Sullivan, "The Relationship of Reference Groups and Self Esteem to Women's Political Participation," Ph.D. Dissertation, University of Maryland, 1974. NS = Not Significant. Probability (p) of findings occurring by chance are reported where p is less than 5 times out of 100 (p< .05). The data on which the analysis is based were provided by the InterUniversity Consortium for Political Research and are from National samples of the American electorate.

Using another method of analysis (evaluation of factor scores), no significant differences were found between men and women in participation in four modes of election related activity (voting, campaign activity, communicating, and communal activity) in 1972. The author further substantiated this finding through analysis of another 1972 national survey, in which three modes of political participation (voting, campaign activity, and communal activity) were examined. [3]

In contrast to the findings of these studies, when we examine individually seven specific types of election related participatory actions, women are less likely than men to engage in certain types of citizen activity. An examination of participation in three recent presidential elections (see Table 1) indicates no significant differences between men and women in displaying political insignia and, in the 1968 and 1972 presidential elections, in attending political functions. However, men more frequently made a financial contribution, tried to influence others as to how they should vote, had a slightly higher rate of voting turnout, and in the 1968 and 1972 presidential elections reported a higher level of interest in the campaign. Most interesting for our concern here is that in the 1972 presidential election, women were more likely to report being a member of a political organization, although among both men and women membership in political organizations was quite infrequent and lower than in previous presidential election years. [4]

How can these patterns of political participation among women be explained? What factors have resulted in changes in the political socialization of women? One important influence, already noted, is participation in the work-for-pay work force. Involvement in employment outside the home either creates or reinforces a sense of personal political effectiveness which is necessary for and supportive of increased political participation. [5]

The increase in political activism among blue collar women, which is particularly noticeable in the early 1970's, could be a consequence of several factors. One is the drive to open higher paying blue collar jobs to women, using as a device political pressure to enact or enforce laws, government regulations, or court decisions. Another is the increased media coverage given to government requirements for equality and to women's organizations working for social and economic equality for women. Other explanations include the effects of changes in school curriculum which result in a

more positive view of women's role in the political system.
Increased political participation by blue collar women may
also have been stimulated by populist and other candidates
who have attracted significant blue collar support (this would
include the various presidential candidacies of George Wallace). Yet another is the mobilization of women in opposition to public policies which are seen as a threat to a valued
way of life, such as school busing and the abolition of the
neighborhood school system. Political skills developed in
organizations arising in opposition to a particular government
policy are easily translatable into political party or candidate
organization work.

How can we explain higher levels of political participation among younger women now than among similar age cohorts ten years ago? The agents of political socialization
may be presenting different role models and behavior norms
for women, with women's participation in political life being
presented now as more appropriate. Furthermore, social
roles assigned to young women, particularly for the stay-at-
home wife and mother of young children, have also significantly altered.

Women as Political Elite Members
in Voluntary Political Activity

Turning to political participation in party and campaign
organizations, what factors are associated with patterns of
political organizational activity among women? Do they differ
in social characteristics, or political orientations from the
men who are active? Studies have been conducted of campaign workers, precinct leaders, state and national convention delegates, county party leaders, and state party chairpersons. [6] The number of national studies is quite limited;
therefore, we must attempt to generalize on the basis of a
limited number of studies which most frequently focus on one
or a few local areas or states.

Studies of precinct organizations indicate that women's
occupancy of this basic political party office varies with the
nature of the political and socio-economic environments, the
proportion of precinct leaders who are women ranging from
five percent to forty-five percent. Women are least likely
to serve as party leaders in rural areas, in central city
machine controlled organizations, or in districts populated
largely by more recent immigrant groups, where cultural

norms have not been supportive of a political leadership role
for women.   Women are most likely to serve as party leaders in urban or suburban middle class areas. [7] While only
limited cross-national comparative studies have been conducted, the proportion of women holding party office in other
developed democracies has generally been reported to be
lower than in the United States, being in the range of ten to
twenty percent. [8]

Women are much less likely to serve in higher level
party office or in posts such as state or national convention
delegate, although some change has occurred in recent years.
Under pressure of McGovern Commission generated rules reforms, the proportion of women delegates in the Democratic
National Convention increased from 14 percent in 1963 to 36
percent in 1972, dropping to 34 percent in 1976.   A change
also occurred in the representation of women at the Republican National Convention, the proportion increasing from 17
percent in 1968 to 30 percent in 1972 and to 31 percent in
1976. [9] Relatively few women serve on party executive committees or as chairpersons of county or state party organizations, however. [10]

Characteristics of Women in Political Leadership Roles

Where women are active in voluntary political work,
their motivations for political work, future political ambitions,
political roles occupied, and role performance have been
found to differ from those of male political activists.

The motivations of men and women political party
activists differ.   Men more frequently than women cite reasons which are self-serving and focusing on personal and
career advancement.   Women are more likely to cite party
loyalty, candidate orientations, or specific issues as reasons
for involvement.   However, both men and women rank as
most important a concern for public issues and a sense of
community obligation.   When questioned as to what they would
miss most if they were to leave party work, men and women
are equally likely to report they would miss the social relationships which are developed in political party work, while
men are more likely to indicate they would miss material
rewards which become available because of their political
party work. [11]

Male political activists are more likely than women to

be motivated to seek public elected office at the state or national level and to have held public office. [12] Women may be more oriented toward local policy programs and issues, although some studies report no such differences. [13]

Women are also more likely to participate in nonpartisan than in partisan office seeking. If such offices are not part of the political career ladder in a state, those with ambitions for higher office would be less likely to seek those non-partisan offices. Such offices may also be less visible to the public, and hence political culture norms for office holding may be less restricting or exclusionary.

Some differences have been found between men and women political party activists in their party work patterns. Men tend to serve for a longer term in party offices; reasons for shorter tenure among women can only be suggested. Women may tend to enter political party office holding at an older age, or they may more frequently have to relinquish party office because of family responsibilities. Women precinct leaders are much more likely to report working in party headquarters or performing other administrative work during non-campaign periods, which is not too surprising considering the types of work to which women political activists have traditionally been assigned. Women in suburban areas are more likely to report devoting more hours to party work than are men; the reverse is true in rural areas. Women tend to cite as their most important party organization task getting out the vote on election day and communicating party principles, while men are more likely to emphasize the building of the party organization. When questioned about their plans for future party work, women are slightly more likely than men to report that they will devote more time to party work in the future. This could be accounted for by employment patterns, with fewer women being employed outside the home and those women not working outside the home having more time for political party activities. [14]

Why Don't Women Participate More?

A number of different explanations for patterns of women's political participation can be suggested. These include: physiological constraints; male conspiracy; childhood socialization; personality characteristics; and adult social role distribution. That physiological characteristics are responsible for women's low rates of political participation is generally discounted. [15]

Another explanation proposed for political inactivism
among women is that they were socialized as children to believe that political participation would be inappropriate behavior for them as adults. Some evidence is provided for
this in age cohort differences in women's political activism,
with participation rates being lower among older cohorts.
Studies of the political socialization of children and adolescents frequently cite research done in the 1950's and 1960's
as evidence that boys and girls develop at an early age dis-
tinctly different political attitudes, levels of political interest,
and orientations toward political participation. [16] Charges of
a sexist bias in the questions used and in their interpretation
in that research have been made and substantiated to a considerable degree, [17] but that does not inhibit a number of political scientists and other social scientists from continuing
to cite these research results. In contrast, more recent research on children's political orientations has found few differences between the sexes in political attitudes, knowledge,
or participation. [18] Some recent research does report sex
differences in pre-adult political orientations, in that the
subgroup of adolescents to whom politics is highly salient is
disproportionately male. [19] Those girls to whom politics is
highly salient could be characterized as feminist in their beliefs about the capabilities of women to perform in responsible economic and political roles--an important point to
which we will return later in this paper. While culturally
prescribed roles may in the past have inhibited women's political activism, it is argued here that this is declining rapidly and will continue to decline as a significant factor in patterns of political activism among women.

Non-participation or low rates of political participation
by women can also be explained as a consequence of political
socialization processes experienced as adults. According to
this view, women who seek to become active are discouraged
either by other women (public opinion studies indicate that until 1972 women indicated less willingness to vote for women
candidates for high level elected offices than did men[20]) or
by those who in some fashion (such as control of the party's
nominating machinery or control of financial support for candidacies) exercise substantial influence over the nominating process. Studies of both traditional political cultures, such as
those found in rural areas or in political machine cities, and
suburban political activists lend support to this explanation. [21]

Yet another explanation for low rates of women's political participation is that the distribution of adult roles works

against women's political participation.   Those who focus on
a role system explanation cite two major aspects of the role
system as inhibiting women's political activity.   These are
women's relative absence from the occupations, such as law,
insurance, and real estate, from which political activists are
disproportionately recruited, and women's assignment to family roles which limit the opportunity for political participation
during the young adult years in which political careers are
usually established.   The presence of young children in the
home has been found to be associated with a disinclination to
seek political offices among both sexes, but it is a particularly inhibiting factor among women. [22]

Some would explain women's lower rates of political
participation as a result of an overt conspiracy, with women
viewed as an oppressed class deliberately excluded from political participation.   The institutional mechanisms which result in psychological attributes or social roles excluding wom-
en from political participation are seen as deliberately structured for that purpose.   This explanation for non-participation
is one which enjoys some popularity among radical feminists.

Certain psychological characteristics, such as motivations or needs deemed necessary for seeking and attaining
political elite roles, are alleged to be lacking or to be present to a lower degree in women than in men.   Supposedly
politically relevant motivations or needs include aggressive-
ness, need for dominance, and need for achievement. [23]
These needs, however, are not innate, but are the product
of socialization processes, and can be acquired by women.
Some research also calls into question their relevance as a
causal or accompanying factor in political office seeking. [24]

One element of psychological characteristics which is
gaining increasing support as the major determining factor
in women's political participation in political elite roles is
that which has previously been labeled feminist consciousness.
Feminist consciousness can be defined as a belief that men
and women are equally capable of performing political roles
and that the role of wife and mother is compatible with performance of high level political roles. [25]   A comparison of
1972 female convention delegates and women in the 1972
electorate found this set of beliefs was a highly significant
distinguishing factor. [26]   This leads to the conclusion that
the most successful way to encourage women to seek higher
level political roles would be to increase feminist consciousness among a much greater proportion of American women.

What learning processes might operate to increase
that set of beliefs which have been labeled feminist consciousness?   There are four major socializing agents which can
significantly affect children's orientations toward the political
system.   These are the family, the schools, peer groups,
and the mass media.   Research cited earlier which focuses
on high school seniors suggests that adolescent girls who
possess a feminist consciousness tend to come from families
where the mother is employed in a profession.   A role model
is provided within the family of a woman who has successfully combined performance of a demanding occupational role
with family responsibilities.   The observed success in an
economic role is apparently generalized into the political
sphere; the daughters of professionally employed women tend
to be more interested in politics and to be, even as teenagers, highly participant in school, community, and political
activities. 27 We can ask, is the maternal role model the only
way in which feminist consciousness can be developed? If
so, then the number of women who will develop such consciousness will increase very slowly--and several generations
will be required in order to form a base for a much greater
proportion of political elite roles being filled by women.   I
will argue that other major sources of political socialization
can help instill feminist consciousness in girls and also in
women.

        The role of the mass media as a socializing agent has
in the past been discounted, but a reassessment of its influence is currently underway.   Several types of mass media
content can be a positive influence in the development of feminist consciousness.   For example, elected and appointed public and party officials frequently receive considerable local,
state, and national news coverage.   Female role models will
be more frequently provided in these offices as those who control access to party, campaign, or public posts realize that
women must be included in these offices; demands by women
can result in the concept of the "balanced" ticket being expanded to include fair representation of women in party, campaign, and public office.

        We should also not discount the political effects of the
female role models presented in television entertainment programs.   It is only since the early 1970's that a substantial
number of females could be found in lead roles in politically
relevant programs.

        One element of feminist consciousness--the belief that

women can perform, equally as well as men, a multitude of
economic roles previously restricted to men only--has only
recently received emphasis in television advertising.   While
such advertising may have been inspired in many instances by
court ordered or negotiated settlements of sex discrimination
cases, the stimulus for the advertising is unimportant.   The
politically relevant consequences--learning about women's
capabilities to perform what were formerly classified as
men's jobs--is significant.

The impact of the educational process on changing beliefs also gives some hope for higher levels of political activism among women.   Higher levels of education are associated with higher levels of political participation.   Thus, as
more women join the college educated group, we can expect
greater levels of political participation among women.   The
relative level of participation of men and women with equal
amounts of education varies with the level of educational attainment.   Thus, women with some college or a bachelor's
degree are more likely to be politically active than men with
the same level of education.   However, women with advanced
college degrees are less active than men with advanced degrees.   The demands of a profession plus the constraints of
family roles may result in women having less time for political activity than men have. 28   A second possible explanation is that men with advanced degrees engage in unusually
high levels of political participation.

The role of peer groups in socializing women to political activism has received limited study, but the encouragement given by women already active in politics to other wom-
en can surely be a major force in increasing the power of
women in American politics.   Such encouragement has recently been institutionalized in the National Women's Political
Caucus and in academically affiliated institutes such as the
Washington Institute for Women in Politics at Mount Vernon
College and the Center for the American Woman and Politics
associated with the Eagleton Institute of Politics at Rutgers.
Individual women who are active in politics could make a major contribution through their personal activities to stimulate,
encourage, and support political activism among other women.

While it may seem unduly optimistic to some, it appears that the general level of political participation among
women in the United States has increased significantly in the
past decade.   The necessary ingredient for another advance,
to that of having more women in the role of voluntary activist

in political party and campaign organizations, is the development in women of the belief that women are equally as capable as men to perform political roles and that family roles are compatible with that type of voluntary activism. An optimistic conclusion which can be drawn is that several trends in changing social patterns will foster development of such a belief among a much greater proportion of women in the next decade.

NOTES

1. The inference is, if more women are to be elected to public office, they must be encouraged to engage in voluntary political activities of this type.

2. Kristi Andersen, "Working Women and Political Participation," American Journal of Political Science, 19 (1975): 439-454.

3. Maureen Fiedler, R. S. M. , "The Participation of Women in American Politics," paper prepared for delivery at the American Political Science Association Meeting, San Francisco, 1975.

4. For an extended discussion of patterns of performance of these seven types of political participation from 1960 to 1972, see Elizabethann O'Sullivan, "The Relationship of Reference Groups and Self Esteem to Women's Political Participation," Ph. D. Dissertation, University of Maryland, 1974.

5. Morris J. Levitt, "Political Attitudes of American Women: A Study of the Effects of Work and Education on Their Political Role," Ph. D. Dissertation, University of Maryland, 1965.

6. See, for example, Thomas A. Flinn and Frederick M. Wirt, "Local Party Leaders: Groups of Like Minded Men," Midwest Journal of Political Science, 9 (March, 1965): 77-98; C. Richard Hofstetter, "The Amateur Politician: A Problem in Construct Validation," Midwest Journal of Political Science, 15 (February, 1971): 51-56; Jeanne Kirkpatrick, The New Presidential Elite: Men and Women in National Politics (New York: Russell Sage Foundation, 1976); Dwaine Marvick and Charles R. Nixon, "Recruitment Contrasts in Rival Campaign Groups," ed. Dwaine Marvick, Political Decision Makers: Recruitment and Performance (Glencoe, Ill. : The Free Press, 1961), pp. 193-216; Charles W. Wiggins and William L. Turk, "State Party Chairmen: A Profile," Western Political Quar-

terly, 23 (June, 1970): 321-32; Cornelius P. Cotter
and Bernard C. Hennessey, Politics Without Power
(New York: Atherton Press, 1964).

7. For studies of precinct leader characteristics, see
Robert Hirschfield, Bert E. Swanson, and Blanche
Blank, "A Profile of Political Activists in Manhat-
tan," Western Political Quarterly, 15 (1962): 489-506;
M. Margaret Conway and Frank B. Feigert, "Motivation, Incentive Systems, and the Political Party Organization," American Political Science Review, 62
(1968): 1159-1173; Robert H. Salisbury, "The Urban
Party Organization Member," Public Opinion Quarterly,
29 (1965-66): 553-561; Samuel J. Eldersveld, Political
Parties: A Behavioral Analysis (Chicago: Rand Mc-
Nally, 1964): 277-292; Harold F. Gosnell, Machine
Politics: Chicago Model (Chicago: University of Chicago Press, 1937); Dennis Ippolito, "Political Perspectives of Suburban Party Leaders," Social Science Quarterly, 49 (March, 1969): 800-815; Dennis Ippolito and
Lewis Bowman, "Goals and Activities of Party Officials in a Suburban Community," Western Political
Quarterly, 22 (September, 1969): 572-580; Lewis Bowman, Dennis S. Ippolito, and William Donaldson, "Incentives for Maintenance of Grassroots Political Activism," Midwest Journal of Political Science 13
(February, 1969): 129-39; Peter Gluck, "Incentives
and the Maintenance of Political Styles in Different
Locales," Western Political Quarterly, 25 (December
1972): 753-760; Glen Browder and Dennis Ippolito,
"The Suburban Activist," Social Science Quarterly,
53 (June, 1972): 168-175; Philip Althoff and Samuel
Patterson, "Political Activism in a Rural County,"
Midwest Journal of Political Science, 10 (February,
1966): 39-51; M. Margaret Conway and Frank B.
Feigert, "Incentives and Task Performance Among
Party Precinct Leaders," Western Political Quarterly,
37 (December, 1974): 693-709.

8. See, for example, Henry Valen and Daniel Katz, Political Parties in Norway (Oslo: Universitetforlaget,
1964); Allan Kornberg, Joel Smith, and David Brom-
ley, "Some Differences in Political Socialization Patterns of Canadian and American Party Officials: A
Preliminary Report," ed. William E. Wright, A Comparative Study of Party Organizations (Columbus:
Charles E. Merrill Company, 1971), pp. 135-169.

9. See Congressional Quarterly, 1972, passim; 1976,
passim; data on 1976 Republican National Convention

were obtained from the Republican National Committee.

10. Charles W. Wiggins and William L. Turk, "State Party
    Chairman: A Profile," Western Political Quarterly,
    23 (June, 1970): 331-332; Samuel Eldersveld, Political
    Parties, pp. 158-9, 171.

11. Edmond Constantini and Kenneth H. Craik, "Women as
    Politicians: The Social Background, Personality and
    Political Careers of Female Party Leaders," Journal
    of Social Issues, 28 (1972): 217-236; M. Margaret Con-
    way, unpublished research.

12. Constantini and Craik, "Women as Politicians"; M. Kent
    Jennings and Norman Thomas, "Men and Women in
    Party Elites: Social Roles and Political Resources,"
    Midwest Journal of Political Science, 12 (1968): 469-
    492.

13. See, for example, Marcia Manning Lee, "Why Few Wom-
    en Hold Public Office: Democracy and Sexual Poli-
    tics," Political Science Quarterly, 91 (Summer, 1976):
    297-314.

14. M. Margaret Conway, unpublished research.

15. Jeane J. Kirkpatrick, Political Woman (New York:
    Basic Books, 1974).

16. Andersen, "Working Women and Political Participation,"
    Table 3, p. 449.

17. Susan C. Bourque and Jean Grossholtz, "Politics as an
    Unnatural Practice: Political Science Looks at Female
    Participation," Politics and Society, 4 (1974): 241-252.

18. Robert E. Dowse and John A. Hughes, "Girls, Boys,
    and Politics," British Journal of Sociology, 22 (1971):
    56-67; Anthony Orum, Roberta S. Cohen, Sherri Grass-
    much, and Amy Orum, "Sex, Socialization, and Poli-
    tics," American Sociological Review, 39 (1974): 197-
    209; M. Margaret Conway, Eleanor Feldbaum, and
    David Ahern, "Sex Differences in Children's Socializa-
    tion to Political Regime Orientations," mimeo., 1975;
    M. Margaret Conway, "Sex Differences in Children's
    Political Orientations: Continuity and Change," paper
    prepared for presentation at the Southern Political Sci-
    ence Association, Atlanta, Georgia, Nov. 4-6, 1976.

19. Roberta S. Sigel, "The Adolescent in Politics: The Case
    of American Girls," paper prepared for delivery at
    the 1975 American Political Science Association Meet-
    ing, San Francisco, September 2-5.

20. See Hazel Erskine, "The Polls: Women's Role," Pub-
    lic Opinion Quarterly, 35 (1971): 277-279; The Gallup
    Poll, Baltimore Evening Sun, September 18, 1975:
    A3; Myra Marx Ferree, "A Woman for President?

Changing Responses: 1958-1972," Public Opinion
Quarterly, 38 (Fall, 1974): 390-399.

21. See, for example, Mary Cornelia Porter and Ann B.
Matassar, "The Role and Status of Women in the
Daley Organizations," in J. Jaquette (ed.), Women in
Politics (New York: Wiley Interscience, 1974), 85-
104.

22. See, for example, Lee, "Why Few Women Hold Public
Office," pp. 304-306.

23. Constantini and Craik, "Women as Politicians."

24. Rufus Browning ("The Interaction of Personality and
Political System in Decisions to Run for Office: Some
Data and a Simulation Technique," Journal of Social
Issues, 24 (July, 1968): 93-100) isolates five different
patterns of needs and styles of political leadership.
See also Jeane Kirkpatrick, Political Woman, pp. 9-
13.

25. Fiedler, "The Participation of Women in American Politics," p. 4.

26. Ibid. , pp. 12-13.

27. Sigel, "The Adolescent in Politics," pp. 8-9.

28. Fiedler, "The Participation of Women in American Politics," p. 7.

Chapter 15

REPUBLICAN WOMEN AND THE FUTURE OF
THE REPUBLICAN PARTY

by Sarah F. Liebschutz

> The public has lost confidence in everybody and
> everything except garbage men. American society
> is riddled with disbelief. Politicians, doctors,
> journalists, the oligarchs of business and labor--
> everyone we used to trust has simply turned to dis-
> belief. [1]

During the past decade, support for American political
parties seems to have eroded faster than for other political
institutions and has fallen to lower levels. Such indicators
of public support for the parties as levels of voter turnout,
proportions of partisan identifiers and incidence of split ticket
voting, all seem to confirm the present low state of party
legitimacy. [2] Concurrent with the trend of declining support
for parties is a kind of counter trend, the increasing involvement of women in the work of the political parties.

Women have long participated in the work of the parties, but, as has been amply demonstrated, their activities
have overwhelmingly consisted of auxiliary roles to the males
who made decisions about who should run for political office
and what policy decisions should be taken. [3] What is of particular interest is that while general support for political
parties has been declining, women are actively seeking to
play new non-auxiliary roles in them. Increasing proportions
of females are delegates to national Republican and Democratic conventions and increasing numbers of women are running on major party tickets for local, state and national offices. The general stimulus for the research reported here
was the desire to understand why women are increasing their
involvement in conventional political institutions at the same
time that the general public is increasingly alienated from
them.

Of the two major parties, the Republican party has

suffered greater losses in numbers of adherents since 1960.
In 1975, only 21 percent of adult Americans identified themselves as Republicans, down from 30 percent in 1960. [4] Victories for Democratic candidates for Congress and state
legislatures in 1972, 1974 and 1976 pointed to the unmistakable disfavor of the Republican party with the voting public. [5]
As of January, 1977--despite the fact that Gerald Ford had
received 49 percent of the 1976 popular vote for president--
only 24 percent of the nation's governors and 34 percent of
the members of Congress were Republicans. Some observers
believe that shrinking numbers of self-identifiers with the Republican party and lower electoral support for Republican
candidates may mean permanent transformation of the Republican party to the party of opposition. Other observers suggest that a strategy to rebuild the party's electoral base can
be successful. [6]

During this period of general decline in electoral success of the Republican party, Republican women have been
achieving greater visibility in the party. Women comprised
approximately 31 percent of the delegates to the 1976 Republican national convention, compared with 17 percent in 1968.
Eighteen women were Republican candidates for Congress in
1976--up from fifteen in 1974 and ten in 1972. Five hundred
eighty-three women were Republican candidates for state
legislatures in 1976--a gain of more than 5 percent over
1974. [7] It is apparent, of course, that even with these gains,
Republican women do not begin to reflect their proportions
of the total population, of which women are 51 percent, or
of Republican party identifiers, of which women are about 53
percent. Nonetheless, the increase within recent years in
the numbers of Republican women in political roles historically monopolized by men do contrast with the decline in public
preference for the Republican party.

The question of whether the increased public presence
of Republican women as convention delegates and as candidates
is due to the fact that they have been co-opted by male party
leaders, aware of increasingly favorable public opinion toward
political activity of women[8] and the responsiveness of the
Democratic party to the notion of greater representation for
women, [9] or whether it is due to the initiative of the Republican women themselves[10] has not been explored. How do
Republican women activists view the Republican party? Do
they feel less loyal as a result of Watergate? How do they
view the efficacy of their own participation in party affairs?
How do their attitudes contrast with those of Republican male

activists? There would seem to be considerable merit in
the exploration of these questions, for if Republican women
do succeed in attaining positions of real influence in party
affairs in addition to their present increasing visibility, their
attitudes toward the role of the party and the political process
generally may help to determine the future course of the Republican party.

Methodology and Sample Description

The present study was undertaken to explore these issues. Mail questionnaires were distributed to delegates to
an unusual Republican convention, held in February 1975, of
the Monroe County (New York) Republican party. The Convention was conceived and designed for the "party to look at
itself--to rediscover its purpose and reorder its priorities
... so that the Republican party and the two-party system
will continue."[11] The responses of 156 of the 406 delegates,
38 percent, [12] who returned the questionnaire, constitute the
data base upon which the following discussion is based.

Convention delegates were selected according to criteria which included stipulations that delegates be enrolled
Republicans, that between 25 and 50 percent be Republican
party committee members, and between 50 and 75 percent
be Republicans not holding party positions, and further, that
delegations from each political subdivision within the county
be balanced by sex. These selection criteria were intended
to ensure both participation of women in greater proportions
than their party committee positions (21 percent as of May
1975) and representation of views of non-party members.

The sample (see Table 1) can be characterized as
white, highly educated, middle-aged and upper middle income. [13] Differences between male and female respondents
were evident with respect to education and total family income levels, with the difference favoring the males. Female respondents were typically self-reported housewives or
held such traditional female jobs outside the home as secretary, nurse or teacher, while male respondents tended to be
professionals (lawyers, engineers) and managers. In this
regard it is interesting to note that the proportion (55 percent)
of female respondents employed outside the home was not far
from the national (1970) labor force participation rate range
of 49 to 54 percent for women in the 35-59 age group. [14]

TABLE 1

Sample Characteristics by Sex of Convention Delegates*

	Males	Females
Age:		
under 30	12%	9%
between 31-50	54%	66%
over 51	35%	25%
Education:		
(highest level completed)		
college	18%	21%
graduate	44%	26%
Total Family Income:		
0-$9,999	8%	15%
$10-$19,000	31%	27%
over $20,000	62%	58%
Employment Status:		
not employed	9%	45%
employed	91%	55%
Major Employment Classes:		
professional	34%	
managerial	13%	
secretary, nurse, teacher		40%
housewife		38%
Current Committee Membership	63%	59%
Number of Respondents	80	76

*Source: Survey of Republican Convention Delegates, Monroe County, New York, 1975.

This high socioeconomic status sample, of course, in-accurately reflects the distribution of national income levels. As is well known, political party elites are not typical of their rank and file. Kirkpatrick, in a description of dele-gates to the 1972 Republican and Democratic National Conven-tions, writes:

> Delegates to both conventions ... shared the char-
> acteristics that identify political elites everywhere;
> they had gone to school longer than most other peo-
> ple, had made more money and had better jobs.
> The social characteristics of the women ... were

> not exactly those of middle-aged white males; but
> the differences were marginal.... The delegates
> to both conventions were an overwhelmingly middle
> to upper-middle class group, and they knew it. [15]

In the sense that this sample of delegates reflects the middle
class bias of party elites in America, the data which follow
may be useful for broader generalization. Specifically, since
the intent of the paper is to explore the coincidence of declining attachment to the Republican party and increasing redefinition of political sex roles, the findings may have relevance
for the participation of Republican women in a context broader than the Monroe County Republican party.

This coincidence of trends is explored with respect
to personal motivations for participation in the convention,
attitudes towards women and politics, and expressions of
directions for change for the Republican. Differences in attitudes among male and female delegates are first separately
presented; then relationships among the variables are considered in an effort to deal with the broader issue of Republican women and the future of the party.

Motivations for Activism

Motivation for attending the convention was ascertained
by asking respondents about initiative exerted in becoming
delegates, and through assessments of the relative importance
of several types of possible motivational goals. Less than
one-fifth (18 percent) of the females reported that they sought
to be delegates; almost one-third (31 percent) of the males
took the initiative. These differences in self-initiative may
have been due to more widespread information about the delegate selection process among males. It clearly cannot be
explained by greater male loyalty to the Republican party.
The sample as a whole was strongly loyal, with 71 percent
of the delegates identifying themselves as strong Republicans.
Among female delegates, as seen in Table 2, loyalty levels
were higher than for male delegates, and highest of all among
female committee members. And the persistence of loyalty
even in the face of the events associated with Watergate was
borne out by the finding that only 9 percent of the female respondents, in contrast to 16 percent of males, reported that
Watergate had weakened their attachment to the party.

Personal motives for convention participation were

TABLE 2

Intensity of Party Identification,
by Sex and Committee Membership*

| | Males | | Females | |
	Comm.	Non-Comm.	Comm.	Non-Comm.
Strong Republican	76%	59%	84%	61%
Moderate Republican	10%	3%	11%	13%
Other	14%	38%	5%	26%
TOTAL	100%	100%	100%	100%
Number of Respondents:	49	29	44	31

*Source: Survey of Republican Convention Delegates, Monroe County, New York, 1975.

investigated through a series of items designed to identify material (monetary), solidary (social and psychological) and purposive (ideological, policy, organizational success) goals.[16] All delegates were more motivated toward purposive than material or solidary goals. Differences between male and female respondents ranged from 1 to 11 percentage points: in every instance the direction of difference pointed to greater intensity of motivation for females (see Table 3). Female respondents, in sum, displayed a high degree of interest in improving government at all levels and in fulfilling a strong sense of citizen duty through participation in the work of the convention.

Attitudes Toward Women in Politics

Is the achievement of these purposive goals related to attitudes toward women in politics? To explore this relationship, inquiry was made as to whether politics was viewed by delegates as an appropriate endeavor for women, and whether greater political participation by women would make any difference. Two items were used from the 1972 Virginia Slims American Women's Opinion Poll conducted by Louis Harris and Associates. The first item concerned attitudes toward politics and femininity,[17] and the other, attitudes toward women in politics and the state of the nation. Strong majorities

TABLE 3

Motivation for Attending Convention, by Sex*

Reason	% Rating as Very Important	
	Males	Females
Fulfill my sense of deep attachment to the Party (P)a	39	45
Launch a personal political career (M)b	11	10
Improve the National Government (P)	51	62
Improve the State Government (P)	57	66
Improve the County Government (P)	84	87
Improve the City or Town Government (P)	82	86
Expand friendships and social contacts (S)c	5	10
Be close to important people (S)	9	16
Make business contacts (M)	1	2
Fulfill sense of community obligation (P)	62	63
Number of Respondents	80	76

*Source: Survey of Republican Convention Delegates, Monroe County, New York, 1975.
a) P= Purposive goal; b) S= Solidary goal; c) M= Material goal

of the entire sample gave support for the feminist position on both items. That is, 86 percent disagreed that "Women who insist on competing in the male world of politics tend to lose their femininity," and 63 percent agreed that "This country would be better off it women had more to say about politics." As can be seen in Tables 4 and 5, however, females were much more supportive of both ideas, that politics and femininity are compatible and that beneficial consequences would flow from greater female participation.

In addition to the analysis of responses by sex, the separate impacts of two intervening variables, female employment status and committee membership on responses, was examined. [18] Neither committee membership nor female employment status had a separate effect on response rates for the politics and femininity item. With respect to the beneficial

TABLE 4

Politics and Femininity, by Sex*
(Item: Women who insist on competing in the
male world of politics tend to lose their femininity.)

	% Males	% Females
Strongly agree	4	3
Agree	9	3
Not sure	4	4
Disagree [Feminist response]	48	24
Strongly disagree [Feminist response]	35	66
TOTAL	100%	100%
Number of Respondents	80	75

*Source: Survey of Republican Convention Delegates, Monroe
County, New York, 1975.

TABLE 5

Women in Politics and the State of the Nation, by Sex*
(Item: This country would be better off if wom-
en had more to say about politics.)

	% Males	% Females
Strongly agree [Feminist response]	12	31
Agree [Feminist response]	41	42
Not sure	29	12
Disagree	13	14
Strongly disagree	5	1
TOTAL	100%	100%
Number of Respondents	76	74

*Source: Survey of Republican Convention Delegates, Monroe
County, New York, 1975.

consequences of greater female participation in politics, female respondents employed outside of the home indicated
greater agreement (76 percent) than did housewives (69 percent).

The independent effect of sex rather than committee membership was particularly striking in that only 48 percent of male
committee members agreed with the item, in contrast to 75
percent of female members.

It is noteworthy that sentiment supportive of a greater
role for women in political decision-making was found here
for the entire sample, even though levels of support for such
a position were not uniform for males and females.   As indicated, the strongest advocates of greater female participation were females, particularly those who already hold committee positions within the party.

Women's Role and Party Change

Thus far it has been demonstrated that delegates to
this local Republican convention were motivated toward the
purposive and impersonal goals of improving the Republican
party and the institutions of government, and that they supported greater participation for women in politics.   Response
levels for female delegates indicated greater intensity than
for male delegates around both these issue clusters.   On the
basis of these findings, it is logical to advance the hypothesis
that the attainment of these purposive goals is positively related to involvement of females in determining the direction
of the Republican party.   One would expect additionally that
female delegates would cite greater involvement of women in
the party as a goal of higher priority than would male delegates.

Responses to an open-ended term, "In what ways would
you like to see the party change?" revealed that delegates as
a whole regard greater inclusiveness of party appeal, that is,
greater responsiveness to a broadened base of people, as the
primary direction for party change.   Eighty-eight percent of
males and 75 percent of females gave such responses as this
one, "The Republican party should become more open and responsive, more accessible, be a party of all the people, not
a privileged few."   The second, much less frequent type of
response, stressed the need for candidates of greater integrity and ability.   Twenty-five percent of males and 20 percent of females gave such responses as, "Candidates should
not make so many definite promises they know they cannot
keep.   They should say they will try to correct evils to the
best of their abilities."   Taken together, these types of responses imply that the party's electoral base needs to be

broadened, and that more credible candidates will help to attract and sustain Republican supporters. Some delegates
stated that the party "needs more women and youth, " but
most respondents did not specify which sectors of the electorate should have greater representation. Only 10 percent
of the sample specifically responded that there should be
greater involvement of women. The distribution by sex of
responses mentioning greater female participation, 14 percent
of female respondents and 6 percent of male respondents,
lends support to the hypothesis that this direction of change
has higher priority for female Republican elites.

In view of the strong majorities displayed among female delegates for the general value of women in politics,
the 14 percent response level seems inconsistent. Even
among female committee members whose belief that the participation of more women will make a difference in the state
of the nation is especially strong, only 13 percent cited female participation as a direction for change. The response
levels, however, may be entirely consistent. The explanation may well be that survival of the Republican party qua
electoral institution was perceived as the primary goal, with
greater participation of women in the party viewed as one
means to that end. The following response to the party
direction-of-change item, supplied by a female committee
member, is illustrative of that point:

> The party is narrow in actions and thinking. The
> Party should be more open and encourage the blue
> collar participation. They should discourage their
> snobbish attitudes. They should seek out qualified
> women to run for office. They have ignored women
> in the past. They need to run honest, highly eth-
> ical people for office, people who are dedicated to
> serving the public and not their own self-interest.

The delegates to this convention of a local Republican
party in upstate New York, while atypical in socioeconomic
status and party loyalty of the American electorate, share
one predominant characteristic with other political elites:
the commitment to winning elections. While both male and
female delegates expressed solid support for the participation
of women in politics, this was not a free-standing priority.
Rather, it seemed to be one pragmatic means to the primary
end of rebuilding the electoral base of the Republican party.
Viewed in this way, greater participation of Republican women
in decisions shaping the party's future may come about faster

than if such participation were valued solely on grounds of intrinsic merit.

NOTES

1. Rod MacLeish, "The Great American Blah," The Washington Post, 17 July 1975.
2. For elaboration of these points, see David Broder, The Party's Over (New York: Harper, 1971); Jack Dennis, "Trends in Public Support for the American Party System," British Journal of Political Science, 5 (1975): 187-230; and James Sundquist, Dynamics of the Party System (Washington: Brookings, 1973).
3. Documentation of auxiliary female party roles can be found in Susan and Martin Tolchin, Clout (New York: Coward, McCann and Geoghegan, 1974); and Jeane Kirkpatrick, Political Woman (New York: Basic Books, 1974).
4. Data of the Gallup Poll (American Institute of Public Opinion) for selected years over the period 1960-1974 clearly show diminishing proportions of voters identifying themselves as Republicans, increasing proportions identifying as Independents, and nearly stable proportions of Democratic identifiers.

	1960	1964	1970	1974	1975
Democrats	47%	53%	45%	46%	44%
Independents	23	22	26	32	35
Republicans	30	25	29	22	21

Source: Gallup Opinion Index (1975), Report No. 120: 22; New York Times, Sept. 21, 1975.

5. These Democratic victories were accompanied by decreasing voter turnouts, themselves probably indicative of widespread alienation from both parties. The estimated national turnout in 1976 of 54 percent of eligible voters marked a further decline in an already negative turnout trend since 1960. For data and discussion of these points, see Dennis, pp. 191-192.
6. For expositions of the view that the Republican party appears to be a permanent party of opposition, see James Sundquist, Dynamics of the Party System, and George Will, "Liberalism in Trouble," The Washington Post, 8 July 1975. Congressman Barber G. Con-

able, Jr., of New York, ranking Republican member
of the House Ways and Means Committee has noted
that 45 percent of the voters voted for Republican candidates for Congress in 1976 (although only 33 percent
of those who won were Republicans) and has suggested
that "A good Republican strategy would be to concentrate on trying to get control of state legislatures and
governorships before the next Congressional reappor-
tionment and redistricting in 1982." Washington Report (December 16, 1976).

7. The following table lists women candidates for Congress
    for 1972, 1974 and 1976:

	U.S. Senate			House of Rep.		
	Rep.	Dem.	Other	Rep.	Dem.	Other
1972[a]	2	0	4	8	24	30
1974[b]	1	2	10	14	30	47
1976[c]	0	1	NA	18	34	NA

Women Candidates

a. Congressional Quarterly Weekly Report, 1972, 30
    (October 28) 2800.
b. Congressional Quarterly Weekly Report, 1974, 32
    (October 26) 2973-2974.
c. National Women's Education Fund (verbally trans-
    mitted to the author).

        An accurate count of female candidates for state
legislature is available for 1974 and 1976. The total
number of female state legislative candidates, as compiled by the National Women's Education Fund of the
major parties, was 1118 (553 Republicans and 565
Democrats) in 1974 and 1260 (583 Republicans and 677
Democrats) in 1976. The author thanks Cynthia Ulman,
Project Associate of NWEF and Joanne Howes, former
Project Associate, for this information.

8. There are many indications of great public acceptance
    of female political activity. For example, the 1972
    Virginia Slims American Women's Opinion Poll found
    clear majorities of men and women agreeing that
    "Women should become more active in politics" and
    favoring "Organizations to strengthen women's partici-
    pation in politics." See also Hazel Erskine, "The
    Polls: Women's Role," Public Opinion Quarterly, 35
    (1971): 275-290.

9. The Guidelines of the Democratic party's Commission on
    Party Structure and Delegate Selection, more popular-

ly known as the McGovern Commission or the Mc-
Govern-Fraser Commission, stated the case for the
elimination of discrimination against women, blacks
and youth. For a full explanation of the Guidelines,
see Jeane Kirkpatrick, "Representation in the American National Convention," British Journal of Political
Science, 5 (1975): 273-280. Women made up approximately 34 percent of the 1976 Democratic National
Convention, down from 40 percent in 1972 and up from
13 percent in 1968.

10. Kristi Anderson, "Working Women and Political Participation," American Journal of Political Science, 19
(1975): 439-454, presents data indicating that while the
McGovern candidacy in 1972 was a potent mobilizing
force for working women, the impact of the Nixon
candidacy on campaign participation levels of women
was negligible. Susan and Martin Tolchin, Clout, pp.
231-232, recount the initial hostility of Republican
women delegates to the 1972 convention toward the
women's liberation movement. But they show how it
moderated as the delegates began to share their common experiences in politics and their common lack of
influence in party decisions.

11. Letter to Delegates from Graham Annett, Chairman,
Monroe County Republican Committee, February, 1975.

12. The major weakness of the mail questionnaire is the
problem of non-returns. In view of the facts of no
follow-up and no provision of postage to return the
questionnaire, 38 percent can be considered a good
return rate. See Delbert Miller, Handbook of Research Design and Social Measurement (New York:
McKay, 1970).

13. The sample, 48 percent female, slightly over-represents
female delegates, who were actually 40 percent of the
registered convention delegates, and under-represents
male convention delegates. The actual distribution of
committee membership among convention delegates was
not ascertained by the convention committee; an es-
timate by an officer of the County Committee was that
65 percent of the delegates were committee members
and 35 percent were not. The sample breakdown is
61 percent committee persons, 39 percent non-
members. Among committee persons in the sample,
females are 48 percent, more than double their actual
proportion of the County Republican Committee. On
this basis, it would appear that female delegates were
more likely to respond to the survey questionnaire

and the response rate was highest for female commit-
teepersons.

14. See Valerie K. Oppenheimer, "Demographic Influences
in Female Employment and the Status of Women,"
American Journal of Sociology, 78 (1973): 947-948.

15. Kirkpatrick, "Representation," pp. 283-285.

16. These questionnaire items were adapted from M. Margaret Conway and Frank Feigert, "Motivation, Incentive Systems and the Political Organization," American Political Science Review, 62 (1968): 1159-1173;
and Frank Sorauf, Party Politics in America (Boston:
Little, Brown, 1972).

17. The item used in this survey, "Women who insist on
competing in the male world of politics tend to lose
their femininity," is a modification of the statement,
"Women who succeed in politics usually have to sacrifice their femininity to get there," used by Louis Harris and Associates, The 1972 Virginia Slims American
Women's Opinion Poll (New York: Philip Morris,
1972).

18. See M. Kent Jennings and Norman Thomas, "Men and
Women in Party Elites," and Midwest Journal of Political Science, 4 (1968): 469-492, for examination
and support of the hypothesis that women employed
outside the home have greater attitude congruence with
men than with housewives. See Conway and Feigert,
and Sorauf for a summary of the literature on attitude differences between party activists and identifiers.

BIBLIOGRAPHY

Anderson, Kristi. "Working Women and Political Participation." American Journal of Political Science, 19 (1975):
439-454.

Broder, David. The Party's Over. New York: Harper,
1971.

Conable, Barber B., Jr. Washington Report, December 16,
1976.

Congressional Quarterly, Weekly Report. "Republican Delegates: Representation Being Widened." 30 (1972): 1998-
2000.

Congressional Quarterly Weekly Report. "Women Candidates: A Big Increase Over 1972." 32 (1974): 2973-
2974.

Conway, M. Margaret, and Frank B. Feigart. "Motivation,
Incentive Systems and the Political Organization."

American Political Science Review, 62 (1968): 1159-1173.

Dennis, Jack. "Trends in Public Support for the American Party System." _British Journal of Political Science_, 5 (1975): 187-230.

Erskine, Hazel. "The Polls: Women's Role." _Public Opinion Quarterly_, 35 (1971): 275-290.

Harris, Louis and Associates. _The 1972 Virginia Slims American Women's Opinion Poll._ New York: Philip Morris, Inc., 1972.

Jennings, M. Kent, and Thomas, Norman. "Men and Women in Party Elites." _Midwest Journal of Political Science_, 4 (1968): 469-492.

Kirkpatrick, Jeane. _Political Woman._ New York: Basic Books, 1974.

_____. "Representation in the American National Conventions: The Case of 1972." _British Journal of Political Science_, 5 (1975): 265-322.

MacLeish, Rod. "The Great American Blah." _The Washington Post_, July 17, 1975.

Miller, Delbert. _Handbook of Research Design and Social Measurement._ 2nd edition. New York: McKay, 1970.

Oppenheimer, Valerie K. "Demographic Influences in Female Employment and the Status of Women." _American Journal of Sociology_, 78 (1973): 946-961.

Sorauf, Frank. _Party Politics in America._ Boston: Little, Brown, 1972.

Sundquist, James. _Dynamics of the Party System._ Washington: Brookings, 1973.

Tolchin, Susan and Martin. _Clout._ New York: Coward, McCann and Geoghegan, 1974.

Will, George. "Liberalism in Trouble." _The Washington Post_, July 8, 1975.

PART VI

WOMEN AND THEIR EQUAL RIGHTS

INTRODUCTION

In the first essay of this section Liz Carpenter allows us a brief look at the discriminatory past and moves us to a future filled with hope and determination. Her no-nonsense discussion of injustice, her positive attitudes toward change, give us the fervor for the trip ahead. The reader will respond to the distinct sense of power in Liz Carpenter's essay, which carriês with it the message that fighting for one's rights of freedom of choice and control over one's life is just and possible.

Claudine A. Schweber gives the reader an understanding of the politics of the jury system in the United States. Schweber illuminates the discriminatory practices that until recently denied women equal participation on federal and state juries and she develops an historical perspective to the problem.

Jean Lipman-Blumen develops a crisis framework for understanding role changes and then applies that framework to the problem of emerging roles in the health profession. Special implications of crisis-induced occupational role changes for women and other minorities then are explored.

Combining knowledge of law and political science, Mary L. Shanley defines, in new perspective, the pressing need for ratifying the Equal Rights Amendment. She examines the tensions between individual and family, and single and married persons, which are of fundamental theoretical

319

and married persons, which are of fundamental theoretical and practical importance in the effort to achieve an equitable social order for women and men.

Chapter 16

GOD, BUT WE'RE GETTING SMART!

by Liz Carpenter

Back in the Bible belt there is an old joke handed down by the storytellers.

A country bumpkin was being interviewed by a Harvard expert researching the extent of the bumpkin's ignorance and the cause for it.

He asked all sorts of questions about the family ... and the historic lack of education. "You have a brother?"

"Yep, he's up at Harvard," the bumpkin replied.

Shocked, the researchist replied, "A brother at Harvard?"

"Yep, he's got two heads and he's in a bottle of formaldehyde."

That is where the women's movement is today. Women have discovered we have two heads, and here we are at Harvard--under the scrutiny of the experts!

Most women feel two-headed. We are pioneers in the world of women; we are guinea pigs in our personal world.

So quickly has the women's movement grown, so catalytic has it been since 1971 that we who are deeply involved in it find ourselves both pioneers and experts, charting the course and receiving the pot shots.

So newly have we thought about our own personal destinies, our own reasons for spending a span of time on this planet as daughter, wife, mother, widow--75.9 years of it-- that we are still timid about saying "If I had my life to live over, let me live it--not as a blonde--but a human."

"I have met brave women," Gloria Steinem has said, "who are exploring the outer edge of possibility with no history to guide them--and with a courage to make themselves vulnerable--that I find moving beyond words."

This is not a lonely effort. There is no woman today who thinks the same way she did five years ago. She has either run in fear to those franchised sick sex classes (some operating in the name of religion) that encourage you to believe that all women want is to hover behind the kitchen door, wrapped in cellophane with boots and jump out each evening, sprayed with whipped cream in all the erogenous zones, to surprise her stomach-ulcered breadwinner--master of the house.

Or, she is refashioning her life to grow. Women are coming alive. There are new risks. There are new satisfactions. "Where danger is near, so also is salvation."

Yes, we are coming alive ...

... in politics. Women are running for office and getting elected. In the 1974 election, more than half the women who ran for office won. So we must be doing something half right. Barbara Jordan was the star of the Democratic Convention by all odds. There are women from the Junior League and from the civil rights fights who are on city councils, who are mayors, who are in the state legislatures and headed upward. (Most of them since July 1971 when the feminist movement moved into the public arena with the birth of the National Women's Political Caucus). How organized and smart we have grown since them! A 27-year-old lawyer, Sarah Weddington, won the abortion case before the U.S. Supreme Court, ran for the Texas state legislature and won, even with that abrasive issue.

She worked on a statewide race for Attorney General in 1978--and formed an advisory committee of men and women in strategy sessions, booking speeches--in the kind of respectable political world of power once reserved only for men.

... in the courts. And I do not have to tell you what the judgments are. Martha Griffiths, that remarkable former congresswoman who retired to become an activist on five large corporate boards, spoke to an assemblage of businessmen recently to shove them faster on affirmative action programs within their corporations. "Gentlemen," she said, "there will be no peace. Behind every door, including the kitchen door, women are 1) listing their grievances, 2) organizing political efforts to alleviate them, 3) researching the law for possible suits, 4) finding the exact person to fit the situation and the most likely to win the suit, and 5) others are raising money to pay for the suit."

... in the marketplace. Barbara Walters makes a million dollar salary on the networks. Betty Talmadge sells chicken wieners in Tokyo. AT&T puts a woman on its board. The First Women's Bank is born in New York.

... in most of the homes in this country, and in the soul of every woman, there is a reawakening to what Tom Wolfe calls "The Me Decade" in which "we can follow and believe in the heresy of our own eyes."

We are going to have a piece of life for ourselves. We are going to sort out our two heads and piece them into one whole person.

Where is the women's movement at? It's exactly where you and I are at. Right now. Right here. And proceeding all around the world where thinking women meet.

One of my "two heads" is Liz Carpenter, co-chair of ERAmerica, the umbrella effort focusing on ratification of the Equal Rights Amendment which has been haunting us so long. It is the first basic step for women to gain confidence, nationally and individually, for it gives us the dignity of being in the Constitution of our own country. It is just that simple. But what a psychological boost, across-the-board, for all women, to have that dignity which all males, black and white now have, being a recognized part of the basic law of the land. "Equality of rights shall not be denied or abridged on account of sex." What a travesty of justice that we still have to stand and beg for it.

My other head is me--55 years old, widowed, and now sorting out how I want to spend the last lap--which, with luck and, as the ad says, "by taking good care of myself, and a spoonful of Geritol each day," gives me 20 or more years and 8 months to live. Women are just beginning to face the fact that most of us will spend a third of our lives alone. And make no mistake about it. There is a tremendous cultural shock of living alone after 31 years of a happy

partnership marriage. I still flinch from the word "widow."
Aside from the painful fact of it, it connotes being shelved,
being old. Lynn Caine's book by that title (Widow) has done
much to bring those feelings off the shelves and into the con-
versation, so that we can hopefully face widowhood as a second life.

Let us look back to 1776 and the framers of the Declaration of Independence, the Constitution in 1787, and the
Bill of Rights in 1791. We know who was there and we know
who was left out. Women missed that meeting. We aren't
going to miss any others.

Using English common law, the framers treated wom-
en, and slaves, as chattels without individual rights or recognition under the law as persons or citizens.

We weren't even in any discarded drafts. Having
worked on many speeches during my days in the White House,
I know how many writings a document can go through before
publication. I checked this out thinking surely it might have
occurred to someone, in an old discarded Constitution draft,
to have included women.

The answer is no--not one! Indeed only two people
mentioned us at all--Abigail Adams who wrote John "to remember the ladies," which he promptly forgot, and Tom
Paine, liberal pamphleteer, who was not invited to the drafting.

There was one petition, signed by 14,000 women in
New England asking the Constitution drafters to see that slave
girls be treated equally with slave boys. This petition was
not even considered by the forefathers because it was signed
by the foremothers.

It seems to me our problem is that we spent 200
years fighting other people's battles instead of our own. No
one else spoke up for us then and not enough since because
it has been conceived as a "woman's issue" or a "feminist
issue," instead of what it really is--an extension of civil
rights.

Many people wonder why at this late date we need a
federal equal rights amendment at all? They point to the
Fourteenth Amendment's Equal Protection Clause, to equal
employment legislation passed in the 1960's and '70's, to

recent laws prohibiting discrimination in education and credit,
to court cases requiring sex equality in jury duty, child custody and many other areas, to state equal rights amendments.
Why, they ask, with all of these legal requirements for
equality, do we need to amend the United States Constitution?
Aren't men and women "equal" already?

We need an equal rights amendment because men and
women are not now, and never have been, equals under our
country's law.   Thomas Jefferson explained the position of
the country's founders in this way:

> Were our state a pure democracy there would still
> be excluded from our deliberations women, who, to
> prevent deprivation of morals and ambiguity of is-
> sues, should not mix promiscuously in gatherings
> of men.

The Fourteenth Amendment to the United States Constitution,
enacted after the Civil War to guarantee racial equality, introduced the word "male" (as a modifier to "citizen") into
the Constitution, making it clear that a country which was
ready to free its slaves still considered women as inferior
social and legal beings.   Two generations later, after nearly
a century of struggle, women were granted the right to vote--
the first step in a long journey toward equality.   Three years
thereafter, in 1923, the federal ERA was first introduced in
Congress.   More than 50 years later, women are still working for legal recognition of the principle that the law should
not treat them differently simply because of their sex.

I get pretty chagrined when I visualize the scene in
Philadelphia where the all-male, all-white drafters left us
all out.   But I recognize they were gluing together a new
nation and realizing it would not be static, if it was to live,
they wisely provided Article V to fill in the gaps with future
amendments.

This has been done 26 times, usually with tremendous
effort.   Indeed, the original Constitution was ratified by New
York State by only 3 votes, and by Virginia, which produced
many of the writers, only after 8 other states had ratified it.
I am not sure it could pass some states today.

Blacks have fared better in amendments than women.
The 14th Amendment and the 15th, adopted in the post-Civil
War period, extended to former slaves the guarantees of due

process, equal protection under the law, and black males the
right to vote. The 19th amendment in 1920 gave all women
the right to vote, but as voiced by the Supreme Court, the
right to vote was all it gave them.

Only recently--and on a very catch-as-catch can, willy-
nilly basis, has the Supreme Court interpreted the 14th
Amendment to include sex--as well as race--as a point of
discrimination.

Indeed, not until Congress passed ERA in 1972, did it
really put its mind to it and it is still no fixed thing.

The burden is still on each woman to prove her case.
ERA would give every man and woman freedom from sex
discrimination without going to court case by case.

We do take heart from occasional recent decisions.
In Frontiero v. Richardson, Justice Brennan and three other
judges stated:

"There can be no doubt our nation has a long and unfortunate history of sex discrimination. Traditionally, such
discrimination was rationalized by an attitude of romantic
paternalism which in practical effect put women, not on a
pedestal, but in a cage. "

Dissenting, we find that Virginia gentleman Mr. Justice Powell practically pleading for ratification "for if the
amendment is duly adopted, it will represent the will of the
people accomplished in the manner prescribed in the Constitution. "

Why hasn't it passed? Two reasons: ERA opponents
have done a very effective job of spreading myths and lies
about ERA. When you listen to them you realize Merrill
Lynch isn't the only one who has bull for America. They
would have you believe that it would bring about abortion,
co-ed bathrooms, unisex marriages, and even fluoride in
drinking water, yet, not one of these allegations has anything to do with the Equal Rights Amendment.

Who are the opponents? Well, it's a strange crew:
the John Birch Society, the Ku Klux Klan, and too many well
meaning people who, I hope, are beginning to realize they
have been the victims of smear and fear. Oh yes, the Com-
munist Party and Gus Hall are on record against it. They
do not want any change to improve life in this country.

Five governors in states which have ratified, and put
the amendment into effect in state law (for each state has
two years in which to bring its old out-moded laws into conformity) have written that none of the charges of the opponents has been true.

The second reason we are racing with the clock is
that we--who support ERA--never suspected its troubles and
we have only recently gotten our act together. We are now
organizing to lobby the key states where governors and legislators have given it lipservice, but stalled, stalemated and
kept it in committees.

I believe that the Equal Rights Amendment is going to
strengthen, not weaken family life. for it strengthens all of
the members of a family.

"Love, real love, the love that unites the mind as
well as the flesh, can only occur between equals. When
someone starts treating you as an inferior, you can be sure
they no longer love you, if indeed they ever did."

Not my quote ... but Clare Luce's, and I like it.

Pushy, noisy, strident. These are often the words
used to describe women who are in the forefront of the effort
to take our place in society. What do men expect after 200
years? For us to just keep on telling you how wonderful
you all are?

There is a new kind of man emerging, and he--as
well as WE--are learning how to put a stop to the bad-
mouthing and putdowns of all those questions so thoughtlessly
asked of both sexes: Like how does it feel to be a Mr.
Bella Abzug? Mr. Betty Ford?

We've learned to bite back, with humor and with sting.

Martin Abzug used humor in the TV interview on the
wedding anniversary (the 34th, I think) with Congresswoman
Bella Abzug. Martin is a stockbroker and a great guy.
The interviewer had a hard time understanding this arrange-
ment. "You seem so happy. How can you get along... ?"
he asked, in awe. "I mean, what holds you together when
she is in the limelight and you are... ? What keeps you together?"

Martin didn't bat an eye. "Sex!" he said.

We use sting, like Congresswoman Pat Schroeder of Colorado and her husband used the day she arrived in Congress. Think of it--26 years old, a lawyer, a briefcase, two babies under four, and a husband who is a lawyer.

When reporters asked Jim Schroeder why HE wasn't the Congressman, he replied, "We found a better candidate."

The first day Pat arrived in the halls of the House of Representatives, an old codger said in wonder, "But how can you be a mother of small children and a congresswoman too?" he asked.

"Because I've got a brain and a uterus and I use both," she retorted.

That has virtually stopped those kind of questions in Congress.

Women and their fight for equality cannot be stopped by the inanities and ignorance of idiots. Congresswoman Barbara Jordan--in her no-nonsense way--in speaking of ERA said:

> All we are trying to do is make this government of the United States of America honest. We only ask that when we stand up and talk about one nation under God, liberty, justice for all, we want to be able to look at the flag, put our right hands over our hearts, repeat those words and know that they are true.

We know--you and I--it could have been a better country if our grandmothers and mothers, had been a recognized part of the past.

It will be a better country because our daughters and granddaughters are.

Chapter 17

BUT SOME WERE LESS EQUAL ...
THE FIGHT FOR WOMEN JURORS

by Claudine A. Schweber

Introduction

The feminist movement has once again drawn attention
to the range of activities which have excluded women solely
on the basis of their femaleness. Jury service is one such
activity. Until recently, women were denied equal participation on federal and state juries in the United States by a
variety of exclusionary devices not permitted for men. (The
exclusion of women from jury duty occurred in several forms
such as: absolute exclusion/prohibition--prohibited women
from any participation; non-compulsory service--women were
eligible, but not required to serve via (a) compulsory registration, which required that women desiring to serve personally sign up with the local clerk; or (b) exemptions based on
sex, which allowed women to obtain a permanent waiver from
jury duty; questionable random selection--administrative procedures whereby men and women did not have the same chance
to become potential jurors.)

Trial by jury is a basic American right, guaranteed
by the Sixth Amendment to the Constitution. [1] Participation
in the process by which the community judges a member's
guilt or innocence is an important responsibility of citizenship.
Jury duty is often promoted as a chore to be evaded. [2] Laws
enabling only women to abstain indicate that some citizens
are less equal. Furthermore, the absence of women jurors
may affect women directly, as parties to a legal process.
Rape cases are the best example. Many women have hesi-
tated to bring charges because the victim is often publicly
humiliated, her morals and motivation challenged. Women
jurors are likely to understand that any woman is prey, not
just half-dressed voluptuous ones.

Women have only recently won the right to be subject
to the same juror standards as men. In June 1975 the United

States Supreme Court held that differential rules were unconstitutional. [3] States with sex-based differences, such as New
York and Louisiana, had to change their laws. [4] This equality had been sought by suffragists since 1920 when votes for
women had been obtained. [5] By 1975 the Supreme Court had
reacted to changing notions of women's roles. A look at the
historical patterns similarly reveals the interface between
social mores and legal decisions.

This paper discusses in three parts the politics of
jury service for women: first, a brief historical overview
of national developments from the eighteenth century to the
present; second, highlights from the post-suffrage battle to
eliminate the outright prohibition against women jurors in
New York State; third, a study of a recent legal case which
successfully used the argument of sex discrimination in jury
selection as the basis for the claim that equitable jury trials
were not possible.

Overview of National Developments[6]

The exclusion of women from juries was an inheritance
of the English common law from which American law is derived. Colonial law permitted twelve women to sit as jurors
when the defendant was pregnant, but only for two situations:
requests for stays of execution until after the child's birth;
requests by a widow for a delay in disposing of her late-
husband's estate until after the child's birth. But the women
jurors' function was limited to a determination of the existence
of pregnancy. The twelve male jurors who were also present were the "triers of fact." The examination function of
women was soon assumed by the (male) medical profession,
thus totally excluding women by the revolutionary period. [7]

In the years immediately following independence, the
state constitutions adopted common law guarantees of trials by
jury for the citizens. Unfortunately, since the common law
did not expressly include women jurors, courts often upheld
their exclusion in the absence of clear affirming statutes. In
Wyoming, for example, women had served on juries for a
while after the state constitution had been ratified in 1890.
But in 1892, the court held that as in the common law, wom-
en had no right to sit on juries unless specifically permitted
to by statute. [8]

In the post-civil war period, women's rights advocates

argued that the Fourteenth Amendment which entitled black
men to jury service, should also apply to black women, and
all women.   In 1879, the United States Supreme Court ruled
in Stauder v. West Virginia[9] that denying black men jury
service violated their constitutional rights under the Fourteenth Amendment.   The justices believed that the Fourteenth
Amendment did not prevent states from setting other limitations for jurors, such as age, education or sex.   The Court
wrote that:

> In [prescribing] the qualifications of its jurors ...
> [a state] may confine the selection to males, to
> freeholders, to citizens....   Looking at [the his-
> tory of the Fourteenth Amendment] it is clear ...
> its aim was against discrimination because of race
> or color. [10]

The situation in this period was further complicated
because states which permitted women to vote did not necessarily also grant them other privileges.   Until ratification of
the Nineteenth Amendment, most state courts held to some
variations of Stauder, which permitted states to exclude wom-
en from jury service regardless of the existence of other
correlated rights, such as state suffrage. [11]

In August 1920 the Nineteenth Amendment enfran-
chised women nationally.   Afterwards, women's organizations
like the National Women's Rights Party and the League of
Women Voters concentrated on the jury issue. [12]   They fought
in the courts and legislatures to overturn the absolute exclusion against women jurors.

The courts divided on the interpretation of the Nineteenth Amendment as it relates to jury service. [13]   Some
state courts were disposed to grant jury participation for
women if the only requirement for jury duty was being a
voter. [14]   Others interpreted specific statutory references to
jurors as "men" as excluding women.   For example, the
New Jersey courts interpreted their statute which referred to
electors as "he" as "a recognition [by the use of the above
pronoun] of the common law rule that men only shall be im-
panelled...."[15]   A few courts interpreted the voting requirement to mean the exclusion of women from jury service.   In
1924 an Idaho court held that although electors were statu-
torily defined as "male and female citizens" this did not
qualify women for jury duty, because "when the people gave
women suffrage they cannot have had in mind conferring the
right to jury duty."[16]

Since the courts were not very helpful, it was in the
political arena of state legislatures writing the statutes that
most changes in jury laws were sought.[17] Between 1921
and 1962, the number of states which totally excluded women
from jury service declined from 37 to 3. In the same period, states which permitted women to serve on the same basis
as men increased from 3 to 20. In the remaining states,
jury service was permitted but not obligatory for women.[18]

In 1957 the United States Congress made the absolute
exclusion of women virtually extinct. Under the Civil Rights
Act of 1957 all women were eligible for federal jury duty,
regardless of state limitations.[19] Consequently, states which
prohibited women on state juries could either change the law,
or maintain a costly dual jury selection system, one for federal and one for state cases. By 1965 only Alabama, Mississippi, and South Carolina excluded women from state juries.
By 1972, women were eligible in all states.[20]

None of this is to suggest that opposition to women
jurors had disintegrated. Even before 1957, many states
with absolute exclusions had changed their statutes to provide
special accommodations for women.[21] While acknowledging
that men and women were equally eligible to serve, these adjustments made jury service non-compulsory for women.
Compulsory registrations and exemptions based on sex were
the dominant varieties of the non-compulsory model. The
former, also known as affirmative registration, required interested women to formally sign up for jury service with the
local clerk; the latter permitted women to claim an exemption* on the grounds that they were female, whereby service would be an undue hardship or would interfere with
childcare.[22] In addition, there were indirectly discriminatory
devices, such as the use of predominantly male tax lists to
collect juror names.[23] While striking down laws which
totally excluded women from being eligible, courts upheld the
constitutionality of these non-compulsory approaches. Mixed
in with the legal reasoning were the judges' attitudes towards
women's proper role, as in the following sample from a 1966
Mississippi court:

*"Exemption" refers to the general category of conditions
under which persons may request to be excused from jury
duty, such as occupation (i.e., journalist, lawyer) or health.
Femaleness was another excusable condition in this category.
(See note 27 for the New York State application.)

> The legislature has a right to exclude women so
> they may contribute their services as mothers,
> wives and homemakers and also to protect them ...
> from the filth, obscenity and noxious atmosphere
> that so often pervades a courtroom during a jury
> trial.... 24

In June 1975 the United States Supreme Court put an
end to the various devices by which jury service could be
non-compulsory for women.   They held that women as a class
could not be excluded or permitted special waivers, because
the effect was to deny a defendent the constitutional right to
a jury drawn from a cross-section of the community. 25   Concerning woman's role in society, the Court wrote:

> If it was ever the case that women were unquali-
> fied to sit on juries or were so situated that none
> of them should be required to perform jury service,
> that time has long since passed....   It is untenable
> to suggest these days that it would be a special
> hardship for each and every woman to perform jury
> service or that society cannot spare any women
> from their present duties. 26

New York State Develops in the Post-suffrage Period

New York was one of the states which had eliminated
the absolute exclusion in favor of non-compulsory service
before the 1957 Civil Rights Act.   Twenty years earlier the
state legislature had agreed to allow women to be eligible for
jury duty with the proviso that they could elect not to serve
by requesting an exemption for their femaleness. *   This
change27 was the culmination of an eighteen year struggle by
women's groups and their supporters who had fought for equal
status, but had had to compromise with the exclusionists. 28

The fight over permitting women to be eligible for
juries climaxed in the early 1930s.   The following highlights
from that period indicate the conflicting opinions about wom-
en, and the fears at a time when jury service in the state
still totally excluded women.

---

*Among the many conditions which permitted New Yorkers to
request an exemption was: "number 7:   A Woman" (N. Y.
Judiciary Laws, secs. 665-7).

Opponents of equality were led by the local bar associations. Their arguments may be summarized as claiming
that the personality, sexuality and mentality of women had
inherent defects which needed protection and eliminated them
as jurors of competence. Those who felt women needed protection made such statements as "the burden of jury duty
shall not be imposed on women,"[29] and "Women need to be
saved from themselves. Women do not know where they are
going and are too delicate and too sweet for all that goes
with jury service."[30] The challenge to women's competence
included a gamut of attacks on mental stability, intelligence
and nymphomania that it's surprising any of the men would
even associate with females. Here are examples:

> The majority of women lack the intelligence for
> jury service.
>
> They have not had enough business experience for
> civil cases.
>
> It's a man's job to try lawsuits.
>
> No man would want a woman of intelligence on a
> jury. A lawyer wants no intelligence equal to his
> own concerning the facts.
>
> Trying a case is difficult.... No man can under-
> stand a woman's reasoning or present facts to her
> which she will understand.
>
> Women might be appropriate for "effeminate leg-
> islation," such as "women's and children's courts."
>
> Courthouses are not built to accommodate the in-
> creasing number of jurors, particularly the special
> needs of women, such as bathrooms.
>
> Sequestering women overnight with men was danger-
> ous. According to the Governor: "(I) would not
> care to have (my) daughter locked up all night with
> a lot of men."[31]

And, finally, opponents of equality claimed that "most women
don't want to serve."[32]

Male and female supporters of women's full and equal
participation in jurywork responded in various ways. They

came to legislative hearings with evidence that women did
want to serve.   One woman, Jane Norman Smith, had tested
opponents' claims in states where women were permitted to
serve.   The respondents, attorneys general and judges in
these states, all denied that women were any hindrance and
several especially commented that women took jury work more
seriously than men did, requesting fewer exemptions. [33]

Other supporters challenged that opponents held wom-
en to a different standard than men by permitting ostensible
lack of interest on the part of women to be an argument
against their serving, while most men also felt jury duty was
a burden:

> Whether or not some women want to accept this
> responsibility has nothing to do with the question....
> Men clergymen, attorneys, physicians, professors,
> teachers, and other classes ... (have not been
> asked) whether or not they want to serve.   Doubt-
> less many of them do not want to.... [34]

Indeed, women on juries would enable more men to be excused.   But the real issue, according to advocates, was the
nature of citizenship in the society:

> Jury service is one of the responsibilities of citi-
> zenship....   Women, too, are citizens and are
> well qualified for jury service ... [they should]
> share the duties and responsibilities of citizenship
> with men, just as they share every other duty and
> responsibility of life with men. [35]

The supporters pointed to other effects of discrimination.   Two points were emphasized.   First, subjecting a rape
victim to humiliation and questioning which challenged her
morality often deterred complaints and allowed the alleged
rapist to go free.   Mary Hamilton, the first New York City
policewoman, testified in 1931 that a man had not been convicted of rape in New York City in twenty years. [36]   As for
the potential voyeurism of the courtroom experience, an
Oregon judge wrote:

> Anyone who has seen a poor frightened girl ...
> forced to detail the facts in regards to her injury
> or shame to a jury composed of strange men, has
> felt that the presence of a few of the mothers of
> children in the jury box would be more in accord-
> ance with humanity and justice. [37]

Second, in some jurisdictions where women jurors
were permitted, jury administrators were refusing to call
them. In 1930, for example, Lillian M. Linebarger of the
National Women's Party wrote to the Jury Commissioner in
Washington, D. C. charging that "the almost total absence of
women jurors ... is not due to claims by women for exemptions, but to the fact that women are given little or no opportunity for service. Of the several hundred people recently
summoned for jury service, almost no women were included."[38] Her analysis was unfortunately prophetic of discriminatory actions which continued to prevent women's participation, as the 1974 case described below will show. Several
challenges to the constitutionality of exclusions and exemptions
based on sex were brought, but none were successful.[39]

New York had created the exemption for women in
1937. In 1974, enough pressure had been generated against
it* that the legislature had amended the Judiciary Law to allow an exemption by:

> ... a parent, guardian or other person who resides
> in the same household with and is legally charged
> with the care and custody of a child or children
> under sixteen years of age, and who is actually and
> personally engaged in the daily supervision ... dur-
> ing a majority of the hours between 8 am and 6
> pm.... [40]

The bill was vetoed by Governor Malcolm Wilson (1974).[41]
It passed again and was signed by Governor Hugh Carey after
the Taylor Decision (1975).

The Jury Challenge in Erie County, New York (1973-74)

The random selection process required to obtain a

---

*Two suits challenging the constitutionality of the women's
exemption had been filed in federal court in 1974. One in
New York City: National Organization for Women, New York
chapter, et al. v. Goodman, #73 civ 4831 complaint filed in
United States District Court for the Southern District of New
York in February 1974; one in Buffalo: NOW, Buffalo chapter v. Grimm et al., complaint filed in United States District Court for the Western District of New York on March
8, 1974.

jury fairly drawn from a cross-section of the community, is
another source of discrimination. [42] In the summer of 1973
a group of volunteers studied the jury system in Erie County
(Buffalo and Lackawanna are the major cities in the county)
in connection with the Attica trials which were to begin in the
fall. This preliminary study revealed that very few women
appeared on juries or in the panels from which the twelve
people and alternates were selected. The jurors were mostly
white, male and over 45. In order to discover how and why
this occurred, an analysis of the process by which people
got to be on juries was undertaken. Demographic data were
collected. The purpose was to find out whether there was
discrimination against women, the points at which it occurred,
and the implications for a fair trial in the county. [43]

After six months of research, the investigators concluded that discrimination against women did indeed exist. It
occurred early in the selection process, in the phase controlled by the jury commissioner. A suit was filed in state
court to throw out the entire pool of jurors and to begin the
selection anew. After three months of hearings, the judge
agreed. [44] County trials were temporarily halted until
enough new jurors could be selected. [45] The Erie County
case demonstrates how the systematic, albeit illegal, exclusion of women from jury duty can occur. [46]

The jury of peers concept has been interpreted as requiring that the panels from which jurors are selected (the
jury pool), must be chosen from a cross-section of the community. [47] The cross-section need not be exact, but "the
original sources of names must be representative; ... and
prospective jurors (must be) drawn from this group at random. "[48] Erie County used voter registration lists as the
source of potential juror names. Women were 50 percent of
the county's registered voters. Normally, one would expect
the jury pool from which names were selected monthly for
the forthcoming trials to contain approximately equal numbers
of men and women.

Yet, the pool* did not. Instead, there were 83. 2 per-

---

*In 1973, in order to be qualified to serve as a juror and
thus be in the pool, a person needed to be a citizen and
resident of the county, between 21 and 75 years, in good
health, and never convicted of a felony or misdemeanor involving moral turpitude. Elected officials, sheriffs and other

cent men and 16.8 percent women. This seemed to explain why few women in fact became jurors; there were not many of them in the jury pool. But it did not explain why there were only 16.8 percent women in the pool. After all, women were 53 percent of the county population and 50 percent of the registered voters.

The investigators assumed that most women had used the exemption, which permanently eliminated them from the pool, as the reason for the small proportion of women jurors. County officials had confirmed this interpretation. But contrary to expectations, most women were not given a choice of jury service. The initial decision was made by staff members of the jury commissioner and they deliberately selected few women's names from the lists. [49] The clerks later testified that they had been assured the exemption would eliminate most women anyway. Thus, calling too many women would entail unnecessary extra staff work. Investigators and clerks also testified that women who were selected and who seemed hesitant about serving might be encouraged to request the exemption. [50] Such evidence resulted in a ruling that discrimination against women jurors had occurred. The judge ordered that the jury pool selected before January 1, 1974, was to be discarded (about 110,000 names) and replacements were to be chosen at random. [51]

Almost thirty years earlier, the United States Supreme Court had dealt with a case involving exclusion of women from federal juries (Ballard v. United States, 1946). [52] Justice William O. Douglas writing on behalf of the Ballard majority said:

> The systematic and intentional exclusion of women ... deprives the jury system of the broad base it was supposed to have in our democratic society....

[cont'd from p. 337] specified governmental positions were specifically disqualified. Clergy, members of the news media, attorneys, volunteer firemen and other specified full-time professionals, and women, were entitled to an exemption. An exemption, once obtained, constituted a waiver of jury duty as long as the claimant remained in the condition which qualified for the exemption. For women, then, this was in perpetuity. The jury commissioner qualifies and disqualifies people, according to the statutory conditions. N.Y. Judiciary Law, sec. 665 (prior to 1975 amendments).

> The injury is not limited to the defendant--there is
> injury to the jury system, to the law as an insti-
> tution,. to the community at large.... 53

The Erie County case indicates how decisions such as
Ballard may be inoperative at the local level and how only by
assertive action on behalf of the injured class--women--did
compliance result.

Conclusion

We have seen that the absence of women from juries
had been fostered by a variety of exclusionary devices ranging from absolute prohibition to non-compulsory service.
The result--few women were jurors--was then cited as evidence that most women were not interested in jury duty.
The possible consequences of such prejudices was demonstrated by the recent Erie County (N. Y.) case, in which the
Jury Commissioner's office was limiting the number of wom-
en who could become jurors. This action by county officials,
besides being unconstitutional, meant that women were not
even permitted to decide for themselves whether they would
serve.

The jury issue provides a) a concrete example of how
a dominant group can integrate its values and attitudes into
the political structure of the society and b) a clear example
of the ensuing difficulties for excluded groups desiring change.
Jury service for women was restricted by mechanisms such
as legislative statutes, court rulings, decisions of administrative agencies. Furthermore, the rationalization that wom-
en were uninterested or incompetent obscured the real point
about citizenship in this society: that it entitles the recipient
to both rights and responsibilities wherein limitations in one
area similarly affect the other. Thus, the granting of exclusions to all women from the responsibilities of jury duty
also meant that women lost the benefits of the fundamental
right to trial by a jury of peers. Clearly, it was not an
equal exchange.

NOTES

1. Ballard v United States 329 U. S. 187 (1946).
2. Ask among your friends, relatives or colleagues.
3. Taylor v Louisiana 95 S. Ct. 652 (1975).

4. Louisiana was the state in the 1975 Supreme Court case
    (see note 3). It required compulsory registration.
    New York permitted an exception for women, N.Y.
    Judiciary Law, sec. 665 (7).

5. The Nineteenth Amendment to the Constitution, ratified
    August 18, 1920.

6. Most of the original research on the legal history was
    done by Karen O'Connor, at the time a law student
    at SUNY/Buffalo. I am indebted to her for the un-
    published paper on this topic (June 1974).

7. 3 Blackstone Commentaries 362, 394, 395 (6th ed. 1974);
    R. J. Miller "The Woman Juror" 2 Or L Rev, 34-6
    (1922); Patton v United States 281 US 276 (1930) in
    O'Connor pp. 4-5.

8. McKinney v State 30 P. 293 (1892), in O'Connor, p. 6.

9. Stauder v West Virginia 100 US 303 (1879), in O'Connor,
    p. 7.

10. Ibid.

11. O'Connor, pp. 7-8.

12. Burnita Shelton Matthews, "The Status of Women as
    Jurors," in Equal Rights (June 14, 1930), 148-91;
    Burnita Shelton Matthews, "Shall Women Serve on
    Juries? An Interesting Phase of Equal Rights," in
    Women's Weekly (April 7, 1923), 4: "A New Slant
    on Jury Service," in Equal Rights (December 19, 1931),
    362; June Provine, "Laws Which Enslave Modern Wom-
    en: Do You Know Your Legal Status in Your State?
    It May Surprise You." in Women's Weekly (November
    18, 1922), 5; Equal Rights, entire issue of February
    14, 1931.
        Burnita Shelton Matthews was the leading Na-
    tional Woman's Party attorney in the post-suffrage
    period. She is presently (1977) Senior Judge of the
    United States District Court for the District of Colum-
    bia.

13. Comment, "Women on Jury," 2 Ind L R J (1927); Note,
    "Constitutional Law: The Nineteenth Amendment, ef-
    fect on Jury Duty" 13 Cal L Rev (1926) and O'Connor,
    pp. 9-10.

14. Michigan, Pennsylvania and Ohio are examples: People
    v Barlitz 212 Mich 580, 12 ALR 520; Commonwealth
    v Maxwell 114 A 825; Browning v State 120 Oh 62, 12
    ALR 520, cited in O'Connor, pp. 9-10.

15. "The Juror," 71 US L R 76 (1937); the quote is from
    State v James 16 ALR 1141, 1154 (1921), both cited
    by O'Connor, pp. 9-11.

16. State v Kelly 229 P 659 (1924); see also In Re Opinion

of the Justices 130 NE 685 (1921), both cited in
O'Connor, pp. 11-12.

17. O'Connor, p. 12.

18. Title 28 USC 1861. Together with Ballard v U.S., supra
     note 1, the Civil Rights Act became an important le-
     gal tool for equality proponents. Ballard held that a
     conviction would be reversed and an indictment dis-
     missed where women, although eligible for service,
     were intentionally excluded from the jury panels, even
     though jury service was not obligatory for women.
     Ballard required the use of random selection proce-
     dures by states in order to obtain juries composed of
     a cross-section of the community.

19. See note 18.

20. O'Connor, table p. 14.

21. O'Connor, tables p. 13 and p. 14.

22. Hoyt v Florida 368 U.S. 57 (1961); State v Hall 187 So.
     2d 861 (Miss. 1966), cert. denied 87 S Ct 331 (1966),
     Taylor v Louisiana 95 S Ct 652 (1975); N.Y. Judiciary
     Law, former sec. 665(7).

23. O'Connor, p. 17.

24. State v Hall, supra note 22.

25. Taylor v Louisiana, supra note 22. 95 S Ct 652 (1975).

26. Ibid., at 692.

27. N.Y. Judiciary Law, former sec. 665.

28. "County Bar Fights Women on Juries," in New York
     Times (February 20, 1931), p. 28; Anne Harbottle
     Whittic, "New York Denies Jury Service to Women,"
     in Equal Rights (March 21, 1931) p. 52-3; "Women
     Plead for Right to Serve on Juries; Retort Sharply to
     Men at Albany Hearing," in New York Times (March
     5, 1931), p. 6; "Women on the Juries, A continuing
     debate," in New York Times (March 15, 1931) p. 9.
     Readers may be interested to learn that Maryland
     women were organizing at the same time to pressure
     the Maryland legislature, and even composed a song
     which they sang up the steps to the State House in
     Annapolis. Sung to the tune of "Maryland, My Mary-
     land," the words were:
                We're voters all, we would be free
                Maryland, my Maryland;
                To fullest meed of liberty,
                Maryland, my Maryland;
                We seek the right denied for years
                To sit as jurors and as peers,
                Forget your Mid-Victorian fears,
                Maryland, my Maryland.

Cited by Florence Kennard, "Maryland Women Demand Jury Service," in Equal Rights (March 7, 1931), p. 36.

29. Matthews, Women's Weekly (1923), 4; underlining is mine.

30. "News from the Field," in Equal Rights (February 1932?), p. 23.

31. Mrs. S. Pell, "Jury Service for Women," in Equal Rights (November 14, 1931), p. 326-7; Whittic, Equal Rights (1931), p. 52-3.

32. "Mrs. Smith Presents the Case," in Equal Rights (February 1931), p. 12; Pell, Equal Rights (1931), p. 326-7; Whittic, Equal Rights (1931), 52-3.

33. Whittic, Equal Rights (1931), p. 53; Pell Equal Rights (1931), 326-7. "A Judge on Women Jurors," Equal Rights (January 30, 1932), p. 413.

34. "Mrs. Smith ...," Equal Rights (1931), p. 12.

35. Ibid.

36. Whittic, Equal Rights (1931), p. 53.

37. Matthews, Equal Rights (1930), p. 148.

38. Letter of Lillian M. Linebarger, in Equal Rights (October 25, 1930), pp. 302-3.

39. Burnita Shelton Matthews, "Massachusetts Rules Against Women Jurors," in Equal Rights (September 1931?), p. 276.

40. An Act to Repeal Articles 16, 17, 18 and Articles 18-a of the Judiciary Law and to Insert a New Article 16. S8254-B/A9721-B, (February 14, 1974), Albany, New York.

41. Governor Malcolm Wilson's veto was June 6, 1974. "Wilson Veto Stirs Debate on Role of Grand Jurors," New York Times (June 23, 1974), p. 1+: "Jury Exemptions Scored as Sexist," New York Times (November 12, 1973), p. 25.

42. Ballard, supra note 1.

43. Affidavit of B. Bonora, sworn to March 25, 1974 filed in Erie County (New York), pp. 2-4; Louise Leiker, "Women Jury Exemption Challenged," Courier-Express (March 3, 1974), n. p.

44. People v Attica Bros. petition filed March 18, 1974 in Additional Special and Trial Term, Supreme Court, Erie County; memorandum decision dated June 27, 1974.

45. Fred Feretti, "Court Edit Leads Buffalo to Drop 110,000 as Jurors," in New York Times (July 4, 1974), p. 1+.

46. The statistical complications and detailed analysis of

the Erie County case are available in A. Levine and
C. A. Schweber, "Jury Selection in Erie County,"
11 Law and Society Rev (Fall 1976).

47. Ballard, supra note 1.

48. Beesner, "Are Juries Representative?" 57 Judicature
334 (December 1973) in O'Connor, supra note 6,
p. 25.

49. When it was discovered that some clerks in the central
office infrequently selected women's names, the process in all districts of the county was also examined.
The discriminatory selection was observable to anyone,
since the clerks underlined in the voter registration
books the names of the persons whom they had selected and sent questionnaires. A sample of 1880
voter names revealed that 15.7 percent were females
(295) and 84.3 percent were males (1585). It should
be remembered that the county had an equal proportion
of men and women registered to vote. Thus the small
proportion of women in the jury pool (16.8 percent)
was not so surprising--it was about the same percent
as the women selected by the clerks from voter registration lists (15.7 percent). See A. Levine and C. A.
Schweber, supra note 46, p. 50.

50. Author's notes from trial attendance, March-May 1974.
These developments were uncovered during the detailed
investigation of the administrative process which was
controlled by the jury commissioner's office. Briefly,
the process began with the (supposed) random selection
of names from voter registration books to whom questionnaires were sent--the potential jurors. It ended
with the summoning to court of panels from which
twelve jurors and alternates were chosen. In the in-
terim, people had been qualified, disqualified, granted
exemptions from jury service based on their responses
to the questionnaires. Monthly drawings from a large
drum with names of qualified people--the Jury Pool--
were held to select the number of persons necessary
for forthcoming trials. The entire operation was done
by hand by the jury commissioner's clerical staff.
Most other counties used a computer, yet only after
the court case had been decided did Erie County institute such a system.

51. People v. Attica Bros., supra note 44. Without such
an order, defense attorneys could challenge all county
trials on the grounds that women had been deliberately
and systematically excluded from the juries. Precedent for such action comes from Ballard, supra notes

1 and 18.
52. Ballard, supra notes 1 and 18.
53. Ballard, supra note 1.

Chapter 18

A CRISIS PERSPECTIVE ON EMERGING HEALTH ROLES:
A Paradigm for the Entry of Women
into New Occupational Roles

by Jean Lipman-Blumen

The processes through which roles change, expand, become obsolete or spin off to structural independence represent a critical area of research that should concern all students of social change. Changing roles have substantive and political implications for all groups within society--those who traditionally have had access to various roles and those who have been excluded.

Emergent roles within the health field are particularly useful models for understanding occupational role change. They offer a paradigm for understanding the dynamics of emergent roles throughout the occupational spectrum in much the same way that the medical profession has provided a model for analyzing the multiple dimensions of the entire range of professions. In Weber's sense[1] they provide the ideal typical case from which social scientists can develop an understanding of the spectrum of alternatives.

Taking emergent health roles as its context, this chapter attempts to convey five major points:

--crisis provides a set of conditions under which roles are easily changed and which allow for the emergence of new roles;

--crisis periods seriously affect the stratification system, whose impairment allows the emergence of new ideologies and new roles;

--once the stratification system is weakened, the criteria for entry into roles change and previously excluded categories of occupants are allowed entry into those roles;

--affirmative action strategies represent a new ideology which questions previous criteria for role entry;

--during crisis periods, new roles begin to emerge,
roles not yet marked by sex, race, or age restrictions.

This chapter first develops a crisis framework for
understanding role changes and then applies that framework
to the problem of emerging roles in the health professions.
Special implications of crisis-induced occupational role
changes for women and other minorities then are explored.

CRISIS AND ROLE CHANGE

Crisis and the State of the System

Social science has shown repeatedly that meaningful
role change occurs not as a random process, but as a response to a perceived social system need. Crisis[2] represents a sufficient (but not a necessary) cause of role change.
In this chapter, we shall try to apply a crisis framework,
developed elsewhere in greater detail,[3] to the phenomenon
of role emergence in the health care field.

Role change may be conceptualized as a system response to crisis.[4] The type of role change to be expected
in any given crisis depends upon both the nature of the crisis
(identified by the dimensions outlined in note 3) and the state
of the system[5] at the onset of crisis. Emerging roles represent just one form of role change.[6]

Two Types of Role Change: Structural and Occupant Role Change

Crisis promotes role change primarily because it requires a reallocation of resources, including the perception
of previously unrecognized resources. Roles, being the basic
units of social systems, constitute important resources in
times of crisis. Roles undergo two types of change: structural change in which the role tasks, expectations, obligations,
and privileges, etc., are reorganized, and occupant or cate-
gorical change in which individuals or categories of individuals
ordinarily excluded from these roles are allowed entry or

actively recruited into these roles. During crisis the criteria for role entrance and performance change.

       The history of medicine is replete with both structural
and occupant role changes in the face of crises. The Cri-
mean War was the crisis during which the previously all-
male nursing profession underwent occupant role change to
permit the entry of women. Artificially generated crises
occur in which technology creates a new method for advancing diagnosis or treatment of disease while simultaneously
precipitating a shortage of trained personnel to carry out the
procedure(s). Which medical role should encompass the new
technology may become the focus of controversy. New roles,
involving structural role change, often emerge through this
process.

       The development of cardiac catheterization techniques
prompted a situation in which both cardiologists and cardiac
surgeons faced unclear role demands. This led to structural
role change by which the role of cardiac technician eventually emerged, absorbing several role components previously
embedded in the physician's role. This structural change
created room for catheterization tasks within the physician's
array of role tasks.

       More recently, World War II, with its severe short-
ages of medical personnel, saw medical care administered
through a wide range of medical and paramedical roles. As
Ford[7] noted in 1975, the direct patient care component of
the nurse's role became the responsibility of nurses' aides,
vocational nurses, technicians, as well as diploma and degree program graduates. The professional nurse's role
changed to incorporate more managerial tasks. These all
represent structural role changes. In addition, structural
role change may lead to occupant role change, and vice
versa.

The Disruption of the Stratification System

       Crisis is a time when the stratification system, the
system for ordering individuals and groups according to various criteria and credentials, is shaken, if not totally dis-
rupted. In times of stability, goals may be diffuse, unclear,
often long-term, and difficult to order in terms of priority.
As a result, means often become more important than ends,
leading to goal displacement.[8] Who is performing a given

task is of greater concern than what is being done.   Characteristics of role occupants assume more importance than task
performance or goal achievement.   The stratification system
rigidly holds everyone in places preordained by formal rules
of professional or occupational selection and training (i. e. ,
credentials).

In times of crisis, goals are clear and short-range.
Most commonly, they are focused on survival or sustenance.
Goals, clearly articulated, are almost self-ranking.   As a
result, individuals or categories of individuals who can contribute effectively to survival or other aspects of crisis resolution are recognized--sometimes for the first time--as important resources.   The stratification system, with its emphasis upon who rather than how or what, cannot withstand this
reallocation of resources and thus begins to give way.   In
its wake, categories of occupants--such as women, Blacks,
the handicapped, immigrants--who previously have been excluded may experience the surprise of recruitment in crisis
periods.

Role Emergence

Role emergence is one of the many types of role
change.   It usually occurs as an established role divests itself of selected role elements or as the result of a techno-
logical breakthrough.   Relinquished role components may
form the nexus of a totally new or an emergent role.   Sometimes these elements are incorporated into other existing
roles, changing the nature and often the status of the role
into which they are assimilated.

There may be a chain reaction, whereby the receiving
role which has just assimilated new role elements relinquished by the first role jettisons parts of its own previous
role components.   A third role may assimilate the role components cut off from the second role, or the relinquished elements may form a true emergent role, which is structurally
separate and distinct from the existing roles.   Major and
complex patterns of role change can occur within a network
of interrelated roles.

The roles of nurse practitioner and physician's assistant provide clear examples of emergent roles.   The mutual point of reference for both of these emergent roles is
the physician's role.   Role elements relinquished from the

physician's role may be incorporated into the traditional and existing role of nurse, thereby transforming the nurse's role into the nurse practitioner. Simultaneously, the same or other role elements from the physician's role may coalesce and develop into a totally new role--midway organizationally, economically, and structurally between that of the physician and nurse.

During the initial stages of role emergence, competition may develop between an established role which feels its turf threatened--often rightfully--and an emergent role. This clearly has been the historical pattern of the nurse, nurse practitioner and physician assistant roles. [9]

Oftentimes, the role elements relinquished by an established role in a technologically-induced role transformation are those which are least valued by the occupants of the original role. The role which subsequently incorporates these role elements often is characterized by lower professional status than the original role. Although the discarded role elements may have had the lowest priority or value for the original role and, thus, were easily relinquishable, they may increase the status of the new role that has assimilated them. Their previous inclusion in a higher status role creates a halo effect, which increases the status of the role to which these role elements have been transferred.

Competition, Dependence, Independence, and Interdependence of Roles

The relationships among traditional and emerging roles are highly complex. Issues of competition, dependence, independence, and interdependence arise. Competition for professional territory, economic rewards, status and independence, particularly in the early stages of role transformation, presents serious problems.

Competition may inhibit or preclude professional role interdependence that would aid in goal attainment. For example, interdependence rather than competition among the physician, nurse, nurse practitioner, and physician's assistant presumably would lead to quality increases in patient care and possibly reduced cost (although there is some dispute about the possibility of reducing cost of quality health care). Until roles can be clearly articulated--and sometimes not even then--reduction in competition among established and emergent roles is not likely to occur.

Difficulties among traditional and emerging roles may
be prompted by concerns about legal responsibilities. Supervision of emerging roles and the setting within which they
are performed pose problems of legal liability. The questions that have been raised about the nature of the relationship between the physician and the physician's assistant are
a case in point. If a physician's assistant must work under
the supervision of a physician in an office or hospital setting,
is s/he merely a dependent assistant for whose professional
actions the physician is legally responsible? Or can the role
be fashioned so that the physician's assistant may work in a
relationship of interdependence with the physician, with the
emerging role characterized by structural integrity and autonomy?

When we superimpose the question of how the role of
the nurse or nurse practitioner fits into this set of relationships, the issues, as well as the relationships, develop increased complexity. An overriding question becomes, "To
whom is the new practitioner responsible--the professional
to whose work s/he contributes, to the organization, to the
professional association, or to the patient-consumer?"

Ideology, Values, and Norms

In a crude way, ideology is the social glue that holds
together social systems. More specifically, ideology refers
to any belief system which interprets reality and factuality by
providing strategies for reconciling the contradictions that
stem from the complexities of social situations. Ideology
acts as a rationalization, explanation, and legitimation of the
social situation in which the individual or group is embedded.
It is a way of reducing the complexities of everyday reality
and providing a set of handles for dealing with the often contradictory realities that constitute our objective reality.
Such contradictory realities create strain at the individual,
group and social system level.

Different forms of ideology[10] are associated with the
movement from rigid, sharply differentiated roles of stable
periods, to more fluid, dedifferentiated roles that charac-
terize a system's response to crisis. Here we shall concern
ourselves with only two types of ideology in relation to crisis
and emergent roles: major and minor ideology.

Major and Minor Ideology: Major ideologies are ac-

cepted by relatively large collectivities as reasonably adequate interpretations of reality.   They offer strategies for
confronting a complex, contradictory existential reality.   Major ideologies usually are addressed to large, loosely organized collectivities, which acknowledge the long-term complex and enduring nature of the major religious faiths, political systems, and traditional professions.

The more comprehensive and enveloping the ideology,
the more diffuse it becomes as it attempts to weave together
in some integrated whole a multiplicity of potential contradictions.   Simultaneously, large scale ideology becomes more
distant from the very reality which it attempts to explain.
The major world religions are examples of major ideologies.

Somewhere in the mid-range of the ideology continuum are located segmented or minor ideologies, which are
less complex, less comprehensive, less formal (although not
necessarily less explicit) ideologies, delimited in terms of
the scope of the reality they claim to interpret.   The collectivities or groups to which they speak accept the segmented ideology as an orientation to reality.   These collectivities usually are smaller, more circumscribed segments of
society.

A minor ideology is less diffuse, more specific, and
often more detailed, than a major ideology.   It may be stated
in more dramatic terms and usually addresses the question
of pressing, present and imminent reality and social conditions.

Minor ideologies attempt to reconcile fewer, but often
sharper antinomies and contradictions than comprehensive
major ideologies, and they commonly remain very close to
the reality which they attempt to explain.   Minor ideologies
may evolve into major ideologies, as they attempt to broaden
1) the range of social phenomena they interpret, and 2) the
size and complexity of the collectivities they serve.   Crisis,
as we shall see, provides one set of conditions under which
minor ideology may supplant major ideology.

In periods of stability, major ideologies, encrusted
and upheld by tradition, buttress the stratification system.
When crisis occurs, the deficiencies of major ideologies become apparent.   They begin to lose their hold on their audi-
ences, whose confidence in the effectiveness of the related
coping strategies begins to wane.   That is when the appeal

of minor ideologies is greatest.   Minor ideologies, closer to
reality, may be seen as encompassing more plausible alternatives.

      Health Care Ideologies--Major and Minor: Major health
care ideology involves an integrated set of beliefs about both
the nature and importance of health and the complex system
by which health may be protected and maintained.   A major
health care ideology is robust in periods of stability, and the
stratification system it buttresses acts as a restraining grid
on the health care system.   Acceptance, if not reification, of
health care systems, norms and goals exists in stable periods.
Efforts to change the system whereby health care agents are
trained and certified and patients are treated are strongly resisted.

      Minor ideology about health care presents an alterna-
tive set of solutions to the health care dilemma.   During
stability, acceptance of these alternative interpretations of
health care reality represented by minor ideology is limited
to small groups, often of dubious status.   Health "freaks,"
Seventh Day Adventists, Christian Scientists, acupuncturists,
and self-help groups accept differing minor health care ideologies unshared by the larger society.   Unlike major health
ideology, minor health care ideology does not revolve around
a "professional mystique," with special training hurdles that
must be overcome in a specified and graduated order.   Minor
health ideology regards nontraditional health care agents, including nonprofessionals, perhaps even the patient as potential sources of health care. [11]

      Thus, in times of crisis, the major health ideology,
with its emphasis upon long-term training and strict prerequisites, becomes unwieldy.   Minor ideology begins to gain
ascendancy, and the stratification system is weakened.   Under these circumstances the structure of health roles changes,
and the criteria for entry into and performance of these roles
also change.

      The organization of health care roles reflects the
values regarding the medical hierarchy embedded in major
health care ideology.   The physician's role at the apex of
the medical structure connotes the value placed on traditional
knowledge and skill in the restoration of health.   The ascend-
ency of the physician's role reflects a dependence upon formal credentials that is likely to be entrenched during periods
of stability.

In crisis periods, the traditional value system, including norms that describe acceptable ways of meeting system goals, undergoes serious revision. While core values may withstand the upheaval of crisis, more peripheral values give way. Core values may be violated or exaggerated if the crisis is sufficiently severe. Thus, while the power to heal may retain or increase its value in crisis, the worth of standard credentials may be seriously diminished. For example, on the battlefield anyone who can treat illness or deal with trauma--not only physicians--will be accepted without concern for credentials. [12]

When the value system undergoes change during crisis periods, the normative system reflects analogous changes. As a result, the conditions under which roles may be performed--in this case, the conditions under which medical care may be dispensed--change. Further, restraints upon who may perform as health care deliverers are relaxed. The health care ideology may be shown to be inaccurate--the traditional healers may not be able to deal with a particular health problem. When this occurs, the social glue of health care ideology loosens and the stratification system gives way to allow the influx of "nontraditional" healers, who stem from a minor health care ideology.

The recent history of drug abuse treatment serves as an excellent example. When drug abuse was considered a small and relatively contained health care problem, only traditional professional health care agents--physicians, nurses, social workers, clergy--were allowed to treat patients. With the escalation of the drug abuse problem to a crisis situation, nontraditional health care agents, representing a minor health care ideology, emerged as important resources. Former drug addicts and "community workers" became important healers of drug users. Personal experience as a drug abuser was recognized as a credential superior to professional health care degrees and diplomas. The definition of a crisis situation brought with it the weakening of the health care hierarchy and the ascendence of nonprofessionals who represented a minor health care ideology.

Segregation in the Health Professions and Affirmative Action

Sex and race segregation within the health field offer a vivid example of the rigid stratification system which locks roles and role occupants in place during periods of stability. Established medical roles have been marked by pervasive sex segregation, with high status, high-paid, action-initiating and direct achievement roles being male-dominated.   Lower status, low-paid, responsive and indirect (i. e. , vicarious) achievement roles traditionally have been female-dominated. Males represent 91. 7 percent of physicians in the U. S. , and women represent 98. 7 percent of the nurses.   Race segregation follows a similar pattern with minorities channeled into lower-status, lower-pay health roles.   When women and other minority group members manage to enter male health care professions, they are relegated to the lower-status specialties within those fields.

The multiple crises represented by the Civil Rights Movement, the Vietnamese War, and the Women's Movement have brought in their wake the affirmative action strategy, which represents a direct attack on the traditional stratification system in the marketplace and academia.   The ideology of affirmative action rejects the major ideology revolving around traditionally limited criteria for entry into educational and occupational roles.

Affirmative action, whose essence is the demand for role change--particularly occupant change--has been perceived in some quarters as a source of crisis.   And this, too, is consistent with the crisis framework, which suggests, almost paradoxically, that role change itself can lead to crisis-- particularly if there are no institutional supports available during the transition period.

Institutional supports may mean rites of passage or systematic introduction of mechanisms for reducing the strain and easing the transition.   Such institutional supports could take the form of counseling to the individuals and institutions involved in role change--to doctors, nurses, physician's assistants, nurse practitioners, and patients, as well as to clinics, offices, and hospitals.

Other institutional supports take the form of remedial or update training and the introduction of cadres, rather than token individuals, from previously excluded groups.   Expanding and updating the knowledge and skills of older members of an occupation will ease the transition stage by reducing both attrition and resistance to change.

Emergent Roles, Sex/Race Segregation, and Crisis

Emergent roles, particularly those which represent the new spin-off variety, rather than enlargement of a previous role, are least likely to be sex- or race-linked in the early stages. Occasionally, the circumstances of their emergence may tip the scales from the outset. Such was the case with the Medex program for physician's assistants, which was designed to utilize the medical expertise of Vietnam veterans who had served in the medical corps.

In cases where a prior sex-linked experience or knowledge--such as military service--is required for admission into the emergent role, the seeds for sex-segregation exist. More often, however, in the early stages, emergent roles are likely to be sex- and race-neutral. This is the most favorable time to articulate social policy, so that an adequate mix of sex and race can be established in these roles.

The channeling of groups into emergent paraprofessional, rather than professional, roles creates a potential pitfall for women and other minorities. Efforts to create avenues of mobility between paraprofessional and professional roles are beset by serious questions. How do individuals who have been in paraprofessional roles move into professional roles? And how can movement from a lower-status to a higher-status professional role be accomplished without serious loss of the investment already made in time, money, education, and work experience?

A related issue is the problem of performing professional tasks within a context that now is defined as paraprofessional. For example, when tasks previously performed by the physician are transferred to the physician assistant's role, how shall these tasks be defined and rewarded? Salary schedules must be devised that adequately recognize the contributions of paraprofessionals and new professionals. At the same time, some balance must be sought to insure that increased quality and efficiency lead to cost savings, not cost escalations. Otherwise, public acceptance of new roles in the health field will prove very difficult to win.

Resources for training (e.g., materials, teachers, money, and time) usually are scarce in crisis periods. Increasingly, we may face periods of overall or quasi-stability where resources are more and more limited. In recent

years, we have witnessed serious cutbacks in federal support
for training programs. The lessons we fail to learn from
crisis--that is, that short-term training is often as effective
for a given type of role as longer-term training[13]--may have
to be re-emphasized and adapted to more ordinary circumstances. Institutional affiliations or settings for training,
easily foregone in periods of crisis, may be equally dispen-
sable in more stable times.

During crises, we have seen short-term or "crash"
training programs designed to transform lower-status to
higher-status professional roles and paraprofessional to professional roles. The dogmas of credentialism disintegrate
in crisis periods. In more stable periods, the lessons
learned in crisis may be forgotten: that individuals who have
entered such "crash" training programs have served respon-
sibly and well in their new roles. Careful consideration of
actual requirement for entry into emergent roles must be undertaken to avoid creating paraprofessional dead ends.

The historical development of many professional roles
has been marked by the call for redundant layers of training
and certification. The demand for increased training may be
couched in terms of the need to protect the patient/consumer;
the impetus for those demands actually may emanate from
the need to protect existing professionals in closely related
roles. In stable periods, when the stratification system is
viable, layering training programs and credentials on emerging roles is one mechanism for strengthening the stratification system. This process excludes all but the persistent
and/or fortunate few who have the time, money, and endur-
ance to comply with the seemingly endless demands. Women
and other minorities often fall by the wayside in the movement to add more "stringent" qualifications to emergent roles.
The reassessment of credentials, the serious questioning of
their validity and necessity, can help us expand emergent
roles to include individuals and groups previously excluded
because of their lack of access to sacrosanct prerequisite
qualifications through formal training.

Reconsideration of the prerequisites for training may
lead to expanded opportunities for women and other minorities who often bear the brunt of unnecessary formal training requirements. Medical educators and social policy plan-
ners who wish to address seriously the question of increased
participation of women and other minorities, as well as older
and partially disabled workers, must examine closely the
necessity of long-term training programs.

Our experience with baccalaureate training programs
for nurses has shown that increasing the length and rigor of
a given training program does not necessarily produce better
primary care professionals. Such educationally elevated programs may have the ironic effect of creating a greater disparity between what one learns in school and what one faces
in the real world of work. The result may be that the trainee
is rendered unfit, both by reason of inadequate practical experience and by disenchantment, for the very role for which
s/he was trained.

Finally, the problem of proper utilization of emergent
roles, both by other professionals and patient-consumers, is
a serious concern. Differential types or levels of supervision
linked to differential training or role demands should help to
eliminate redundancy. Underutilization and inappropriate
utilization are two vulnerabilities of the emergent role. Education of health professionals and paraprofessionals, as well
as patient-consumers, is one avenue to more proper use of
emergent health practitioners. And a clearer definition of
these roles, with their interdependencies spelled out, will
serve as an important first step. If the individuals who occupy these roles are unclear about the parameters of their
roles, as well as the nature of their relationships with other
paraprofessionals, professionals, and patients, then those
further removed from these emergent roles can hardly hope
for clarification. If the occupants of these emergent roles
can articulate the dimensions and responsibilities of their
roles, they can act in concert to convey their expectations
and understanding to those with whom they hope to have meaningful professional relationships. The problems of training,
credentialism, and utilization that emergent roles face in the
health field are recapitulated in the wide spectrum of occupations which face role expansion and emergence.

Public Acceptance of Emergent Roles

Public acceptance of emergent roles is essential to
the integration of these roles into the established occupational
structure--in health as in other occupational fields. Public
acceptance means several things: 1) acceptance of established
professionals, both at the individual and professional association levels; 2) acceptance by potential candidates for recruitment; 3) acceptance by the consumer (i.e., the patient);
4) acceptance by the institutions within which these roles will
be performed; and 5) acceptance by other sectors of the econ-

omy that are affected (i. e. , third-party payment institutions, regulating agencies of the federal government, etc.). Since it is clear that each of these groups has different priorities, strategies for gaining acceptance from each group must be individually tailored.

One important strategy is to convince the opinion-makers and leaders, particularly in the professional sector, whose endorsement may be essential to acceptance by consumers. An important part of this strategy (which admittedly will be difficult to sell to highly specialized professionals) is the understanding that professional specialists at the highest levels are not necessarily needed to perform certain tasks. In order to convince professional medical specialists that certain elements of their role could be handled equally well by a paramedical specialist, specialists need to be reassured that their own role will not suffer.

Medical specialists will need substantial and meaning-ful reorientation to help them recognize that the introduction of paraprofessional and new professional associates will offer the specialists several distinct advantages. For example, such arrangements will free the specialist to devote more time to those tasks which truly must be performed by the established specialists. The development of paraprofessional roles will allow the established specialist more time to see patients or time to see more patients. Further, these arrangements will permit time for necessary and desirable continuing education programs and will introduce more opportunity for leisure and relaxation for professional specialists.

The patient as consumer needs to be informed of the availability and advantages of emergent practitioners in the health field. The potential reduction in medical costs as well as queuing time, without reduction in quality of care, can be potent persuaders, particularly in a tight economy.

Exposing patients to new practitioners in settings where it is clear they have the endorsement and confidence of the established health professionals would promote acceptance. Presenting the new practitioner as an alternative, rather than a substitute, for traditional medical practitioners would enable patients as consumers to exercise their legitimate options in health care.

Educating the patient as consumer to be able to judge when s/he requires the treatment of a paramedical, rather

than a medical specialist, is an important step forward.   It
should be part of the larger effort to make patients participate in and take more responsibility for their own health.
The serious economic difficulties faced by patients, professionals and health care delivery systems, compounded by decreased federal spending in medical research and health care,
set the stage for emerging health roles.   The opportunity to
prove the utility, efficiency and effectiveness of emerging
health roles that an economic crisis provides can be stabilized and institutionalized so that the hopeful return of economic stability will see them well rooted in the health field
landscape.   The entry of women and other minorities into
these roles requires additional public education, both for the
recruits, their colleagues and their patients.

SUMMARY

The present paper has used emergent roles in the
health field as a paradigm for analysis of emergent roles
throughout the occupational structure.   A crisis framework
has been applied to emergent health roles to provide an understanding of how barriers between roles in all fields may
be broken down more easily.   The crisis framework focuses
on the disruption of the stratification system, which in times
of stability acts to rigidify roles.   Crisis periods, which involve changes of criteria for role entry, historically have
been periods marked by the entry as well as the recruitment
of previously excluded groups, including women and other
minorities.   Lessons on the fruitlessness of artificial entry
and training requirements are learned in crisis and should
be institutionalized during periods of stability.   Only then can
women and other minority groups look to emergent roles as
new opportunities, rather than new dead ends.

NOTES

1.   Max Weber, "Religious Rejections of the World and
       Their Directions, " in H. H. Gerth and C. Wright
       Mills, eds. , From Max Weber: Essays in Sociology
       (New York: Oxford University Press, 1946), pp. 323-
       359.
2.   Crisis is used here to mean any situation recognized by
       the participants of the system as a threat to the sur-
       vival, status quo, or sustenance of the system, whose
       ordinary coping mechanisms and/or resources are in-
       adequate to resolve the situation confronting it.

3. For a more detailed description of the crisis and role
   change framework, see Jean Lipman-Blumen, "Role
   De-Differentiation as a System Response to Crisis:
   Occupational and Political Roles of Women," Sociolog-
   ical Inquiry, 43, no. 2 (1973): 105-129; Jean Lipman-
   Blumen, "A Crisis Framework Applied to Macrosocio-
   logical Family Changes: Marriage, Divorce, and Occupational Trends Associated with World War II,"
   Journal of Marriage and the Family, 37, no. 4 (1975):
   889-902; Jean Lipman-Blumen, "A Crisis Perspective
   on Divorce and Role Change," in Women into Wives:
   The Legal and Economic Impact of Marriage, eds.
   Jane Roberts Chapman and Margaret Gates (London,
   England: Sage Yearbooks in Women's Policy Studies,
   1977).

4. Crises may be characterized along at least 10 dimensions, thereby creating a typology. They may be
   1) large-scale or limited (pervasive or bounded), 2) intense or mild, 3) precipitous or gradual in onset,
   4) perceived as solvable or insolvable. Crises may
   stem from causes 5) internal or external to the system being stressed and, further, they are the result
   of 6) natural generation (i. e., tornadoes, earthquakes)
   or artificial (or human) generation (i. e., technology).
   They may be 7) random events or events that occur
   with some expectability, if not predictability. Crises
   may be marked by 8) transitoriness or chronicity, and
   they may be characterized by 9) surplus or scarcity.
   In addition, there is the 10) substantive content of the
   crisis, which may stem from the realms of politics,
   economics, medicine, religion, law, sexuality, or
   some combination thereof.

5. The state of the social system (whether it is the entire
   society, the medical profession, a hospital, a doctor's
   office, a nursing school, a family, or a doctor-patient
   relationship) may be assessed in terms of at least 11
   factors: 1) its level of organization/disorganization
   (i. e., the degree to which the system is organized into a set of integrated, effectively functioning parts);
   2) the adaptation coefficient of the system or its degree of flexibility (i. e., the degree to which the system is able to adjust its organized pattern to new situations by creative, meaningful, and effective realign-
   ment of its parts); 3) the available resources at the
   time of crisis, material and non-material, as well as
   human resources; 4) its previous experience with
   analogous crises, including the development of coping

mechanisms and strategies; 5) the effectiveness of the
social system in resolving previous similar crises;
6) the breadth and complexity of roles prior to the
crisis; 7) the characteristics of the previous crisis
(e. g., time elapsed since last crisis; nature of crisis;
residue from previous crisis); 8) its relation to other
external systems; 9) its information processing system;
10) its autonomy; and 11) the availability of tension
release mechanisms.

6. Other patterns include role reversal, role submergence,
role obsolescence, institutional substitution, role com-
partmentalization, as well as unilateral and reciprocal
patterns of assimilation and overlap. In addition, role
expansion, role depletion, role highlighting, role im-
mobilization, increased role differentiation and forms
of collective behavior are alternative role responses
to crisis. For an extended description of these patterns, see Jean Lipman-Blumen, "Role De-Differentiation as a System Response to Crisis: Occupational
and Political Roles of Women," Sociological Inquiry,
43, 2 (1973): 105-129.

7. Loretta C. Ford, "Emerging Professional and Paraprofessional Models for Expanding the Nurse's Role,"
paper presented at Annual Meeting of the American
Association for the Advancement of Science, New
York, New York, January 30, 1975.

8. Robert K. Merton, Social Theory and Social Structure,
The Free Press, Glencoe, Illinois, 1957.

9. Alfred M. Sadler, Jr., Blair L. Sadler, and Ann A.
Bliss, The Physician's Assistant--Today and Tomor-
row, Yale University Press, New Haven, Connecticut,
1972.

10. Ideology is best conceptualized as a continuum, ranging
from major to minor (i. e., partial or compartmental-
ized) ideology to fragmentary ideology. For a more
detailed description of types of ideology, see Jean
Lipman-Blumen, "Ideology, Social Structure and Crisis:
The Case of the Feminist Movement," paper presented
at the American Sociological Association Annual Meeting, Montreal, Canada, August 1974.

11. Sheryl K. Ruzek, "The Women's Medical Self-Help
Movement: A Challenge to Traditional Professional-
ism," paper presented at Annual Meeting of Pacific
Sociological Association, San Jose, California, 1974.

12. Another interesting case may be seen in small rural
towns where medical imposters occasionally have successfully practiced medicine. Oftentimes, after ex-

posure of the fraudulent credentials, the medical establishment which faces no direct threat, demands ouster and punishment of the imposter. The patient community, confronting the crisis of no medical care, commonly has offered acceptance of the practitioner, despite the lack of traditional training.

13.   Sadler, et al. , op. cit.

Chapter 19

INDIVIDUALISM, MARRIAGE, AND THE LIBERAL STATE:
Beyond the Equal Rights Amendment

by Mary Lyndon Shanley

Introduction

Anglo-American political thinking has long been beset
by a deep conceptual duality which so far has received virtually no attention in the works of either political theorists
or feminists. On the one hand, liberal theory assumes that
the individual is the "basic unit" of the polity, that it is the
individual who will gives legitimacy to government and who
is the object of the regulations imposed for the public good
by the government. On the other hand, political observers
similarly think of the family as the basic unit of society, as
that collective entity which bonds adults together, socializes
the young, and gives stability to all social relationships.
The works of early liberal theorists such as John Locke,
for example, speak of the pursuit of individual rights and of
family unity in virtually the same breath. American law and
public policy have traditionally been concerned with the protection and promotion both of individual rights and of family
unity. These goals have been pursued simultaneously and
without any recognition that the realization of one goal might
be purchased at the expense of the other.

Contemporary feminists have pointed out that notions
of family unity have frequently resulted in, or been the ex-
cuse for, depriving married women of various rights. Most
blatantly, until the latter half of the nineteenth century the
doctrine of spousal unity took away a married woman's control of her own property, her right to contract, and her
right to sue or be sued without being joined by her husband.
More recently, notions of proper male and female roles within the family and society have deprived married women of
the use of their birth names after marriage, the ability to obtain credit on their own, and the right to choose their own
domicile.

363

The Equal Rights Amendment is the single most obvious and powerful tool aimed at insuring that the law endows married women with the same civil rights and responsibilities as their husbands. The Equal Rights Amendment would eradicate gender-based distinctions in the law. Ratification of the amendment is therefore an important step in the extension of the principle of individualism in our society.

The Equal Rights Amendment alone, however, does not resolve all the tensions between individual rights and legally recognized marital roles. The elimination of gender-based distinctions from the law leaves open the question of whether it is proper or desirable to treat married persons differently from single persons. The law currently treats those who are married not strictly as individuals but as members of a matrimonial pair--for example, in matters relating to income tax, social security, and marital property rights. One may ask whether this practice is justifiable in a society committed to individualist principles.

I want to explore these questions with respect to contemporary American society. I outline the theoretical origins of the tension between individualism and recognition of the unity of the matrimonial pair, and describe the ways in which the law has dealt with this problem in the past. I then discuss the changes in the law which will occur should the ERA become part of the Constitution. This is followed by a brief description of several policy areas which distinguish between married and single persons regardless of sex, and which therefore pose questions concerning the further extension of individualistic principles in our society. Finally, I attempt to evaluate the possibility and the desirability of moving toward a totally individualistic polity. Such a system would require enormous changes in our social, legal, and economic structures. The radical changes which would be necessary were the state always to treat each person--married or single--as an individual, demonstrate the degree to which we have built our society on the assumption that married women will perform very different social tasks than will either married men or single men and women. An imaginative examination of a more individualistic social order reveals the origins, depth, and great complexity of impediments which strew the path to a more egalitarian society of the future.

I wish to acknowledge the financial and intellectual support of the Wellesley Center for the Study of Women in Higher Education and the Professions in the preparation of early version of this essay.

Individualism and Familialism in
Anglo-American Political Thought

Since the rise of individualism and particularly since
the political writings of John Locke provided the major formu-
lation of the theory of individualism, Anglo-American political
thought has contained two distinct theories about the origin
and basis of political and social life.   One theory asserts
that the basic unit of society is the individual, the other that
it is the family.

Both notions can be found in Locke's classic Second
Treatise on Government.   Locke firmly ensconced in Anglo-
American thought the notion that the individual is inviolable,
a being endowed with "inalienable rights" which neither other
men nor the government may transgress.   Only by his or her
own consent can anyone be divested of any part of these rights.

> Men being ... by nature, all free, equal and in-
> dependent, no one can be put out of this Estate,
> and subjected to the Political Power of another,
> without his own Consent.   The only way whereby
> anyone devests himself of his Natural Liberty, and
> puts on the bonds of Civil Society, is by agreeing
> with other Men to joyn and unite into a Community,
> for their comfortable, safe, and peaceable living
> one amongst another, in a secure Enjoyment of
> their Properties, and a greater Security against
> any that are not of it. [1]

Not simply political obligations and associations were
generated by contractual agreements, but all other associations as well, for the individual could not be thought to be
bound to any agreement to which he had not given his consent.   Locke even represented marriage as a contractual relationship, rather than as the "natural" and "Sacramental"
relationship of medieval thought:

> Conjugal society is made by a voluntary Compact
> between Man and Woman: and tho' it consist chief-
> ly in such a Communion and Right in one anothers
> bodies, as is necessary to its chief End, Procre-
> ation; yet it draws with it mutual Support, and As-
> sistance, and a Communion of Interest too.... [2]

But while individuals formed both civil and matrimonial societies freely, a conjugal pair once formed was a

"unit" which in matters of common concern needed to be determined by a single will.

> But the Husband and Wife, though they have but one common Concern, yet having different understandings, will unavoidably sometimes have different wills too; it therefore being necessary, that the last Determination, i. e. the Rule, should be placed somewhere, it naturally falls to the Man's share, as the abler and the stronger. [3]

Other influential strains in seventeenth-century political thought contributed to the notion of the family as a male-headed unit whose existence was crucial to the larger society. The English and American Puritans regarded the family as a "little commonwealth" and conceived the political commonwealth as made up of these "little commonwealths." God placed the husband at the head of the family, and the husband was responsible both to the commonwealth for the behavior of the members of his family and to God for the salvation of their souls. [4]

Thus there was an important caveat to the seventeenth-century concept of individualism and of the equality of all human beings. This equality (at least in certain matters to be explained and enumerated below) could be altered by entering into a marriage; marriage created a unit which transcended the individuals who composed it, and State as well as Church felt called to protect that association.

Marital Unity and Male Dominance Within the Family

Until the middle of the nineteenth century, the common law doctrine of spousal unity maintained the husband's superiority in marriage. Under the common law, the state based its regulation of the family on the assumption of the unity of husband and wife. Here the assumption of the law was akin to but not identical with that of John Locke: all men and women are equal individuals, but when they marry they form a unit. The roots of this attitude go back much further than Locke, of course; they are Biblical: "Therefore shall a man leave his father and his mother, and shall cleave unto his wife and they shall be one flesh." [5] If "one flesh," then the husband and wife could only be one "person" in law.

The consequences of this assumption in the common law was the doctrine of coverture, which Blackstone explained as follows:

> By marriage, the husband and wife are one person in law; that is, the very being or legal existence of the woman is suspended during the marriage, or at least is incorporated and consolidated. [6]

Since husband and wife had to be treated as one, women forfeited the right of choice of domicile; husbands were given the right to manage their wive's real estate and the income therefrom; wives could not retain their wages but had to give them over to their husbands. It also became customary for a woman to take her husband's name. Because of the doctrine of coverture husbands and wives could not sue one another (interspousal immunity), for such an action would suppose that a single person could act against himself; nor could husbands and wives be held to have conspired together, since two or more persons must act in concert for a conspiracy, and husband and wife in the eyes of the law were one.

The assumption of the identity of husband and wife was undercut in the latter half of the nineteenth century by the passage in most states of Married Women's Property Acts. Such Acts gave a woman the management and control of the property which she brought to her marriage, the right to earn wages and to keep them, the right to enter into contracts, and the right to sue and be sued without being joined by her husband. [7] Thus the Married Women's Property Acts implicitly asserted that--Genesis and Blackstone notwithstanding--there could be two persons in the unit of the family.

Other laws which had rested upon the notion of spousal unity were gradually abandoned following the passage of the Married Women's Property Acts, until a century later only a few (albeit important ones) were left. The wife's immunity from suit for tort damages and the husband's liability for her torts had virtually disappeared by the mid-twentieth century;[8] in 1960 the Supreme Court rejected the notion that a husband and wife, being one, could not be held to have conspired;[9] and several states adopted the principle that a married woman could maintain a legal domicile of her own for such purposes as voting, running for office, jury duty, and taxation. [10]

But although the passage of the Married Women's
Property Acts and the concept of individual rights and responsibilities which lay behind them undercut the notion that "husband and wife are one person, and that one is the husband,"
the state did not abandon the idea that women forfeited certain rights upon marriage in order that family unity be maintained.   What had previously been justified on the grounds
of spousal unity now became justified on the grounds of the
"public interest" in the maintenance of the family.

In a decision rejecting a married woman's argument
that she be able to establish her own domicile, the Supreme
Court of Tennessee argued:

> The rule of the common law that the domicile of
> the wife follows that of the husband was based on
> (1) the doctrine of marital unity, and (2) that pub-
> lic policy demanded that the family unity be pro-
> tected by allowing one family to have one domicile.
> [Emphasis added.]11

If the family need have only one domicile, who then was to
decide where that domicile was to be?   Blackstone and the
doctrine of coverture unequivocally answered, "the husband,"
basing that response on the notion of spousal unity.   Without
that doctrine the courts just as clearly responded "the husband," basing their decisions on the role of man and woman
in society and in the family:

> The law imposes upon the husband the burden and
> obligation of the support, maintenance and care of
> the family and almost of necessity he must have
> the right of choice of the situs of the home.   There
> can be no decision by a majority rule as to where
> the family home shall be maintained, and a reason-
> able accompaniment of the imposition of obligations
> is the right of selection.   The violation of this
> principle tends to sacrifice the family unity, the
> entity upon which our civilization is based.   The
> principle is not based on the common law theory of
> the merger of the personality of the wife with that
> of the husband; it is based on the theory that one
> domicile for the family home is still an essential
> way of life. 12

Not only does the husband have the right of choice of
family domicile, but if his wife refuses to follow him to a

new domicile, she is in many states guilty of abandonment or desertion. 13 Moreover, in most cases the father's domicile is the domicile of legitimate children. 14

Most marriage law assumes the traditional sex-role division of labor in family and society. As the husband must provide support, so the wife is legally responsible for house- hold services. If a marriage ends in divorce, the assumption that the wife is responsible for domestic chores and child care leads many courts automatically to favor the mother in child custody cases, in detriment to the father's claim. Sim- ilarly, the husband's responsibility for support may be con- verted into an obligation to provide his wife with alimony, while in many states no such requirement falls on econom- ically capable wives. 15 The legal expectations which sur- round marriage are firmly rooted in customary sex roles, and these sex roles set the legal parameters within which those who wish to be married must act. Such gender-based expectations are likely to persist in the law unless the Equal Rights Amendment becomes part of the Constitution.

The Equal Rights Amendment

The Equal Rights Amendment states: "Equality of rights under the law shall not be denied or abridged by the United States or by any state on account of sex." This means that if the amendment is ratified gender will not be allowed to be a factor in determining the legal rights of men and women. The ERA would prohibit the state from creating any different rights or obligations for either husband or wife based solely on gender.

Certain inequities which the ERA was meant to remedy have already been dealt with by legislative action, executive action, and judicial decision. For example, the 1963 Equal Pay Act made it illegal for sex to be used as a factor in determining salary, promotion, and other benefits of employ- ment. 16 Title VII of the Civil Rights Act of 1964 made it illegal to discriminate "with respect to ... compensation, terms, conditions, or privileges of employment, because of [an] individual's race, color, religion, sex, or national ori- gin...."17 In Reed v. Reed the Supreme Court held that different treatment accorded to men and women applying to be estate administrators based solely on their sex was in violation of the Equal Protection Clause of the 14th Amend- ment and invalid. 18 In Frontiero v. Richardson the court

declared unconstitutional a fringe benefit scheme that awarded
male members of the military a housing allowance and medical care for their wives, regardless of dependency, but au-
thorized such benefits for women in the military only if they
were in fact providing more than one-half of their husbands'
support. [19]

Other cases, however, indicate that the courts are
not ready to declare sex a suspect classification or hold differential treatment on the basis of sex a violation of the Constitution or of statute law. A few months after Reed, the
Supreme Court affirmed, without hearing argument and without opinion, a federal district court decision holding constitutional Alabama's law that upon marriage a woman takes her
husband's surname and must use it for such official matters
as obtaining a driver's license, unless she obtains a court
order changing her name. [20] Men, also, have suffered from
the Court's reluctance to strike down gender-based classifications. In Kahn v. Shevin, for example, the Court upheld a
Florida statute which provided a property tax exemption for
widows but not for widowers. The Court sustained the classification based on sex as bearing a "fair and substantial relation to the object of legislation," that is, a reduction of the
disparity of the economic capabilities of a man and a woman. [21] A minority argued in vain that such an end might better be served by a more narrowly drafted statute granting
relief on the basis of economic need rather than sex alone. [22]

Certainly the mixed record of court decisions indicates
that the Equal Rights Amendment is needed to shift the law
from drawing gender-based lines to making distinctions based
on more narrow, functionally-based criteria. The Equal
Rights Amendment would prohibit the use of any concept of
"family unity" which involved gender-based stereotypes to
sustain different legal rights and obligations for husbands and
wives. For example, age differentials for marriage would
be equalized in those states where it now differs for men and
women, although states could of course retain the same minimum age requirement for both sexes. If the state wished to
require that all members of the same family have the same
name, it could not assume or require that the husband's
name be the family name. In the same way the man's domicile could not automatically determine the domicile of the
woman. In community property states, the husband could no
longer automatically be favored as manager of the community property. Moreover, in tort proceedings, "Courts would
not be able to assume for any purpose that women had a

legal obligation to do housework, or provide affection and companionship, or be available for sexual relations, unless men owed their wives exactly the same duties. "23   Obligations of interspousal support would have to be either eliminated or imposed on both spouses based on such criteria as earning power, investments and property holdings, non-monetary contributions to the marriage, and other obligations. And, in the event of the dissolution of the marriage, the grounds for divorce would have to be the same for men and women. 24

The Equal Rights Amendment would not prohibit the states from treating the married couple as a unit, nor from defining what a legally recognizable family shall be, nor from assigning rights and responsibilities based on marital relationship.   Its sole requirement with respect to domestic relations law would be that marital obligations and benefits cannot be based solely on gender, but must be sex-neutral and established by function, or need, or some other more narrowly-drawn criterion.   The Equal Rights Amendment would establish the principle that men and women, even when married, have the right to be treated as individuals, not as members of a gender-defined class.

Individualism and Marriage

The Equal Rights Amendment asserts that every person--man or woman--has the right to be treated as an individual without regard to sex; the adoption of the ERA would therefore overturn much domestic relations law which incorporates gender-based distinctions.   The ERA does not address the further question of whether the law should recognize distinctions between married and single persons.   Does the full recognition of individual rights require that every person--married or single--have the right to be treated as an individual without regard to marital status?   I briefly explore in this section three areas of the law in which marital status creates different rights and obligations for married and single persons.   I will suggest that the elimination of the legal relevance of marital status, and the concomitant move to a more individualistic polity may be theoretically desirable, but is not feasible at present.   This is not due, however, to any characteristics intrinsic to marriage itself, but to the social and economic organization of American life which at present makes it extremely difficult to eliminate the economic dependence of married women on their husbands.

Until these organizational features of society change, it makes
little sense for the law to treat married persons exactly as
it does single men and women.   Marital status is currently
relevant to a wide variety of legal rights and privileges, including income tax rates, eligibility for social security benefits, and, in some jurisdictions, establishing title to property.
Analyzing the rationale for--and the costs and benefits of--
moving toward a more individualistically based policy in each
of these areas points out the tensions between individual and
matrimonial pair in social theory and public policy.

Income Tax

The income tax law as it applies to individuals and
families tries to accomplish several goals simultaneously:
to be progressive (that is to tax those with greater incomes
at higher rates than those with lower incomes); to treat similarly situated persons equally; to treat similarly situated
couples equally; and to provide neither a tax incentive nor
disincentive for people to marry.   The history of changes in
the internal revenue laws reflects lawmakers' assumptions
concerning not only these matters but also concerning the
gender-based division of labor in society and in the family.

The original income tax legislation passed by Congress
after the ratification of the 16th Amendment in 1913 was
dominated by an individualistic approach.   "The right of married couples to file a joint return (first recognized by statute
in 1918) was not an exception to this individualistic bias,
since the same rate schedule applied to both separate and
joint returns, with the result that joint filings were disad-
vantageous except in unusual circumstances."25   In the eight
community property states, however, both partners by law
owned the acquests of the marriage.   The tax savings to
single-earner married couples in community property states,
each paying the tax on one-half of their joint income, was
therefore considerable when compared with the tax paid by
single-earner households in common law states.

In 1948, Congress attempted to equalize the burden
among married couples (and prevent a rush to community
property regimes), and allowed married taxpayers in common law states to file joint returns and to split their aggregate income--one half to each--for tax purposes.   A family
in which only one spouse worked and earned $20,000 a year
therefore paid the same income tax as a family where one
spouse earned $12,000 and the other earned $8,000.   Thus

the tax burden was equalized for similarly situated couples.
Under this plan however, a different discrepancy occurred:
most married couples (particularly in single-earner households) realized a considerable savings over their unmarried
counterparts.   For example, a couple where only one person
worked and earned $20,000 a year could split that income and
pay the tax on $10,000 twice.   The single person earning
$20,000 a year paid the same tax on the first $10,000 as
his married counterpart, but because of progressive taxation
paid a higher tax on the second $10,000.   This system could
make the total tax for a single person as much as 41 percent
higher than that for a married couple. [26]

        In 1969 Congress acted again, this time to eliminate
the disparity between the single person and the married
couple.   To do this, Congress lowered the single taxpayer
rate with respect to the joint rate.   The new law reversed
the discrimination which previously prevailed between single
persons and two earner families.   The couple in which each
partner worked and received $10,000 a year were taxed for
the second $10,000 at a higher rate than if each had been
single and earning the same $10,000.   In attempting to
equalize the tax burdens of single persons and couples who
could file joint returns, lawmakers acted on the assumption
that couples would be "splitting" a single paycheck between
them.   As this short history shows, even a whole-hearted
determination to eliminate gender-based assumptions from the
tax law does not resolve the question of how to regard married couples for the purposes of taxation.   This is so because the tax of a married couple can be one of three things:
greater than the partners paid before marriage, in which
case they are subject to a marriage penalty--as has been the
case for equal-earner families since 1969; less than they paid
before marriage, in which case single persons are subject to
a single's penalty--as they were between 1948 and 1969; unchanged by marriage, in which case equal income married
couples are subject to unequal taxes, with those with single
earners paying a greater tax on the same joint income than
those with two earners. [27]   Add to these considerations the
fact that there are both community property and common law
regimes in the United States, and difficulties of drafting an
equitable tax law become clear.

        The strictly individualistic solution to this dilemma
would be to tax everyone on his or her own income; there
would be no income splitting and no joint return schedule.
This proposal, however, offends the notion that similarly

situated couples should be treated in an equivalent manner.
The "one person, one tax" schedule makes sense, therefore,
only if everyone in society has his or her own income.   It
therefore makes sense only if all adults--men and women,
with children or without--work outside the home, or if people
are paid for doing domestic labor in their own households.
The only "marriage incentive" would then be the advantage
of the economies of scale which would be realized by combining two households into one.

     The notion of "one person, one tax" is appealing in
its conceptual simplicity, but it is not appropriate for a society in which not all adults receive taxable income.   If
adopted at present, such a program would place a greater
tax burden on single-earner than on two-earner families with
the same collective income.   It would again favor those families living under community property regimes.   And it would
discourage marriages where both partners did not expect to
draw salaries.   It therefore seems likely that some form of
the joint return is likely to remain for married couples in
the United States.   But it is important to realize that the
current inequities in the joint return stem from the lawmakers' mistaken assumption that married couples will be single-
income families (even though nearly 50 percent of married
women now work outside the home). 28   Moreover, it is important to recognize the fact that "one person, one tax"
would be a viable principle if married women did not by-
and-large become the economic dependents of their husbands.
That married women do become economically dependent upon
men is a consequence of their generally lower salaries,
more limited job opportunities, and the fact that they are
assigned primary responsibility for child care in our society.
Even a cursory examination of alternative income tax schedules quickly focuses attention beyond tax policy to the much
broader considerations of the dilemmas of combining family
life with equal economic opportunity for men and women,
married and single, alike.   Similar considerations arise
when one shifts attention from the amount to be paid to
government through taxes, to the benefits to be received
from government through social security.

Social Security

     The provisions of the Social Security Act, like those
of the Internal Revenue Act, have traditionally reflected the
assumption that in a marriage the husband acts as bread-
winner, the wife as provider of domestic services.   Recent

Supreme Court decisions have attacked some of the manifestations of this assumption, and the Equal Rights Amendment would prohibit gender-based distinctions in social security benefits. 29   The ERA does not, however, address the
question of whether it is proper that a person be treated differently under Social Security as a married person than he
or she would be treated if single.

The history of amendments to the Social Security Act
illustrates the legislators' intention that social security benefits provide support not only for the wage earner, but for
his or her dependents as well. 30   It also shows the tenacity
of the notion of the "natural" dependency of married women,
but not of married men, on their spouses.

The first Social Security Act covered only salaried
workers.   Congress amended the Social Security Act in 1939
to provide family protection in addition to protection for the
wage earner.   At that time, it expressly limited the amendments to wives, widows, and minor children.   These were
assumed to be dependents; no proof of dependency was required.   In 1950, Congress extended social security protection to husbands, widowers and minor children of working
women.   But husbands, widowers, and minor children of
women workers were not granted the same presumption of
dependency as those relations of working men.   Instead, they
had to prove that one-half of their support came from the
woman.   As a result, by the end of 1971, 5. 8 million wom-
en received social security based on their husband's earnings, while only 12 thousand men received payments as dependents of their wives. 31

Coverage of a wage earner's dependents extends social security protection to many "unemployed" adults; a strictly individualistic system would not cover such dependents.
Even the present system, however, frequently leaves dependent spouses uncovered in the event that a marriage ends
by divorce.   While a widow or widower may obtain social
security benefits if the marriage lasted at least six months
prior to the spouse's death, a divorced person is eligible for
dependent's benefit only after a marriage of twenty years. 32
The twenty-year requirement leaves women of long-term marriages divorced and without any financial security other than
alimony.   A current popular proposal to deal with this problem would abolish both dependency payments and restrictions,
and substitute for them social security benefits for housework
in one's own home.

One of the most persuasive advocates of social security coverage for homemaking argues that

> The only equitable solution to the problem [of grant-
> ing benefits to divorced dependents] seems to be to
> recognize the non-paid work performed in the home
> by a married woman to be economic work, and to
> allow such women to accumulate credits under the
> social security system. This would enable all
> benefits to be paid to individuals on the basis of
> their work and the benefits they had earned accord-
> ingly. I believe that wives who are fully employed
> at home should be granted coverage under the so-
> cial security system, and should be eligible for
> benefits earned on the basis of their own work. ...
> [T]hey should be eligible for income maintenance
> because they have earned it, not because they are
> dependent. [33]

An attractive feature of this proposal from the perspective
of liberal theory is that the homemaker receives benefits in
his/her own name--as an individual--not as someone else's
dependent.

There are problems--both practical and theoretical--
however, with the proposal to give social security benefits
for housework done in one's own home. First is the difficulty of deciding who should pay for the benefit. It one
answers "the employed spouse," either one must assume a
wealthy family or a willingness and ability on the part of all
to give up that part of the family income needed to pay the
homemaker spouse. If one answers "the government," one
must assume that the general public married and unmarried,
is willing to be taxed to pay for this coverage. Second,
this proposal might encourage women to pursue only their
traditional homemaking role, substituting dependency on the
government for dependency on their spouses. Third, there
is the problem of equity between those who receive social
security for full-time homemaking in their own houses and
those who receive social security through their outside jobs
and simply do their housework "on the side." Presumably,
only married persons would be eligible for social security
coverage for housekeeping in their own homes. Providing
social security coverage would aid the divorcee and might
help equalize the situation among couples by giving some
form of financial independence and security to all wives,
whether employed outside the home or not. But the plan in

turn seems to create inequities for two-earner couples where
both partners hold the "two jobs" of homemaking and outside
employment yet cannot draw homemaker's benefits, and for
single men and women who cannot elect homemaker coverage.[34]

    The radical individualist solution to these problems
would be to provide social security coverage only to those
people who are employed for a salary. A person would earn
benefits in his or her own name through the tax on his/her
salary, and would receive benefits only in his/her own name.
The introduction of such a system at present would, however,
be as blind to current social realities and the exigencies of
family life as would the introduction of a wholly individualistic tax law. It would leave millions of married women without adequate economic protection. Again, the individualist
proposal does not make sense given women's economic disadvantages in the labor market, the existing organization of
work, and the structure of child-rearing in American society.
This does not mean that the individualist proposal is necessarily wrong. On the contrary, our inability to structure
our tax and social security laws on individualistic grounds
may equally well point to our failure to provide married
women economic opportunities equal to those enjoyed by their
husbands. It may be that the way we have organized work,
household life, and child-rearing unjustifiably thwarts the
realization of the liberal ideal of individual self-reliance and
independence.

Matrimonial Property

    The different marital property regimes in the United
States reflect the tension between the logic of individualism
and the assertion that marriage creates an entity which tran-
scends the identities of its separate members. Prior to the
passage of the Married Women's Property Acts, the common
law gave the husband control over all matrimonial property,
his own as well as his wife's. Since the Married Women's
Property Acts, each partner in the common law states has
maintained separate title to his or her own property in recognition of each person's individual identity. The situation in
the eight community property states--Louisiana, Texas, New
Mexico, Arizona, California, Nevada, Idaho, and Washing-
ton--is somewhat different. In community property states,
each partner retains title and control of any property he or
she brings to the marriage, but property acquired by either
during the marriage belongs to them jointly. Community
property regimes thus explicitly recognize the partnership
aspects of marriage.

Laws governing the disposition of marital property are typically most important at the time of divorce, when each partner attempts to begin again an independent existence. In common law jurisdictions, a wife who has no property before marriage and who acquires title to none during marriage-- who relies for support on her husband and lets him purchase a home, car, and securities in his name alone--has no legal right to any of the property the family has accumulated and enjoyed during marriage. A New York case provides a famous example of the unfairness which can result:

> [B]oth husband and wife were employed and for 22 years of their marriage their earnings were pooled. She also raised two children. In 1956 it was agreed between them that the husband would start a "crash" savings program and that family expenses would be met out of her income and his would be used for investments.... All the investments were taken in the husband's name and none were held by joint ownership. Upon divorce it was held that she had no interest whatsoever in the assets they had accumulated as a nest egg for both of them, and that although she might be entitled to alimony (after some forty years of marriage), he got to keep all of the investments. 35

In this case the unfairness and the husband's perfidy seem particularly evident as the wife's own earnings were exhausted. Yet even in a case where the wife had never worked outside the home and where the husband made investments in his name alone from his earnings, the wife might be thought to have a claim to that property. The husband's earnings and savings were in part made possible due to the fact that the wife provided household services (currently valued at about $13,000 a year), emotional support, business entertainment, and so forth. No such legal right exists, however.

In common law states the courts recognize the "partnership" aspect of marriage only by granting alimony and support awards to divorced spouses who do not have adequate separate property to maintain themselves. To deal with the resulting inequities, the proposed Uniform Marriage and Divorce Act urges that courts calculate the non-wage-earning spouse's contribution to the marriage in making property settlements upon divorce, if necessary changing title from one person to the other. 36

The precarious financial position of many married women under common law regimes has led many persons concerned about the economic security of married women to advocate community property laws for all states. Community property recognizes the rights of both spouses in the acquisitions of either spouse during the marriage. Recent studies, however, question whether community property is the answer to the economic disadvantages of the married women. Professor Herma Hill Kay argues that the community property system, although attractive in theory, "disappoints in practice by failing to produce equality of result between spouses."37 For example, if a working wife divorces a non-wage-earning but wealthy husband (whose property predates the marriage),

> [n]ot only must she surrender half of the community assets attributable to her efforts if her husband insists on a division, but she is unlikely to receive any spousal support where there are no children and she has a history of working during the marriage. The situation is not a great deal better for a housekeeping wife. There is still no community property to divide, but she will have a better chance of getting spousal support, particularly if the marriage has been one of long duration. 38

And no matter what the pre-marital economic assets of either partner, a woman may lose effective management of her "share" of the community property since (in the absence of the ERA) community property states frequently give the husband exclusive or predominant control of community property during marriage. 39

Professor Mary Ann Glendon argues persuasively that separate property is a far fairer system if both partners have the opportunity to acquire property in their own names. In her article, "Is There a Future for Separate Property," she reasons that

> when the widespread expectation that marriage will last only so long as it performs its function of providing personal fulfillment is put together with the reality of unilateral divorce, a diminished sense of economic responsibility after divorce, the increasing economic independence of married women, and the expansion of social welfare, the resulting state

> of affairs does not lead inevitably to the sharing of
> worldly goods.   Compulsory sharing ... may come
> to be seen by increasing numbers of spouses as
> undesirable, ... [and] the system of separation of
> assets may come to have the most appeal for the
> greatest number of people. 40

The individualistic approach to marital property would be to
maintain the common law rule that the right of possession
accompanies title, and that each person hold title to that
which he or she individually earns.   This is, after all, what
women sought in the Married Women's Property Acts.   The
common law rule creates problems today, however, because
many married women do not work for wages, and because a
large proportion of those who do work outside the home receive lower salaries than do their husbands. 41

The debates between advocates of community property
and common law property regimes, like the arguments over
equitable income tax and social security systems, reveal
that the individualism which lies at the root of Anglo-American political theory, must for the moment necessarily give
way before the actual economic dependency of married women
in contemporary society.

In each of the policy areas sketched above the law
must strike a balance between treating married persons as
independent individuals like their single counterparts and sub-
suming their separate legal identities into a marital entity
with a life of its own.   Legal recognition of the unity of the
matrimonial couple has traditionally resulted in differential
treatment of married men and women, based on the assumption that members of each sex had distinct roles to play in
the family and in society.   The passage of the Equal Rights
Amendment would make differential treatment of men and
women, married or single, illegal.   This consideration does
not, however, answer the question of whether married persons of either sex should be treated differently than their
single counterparts.

This theoretical issue cannot be resolved without giving attention to the actual conditions of society in which such
a change would take place.   A society in which marital status was irrelevant to a person's legal status, where all
adults were treated as individuals and not in terms of their
relations to others, would have to provide all adults with an
opportunity to accept that responsibility and to be capable of

self-support.   Social and economic reality in the United
States make such a proposal visionary at best.

The economic dependency of the American wife stems,
of course, from the fact that women bear, and have assigned
the primary responsibility for raising, children.   This has
in turn led to the assumption that they are rightly responsible
for household management, while men are responsible for
providing for the household's income.   The pervasiveness of
these assumptions has contributed to the structure both of
work and of family life in the United States.   It is possible
to imagine changes which would decrease the economic dependency of the married woman.   I shall quickly sketch a
few of these measures.

One way to mitigate spousal dependency would be to
make it economically worthwhile for married women to work.
Differential pay for men and women performing the same job
was made illegal by the Equal Pay Act of 1963. [42]   Nonetheless, figures from the late 1960's indicate a persistence of
lower salaries for women than for men. [43]   Most of this pay
differential is probably not due to unequal pay for identical
work, but to "occupational segregation, " the fact that women
overwhelmingly predominate in some jobs, and men in others. [44]   For the divorced woman or widow with children low
salaries may create economic hardship; for the married woman low salaries may serve as a deterrent to entering the
paid labor force given the lack of social services and the
exigencies of child care.

A second step towards the economic self-sufficiency
of the married woman would come from the mandatory provision of maternity leaves and from including pregnancy and
childbirth in employees' health insurance plans.   The EEOC
guidelines for administering Title VII state that "Disabilities
caused or contributed to by pregnancy ... are, for all job-
related purposes, temporary disabilities and should be treated
as such under any health or temporary disability insurance...."[45]   But, of course, if an employer does not provide sick leaves, or if an employer terminates the employment of those who take more than two consecutive weeks of
sick leave, these guidelines do not compel employers to provide maternity leaves.   Nor is it established that employee
benefit or insurance programs must cover such absences as
they do other temporary disabilities. [46]   Thus a couple in
which both partners work may face a dilemma if they wish
to have a child--they may have to bear all medical expenses

associated with childbirth and risk the woman's losing her job or seniority.

A third necessary pre-condition for the economic equality of married men and women and the elimination of dependency status for most married women is a restructuring of the conditions of work. Families in which both husband and wife wish to work outside the home face many logistical difficulties, not intrinsic to the work itself. Many of these obstacles could be eliminated. There are measures which would enable couples to have others care for their children while they themselves work. 47 Increased day-care facilities with more highly-trained staffs would aid working couples; particularly helpful would be day-care facilities available to both parents of young children. Other measures would allow the parents themselves to combine family tasks and employment. Part-time work would be a boon to two-worker couples, particularly those with children. 48 Flexible hours, devised initially to deal with pressures on transportation facilities might allow a parent to adjust his or her work to home needs. Leaves of absence without loss (although obviously without accumulation) of seniority, and increased opportunities for continuing education, would also help those who felt the need to withdraw from the job-market temporarily, but did not wish to do so permanently.

Traditionally, one person of a matrimonial pair has worked away from the home, for fixed hours, for five days a week, for close to forty-five years, and preferably has done so without interruption and without change of occupation. There is nothing intrinsic to the nature of most work, however, that dictates it be performed in this manner.

Some such far-reaching reorganization of work, and a concomitant recognition that the woman alone is not solely responsible for the rearing of children is necessary before it makes sense to banish notions of dependency from the law. If an individualistic polity is not at present possible nor desirable, thinking about the preconditions which would make it feasible reveals a great deal about the systemic barriers to the real equality of economic opportunity for married men and women. Such equality is necessary before we can hope to realize that possibility for personal autonomy which the liberal polity seeks to guarantee for all its citizens.

Conclusion

One of the paradoxes of classical liberal political
theory is that while philosophers like Hobbes, Locke, and
Rousseau asserted that all human beings--men and women
alike--were free and equal in the state of nature, they assumed that only males were to be active citizens, while wom-
en presumably would agree to be subordinate members of
male-dominated families. [49] This had the result of making
men the only true "individuals" in civil society; women were
absorbed into the family "unit" which was represented in its
dealings with the outside world by the male head-of-household.
The notion of a family unit implied that the sexes had different and complementary roles to play both in the family and
in society. The law, as well as everyday social practice,
reflected this assumption.

Advocates of women's rights challenged the notion of
prescribed gender-based roles by appealing to the first tenet
of liberal theory: all human beings must be presumed to be
free and equal, and therefore endowed with the same civic
rights and obligations as men. [50] Supporters of both the Married Woman's Property Acts and the women's suffrage amendment to the constitution appealed to this principle. The Equal
Rights Amendment is firmly rooted in this tradition, asserting that sex is irrelevant to ascribing "equality of rights under the law." The ERA would undermine the rationale and
the legal support for different male and female roles within
marriage.

If the relationship between husband and wife is equalized, and each partner is endowed with the same civil rights
within marriage, the question then arises as to whether there
is a continuing justification for treating married persons of
either sex differently from their single counterparts. If married men and women no longer are legally assumed to play
complementary roles in marriage, with the wife dependent
on the husband, should all references to spousal dependency
now be eliminated from the law? Should the fact of marriage
or marital status be irrelevant in the ascription of legal
rights and responsibilities?

I have examined this issue by looking at several areas
of public policy, and by indicating how each would have to be
changed if based on wholly individualistic principles. While
theoretically or conceptually tidy, such policies could not be
adopted at present. The notion and practice of different

familial and social roles for men and women has too profoundly shaped economic and social structures--particularly
the organization of work--to assure the possibility of spousal
economic independence even for those who might desire it.

The Equal Rights Amendment is a necessary step toward the full realization of individual rights in our society.
The ratification of the ERA would mean that the Lockean assumption that in a marriage the man must rule as "the abler
and the stronger" could no longer be sanctioned in law.   It
will nonetheless continue in social practice unless various
measures are taken to assure the equal economic opportunity
of the married woman.   Only when that opportunity is established will it be possible to speak of the realization of individual rights regardless of sex or marital status in American
society.

NOTES

1. John Locke, "Two Treatises on Government," ed. Peter
   Laslett (rev. ed. ; New York: Mentor Book, 1963),
   Treatise II, VIII, Sec. 95, pp. 374-375.
2. Ibid., VII, Sec. 78, p. 362.
3. Ibid., VII, Sec. 82, p. 364.
4. Edmund S. Morgan, The Puritan Family (New York:
   Harper Torchbooks, 1966), pp. 26-30.
5. Genesis II:22-23.
6. William Blackstone, Commentaries, 433 as quoted in
   Leo Kanowitz, Women and the Law: The Unfinished
   Revolution (Albuquerque, N. M. : University of New
   Mexico Press, 1969), p. 35.
7. Kanowitz, p. 40.
8. Ibid., p. 75.
9. U. S. v. Dege, 364 U. S. 51 (1960).
10. Kanowitz, p. 49.
11. Younger v. Gianotti, 176 Tenn. 139; 138 S. W. 2d 448
    (1940).
12. Carlson v. Carlson, 75 Ariz. 308, 256P. 2d 249
    (1953).
13. Barbara Brown, et al., "The Equal Rights Amendment:
    A Constitutional Basis for Equal Rights for Women,"
    Yale Law Journal, vol. 80 (1971), p. 942.
14. Ibid.
15. Ibid., pp. 951-952.
16. 29 U. S. C. A. Sec. 206(d), text printed in Kenneth M.
    Davidson, Ruth B. Ginsberg, and Herma H. Kay,

Sex-Based Discrimination: Texts, Cases and Materials (St. Paul, Minn.: West Publishing, 1974), pp. 955-956.

17. 78 Stat. 253, 42 U.S.C. Sec. 2000e et seq. (1964) text printed in Kanowitz, pp. 207-221.

18. 404 U.S. 71 (1971).

19. 411 U.S. 677 (1973).

20. Forbush v. Wallace, 341 F. Supp. 217 (M.D. Ala. 1971), aff'd mem., 405 U.S. 970 (1972).

21. Kahn v. Shevin, 416 U.S. 351 (1974).

22. 416 U.S. at 361.

23. Brown, et al., p. 944.

24. Ibid., p. 951. An interesting effect of this would be that in those states where a wife's undisclosed pregnancy by another man before marriage is a ground for divorce, it would either cease to be a ground or a woman might sue her husband for divorce if he had concealed the fact that he had impregnated another woman before marriage.

25. Boris I. Bittaker, "Federal Income Taxation and the Family," Stanford Law Review, v. 27 (July, 1975), p. 1400.

26. Davidson, Ginsberg, and Kay, p. 529.

27. See the discussion of this point in Bittaker, pp. 1428-31.

28. By 1975, 45 percent of all married women were in the labor force. Bureau of the Census, U.S. Department of Commerce, Statistical Abstract of the United States, (1975), p. 346, Chart 563.

29. For example, in Weinberger v. Wiesenfeld, 420 U.S. 636 (1975), 95 S. Ct. 1225, the Supreme Court extended social security benefits for widowed mothers with minor children to widowed fathers as well. On the social security system and its impact on women see Martha Griffiths, "Sex Discrimination in Income Security Programs," Notre Dame Lawyer, v. 49, p. 534 (1974).

30. For a brief summary of the history of the Social Security Act and its amendments see Davidson, Ginsberg, and Kay, pp. 144-45.

31. Carolyn Shaw Bell, "Women and Social Security: Contributions and Benefits," in U.S. Congress, House, Joint Economic Committee, Hearings on Economic Problems of Women, 93rd Cong., 1st sess., July, 1973, p. 304.

32. See the comments on this fact in Lenore Weitzman, "Legal Regulation of Marriage: Tradition and Change,"

California Law Review, v. 62, pp. 1190-91 at notes 112 and 113.

33. Bell, pp. 305 and 307.

34. At present, of course, married women who work out-
     side the home are subject to a similar inequity. A
     "working wife" is theoretically eligible for two bene-
     fits: one in her own name as an insured worker, the
     other as a wife entitled to benefits based on her hus-
     band's earning record. Working wives are not given
     both benefits, however, but may elect to receive which-
     ever is higher. When her benefit as a wife is higher
     than that which she would draw in her own name, a
     woman has contributed to the social security system
     with no direct advantage to herself except for disabil-
     ity coverage while she is employed.

35. Henry Foster and Doris Freed, "Marital Property Re-
     form in New York: Partnership of Co-Equals?"
     Family Law Quarterly, v. 8 (1974), pp. 174-75.

36. National Conference of Commissioners on Uniform State
     Laws, Uniform Marriage and Divorce Act (1970, as
     amended 1971, 1973), sec. 307.

37. Judith Younger, "Community Property, Women, and
     Curriculum," New York University Law Review, v.
     48 (1973), p. 258.

38. Davidson, Ginsberg, and Kay, p. 163 (refs. omitted).

39. For a discussion of the management of community
     property see Davidson, Ginsberg, and Kay, pp. 163-
     68.

40. Mary Ann Glendon, "Is There a Future for Separate
     Property?" Family Law Quarterly, v. 8 (Fall, 1974),
     p. 327.

41. This disparity reflects the general differential between
     male and female wages in the United States. See
     below, notes 43 and 44.

42. See above, note 16.

43. In 1966, for example, the median income of year-
     round full-time professional and technical workers
     was $5,826 for women and $8,945 for men; of cler-
     ical workers, $4,316 for women and $9,103 for men;
     of service workers (except private household), $2,815
     for women and $5,078 for men. U.S. Department of
     Labor, Women's Bureau Bulletin #294, Handbook on
     Women Workers (1969), Table 62 at p. 139.

44. In 1960, nearly 100 percent of professional nurses were
     women, as were 70 percent of clerical workers and
     non-college teachers. Conversely, nearly 100 percent
     of technical engineers were men, as were nearly 90

percent of the lawyers, physicians, and natural scientists. U.S. Department of Labor, Manpower: Report of the President (1970), Chart 24 at p. 186. See also the special issue of Signs: Journal of Women in Culture and Society, v. 1, no. 3, part 2 (Spring, 1976) which is entirely devoted to occupational segregation.

45. Equal Employment Opportunity Commission, "Guidelines on Discrimination because of Sex," Title 29 CFR, Chapter XIV, Part 1604, Section 1604.10(b). The text of the "Guidelines" is given in Davidson, Ginsberg, and Kay, pp. 1101-1105.

46. See Geduldig v. Aiello, 417 U.S. 484 (1974).

47. During World War II, many industries established successful on-site nurseries and day-care centers. See William Chafe, The American Woman: Her Changing Social, Economic and Political Role 1920-1970 (New York: Oxford University Press, 1972), pp. 161-171.

48. For a discussion of the issues involved in child-care deductions on federal income tax see Carol Faye Simkin, "Child Care and Household Expense Tax Deduction Under the New Section 214: Is This Really the Reform We Were Waiting For?" Women's Rights Law Reporter, v. 15 (Fall/Winter 1972-73).

49. On Locke, see above, pp. 4-6 and notes 1-3. Thomas Hobbes' reasoning is set forth in his Leviathan, Part II, ch. 20. Jean-Jacques Rousseau presented his ideas on the family in Emile, Book V, and in Julie, ou la novelle Heloise, Part III, letter XX, and Part IV.

50. Recent court decisions and legislative actions have affected the laws dealing with income tax, social security, and matrimonial property. A readily available source for such changes are the 1978 supplements to Davidson, Ginsberg and Kay. These changes, however, are not of such magnitude as to resolve the conceptual and policy dilemmas posed in this article. The tensions between individual and family, and single and married persons, remain of fundamental theoretical and practical importance in the effort to achieve an equitable social order for women and men.

NOTES ON CONTRIBUTORS

Each author has received honors and awards, published many papers and books and has participated in other professional activities. They are numerous and we regret that space does not permit specific mention of them here.

Yvonne Brathwaite Burke was elected to the House of Representatives from the twenty-eighth Congressional District in Los Angeles, California, in 1972. The first woman to be elected to Congress from California, she was also the first black woman ever elected to the House from her state. In the area of women's issues, Congresswoman Burke, an attorney, initiated and advocated important affirmative action legislation: She called for legislation authorizing assistance to displaced homemakers, and was legal advocate for the New Legal Services Corporation where she sought legal services and policy-level participation by women and minorities in its activities.

Karen Burstein was appointed in 1978 by Governor Hugh L. Carey to the New York State Public Service Commission as one of two consumer representatives. Ms. Burstein is an attorney and a Fellow at the Institute of Politics, Kennedy School, Harvard University. She was elected to the New York State Senate in 1974 and 1976 and resigned to accept the Public Service Commission post. As Senator, Karen Burstein earned a reputation for being an outspoken consumer advocate and champion of equal rights for women. She led the fight for the Equal Rights Amendment and was a leading proponent of the bill which ended credit discrimination against women. Karen Burstein received her law degree from Fordham University.

Liz Carpenter is well known in the news media and government, as an author and journalist. She founded and co-directed the Carpenter News Bureau and was President of the National Women's Press Club. Ms. Carpenter joined Senator

Lyndon B. Johnson in the campaign for the Kennedy-Johnson ticket, was executive assistant to Vice President Johnson and press secretary and staff director for Ms. Johnson. Currently, Liz Carpenter serves as part-time consultant to the Friends of the LBJ Library, writes for Redbook and other magazines and syndicates a column for the Dallas Times Herald. Ms. Carpenter is co-chairperson of ERAmerica and was a founder of the National Women's Political Caucus. She is also a member-at-large of the Democratic National Committee and is working on a book about the women's movement.

Ruth C. Clusen is Assistant Secretary for Environment in the Department of Energy. She was National President of the League of Women Voters from 1974 to 1978 and was responsible for initiating the 1976 Presidential Debates, sponsored by the League. From 1966 to 1974, Ruth Clusen served as the League's Vice president and National Board member and chairperson of Environmental Quality. Ms. Clusen has been a leader in promoting an integrated approach to environmental improvement through public education and attention to natural resources production and conservation. In addition, she has been a leader in civil rights and women's issues.

Mary Margaret Conway is Associate Professor of Government and Politics at the University of Maryland. She has written and lectured on such subjects as social learning theory and political socialization, party workers: their attitudes and motivations and public opinion on crime and law enforcement. M. M. Conway received her Ph. D. in Political Science and Sociology from Indiana University.

Anne Nicholas Costain is Associate Professor in the Department of Political Science at the University of Colorado at Boulder. Her fields are American politics, public policy, administration and methodology. Anne N. Costain's work in the area of women's issues has included such subjects as women and the law; lobbying for women's organizations; and eliminating sex discrimination in education. A. N. Costain obtained her Ph. D. in Political Science from the Johns Hopkins University

Bernice Cummings is a Sociologist whose interests and work have engaged her in both scholarly and such activist pursuits as teaching; conducting community surveys about women; developing and directing conferences and organizations; writing, reporting and consulting nationally on the women's movement; and serving as chief of anthropological studies for a medical

research group interested in sex role differences. As a
Sociologist, Bernice Cummings has studied the women's movement since 1966, always with the belief that women must
legislate for their own priorities. Because of her conviction,
she founded the Women's Political Caucus of Long Island.
Continuing her abiding interest in the status of women,
she co-edited the present anthology which grew out of the
North American Women in Politics Symposium that she directed at Adelphi University. Her current research focuses
on group influences and the role of women as well as on developing a new methodology for helping women implement
their creative concepts.

Arlene Kaplan Daniels is Director of the Program on Women
and a Professor on the Department of Sociology at Northwestern University in Evanston, Illinois. She has been the
Chief at the Center for the Study of Women in Society at the
Scientific Analysis Corporation and the principal investigator
for many programs concerned with women and social problems. Professor Daniels teaching fields include social psychology; sex roles and socialization, occupations and professions; women in the mass media; and the sociology of mental
illness, medicine, large-scale organizations and education.
Arlene Kaplan Daniels received her Ph. D. from the University of California at Berkeley.

Irene Diamond is Assistant Professor of Political Science at
Purdue University, in Indiana, where she teaches courses in
public policy and women's studies. Her book, Sex Roles in
the State House, was published by Yale University Press in
1977. Irene Diamond received her Ph. D. from Princeton
University.

Rona F. ("Ronnie") Feit is a graduate of Bryn Mawr College
and Columbia Law School. Formerly a practicing corporate
lawyer in New York City, she is currently serving in the
Carter administration in Washington, D. C. , as Special Assistant to the Chief Counsel for Advocacy in the United States
Small Business Administration where she is also Executive
Director of the Interagency Committee on Women's Business
Enterprise, established by President Carter. She has also
served as a member of President Carter's White House staff
and as Special Legislative Counsel to Congresswoman Barbara A. Mikulski of Baltimore, Maryland. Ms. Feit was the
coordinator of the organizing conference of the National Wom-
en's Political Caucus in 1971 and is a permanent member of
its National Advisory Board.

Maureen Fiedler is a co-director of the Quixote Center, a
national Catholic justice center with a special interest for
women and men in the church and in civil society. She is
also a founder and national co-ordinator of Catholics Act for
ERA, a companion organization to the Center. Dr. Fiedler
has lectured nationally on Women in Politics, Women in the
Church, and the Equal Rights Amendment. She is the principal author of a recently published study Are Catholics Ready?
An Exploration of the Views of "Emerging Catholics" on Wom-
en in the Ministry (Quixote Center, 1978). Maureen Fiedler
obtained her Ph. D. in Government from Georgetown University
where her dissertation dealt with women in American politics.

Nancy C. M. Hartsock is an Assistant Professor of Political
Science at The Johns Hopkins University and is an editor of
Quest: A Feminist Quarterly. She has written on feminist
theory and the philosophy of social science and is currently
working on a feminist interpretation of the history of Western
political thought. She holds a Ph. D. from the University of
Chicago.

Marilyn Johnson is Director of Research at The Center for
the American Woman and Politics, Eagleton Institute of Politics, Rutgers University. She is also a part time lecturer
at Rutgers University and was an Assistant Professor of Sociology at Fairleigh Dickenson University. Dr. Johnson has
written extensively about women (in careers, in politics, in
adolescents), and is a consultant/specialist in the area of
women in politics. She is currently researching the subjects
of gender and school board activity, voluntary organizations
and perceptions about women in politics. Marilyn Johnson
obtained her Ph. D. in Sociology from Rutgers University.

Sarah F. Liebschutz is Associate Professor of Political Science at The State University at Brockport. She is also a
Consultant with The Brookings Institution where she was both
a Field and full-time Research Associate. She has devoted
much of her teaching and research to the areas of fiscal and
community problems. Sarah F. Liebschutz received her
Ph. D. in Political Science from Rochester University.

Jean Lipman-Blumen is currently a Fellow in Residence at
The Center for Advanced Study in the Behavioral Sciences at
Stanford, California. She is also a Fellow with the National
Endowment for the Humanities and is on leave from the Na-
tional Institute of Education, Washington, D. C. , where she
is Assistant Director; Senior Research Associate, Women's

Research Program.   In her recent post as Special Assistant
in Domestic Policy at the White House, Dr. Lipman-Blumen's
areas of responsibility were in the fields of education, and
women's issues.   Among her teaching and research interests
are such subjects as: social policy, sex roles, and crisis
theory.   Jean Lipman-Blumen received her Ph. D. in Sociology
from Harvard University.

Lucy B. Mallan is an economist with the Office of Research
and Statistics, Social Security Administration, Washington,
D. C.   Prior to 1972, she was a Research Associate at The
Brookings Institution; an economist with The Office of Economic Opportunity and with a Presidential Commission.   Dr.
Mallan's research and publications are in the areas of the
working poor, adequacy of income maintenance benefits, employment and earnings of women, as well as social security
retirement and retirement benefit provisions and the financial
characteristics of households with working wives.   Lucy B.
Mallan received her Ph. D. in economics from Northwestern
University.

Inez Smith Reid is Deputy Counsel for Regulation Review,
Department of Health, Education and Welfare, Washington,
D. C.   Dr. Reid was formerly General Counsel in the New
York State Executive Department for the State Division for
Youth, Albany, New York; Associate Professor of Political
Science at Barnard College, Columbia University and Execu-
tive Director for the Black Women's Community Development
Fund, Washington, D. C.   Dr. Reid has practiced law pri-
vately and has taught such subjects as African Studies, Crim-
inal Law and American Politics.   Inez Smith Reid received
her Ph. D. from Columbia University and her Law Degree
from Yale University.

Victoria Schuck has been president of Mount Vernon College
since fall of 1977.   Since 1974 she has also been a contributing editor to the Social Science Quarterly.   In Washington, Dr. Schuck has served on the President's Commission
on Registration and Voting Participation.   Last year she was
appointed to the House of Representatives Commission on Administrative Review.   Her professional activities include being
the former Vice President of the American Political Science
Association; the President of the New England Political Science Association; and the President of the North Eastern Political Science Association.   She presently is a member of
the Advisory Committee of the United States Civil Rights
Commission; a Council Member of the National Municipal

League; and a Member of the Federal City Council of Washington, D. C.   Victoria Schuck received her Ph. D. in Political Science from Stanford University.

Claudine A. Schweber is Assistant Professor in the Department of Criminal Justice at The State University College at Buffalo, New York, where she teaches graduate and undergraduate students, specializing in corrections, administration, institutions and change.   Dr. Schweber's research on women and the criminal justice system includes both historical and contemporary problems.   Her present projects in this area include a study of inmates and administration at the first federal women's prison and a study of the implications-complications of co-ed prisons.   Claudine A. Schweber received her Ph. D. from the State University College of New York, at Buffalo.

Nancy Seifer is the author of Nobody Speaks for Me! Self Portraits of American Working Class Women, released by Simon and Schuster in October 1976.   Ms. Seifer was formerly Director of the American Jewish Committee Center on Women and American Diversity, where she wrote Absent from the Majority: Working Class Women in America in 1973.   Nancy Seifer is currently a freelance writer.

Mary Lyndon Shanley is Assistant Professor of Political Science at Vassar College.   She was formerly Assistant Professor at Regis College and a Teaching Fellow and Tutor at Harvard University.   Mary Shanley's fields are Political Theory; Ancient and Modern Women; and Politics and the Law. Some of her research has been in the areas of women and politics; matrimonial law; methodological issues and the study of political woman and contract marriage and autonomy. Mary Lyndon Shanley received her Ph. D. from Harvard University.

Kathy Ann Stanwick is a Research and Information Associate at the Center for the American Woman and Politics at the Eagleton Institute of Politics at Rutgers University.   Some of her research includes devising and maintaining a system for collecting and disseminating data on women officeholders, nationwide.   Kathy Ann Stanwick is a Sociologist with a graduate degree from Rutgers University.

Barbara Wertheimer is Associate Professor of The Institute for Education and Research and Work, of The New York State School of Industrial and Labor Relations, Cornell Uni-

versity, and directs its Institute.   She is the author of Trade
Union Women: A Study of Their Participation in New York
City Locals (with Anne Nelson).   Her most recent book, We
Were There: The Story of Working Women in America, was
released in April 1977, by Pantheon Books.

INDEX

397